BUSINESS CYCLES AND ECONOMIC GROWTH

Leading Indicators, follow me
I will your protector be,
As you go down the coincident trail
And all economists stand up and hail,
Waiting for the laggers to give way and turn
Marking the time for which investors yearn.
When the two Kleins, Philip and Larry
Sit down together, with Tom, Dick and Harry,
It means that the Indicators have come out of hiding,
And will always be there when we look for a tiding.
User-friendly Indicators, you've come a long way
Since we charted by hand and punched cards the whole day.
To seasonally adjust we studied the data,
No X-11 to tell us, we simply knew it-
Christmas was a time, when customers blew it.
Then here's to the Indicators, victory won.
They've truly earned their place in the sun.

—Geoffrey H. Moore, April 1990

BUSINESS CYCLES AND ECONOMIC GROWTH

An Analysis Using Leading Indicators

Edited by
Pami Dua

OXFORD
UNIVERSITY PRESS

OXFORD
UNIVERSITY PRESS

YMCA Library Building, Jai Singh Road, New Delhi 110 001

Oxford University Press is a department of the University of Oxford. It furthers the University's objective of excellence in research, scholarship, and education by publishing worldwide in

Oxford New York
Auckland Bangkok Buenos Aires Cape Town Chennai
Dar es Salaam Delhi Hong Kong Istanbul Karachi Kolkata
Kuala Lumpur Madrid Melbourne Mexico City Mumbai Nairobi
Sao Paulo Shanghai Taipei Tokyo Toronto

Oxford is a registered trademark of Oxford University Press in the UK and in certain other countries

Published in India
By Oxford University Press, New Delhi

First published 2004

ISBN 0 19 5662156

Typeset in 10.5 A.Gramond by Laser Printcraft, Delhi 110 051
Sai Printopack Pvt. Ltd. Y-56, Okhla, Phase-I, New Delhi-110 020
Published by Manzar Khan, Oxford University Press
YMCA Library Building, Jai Singh Road, New Delhi 110 001

Acknowledgments

This compilation of articles is drawn largely from the *Indian Economic Review's* Special Issue on 'Analysis of Business Cycles' published in 2001. Most of the articles reprinted in this volume have been revised and updated to include the recent global recession. New papers include those by Victor Zarnowitz, Andrew Filardo, Lawrence Klein and Suleyman Ozmucur, and Pami Dua and Anirvan Banerji (article on exports sector).

I am deeply indebted to the *Indian Economic Review,* Department of Economics, Delhi School of Economics for support in the publication of the Special Issue. I am also extremely grateful to Srividya Subramaniam for her diligent and meticulous editorial assistance. I would like to thank the editors at Oxford University Press, India for their support.

I dedicate this book to Geoffrey H. Moore, the Father of Leading Indicators.

Geoffrey H. Moore (1914–2000)

Geoffrey H. Moore

Geoffrey H. Moore (1914–2000) was one of the leading scholars of business cycles of the world for over half a century. Many of his pioneering innovations have passed into common parlance as part of the vocabulary of business cycle analysis, and his contributions to business cycle analysis are applied the world over.

In 1939, Moore joined the National Bureau of Economic Research (NBER) and in 1950 he created the first list of leading indicators of recession and revival—namely, leading indicators as we now know them—following on the work of Mitchell and Burns (1938) who had published the first list of leading indicators of revivals. The robustness of these indicators was proven by Moore and Cullity (1994) who showed that Moore's 1950 set of eight leading indicators selected on the basis of economic theory and empirical performance between 1870 and 1938, performed equally well in the out-of-sample period in the latter part of the twentieth century. In other words, leading indicators that had correctly predicted turning points in the nineteenth century US economy continued to perform well not only in the US but also in diverse market economies, despite structural differences. This remarkable empirical robustness of the leading indicator approach refuted the criticism that it represented 'measurement without theory', as expressed by Koopmans (1947): such performance is possible only if the approach to leading indicator selection is rooted in sound economic theory about why each indicator should lead.

In the 1950s, Moore and his NBER colleagues worked on the development of the diffusion index that measures the proportion of indicators of economic activity in the overall economy or in sectors that are experiencing expansion over a given span of time (Moore 1955). Moore later devised the method of constructing composite indexes (Moore 1958) by extending the idea of the diffusion index to take into account the magnitude of these cyclical movements. Moore was also responsible for creating the original US indexes of leading, coincident and lagging indicators (Moore and Shiskin 1967). While the list of leading indicators originally proposed by Moore and Shiskin was revised over time, Klein (1983) shows that the variables included in the first five sets of leading indicators show remarkable consistency in timing.

Starting in the 1970s, Moore and Philip A. Klein pioneered the creation of composite leading and coincident indexes for several countries (Klein and Moore 1985). Their work on developing international economic indicators focused mainly on growth cycles based on the deviations of indicators from trend. Their analysis shows that a set of roughly equivalent leading indicators consistently led growth cycle turning points in diverse market-oriented economies.

In 1979, Moore retired as the NBER's Director of Research but continued to pursue work on business cycle analysis at the Centre for International Business Cycle Research (CIBCR), which he originally founded at Rutgers University and later moved to Columbia University in 1983. In 1996, after the closure of CIBCR, he founded the Economic Cycle Research Institute (ECRI) in New York to continue work on the indicator approach. At ECRI, Moore developed the concept of 'growth rate cycles' based on growth rates of the indicators and once again established the robustness of the leading indicator approach in a diverse set of market economies.

Moore remained Director Emeritus of the NBER and a member of its Business Cycle Dating Committee that determines the official dates of US recessions and recoveries. Moore's multidimensional work (see Banerji and Hiris 2001) ranged from the analysis of credit cycles (Moore and Klein 1967), employment cycles (Moore 1981), inflation cycles (Moore and Kaish 1983) to leading indicators for the service sector (Layton and Moore 1989) and the application of signals from leading indicators to the securities markets (Moore *et al.* 1994). Under his leadership, leading indexes for the manufacturing and construction sectors in the US were also created at ECRI. A leading index for the exports sector was also constructed recently (ECRI 1997).

Moore was really more of a practitioner than a theoretician. His main concern was to devise tools to predict recessions and recoveries 'in practice'. Some three decades ago, Moore remarked that if one could forecast a recession when it was starting, one was doing very well as a forecaster. He clearly passed this test and predicted the 1990–91 US recession five months in advance. This was, in fact documented in real time in *The Wall Street Journal* (Sebastian 1990), along with the fact that the 'official' Leading Index whose original version was a creation of Moore himself, as also Stock and Watson's model, as well as the consensus, did not see any recession coming.

This achievement can hardly be dismissed as merely something that Moore did based on his instincts and vast experience, and thus of no scientific or practical value. Based on the latest advances in leading indicator analysis spearheaded by Moore, even after Moore's death in 2000, ECRI was able to correctly predict the 2001 US recession, when once again, others did not foresee it. This is documented in *The New York Times* and *The Wall Street Journal* (19 April 2001) shortly after ECRI made the definitive recession forecast. At the time ECRI made that forecast, according to The Economist (28 September – 4 October 2002), 95 per cent of American economists thought that there would not be a recession. Thus the system of leading indicator analysis advocated by Moore has successfully stood the test of time. In stark contrast to this record, a 63-country study of consensus forecasts (Loungani 2001) concluded, 'The record of failure to predict recessions is virtually unblemished'.

Moore also pioneered the concept of inflation cycles, which he distinguished from economic cycles, reasoning that weak growth did not rule out strong inflation, as in the US stagflation of the late 1970s, while inflation could decline in the face of strong growth, as occurred, to the surprise of many, in the late 1990s. To predict cyclical movements in inflation, he identified leading indicators of inflation, which he combined into a composite Future Inflation Gauge (FIG). During the tenure of one of Moore's students, Alan Greenspan, as Chairman of the Federal Reserve, its pre-emptive interest rate moves have shown a remarkable correlation with earlier moves in the FIG, consistent with Greenspan's 1994 congressional testimony that he closely followed Moore's work. In fact, a biography of Greenspan claims that Moore's FIG 'would prove to be one of Greenspan's favourite indicators as Fed chairman' (Martin 2000).

In 1995, the American Economic Association named Moore, Distinguished Fellow, its highest honour, citing 'his important empirical findings' that 'were eventually incorporated in the regular statistical work of the US and international agencies' and 'a reputation for objective scientific research on significant economic problems that serves to strengthen the basis for sound economic policy' (*American Economic Review* 1996).

Moore published numerous books and articles over a six-decade career. During his career, he served as US Commissioner of Labour Statistics in Washington, DC and as President of the American Statistical Association. He taught at Rutgers University, New York University, Columbia University, and the Colorado School of Mines, and was a senior research fellow at the Hoover Institution at Stanford University. Over two decades, at CIBCR and ECRI, he helped train many economists from central banks and governments from the world over, in the construction of systems of indicators for their respective economies.

Yet his formidable professional legacy is not the most important measure of Geoffrey Moore's greatness. Moore was a man of great integrity. Gentle and unassuming, he was patient and unfailingly generous with his time with anyone who had a question on business cycles, regardless of their social or professional standing. To better understand economic cycles and to convey that understanding to professional economists and lay people alike was his mission in life. His devotion to that cause has left us with a deeper understanding of one of the most complex phenomena in economics, and likely contributed to a better life for millions who never knew his name.

References

American Economic Review (1996), Vol. 86, No. 3.

Banerji, A. and L. Hiris (2001), 'A Framework for Measuring International Business Cycles', *International Journal of Forecasting*, Vol. 17, pp 333–48.

Burns, A.F. and W.C. Mitchell (1946), *Measuring Business Cycles*, National Bureau of Economic Research, New York.

ECRI (1997), 'A New Predictor of US Exports Growth', *International Cyclical Outlook*, October, ECRI, New York.

Klein, P.A. (1983), 'The Neglected Institutionalism of Wesley Clair Mitchell: The Theoretical Basis for Business Cycle Indicators', *Journal of Economic Issues*, Vol. 17, pp 867–99, Reprinted in P.A. Klein (1994), *Beyond Dissent*, New York: M.E. Sharpe.

Klein, P.A. and G.H. Moore (1985), 'Monitoring Growth Cycles in Market-oriented Countries, Developing and Using International Economic Indicators', *NBER Studies in Business Cycles*, No. 26, Cambridge, MA: Ballinger.

Koopmans, T. (1947), 'Measurement Without Theory', *Review of Economics and Statistics*, Vol. 29, pp 161–72.

Layton, A.P. and G.H. Moore (1989), 'Leading Indicators for the Service Sector', *Journal of Business and Economic Statistics*, Vol. 7, pp 379–86.

Loungani, P. (2001), 'How Accurate are Private Sector Forecasts? Cross-country Evidence From Consensus Forecasts of Output Growth', *International Journal of Forecasting*, Vol. 17, pp 419–32.

Martin, J. (2000), 'Greenspan: The Man Behind Money', Cambridge, MA: Perseus Publishing.

Mitchell, W.C. and A.F. Burns (1938), 'Statistical Indicators of Cyclical Revivals and Recessions', *Bulletin*, Vol. 69, National Bureau of Economic Research, reprinted in G.H. Moore Ed., (1961), *Business Cycle Indicators: Contributions to the Analysis of Current Business Conditions*, Vol. I, National Bureau of Economic Research.

Moore, G.H. (1955), 'The Diffusion of Business Cycles', in R.A. Solow (Ed.), *Economics and the Private Interest*, New Brunswick, New Jersey: Rutgers University Press, reprinted in Moore (1961).

——(1958), 'Forecasting Industrial Production—A Comment', *Journal of Political Economy*, February.

——(1981), 'A New Leading Index of Employment and Unemployment', *Monthly Labour Review*, July, 44–7.

——, E.A. Boehm and A. Banerji (1994), 'Using Economic Indicators to Reduce Risk in Stock Market Investments', *International Journal of Forecasting*, Vol. 10, pp 405–18.

Moore, G.H. and J.P. Cullity (1994), 'The Historical Record of Leading Indicators—An Answer to 'Measurement Without Theory'', in K.H. Oppenlander and G. Poser (eds) *The Explanatory Power of Business Cycle Surveys: Papers presented at the 21st CIRET Conference Proceedings, Stellenbosch, 1993*, Aldershot, UK: Avebury.

Moore, G.H. and S. Kaish (1983), 'A New Inflation Barometer', *Morgan Guarantee Survey*, July.

Moore, G.H. and P.A. Klein (1967), 'The Quality of Consumer Instalment Credit', NBER, New York.

Moore, G.H. and J. Shiskin (1967), '*Indicators of Business Expansions and Contractions*', *NBER, New York.*

Sebastian, P. (1990), 'No Recession Yet, Says Panel of Experts: Group Tracking Business Cycle Sees Slow Growth Ahead', *The Wall Street Journal*, 3 March B3B.

Contents

Contributors

Anirvan Banerji	Economic Cycle Research Institute (ECRI), New York
Roy Batchelor	Sir John Cass Business School, City University, London
Ernst Boehm	Melbourne Institute of Applied Economic and Social Research, University of Melbourne
Bryan L. Boulier	George Washington University, Washington, DC
Vikas Chitre	Gokhale Institute of Politics and Economics, Pune
Pami Dua	Delhi School of Economics, University of Delhi; and ECRI, New York
Jeremy Dutra	George Washington University, Washington, DC
Andrew J. Filardo	Monetary and Economic Department, Bank of International Settlements, Basel
Lorene Hiris	Department of Finance, College of Management, Long Island University; and ECRI, New York
Detelina Ivanova	Department of Economics, University of Albany-SUNY
John B. Guerard Jr	University of Pennsylvania, Philadelphia
Lawrence R. Klein	University of Pennsylvania, Philadelphia
Philip A. Klein	ECRI, New York and Department of Economics, Penn State University
Kajal Lahiri	Department of Economics, University of Albany-SUNY

Allan P. Layton School of Economics and Finance, Queensland University of Technology, Brisbane; and ECRI, New York

Mehdi Mostaghimi School of Business, Southern Connecticut State University, New Haven

Michael P. Niemira International Council of Shopping Centers, New York

Suleyman Ozmucur University fo Pennsylvania

H.O. Stekler Department of Economics, George Washington University, Washington, DC

Victor Zarnowitz The Conference Board, New York

Tables

Figures

Abbreviations

AHP	Analytical Hierarchy Process
AR	Autoregressive
ARIMA	Autoregressive Integrated Moving Average
CBI	Confederation of British Industry
CI	Coincident Index
CIBCR	Centre for International Business Cycle Research
CLI	Composite Index of Leading Indicators
CPI	Consumer Price Index
DOC	Department of Commerce
DS	Difference Stationary
ECRI	Economic Cycle Research Institute
EIA	Economic Indicator Analysis
EPZ	Export Processing Zone
EU	European Union
EXIM	Export-Import
FIBER	Foundation for International Business and Economic Research
FIRE	Finance, Insurance and Real Estate
FSCI	Financial Services Coincident Index
FSLI	Financial Services Leading Index
FTZ	Free Trade Zone
GDP	Gross Domestic Product
GNFP	Gross non-farm Product
ICI	Indian Coincident Index
ICS	Index of Consumer Sentiment
IEI	International Economic Indicator
IIP	Index of Industrial Production
IMF	International Monetary Fund

ISM	Institute for Supply Management
LD	Leading Indicator
LEI	Leading Economic Indicator
LI	Leading Index
MA	Moving Average
MAPE	Mean Absolute Per cent Error
MS	Markov Switching
NAICS	North American Industrial Classification System
NAPM	National Association of Purchasing Managers
NBER	National Bureau of Economic Research
NDP	Net Domestic Product
NIPA	National Income and Product Accounts
ONS	Office for National Statistics
OPEC	Organization of Petroleum Exporting Countries
PAT	Phase Average Trend
REER	Real Effective Exchange Rate
RMSE	Root Mean Square Error
SDR	Special Drawing Right
S&P	Standard and Poor
TCB	The Conference Board
TS	Trend Stationary

Introduction

Pami Dua

Predicting the level as well as the direction of change in economic activity is a challenging task even for the best forecasters. Reading the economic tea leaves is, however, made easier by recognizing and understanding the fluctuations in economic activity as represented by the business cycle. One striking aspect of the business cycle is that it is a phenomenon that is reflected in similar patterns in several economic indicators, thus reflecting their interdependence.

Wesley Clair Mitchell wrote one of the earlier major works on explaining business cycles in 1913, and emphasized the need for acquiring factual information about economic instability before attempting to develop theoretical explanations. This was expressed in Mitchell (1927): 'For theoretical uses, there is needed a systematic record of cyclical alternations of prosperity and depression, covering all countries in which the phenomena have appeared, and designed to make clear the recurrent features of the alternations'.

Mitchell proposed to examine the 'cycles of reality' in a large number of countries by collecting statistical records of each of these fluctuations. This systematic statistical record was required to understand the theoretical foundations of these 'cycles of reality'. This was also one of the reasons for founding the National Bureau of Economic Research (NBER) in 1920 that pioneered research into understanding the repetitive sequences that underlie business cycles. Mitchell's contention was that business cycles are 'sequences among business phenomena...that are substantially uniform'. Since each business cycle is in a sense unique, Mitchell recognised that 'a thoroughly adequate theory of business cycles, applicable to all cycles, is ...unattainable'. Mitchell In 1941, however, noted that the common aspects in all cycles imply that 'the theory of business cycles...need not be given up in despair because it cannot satisfy ideal requirements.'

In 1938, Arthur F. Burns and Wesley C. Mitchell compiled the first list of indicators reflecting cyclical activity. In 1946, Burns and Mitchell presented the methodology to analyse business cycles in their pioneering work entitled, 'Measuring Business Cycles' in which business cycles were defined as follows:

> Business cycles are a type of fluctuation found in the aggregate economic activity of nations that organize their work mainly in business enterprises: a cycle consists of expansions occurring at about the same time in many economic activities, followed by similarly general recessions, contractions and revivals which merge into the expansion phase of the next cycle; this sequence of changes is recurrent but not periodic; in duration business cycles vary from more than one year to ten or twelve years; they are not divisible into shorter cycles of similar character with amplitudes approximating their own.

Subsequent work on business cycles was conducted under the leadership of Geoffrey H. Moore, a protégé of Wesley Clair Mitchell and Arthur F. Burns, as Director of Research at the NBER for several years. This work was in collaboration with Charlotte Boschan, Gerhard Bry, Philip Klein, Julius Shiskin, Victor Zarnowitz, and others affiliated with the NBER.

Moore's multidimensional work (see Banerji and Hiris 2001) ranged from the analysis of credit cycles (Moore and Klein 1967), employment cycles (Moore 1981), inflation cycles (Moore and Kaish 1983), to leading indicators for the service sector (Layton and Moore 1989) and the application of signals from leading indicators to the securities markets. Under his leadership, leading indexes for the manufacturing and construction sectors in the US were also created at ECRI. A leading index for the exports sector was also constructed recently (ECRI 1997) and this methodology has now been applied to India (see Dua and Banerji, 2003b).

The papers included in this volume attest to the ongoing efforts in the measurement and forecasts of fluctuations in economic activity.

Papers in this Collection

The papers in this volume are divided into four sections.

A Indicator Approach to Business, Growth and Growth Rate Cycles,

B Evaluation of Leading Indexes,
C Applications of Business Cycles Analysis,
D Business, Growth and Growth Rate Cycles in the Indian Economy.

Some of the papers in this collection were published in the special issue of the *Indian Economic Review* (2001) on 'Analysis of Business Cycles' and most of these have been revised for this volume.

Indicator Approach to Business, Growth, and Growth Rate Cycles

Geoffrey H. Moore's work focused mainly on the indicator approach to monitoring and forecasting business cycles. Ernst Boehm's paper highlights his pioneering role in this area. Boehm discusses the classification of economic indicators and the construction of composite indexes at the national, regional, and sectoral levels. He also reviews the spread of the economic indicator approach to an increasing number of countries in North America, Europe and Asia-Pacific. Boehm adds that Moore's major contribution is evident from the timely assessments that his colleagues are 'continuing to offer and to develop further regarding the business cycle and inflation prospects of the United States and of an increasing number of other countries'.

Victor Zarnowitz in his paper on 'The Anatomy of Recent US Growth and Business Cycles' examines post World War II US business cycles and divides them into stages of expansion and contraction. He discusses how the stages of business cycles can be identified and dated and describes the dimensions of these stages. Zarnowitz also examines the common and uncommon features of individual cycles with special reference to the latest sequence of recovery–boom–slowdown–recession (1991–2001).

Continuing in the tradition of Geoffrey Moore are the papers by Lorene Hiris, Philip A. Klein and Michael P. Niemira. Hiris applies the indicator approach to a major sector of the US economy—the financial services industry comprising finance, insurance, and real estate. A system of coincident and leading indexes is developed for this industry that shows that the Leading Index of Financial Services leads turning points in the financial services reference chronology. This index is important because of the central role of the US financial services sector, domestically as well as globally. It also illustrates the use of such indexes for different sectors and regions of an economy.

Geoffrey Moore examined lagging indicators in a paper in 1950, and later concluded that '...the downturns in the laggers had consistently preceded the upturns in the leaders, while upturns in the laggers had consistently preceded downturns in the leaders' (Moore 1983). This implied that a lagging indicator could be inverted and used as a leading indicator. Klein's paper on this issue shows that the inverted lagging index growth rate leads growth rate cycle downturns as well as the inflation cycle downturns in Sweden and the US. These results corroborate the prediction made by Moore half a century ago.

Niemira suggests an Analytical Hierarchy Process (AHP) for time-variant component weighting for compiling composite indexes. This extends the current indicator methodology by including component weighting. The author notes that the '...flexibility of AHP to derive weights for compiling dissimilar items with differing units of measurement opens up a whole new avenue for research that potentially can customize and optimize the time series component distribution for use in the composite index'.

Evaluation of Leading Indexes

The three papers in this volume discuss the evaluation of the performance of leading indexes. Andrew Filardo's paper evaluates the performance of four recession models in predicting the 2001 US recession. These are the traditional rule-of-thumb model using the Conference Board's composite index of leading indicators (CLI), Neftci's sequential probability model, a probit model, and Stock and Watson's experimental recession indexes. The forecasts of the US 2001 recession from the first three models using the CLI are particularly accurate while the Stock and Watson experimental recession probability indexes do not perform as well. Filardo, therefore, concludes that '...the results stand as a challenge to those who have had reservations, if not doubts, about the marginal predictive content of the CLI'. He further states that '...it seems reasonable to expect with some confidence that the impressive contributions of Geoffrey Moore to the theory and construction of the CLI and to our understanding of business cycles will help to lead to a better synthesis of traditional business cycle analysis and modern econometric practice of recession prediction'.

The papers by Mehdi Mostaghimi and John B. Guerard, Jr. evaluate the predictive performance of the US leading index constructed by the Conference Board. Using a Bayesian probability forecast of a downturn, Mostaghimi shows that the Conference Board's leading index restructured in 1996, requires only one probability over 95 per cent to signal a recession, with no false alarm. To produce the same result, the pre-1996 leading index requires three consecutive probabilities to be over 95 per cent. Mostaghimi, therefore, concludes that the revised post-1996 index has more information to predict a downturn in the US economy. In an out-of-sample application, however, the leading index failed to predict accurately the 2001 recession.

Guerard uses a transfer function model to test the hypothesis that the US leading index is a statistically significant predictor of US real GDP. Guerard performs similar analyses for the G-7 countries and finds that the leading indicators are statistically significant inputs to real GDP during the 1970–2002 period. However, a rolling post-sample comparison with univariate time series models shows that leading economic indicator forecasting errors are not always significantly lower than those from univariate ARIMA models.

Applications of Business Cycles Analysis

Economists continue to investigate the causes and timing of the Great Depression. Bryan L. Boulier, Herman O. Stekler, and Jeremy Dutra examine the dating of the Great Depression using US industrial production data published in 1929–30. These numbers show a sharp drop in production from June to December 1929 and a recovery by February 1930. Revised data, however, show a smaller decline in 1929 and no recovery period. These differences are attributed to differences in seasonal patterns identified by historical methods *vs* the X-11 ARIMA procedure. Thus, while economic forecasters were optimistic in early 1930, this paper shows that the data reported in 1929 and early 1930 did not represent the true economic picture. Nevertheless, what matters is that the 'analyses of the forecasts and actions of economic agents must be related to the information that was available at the time the decisions were made'.

The papers by Roy Batchelor, and Detelina Ivanova and Kajal Lahiri employ the Markov switching model. Batchelor evaluates the usefulness of consumer and business confidence indexes in predicting turning points in economic activity in the US and the UK. The study shows that a fall in business confidence decreases the probability of staying in the high-growth state. Likewise, an increase in consumer confidence lowers the probability of staying in the recession-state.

Generally, the model works better for the US than for the UK. However, the author cautions against the several false alarms that are generated by using a mechanical forecasting rule based on the Markov model.

Ivanova and Lahiri use linear and Markov switching models to evaluate the usefulness of the US Index of Consumer Sentiment in forecasting aggregate consumption expenditure and its components. They find that the index is useful for predicting durables consumption in a linear model. In the case of Markov switching models with regimes of high and low volatility of consumption growth, consumer sentiment and consumption expenditures are strongly related in the high volatility regime. These high volatility periods are, however, not always related to recessions. The predictive ability of the index of consumer sentiment falls in the presence of financial variables such as interest rate spreads and stock returns.

Lawrence R. Klein and Suleyman Ozmucur apply the principal components methodology as a 'short-cut method' to a full-scale structural econometric model. Forecasts of real consumption expenditures, industrial production, employment, and stock market averages are estimated using principal components of economy-wide indicators and a corresponding sample survey (leading indicator). Generally, the models that include survey results perform better than those that do not include this information.

Business, Growth, and Growth Rate Cycles in the Indian Economy

The four papers on the Indian economy apply the economic indicator approach to construct and analyse cyclical fluctuations in economic activity. Chitre's current paper and his earlier works represent the first application of the NBER methodology to the Indian economy. Chitre analyses 94 monthly time series to prepare a systematic list of indicators of recessions and revivals, and tracks growth cycles in India over the period 1951–1982.

Pami Dua and Anirvan Banerji carry Chitre's work forward and construct composite coincident and leading indexes to monitor and predict Indian business cycles and growth rate cycles. The main result is that until the early 1990s, the leading index was roughly coincident with business cycles, while the leading index growth rate was roughly coincident with growth rate cycles. However, a clear pattern of leads has emerged in the last few years since the start of economic liberalization in the early 1990s. This experience is consistent with the logic of leading indicators, which is predicated upon the existence of a free market economy.

Dua and Banerji also construct a leading index for India's exports that illustrates the usefulness of analysing and predicting different sectors of an economy. The importance of sectoral analysis is also highlighted in Hiris' study of the financial sector included in this volume. The leading index of exports comprises an index of the real effective exchange rate and a composite of leading indexes of India's major trading partners. The analysis shows that the leading index of India's exports would have anticipated most of the cyclical turns in real exports, the price of exports, and their value over the past 25 years.

Allan P. Layton and Anirvan Banerji argue that, in addition to an output dimension, there are other important dimensions to aggregate economic activity that must be considered in determining a chronology for the business cycle. This view is in contrast to those who argue that GDP is all that is needed to represent a country's business cycle. They show that basing the Indian business cycle chronology on just industrial production, a much narrower monthly measure of output, is even less appropriate.

The 16 papers in this collection cover a wide spectrum of research in measuring, monitoring, and forecasting economic activity. These papers also vouch for the fact that the business cycle is very much alive and well. It is thus evident from the ongoing efforts of the researchers that tracking, measuring, and predicting cyclical fluctuations can greatly enhance our understanding of the economy as well as improve forecasting accuracy. This, indeed, is a fitting tribute to Geoffrey H. Moore, the father of leading indicators, who devoted his lifetime to better understand and predict business cycles.

References

American Economic Review (1996), Vol.86, No. 3.

Analysis of Business Cycles, Special Issue, *Indian Economic Review* (2001), Vol. XXXVI.

Banerji, A. and L. Hiris (2001), 'A Framework for Measuring International Business Cycles', *International Journal of Forecasting*, Vol.17, pp. 333–48.

Burns, A.F. and W.C. Mitchell (1946), Measuring Business Cycles, National Bureau of Economic Research, New York.

Dua(2003a), 'Monitoring and Predicting Business and Growth Rate Cycles in the Indian Economy', this volume.

——(2003b), 'Economic Indicator Approach and Sectoral Analysis: Predicting Cycles in Growth of Indian Exports', this volume.

Dua, P. and S.M. Miller (1996), 'Forecasting and Analysing Economic Activity with Coincident and Leading Indexes: The Case of Connecticut', *Journal of Forecasting*, Vol. 15, pp. 509–26.

Layton, A.P. and G.H. Moore (1989), 'Leading Indicators for the Service Sector', *Journal of Business and Economic Statistics*, Vol. 7, pp. 379–86.

Mitchell, W.C. (1941), Business Cycles and their Causes, University of California Press, Berkeley.

——(1927), *Business Cycles: The Problem and its Setting*', National Bureau of Economic Research Studies in Business Cycles, No. 1 and General Series No. 10.

——(1913), *Business Cycles*, Berkeley: University of California Press.

Mitchell, W.C. and A.F. Burns (1938), 'Statistical Indicators of Cyclical Revivals and Recessions', Bulletin, Vol. 69, National Bureau of Economic Research, reprinted in G.H. Moore (ED) (1961), *Business Cycle Indicators: Contributions to the Analysis of Current Business Conditions,* Vol. I, National Bureau of Economic Research.

Moore, G.H. (1983), 'When Lagging Indicators Lead: The History of an Idea', in G.H. Moore, *Business Cycles, Inflation, and Forecasting*, Cambridge, Massachusetts: NBER.

——(1981), 'A New Leading Index of Employment and Unemployment', Monthly Labour Review, July, 44–47.

——(1950), *Cyclical Indicators of Revivals and Recessions*, National Bureau of Economic Research, New York, Occasional Paper No. 31.

Moore, G.H. and S. Kaish (1983), 'A New Inflation Barometer', *Morgan Guarantee Survey*, July.

Moore, G.H. and P.A. Klein (1967), 'The Quality of Consumer Installment Credit', NBER, New York.

Indicator Approach to Business, Growth, and Growth Rate Cycles

1

Contribution of Economic Indicator Analysis to Understanding and Forecasting Business Cycles

Ernst A. Boehm

Introduction

Governments and private businesses rely on a large volume of economic (and other) information in the strategies that they follow and in their policy decisions. A major objective of this paper is to describe how economic indicator analysis (EIA) has been playing an increasingly important role in contributing to this information, initially for the United States and then for an increasing number of market?oriented countries in North America, Europe, and Asia-Pacific. Another objective is to recognize the major role of Moore in this development. Which began when he was invited in 1939 to join Wesley C. Mitchell and Arthur F. Burns to participate in formal business cycle analysis at the National Bureau of Economic Research (NBER), New York. It will be seen that in recognizing the contribution of EIA to understanding business cycles and thereby adding to the knowledge of an increasing number of economists, policy makers and others in an increasing number of countries, we shall also be recognising Moore's lifelong contribution to this subject and the close attention paid to his work: witness, for instance, the following statement in his obituary in the New York Times of 11 March 2000:

One of his (Moore's) Statistics 1 students at New York University in 1946 was Alan Greenspan, now chairman of the Federal Reserve, who yesterday called his former teacher 'a major force in economic statistics and business-cycle research for more than a half-century'. Mr Greenspan told Congress in 1994 that he closely followed all of Dr Moore's work, which focused mainly on economic fluctuations and ways of measuring them (Robert D. Hershey Jr.).

Moore's substantial contribution to the ongoing development and application of EIA will also be observed in the references in this paper to a selection of his publications. Some of these were co-authored with colleagues working under his expert guidance and supervision. These papers contributed to: first, a fuller and, in turn, a more accurate understanding of the empirical regularities of business cycles; second, the increasingly widespread dissemination of this knowledge, both nationally and globally, with comparable research being inspired in an increasing number of countries; third, the forecasting of business cycles; and last, but not the least, the ongoing search for theoretical explanations of business cycles, a challenging and interesting subject that is being reviewed in some detail elsewhere by the author.

Economic Indicator Analyses initially involved the construction of leading (referred to here as short-leading), roughly coincident and lagging indexes. Additional indexes have been added in recent years, largely as a result of Moore's initiatives and with the aid of his colleagues. The new indexes include the development of long-leading (as well as the former short-leading) indexes; leading and coincident indexes for major sectors (including services, metals, manufacturing and construction) and regions of an economy; and leading indexes of inflation and employment. These indexes furnish comprehensive summaries about a number of key aspects of an economy, particularly, how the economy has performed in the past with respect to its output, inflation, and employment experiences, and so on; its current economic performance; and its prospects in the coming months. The indexes are usually updated monthly, reporting the latest information, and thus provide broad overall assessments of important aspects of an economy at an earlier date than generally available otherwise.

Our acknowledgement of the contribution of EIA can be highlighted through seven aspects: (i) recognizing the need for a monthly measure of aggregate economic activity; (ii) discussing the selection and classification of economic indicators to permit the construction of the indexes mentioned, especially the leading, coincident and lagging; (iii) defining what we mean by business cycles; (iv) describing how the relevant coincident index and its components can be used to date business cycles on national, regional, and sectoral bases; (v) noting the development of EIA around the world; (vi) making an overall assessment of the contribution of EIA; and (vii) illustrating how EIA may be used to study the co-movements of key economic variables and to forecast the course of economic activity (and of the business cycle) for a particular country, region and or sector in the months ahead.

Selection of Economic Indicators to Satisfy the need for a Monthly Measure of Aggregate Business Activity

Problems in Using Estimates of Real GDP

In order to monitor and forecast the fluctuations in business activity, ideally what is required (for details see Boehm 1987, pp. 3–5; Boehm 1998, pp. 9–12; and Boehm and Summers 1999, pp. 253–5) is a precise and accurate measure of the 'aggregate economic activity' of a nation, region, or sector as soon as possible after the event. In this vein, an increasing number of economists in the 1980s and 1990s—in seeking a theoretical and empirical explanation of the stylized facts of business cycles—have hypothesized in terms of a single measure of real activity to represent the business cycle. The measure chosen has generally been real gross domestic product (GDP) or industrial production. In Boehm (1998) and Boehm and Summers (1999), this methodology and the problems that it may encounter are discussed, in particular, whether it is theoretically appropriate or realistic and empirically justified to represent the business cycle by a single measure such as real GDP or industrial production.

It would certainly be very helpful if we could define the ideal measure of the current level of aggregate economic activity as monthly real GDP or, in addition, for a country like Australia real gross non-farm product (GNFP) in order to allow for irregular weather influences on the harvest. As noted in the references cited though no such ideal series is available, it is nevertheless worth pondering what it would mean to have a series that measures total economic activity accurately and consistently, and does not require later revisions. This series would, therefore, clearly reflect business fluctuations. An important reason for looking at GDP (and or GNFP) as possibly providing the required ideal measure is because it could be the most comprehensive of the official statistical series that reports the level of aggregate economic activity. It would seem appropriate to see the ideal measure as a monthly series since this tends to be the period for which a number of important variables are measured and for which forecasts for the next year or so are made. However, it could be even more helpful for policy purposes if earlier signals of business cycle peaks and troughs were anticipated than those furnished by monthly series. Indeed, Moore's recognition of this fact led to a weekly leading index for the United States being produced by the Centre for International Business Cycle Research (CIBCR New York) for its subscribers and now done by the Economic Cycle Research Institute (ECRI) New York.

Using the Coincident Composite Index Developed At EIA

If we had at least an ideal monthly measure of the current level of aggregate economic activity, it could perform the role of the concept that is widely known in EIA as the coincident composite index. We could also base our theoretical and empirical study of the stylized facts of the business cycle and forecasts of the level of economic activity, particularly changes in it in the months ahead, on the evidence that for some aspects of activity we have statistical series that anticipate actual changes in aggregate economic activity. These series in EIA are, of course, called leading indicators. Other series, known as lagging indicators, follow paths that habitually lag the general course of aggregate economic activity as portrayed by the coincident index and, when inverted, the lagging composite index computed from the lagging indicators provides a long-leading composite index (see Moore 1983, ch. 23).

Thus, in theoretical and applied analyses of the business cycle, our ideal substitute measure for monthly real GDP (or GNFP) would furnish the basis for identifying reference cycle chronologies of the peaks and troughs of business cycles, both classical and growth cycles. However, in reality, as the US Department of Commerce (1984, p. 65) acknowledged in discussing the definition and measurement of aggregate economic activity, '... no single time series measures it adequately, however, a variety of statistical series measure some of its major aspects'. This still applies and will almost certainly continue so, more or less equally to all countries. Thus, in the absence of an ideal single monthly measure of real GDP, we select roughly coincident indicators which, when combined into a composite index, will, as far as possible, truthfully reflect aggregate economic activity. Roughly coincident timing means that an indicator generally experiences a lead/lag relation of between plus or minus three months at coincident index turning points. The ideal, of course, would be a lead/lag of zero months and this does occur to some extent. For the selection of the coincident indicators, criteria are used (as discussed in section 3 below,) to identify the statistical series that historically appear to have accurately represented the current economic activity. (See Stock and Watson's (1991) consideration of the question of 'What do the leading indicators lead?' and their support for the development of the 'coincident indicator model', an idea also approved by Oppenländer 1994, p. 718).

Nevertheless, as mentioned briefly, there has been a strong tendency in recent economic research on business cycles for theories and associated empirical analyses to be developed with the business cycle being defined in terms of a single series such as GDP. But, unfortunately, the real GDP and GNFP series that are available do not completely satisfy our ideal requirements. This is not only because the estimates of GDP and GNFP are not available monthly. The available quarterly series are subject to significant revisions (for varying reasons), as illustrated in Boehm 1998, especially pp. 12–26 and 48–55; and Boehm and Summers 1999, especially pp. 255–63. Nor does any other statistical series individually satisfy our requirements for analysis of the current state of economic activity. To meet these requirements, a reference cycle chronology, as implied by Burns and Mitchell's definition of business cycles (quoted in the Section 'The definition of business cycles'), can best be determined on the basis of the consensus of economic fluctuations experienced in selected, key, roughly coincident indicators, to which we now turn our attention.

The Selection and Classification of Economic Indicators

To Aid Monitoring the Course of Business Activity

This subject was largely pioneered at the NBER through the work of, in particular, Mitchell, then Burns, and later Moore. The widespread development of economic indicator analyses in recent years has aided the analysis, including, monitoring of the course of business activity and identification of the peaks and troughs of business cycles (both classical and growth) on regional and sectoral as well as initially on national bases in an increasing number of industrial market economies. It will be seen how a slowdown or downturn in the economy being foreshadowed by the leading composite index can be monitored to see whether it is only a growth recession (or slowdown) or whether it leads to a classical (real) recession. It shall also be seen that monitoring essentially involves identifying if the declines (or, alternatively, expansions) in the leading index and the following corresponding declines (expansions) in the coincident index are pronounced, pervasive, and persistent (the three Ps as Geoffrey Moore and Anirvan Banerji have appropriately dubbed this aspect of EIA in connection with business cycle experiences (see ECRI 1996 and subsequent issues of this monthly publication; and Banerji 1999, pp. 72–6.)

The effectiveness of EIA in business cycle studies and in economic forecasting depends a great deal on the care and attention paid to the selection and the ongoing monitoring of the indicators themselves. This entails testing whether the indicators perform consistently in the course of the business cycle: in particular, whether they display a consistent relationship with respect to being leaders, roughly coincident, or laggers during each phase of a cycle and at the turning points of economic activity. In short, it is important to ensure that the selected indicators continue to perform for the reasons they were initially chosen.

To Make International Comparisons of Business Cycle Experiences

The rationale for the EIA is that market-oriented countries display, through the selected economic indicators, repetitive alternating sequences (or empirical regularities) that underlie their ever - changing business-cycle experiences. The objective of indicator analysis is to identify these sequences and to monitor their ongoing occurrence in order to identify, through the coincident indicators, the current state of business activity and to aid the forecasting of the course of activity in the months ahead through leading and lagging indicators. A detailed discussion of the cross-classification of the indicators is provided in Moore 1980, pp. 78–9; Moore 1983, pp. 70–1; and Boehm and Moore 1984, p. 39. The rationale and scope of EIA cover a wide range of business activities. It is from these aspects that the tested veracity of EIA will continue to furnish its strength and longevity.

Moore's (and his colleagues', in particular, Philip A. Klein's) 'International Economic Indicator' (IEI) projects—initially at the NBER (see especially Moore and Klein 1977; and Klein and Moore 1985) during the mid-1970s and then at the CIBCR between 1978–97 and at ECRI since its foundation in 1997—allow international comparisons of the state of the business cycles in different countries or groups of countries. This is an important facility since business cycles may be transmitted internationally. International comparisons are especially instructive because of the high degree of the real and financial linkages between industrial countries; for instance, for Australia, notably with the United States and Japan.

In recognition of the international manifestations of business cycles, a research strategy of the IEI projects, especially at CIBCR and ECRI, has been to check to what extent the long-leading, short-leading, coincident, and lagging indicators—that have a recognized success in monitoring the United States economy for more than sixty years (Auerbach 1982)—perform equally efficiently in other market-oriented countries (Moore 1983, ch. 6; Boehm and Moore 1984, p. 34; and Moore and Moore 1985). However, no series has been included for other countries simply because it appeared to parallel, by description, a series in the CIBCR's or ECRI's indexes of economic activity for the United States. Where better long-leading, short-leading, coincident, and lagging indicators have been found for other countries, or it may be expected will be found in ongoing research, they have or will be included. Furthermore, a large number of apparently comparable series have been examined for each country. Some were rejected as unsuitable in the process of selection; and others are being examined further. In short, the indicators included are generally the best that have been found so far. 'Best' here is based on a selection of indicators from an *a priori* knowledge (including a theoretical understanding) of the working of the economy and their evaluation individually in terms of the criteria discussed later. Fortunately, and not surprisingly, a number of the indicators chosen, for instance for Canada, France, United Kingdom, West Germany,

Italy and Japan (Moore 1980, pp. 80–1 and Moore 1983, pp. 72–5); for Australia (Boehm and Moore 1984), and for other countries, parallel quite closely those also found suitable to monitor the economies of the United States and other industrial countries in the IEI projects, thereby enhancing the comparisons of the business cycles in each country. (For reviews of changes in the components of the NBER's indicator system for the United States, see Moore 1983, ch. 24; for revisions to the components of the US Commerce Department indexes, see Hertzberg and Beckman 1989; and Green and Beckman 1993. See also Zarnowitz 1992, ch 11.)

Definition of Business Cycles

Defining business cycles is not a simple matter, partly because cyclical experiences, notably in respect to 'the 3 Ps' mentioned in section 3 above, may vary, sometimes significantly, from one country to another during a given period and from time to time in the same country. These divergent experiences also largely explain why there is not, as yet, and seems unlikely ever to be an accepted 'general' theory of business cycles. However, there are several key elements that are commonly believed to be central to a theoretical explanation.

The term 'business cycle' in this paper, is used to refer to either or both classical and growth cycles. Classical cycles are defined as recurring, alternating expansions and contractions in the absolute level of aggregate economic activity (with the expansion including here the recovery stage of the growth cycle). Growth cycles, on the other hand, are defined as recurring fluctuations in the rate of growth of total activity relative to the long-term trend rate of growth. So growth cycles refer to the deviations of the series from the trend. (See Boehm and Liew 1994, p. 5 for a stylized illustration of business cycles in terms of classical and growth cycles.)

A descriptive definition of business cycles that has been widely acknowledged, at least as a starting point, was first formulated by Mitchell (1927, especially pp. 468–9) at the NBER, and then adapted by Burns and Mitchell (1946, p. 3):

> Business cycles are a type of fluctuation found in the aggregate economic activity of nations that organize their work mainly in business enterprises: a cycle consists of expansions occurring at about the same time in many economic activities, followed by similarly general recessions, contractions, and revivals which merge into the expansion phase of the next cycle; this sequence

of changes is recurrent but not periodic; in duration business cycles vary from more than one to ten or twelve years; they are not divisible into shorter cycles of similar character with amplitudes approximating their own.

This definition applies to classical cycles that were initially the centre of business cycle studies at the NBER. However, the relatively long classical expansion in the United States from February 1961 to December 1969 (106 months) increasingly raised questions as to whether the business cycle had become obsolete (Bronfenbrenner 1969; Boehm 1990, especially pp. 27–8; Boehm 1998, p. 2; and Boehm and Summers 1999, p. 247.), Further, there was an even longer classical upswing in Australia from September 1961 to July 1974—an expansion of 154 months. There were also long classical upswings at this time in other industrialized market economies. These experiences, particularly in the United States, stimulated a revival of interest in growth cycles, especially manifested in research at the NBER by Mintz (1969, 1972, 1974). Mintz's work on growth cycles as well as classical cycles led to the Burns–Mitchell definition of business cycles, as quoted here, being revised to the extent, as Mintz (1974, pp. 6–7) states of '... inserting the words "adjusted for their long-run trends" after "economic activities". This version brings out the identity between classical cycles and growth cycles when long-run trends are horizontal'.

Another aspect (in Boehm and Summers 1999, p. 251,), '...is that, while there was a long classical upswing in the 1960s in both the United States and Australia, nevertheless there were during that time two growth cycles in each country that did not lead on to classical cycles', There were similar experiences in both countries in the 1990s when questions were again increasingly being asked about the continued existence of the business cycle. Indeed, there was a record long classical peacetime expansion in the United States of 120 months from March 1991 to March 2001. During this long expansion there was nevertheless a growth slowdown in 1995. Similarly, in Australia, there was a growth slowdown from December 1995 to January 1997 that did not lead to a classical cycle. The slowdown in the mid-1990s in both the United States and Australia, though not leading on to classical recessions, had important theoretical and policy implications. (On 'the dating of (classical) business cycles' in the United States by the NBER for statistical and historical purposes, see Council of Economic Advisors 1999, p. 21; and Hall *et al.* 2002)

Identifying Business Cycle Chronologies in National, Regional, and Sectoral Bases

Methodology to Identify Turning Points

The procedures for selecting business-cycle chronologies (as described in detail in Boehm and Moore 1984, pp. 38 and 40–2), essentially involve identifying (with the aid of computer programmes) the classical and growth cycle turning points in three parts: first, the turns in the coincident composite index constructed from the widely recognized coincident indicators representing income, production, retail turnover, employment and unemployment; second, the turns in the coincident series themselves; and third, identifying the medians of clusters in which the turning points of the coincident indicators have occurred. The clusters are usually readily identifiable (as illustrated in Boehm and Moore 1984, Tables 3 and 4), since the individual coincident indicators are interrelated in important respects.

The computer programmes used to select the turning points are based on the rules for turning-point selection developed at the NBER over many years and discussed in Bry and Boschan (1971). The method used for constructing the composite index corresponds with that developed by the US Department of Commerce in conjunction with the NBER. (On the construction of composite indexes, see: US Department of Commerce 1977, pp. 73–6 and 1984, pp. 65–70; and CIBCR 1993, Appendix D.)

Development of Regional Business Cycle Chronologies

The success of the economic indicator approach in monitoring the empirical regularities of business cycles in national economies such as the United States, Australia, and other market-oriented countries created an increasing desire (particularly among business and government economists and policy makers) for comparable leading and coincident indexes on a regional basis (see, Orr, Rich, and Rosen 2001 and their references to earlier studies for several other States of the United States). Preliminary leading and coincident indexes have been constructed for the six Australian states (Boehm 1996). The results fully affirm the growing interest in regional leading and coincident indexes. (For more details see Boehm 2001, pp. 13–15, (also see Phillips 1994 and Dua and Miller 1996.).

There is a strong case for regional analyses of countries such as Australia and the United States. This applies equally to the development of econometric models as well as EIA, used to aid economic forecasting. An advantage of regional leading indexes is—as Phillips (1994, p. 347) observed—that they furnish a relatively low cost method of short-term economic forecasting which is also more easy to understand and follows month by month as compared to econometric models. Also regional leading and coincident indexes could be used to supplement and complement alternative econometric techniques to monitor and forecast the course of business activity.

Exploiting EIA to Understand Cyclical Experiences of Major Sectors of an Economy

In addition to the construction of leading and coincident composite indexes on regional and national bases, attention has also been successfully given to the development of leading and coincident indexes for major sectors of an economy. The CIBCR did so for the US service sector and metals industries (for services: see Moore 1987; Layton and Moore 1989; for metals, see Moore and Cullity 1990). Economic Cycle Research Institute has developed, and publishes in its monthly reports, leading and coincident indexes for the United States for employment, services, financial services, manufacturing and construction, and a leading imports index, a leading exports index and a leading trade balance index (ECRI 2001c, p. 5). In addition, ECRI reports for the United States a weekly leading index and a monthly and a weekly future inflation gauge (ECRI 2001e). It also publishes daily the Journal of Commerce (JOC)–ECRI industrial price index. Other indexes that ECRI constructs largely for its own use in order to monitor and achieve a better understanding of the US economy include an unemployment severity index, a leading diffusion index, and a leading credit index. Each additional index and the cycle it exhibits may, of course, be usefully monitored in relation to the corresponding cycles in related variables and in the national and regional indexes. The ECRI also reports future inflation gauges for France, Germany, Japan, and United Kingdom (ECRI 2001d and 2001e).

Leading and coincident indexes have been constructed for Australia's service sector and metals industries. (for services, see Boehm 1991a, 1991b; for metals, see Boehm 1994). The service sector now accounts for more than half and in some cases about two-thirds of GDP in most relatively developed countries such as the United States and Australia; and the metals industries in both countries as well as the manufacturing and construction sectors generally constitute a sufficiently large enough area of productive activity to justify being monitored in their own right in terms of EIA (see Layton and Moore 1989; Moore and Cullity 1990; and Boehm 1993 pp. 8–11, and 1994). It should be noted that the leading and coincident indexes constructed thus far for Australia's service sector and metals were seen as 'experimental', but it is believed that they exhibit pictures for both sectors that are instructive and justify further attention being given to them. Further discussion of sectoral analyses is provided in Boehm 2001, pp. 15–17. Also see Boehm 1991a; Boehm 1993; Layton and Moore 1989; Moore and Cullity 1990.

To summarize, the growth of the service-dominated relative to the goods-producing economy has not meant that the business cycle may (or has) become obsolete, as some have suggested. Nevertheless, classical recessions are less frequent or severe in the service sector. This, together with the growth in the general importance of the service sector, should mean a reduction in future in the general severity and duration of recessions compared with what they may have been otherwise. This means that business cycles may henceforth be more in evidence in terms of fluctuations in growth rates. But, here too the fluctuations in growth rates are likely to be less severe for the service sector than for the total economy.

Cyclical Experience of the Farm Sector

Another important and interesting sectoral aspect worth noting is that there have been a greater number of classical and growth cycles in the farm sector as compared to those in the economy as a whole. It is noted in Boehm 1998 (pp. 19–21 and 52) that was true for both the United States and Australia during the 1960s to the 1990s, though to a slightly greater extent in Australia. Boehm (1998, p. 19) states that Australia's farm sector over the period 1960 to early 1997 '... experienced eleven classical cycles compared with only five in the total economy. There were about the same number of growth cycles as classical cycles in Australia's farm sector, with some differences in the timing of turning points'. (See also Boehm and Summers 1999, pp. 257 and 259). The greater cyclical instability of the farm sector justifies the preference for the use of the GNFP series in studies of

Australia's cyclical experiences. It needs to be recognized that the farm sector has declined significantly in relative importance in industrialized market economies. Real farm product as a share of real GDP has declined in Australia from about 6 per cent in the early 1960s to just under 4 per cent in 1997 (see Boehm 1993, pp. 8–9; Boehm 1998, p. 20; and Boehm and Summers 1999, p. 259). Similarly, the share of farm product in real GDP in the United States has declined from nearly 4 per cent in 1960 to about 2.5 per cent in 1990 (DeLong and Summers 1986, p. 685). This has contributed to a decline in the volatility of GDP, which is also apparent in the coincident composite indexes for the 1990s (Figures 1.1 and 1.2).

The Development of EIA Around the World

Aiding the Continuing Monitoring and Identification of Business Cycle Experiences

There are three interesting and important aspects to acknowledge here. First, the extent to which EIA has spread around the world with long-leading, short-leading, and roughly coincident indicators having been identified for an increasing number of countries. This, in turn, has enabled the construction of long-leading, short-leading, and coincident indexes which together with the respective, carefully identified 'select' indicators included in these indexes have aided the second and third aspects that warrant acknowledgment. The second is the identification of business cycle chronologies for these countries from the coincident indexes and their components, thus manifesting further evidence of the nature of business cycles with respect to how pronounced, pervasive, and persistent they have been (the 3 Ps); and the third is the evidence thus provided for international comparisons of business cycle experiences in each country.

Table 1.1 presents the average duration of growth cycles for twelve market-oriented countries and for three groups of countries; and Table 1.2 does so for classical cycles—also for twelve countries but only one group of countries. The quality of the results used to construct Tables 1.1 and 1.2 is relatively high and equally good for both growth and classical cycles for most countries, but particularly for growth cycles. Classical cycles were much less frequent, or did not occur at all in some countries in the 1950s and 1960s, notably Japan and West Germany. This contributed to the increasing interest in

Table 1.1: Average Duration of Growth Cycles in Twelve Countries and Three Groups of Countries, Various Periods, 1948–98

Country	Period	Number of cycles	Average duration in months[a]			
			Contraction:	Expansion:	Cycle	
			Peak to trough	Trough to peak	Peak to peak	Trough to trough
Australia	1951–98	10	23 (8)	31 (9)	53 (12)	54 (14)
Canada	1950–96	13[b]	18 (6)	22 (11)	40 (13)	40 (15)
France	1957–96	8	24 (10)	31 (17)	57 (18)	56 (22)
Italy	1956–93	8	23 (11)	30 (14)	53 (17)	51 (22)
Japan	1953–97	10[c]	19 (6)	33 (16)	52 (19)	52 (17)
Malaysia	1970–98	9	18 (8)	17 (8)	36 (15)	35 (10)
New Zealand	1966–96	9[d]	20 (6)	21 (11)	40 (14)	37 (8)
South Korea	1966–97	7	20 (5)	29 (11)	48 (13)	52 (10)
Taiwan	1963–98	8	23 (12)	27 (14)	51 (16)	50 (14)
United Kingdom	1951–96	9	27 (9)	31 (10)	59 (10)	59 (17)
United States	1948–97	12	24 (10)	23 (9)	46 (16)	47 (18)
West Germany	1951–97	10	24 (11)	28 (11)	53 (18)	52 (18)
Four countries:						
Europe[e]	1957–90	6[f]	26 (8)	40 (23)	66 (30)	58 (20)

Contd.

			Average duration in months			
			Contraction:	Expansion:	Cycle	
Country	Period	Number of cycles	Peak to trough	Trough to peak	Peak to peak	Trough to trough
Five Countries:						
Pacific[g]	1959–90	6	23 (8)	34 (15)	58 (13)	57 (22)
World Economy:						
Eleven Countries[h]	1957–90	8[i]	20 (8)	30 (12)	50 (15)	49 (20)

Notes:

[a]The figures in parentheses in columns under 'Average duration in months' are standard deviations of the respective average durations rounded to full months;

[b]Thirteen from peak to peak and fourteen from trough to trough;

[c]Ten from peak to peak and nine from trough to trough;

[d]Nine from peak to peak and eight from trough to trough;

[e]Includes France, Italy, United Kingdom, and West Germany;

[f]Six from peak to peak and five from trough to trough;

[g]Includes Australia, Japan, New Zealand, South Korea, and Taiwan;

[h]Excludes Malaysia from the twelve countries listed above;

[i]Eight from peak to peak and seven from trough to trough.

Sources: ECRI, NBER, CIBCR, *IEI*, (various issues), Boehm and Moore (1984).

Table 1.2: Average Duration of Classical Cycles in Twelve Countries and a Group of Four European Countries, Various Periods, 1948-97

Country	Period	Number of cycles	Average duration in months[a]			
			Contraction:	Expansion:	Cycle	
			Peak to trough	Trough to peak	Peak to peak	Trough to trough
Australia	1951–92	6	20 (8)	60 (47)	77 (45)	80 (48)
Canada	1953–92	5	14 (6)	76 (50)	88 (49)	91 (48)
France	1957–93	5	29 (14)	51 (30)	79 (26)	84 (24)
India	1964–97	5	10 (2)	65 (41)	76 (41)	75 (39)
Italy	1963–94	6	14 (4)	44 (33)	57 (34)	58 (36)
Japan	1954–97	2	16 (1)	160 (88)	140 (86)	238 (10)
Malaysia	1974–98	2	10 (2)	131 (12)	140 (14)	143 (12)
New Zealand	1967–91	4	12 (6)	58 (43)	70 (42)	71 (46)
Taiwan	1973–98	5[b]	8 (3)	50 (21)	58 (23)	63 (19)
United Kingdom	1951–93	5	27 (12)	70 (51)	93 (52)	98 (46)
United States	1948–91	8	11 (3)	52 (30)	63 (32)	62 (29)
West Germany	1966–97	4	19 (8)	70 (27)	91 (33)	90 (29)

Contd.

			Average duration in months			
Country	Period	Number of cycles	Contraction:	Expansion:	Cycle	
			Peak to trough	Trough to peak	Peak to peak	Trough to trough
Four countries:						
Europe[c]	1966–93	3	18 (9)	85 (23)	102 (31)	106 (19)

Notes:
[a]The figures in parantheses in the four columns under 'Average duration in months' are standard deviations of the respective average durations rounded to full months;
[b]Five from peak to peak and four from trough to trough;
[c]Includes France, Italy, United Kingdom, and West Germany.
Sources:
ECRI, NBER, CIBCR, *IEI*, (various issues), Boehm and Moore (1984). For India, computed from data in Dua and Banerji 1999, Table 1.

growth cycles in the 1960s. Thus the main business cycle for most countries has been a relatively short growth cycle with an average duration of just over three to under five years (from peak to peak or trough to trough). Classical cycles have averaged about one or two or three years longer than the growth cycles for Australia, France, Italy, New Zealand, Taiwan, and United States. However, the average duration of the classical cycles in other countries listed in Tables 1.1 and 1.2, notably Japan and Malaysia, has been significantly greater than the growth cycles; though an allowance should be made for the fact that both countries experienced only two classical cycles in the period of cyclical record available. It also needs to be allowed that there was considerable variability in duration of individual growth and classical cycles around the average. This is revealed by the relatively high standard deviations (Tables 1.1 and 1.2). The standard deviations are especially high for classical cycles, and generally for the expansion phases, again for the classical cycle.

International Comparisons of Business Cycle Experiences

Another by-product of the international spread of EIA and the identification of corresponding business cycle chronologies for individual countries is the opportunity for a study of the apparent economic linkages between countries. For instance, it is particularly instructive to note the extent to which it appears that growth cycle peaks and troughs in most European and most Asia-Pacific countries (for which data are available) have generally lagged corresponding turns in the United States. Table 1.3 reveals that the lags in of both median and mean measures have tended to be longer at peaks than troughs, probably partly reflecting the fact that in most countries the expansion phases of growth cycles have, on average, been longer than the contraction phases, whereas both phases have, on average, been approximately the same in the United States (Table 1.1). Taiwan is the major exception among these countries to the conclusion about the leadership role of the United States. It has generally led turns in the United States at both peaks and troughs, a subject worthy of more examination. (For more detailed discussions on international comparisons, see Beguelin 1980; Boehm 2001, pp. 20–3; Boehm and Moore 1984, especially pp. 47–8; Kaish 1982; Klein 1976 and 1981; Klein and Moore 1979; Layton 1987; and Moore and Klein 1977).

Overall Assessment of EIA

The general contribution of EIA has been discussed in terms of business cycle chronologies on national, regional, and sectoral bases. These chronologies are largely comparable in terms of concept and method of construction. The techniques developed over a number of years at the NBER in conjunction with the US Department of Commerce. The techniques and quality of the indexes were developed and improved at the CIBCR from 1978; and now at ECRI since 1997, the Melbourne Institute since 1985 and other institutes in an increasing number of countries. These developments largely followed the establishment of the IEI project by Moore and his colleagues. The project initially concentrated on the G7 countries. Australia was the next to join in 1984 (Boehm and Moore 1984); and it has been followed by an increasing number of other countries. A total of 17 countries are now monitored and reported on at least a monthly basis by ECRI. The developments in EIA should result further in facilitating, at least potentially, if not yet in fact, more comprehensive, theoretical and empirical studies of stylized facts of business cycles.

Though the road on which EIA has travelled—since the monumental study by Burns and Mitchell (1946) presented in *Measuring Business Cycles*—has at times been very rocky (being discussed more fully elsewhere by the author), it seems fair and accurate to say that it has never gone 'off course' or posed any serious doubts regarding its merits of being developed further, as indeed it has; and hence justifies is assessment by Romer (1994, pp. 573–4):

> One reason that the NBER reference dates have been so influential is simply that they are very convenient. They provide a quick shorthand that economists can use to summarize a very complex phenomenon. More fundamentally, the NBER dates have been influential because they are thought to be reliable. The amount of work that went into their development is extremely impressive. Arthur Burns and Wesley Mitchell's seminal study Measuring Business Cycles, in which the NBER methodology is described and developed, is surely one of the most respected books in American macroeconomics.

Nevertheless, in their theoretical and empirical studies of business cycles, some economists have been silent on the longevity and usefulness of EIA, (recognized, for instance, by Auerbach 1982). So next we note briefly the contributions of EIA to combined theoretical

Table 1.3: Comparison of Growth Cycle Turning Points in the US With Corresponding Turns from 1960 or Later in Eleven Market-Oriented Countries and Four Groups of Countries, 1960–98

Country	Total period available	Median lead (-) or lag (+) on US's turns in months[a]		Mean lead (-) or lag (+) on US's turns in months[a]	
		Peak	Trough	Peak	Trough
1	2	3	4	5	6
Australia	1960–98	+ 10	+ 6	+ 11 (13)	+ 7 (5)
Canada	1960–96	0	+ 1	+ 4 (7)	– 1 (6)
France	1960–96	+ 8	+ 5	+ 7 (11)	+ 2 (11)
Italy	1960–93	+ 11	+ 6	+ 8 (8)	+ 9 (7)
Japan	1960–97	+ 15	+ 10	+ 18 (8)	+ 10 (7)
Malaysia	1970–98	+ 8	0	+ 8 (8)	+ 5 (10)
New Zealand	1966–96	+ 13	+ 3	+ 11 (8)	+ 4 (10)
South Korea	1966–97	+ 7	+ 1	+ 9 (11)	– 3 (14)
Taiwan	1963–96	– 4	– 3	–2 (7)	– 8 (8)
United Kingdom	1960–96	+ 3	+ 2	+ 2 (8)	0 (10)
West Germany	1960–97	+ 10	+ 2	+ 8 (14)	+ 2 (9)
Four countries:					
Europe[b]	1960–90	+ 7	+ 7	+ 5 (11)	+3 (12)

Contd.

Country	Total period available	Median lead (-) or lag (+) on US's turns in months[a]		Mean lead (-) or lag (+) on US's turns in months[a]	
		Peak	Trough	Peak	Trough
Five countries:					
Pacific[c]	1960–90	+ 4	+ 4	+ 7 (10)	0 (12)
Ten countries:					
excluding USA[d]	1960–93	+ 8	+ 7	+ 2 (15)	+ 5 (11)
Eleven countries[e]	1960–90	0	0	+ 5 (6)	– 1 (9)

Notes:

[a]The median leads or lags in the third columns and fourth and the mean leads or lags and their standard deviations shown in parenthesis in the last two columns are rounded to full months.

[b]Includes France, Italy, United Kingdom and West Germany.

[c]Includes Australia, Japan, New Zealand, South Korea and Taiwan.

[d]Excludes Malaysia from countries listed above (as well as USA).

[e]Excludes Malaysia from countries listed above and includes USA.

Sources: Computed from data used for Table 1.1.

and empirical studies of the business cycle, particularly in terms of a more complete and accurate understanding not only the past and current states of economic activity but also the prospects in the coming months.

Use of EIA for Studying Co-Movements of Key Economic Variables and for Forecasting Classical and Growth Cycles

Advantages of Using The Coincident Composite Index as a Proxy for the Business Cycle and to Compare Cyclical Movements in Other Key Economic Variables

Especially since the late 1980s (and to some extent earlier as well), a key feature of combined theoretical and empirical research on business cycles has been to use a single series such as real GDP (or output) or industrial production as a proxy for the business cycle. As discussed in Boehm (1998, pp. 7–9) and Boehm and Summers (1999, pp. 252–3), influential papers by Lucas (1977) and Kydland and Prescott (1990) led to the methodology of using a single series for the cyclical analysis of empirical regularities and irregularities in studying persistence and co-movements in key macroeconomic variables during business cycles. Papers that have followed the methodology of using such a single series include Hodrick and Prescott (1980) and the revised version of this paper in Hodrick and Prescott (1997), Kydland and Prescott (1982), Long and Plosser (1983), Plosser (1989), Danthine and Girardin (1989), Wolf (1991), Brandner and Neusser (1992), Backus and Kehoe (1992), Blackburn and Ravn (1992), Kim, Buckle, and Hall (1994), Crosby and Otto (1995), Serletis and Krause (1996), Fischer, Otto, and Voss (1996), and Andreou, Osborn, and Sensier (2000).

Reliance on a single series as a proxy for the business cycle has contributed to contrasting and or conflicting findings regarding the pro, counter, or acyclical changes in key economic variables. Evidence for this is examined in some detail in Boehm (1998, pp. 9–21 and 48–51) and Boehm and Summers (1999, pp. 255–63). These findings may reflect the relatively poor and or varying quality of data, or possibly and more likely, revisions in the data that may shift turning points. Boehm (1998) and Boehm and Summers (1999) identify the timing of these changes in real GDP and real GNFP for

Australia. They also show that GDP and GNFP are subject to 'extra cycles' in comparison with the cycles manifested in a comprehensive coincident composite index. Furthermore, the coincident indexes are generally available on a monthly basis whereas the GDP and GNFP series are available only quarterly. They concluded that a more appropriate and helpful methodology would be to use (where available) a country's coincident composite index. This series is not only subjected to fewer revisions but also represents or indicates more closely and accurately the general course and level of economic activity. Moreover, internationally comparable coincident composite indexes—a major product of economic indicator analyses—are now available monthly for most major market-oriented countries, (from data in Tables 1.1 to 1.3).

As observed by Boehm and Summers (1999, p. 266), the coincident composite index is less subjected to revisions or changes than a single series partly because it is a combination of several components—for instance, seven for the United States and six for Australia—which reduces the effects of measurement difficulties relating to errors or later revisions of a series, especially where the early estimates of a series are based on preliminary or inadequate information. It particularly means that the coincident index generally exhibits a more accurate, stable and up-to-date reading of the course of each phase of the business cycle and of the turning points. The combination of key measures of economic activity involving income, production, retail trade and the labour market (through the level of employment and the unemployment rate) comprehensively captures the underlying empirical regularities manifested in the course of business cycles and changes in them in terms of the cumulative expansions and contractions and the associated peaks and troughs.

Using EIA to Forecast Business Cycles

The coincident index can also be used progressively in conjunction with the long-leading and the short-leading indexes both to aid reliable short-term forecasts of the likely course of business activity in the months ahead and to furnish an early identification of the timing of business-cycle turning points, both classical and growth. This is illustrated in Figures 1.1 and 1.2 which use a methodology pioneered by Moore and used by him and his colleagues at CIBCR and continues to be used at ECRI (see Banerji 1999, p. 72; also Zarnowitz and Moore 1982). Boehm (1998, pp. 37–52) and Boehm and Summers (1999, pp. 268–71) show how the growth rates in leading and coincident indexes (as explained below) may be used to forecast the course of economic activity in the months ahead for Australia. Here the analysis is extended to demonstrate this application of EIA to the business-cycle experiences in the United States and also to take advantage of the development of long-leading indexes for the United States and Australia. The traditional leading indexes for both countries are (as noted in section 1 above) here called short-leading indexes that have generally been seen to anticipate likely changes in the coincident index with leads, on average, of about six to nine months at peaks and generally about three to six months at troughs. The CIBCR's long-leading index for the United States '... was required to have an average lead of at least 12 months at peaks and 6 months at troughs for the business cycles from 1948 to 1982' (Cullity and Moore in Moore 1990, p. 59). Since then comparable long-leading indexes have been replicated for Australia, Japan, France, Germany and the United Kingdom (see Cullity and Moore 1988; Boehm and Moore 1991a and 1991b; Moore, Cullity and Boehm 1993, in which Appendix A sets out the components of the long?leading indexes in each country; and Moore, Boehm and Banerji 1992 and 1994). The performance of the long-leading index developed for Australia compares favourably with that for the United States (see the comparison of the respective long-leading, short-leading, and coincident indexes in Figures 1.1 and 1.2.

Summary and Conclusion

This paper has outlined key aspects of the development of EIA and its contribution to providing essential economic indicators and indexes to aid more fully the understanding of business cycle experiences as well as prospects in the coming months for an increasing number of countries in North America, Europe, and Asia-Pacific.

The success of EIA, its longevity and its intensive development in individual countries—initially in the United States and then its global spread—testify to Geoffrey Moore's initiatives and enthusiasm. Further, our much clearer understanding today of economic fluctuations in major market-oriented countries, and our ability to forecast more accurately how these fluctuations are likely to unfold in each country, owe much to Moore's pioneering role. Indeed, without

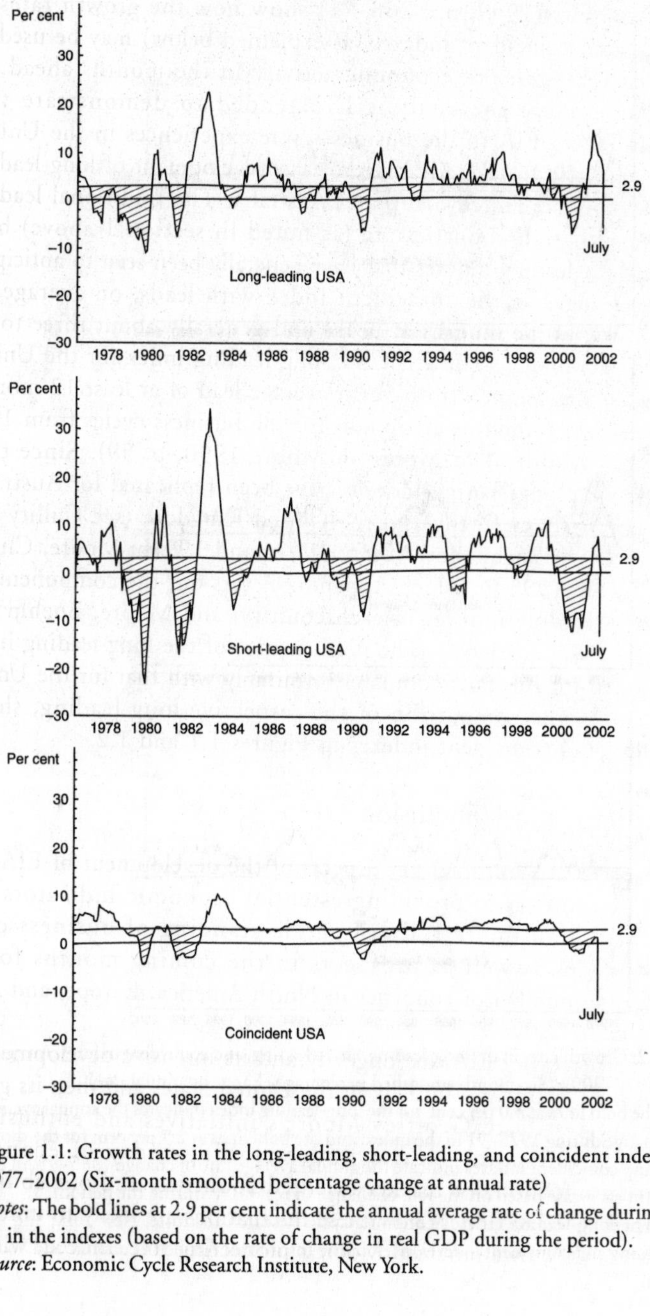

Figure 1.1: Growth rates in the long-leading, short-leading, and coincident indexes, US, 1977–2002 (Six-month smoothed percentage change at annual rate)

Notes: The bold lines at 2.9 per cent indicate the annual average rate of change during 1975–91 in the indexes (based on the rate of change in real GDP during the period).

Source: Economic Cycle Research Institute, New York.

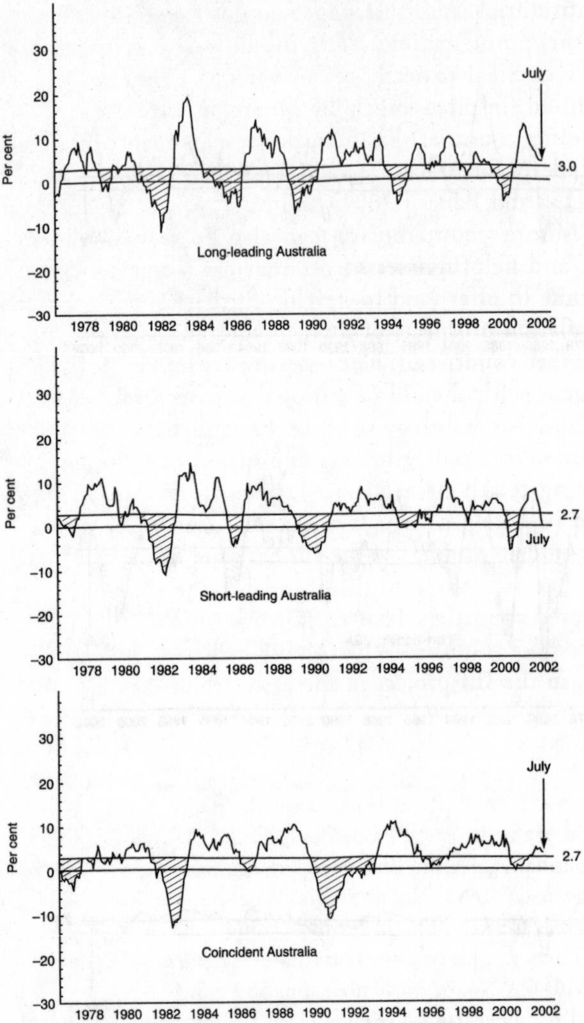

Figure 1.2: Growth rates in the long-leading, short-leading, and coincident indexes, Australia during 1977–2002 (Six-month smoothed percentage change at annual rate)

Notes: The bold lines at 3.0 per cent for the long-leading index indicates the annual average rate of change during 1975–91 in the index; and the bold lines at 2.7 per cent for the short-leading and coincident indexes indicate the annual average rate of change 1985–95, in the indexes (in each case based on the rate of change in real GDP during the period).

Source: The long-leading index, Economic Cycle Research Institute, New York; and the short-leading and coincident indexes, Melbourne Institute of Applied Economic and Social Research.

Moore's substantial role, this paper could largely not have been written at this point in time along the lines it has, regarding the comparative cyclical experiences of various countries. A recent notable addition (inspired largely by Moore, as were the comparable indexes for other countries) has been the development of leading and coincident indexes for India (Dua and Banerji 1999; Banerji and Dua 2000; and Dua and Banerji 2001a and b).

Finally, Moore's contribution can also be seen in the timely, instructive, and helpful assessments that his former colleagues at ECRI continue to offer (and to develop further) about the business cycle and inflation prospects of the United States and an increasing number of other countries. These assessments for the United States are being made with the aid of national and sectoral, leading and coincident indexes. Clearly, the EIA has much to contribute in assisting economists, policy makers and others in following closely and explaining relatively accurately the current state of business activity and its likely course in the near future. The ECRI now furnishes up-to-date readings of the current state of the business cycle and its prospects in the months ahead for the US and 16 other market-oriented countries. That is, just over double the number of countries—the G7 countries—that Moore had set as his initial target when he began the IEI project in the early 1970s.

References

Andreou, Elena; Denise R. Osborn, and Marianne Sensier (2000), A Comparison of the Statistical Properties of Financial Variables in the USA, UK and Germany over the Business Cycle, *Manchester School: Topics in Macroeconomics*, Vol. 68, No. 4, Special Issue, pp. 396–418.

Auerbach, Alan J. (1982), 'The Index of Leading Indicators: Measurement Without Theory, Thirty-Five Years Later', *Review of Economics and Statistics*, Vol. 64, No. 4, November, pp. 589–95.

Backus, David K. and Patrick J. Kehoe (1992), 'International Evidence on the Historical Properties of Business Cycles', *American Economic Review*, Vol. 82, No. 4, September, pp. 864–88.

Banerji, Anirvan (1999), 'The Three P's: Simple Tools for Monitoring Economic Cycles', *Business Economics*, Vol. 34, No. 4, October, pp. 72–6.

Banerji, Anirvan and Pami Dua (2000), 'A Leading Index for the Indian Economy', Paper presented at the 20th International Symposium on Forecasting, Lisbon, Portugal, June.

Beguelin, Jean-Pierre (1980), An International Comparison of Business Cycles, CIBCR, Rutgers University, mimeo.

Blackburn, Keith and Morten O. Ravn (1992), 'Business Cycles in the United Kingdom: Facts and Fictions', *Economica*, Vol. 59, No. 236, November, pp. 383–401.

Boehm, Ernst A. (2001), 'The Contribution of Economic Indicator Analysis to Understanding and Forecasting Business Cycles', *Indian Economic Review*, Vol. 36 No.1, January–June 2001, pp. 1–36.

—— (1998), 'A Review of Some Methodological Issues in Identifying and Analysing Business Cycles', (MIAESR) Working Paper no. 26, November.

—— (1996), 'New Economic Indicators and Business Cycle Chronologies for the Australian States', 1967–95, IAESR, Working Paper no. 2, June.

—— (1994), 'Leading and Coincident Indicators for Australia's Metals Industries', IAESR Working Paper no. 4, August.

—— (1993), *Twentieth Century Economic Development in Australia*, 3rd Edn, Melbourne: Longman Cheshire.

—— (1991a), 'Economic Indicators for Australia's Service Industries', in Lahiri and Moore (Eds) (1991), pp. 373–401.

—— (1991b), Westpac-Melbourne Institute: Indexes of Economic Activity, Report no. 75, September.

—— (1990), 'Understanding Business Cycles Today: A Critical Review of Theory and Fact', in Klein, (Ed.) (1990), pp. 25–56.

—— (1987), 'New Economic Indicators for Australia: A Further Report', IAESR (Institute of Applied Economic and Social Research), Working Paper no. 4, April.

Boehm, and Woei T. Liew (1994), 'A Review of Australia's Recent Business Cycle Experiences and a Forecast Length of the Current Expansion', *Australian Economic Review*, 3rd Quarter, pp. 4–19.

Boehm, Ernst A. and Vance L. Martin (1987), 'Testing Predictability Properties Between the Australian Leading and Coincident Indicators, 1962–85, and a Comparison with Previous Work', Department of Economics, University of Melbourne, Research Paper No. 167.

Boehm, Ernst A. and Geoffrey H. Moore (1991a), 'Financial Market Forecasts and Rates of Return Based on Leading Index Signals', IAESR, Working Paper No. 1, January.

—— (1991b), 'Financial Market Forecasts and Rates of Return Based on Leading Index Signals', *International Journal of Forecasting*, Vol. 7, No. 3, November, pp. 357–74.

—— (1984), 'New Economic Indicators for Australia, 1949–84', *Australian Economic Review*, 4th Quarter, pp. 34–56.

Boehm, Ernst A. and Peter M. Summers (1999), 'Analysing and Forecasting Business Cycles With the Aid of Economic Indicators', *International*

Journal of Management Reviews, Vol. 1, No. 3, September, pp. 245–77.

Boschan, Charlotte and Walter W. Ebanks (1978), 'The Phase-average Trend: A New Way of Measuring Economic Growth', Proceedings of the Business and Economic Statistics Section, American Statistical Association, pp. 332–5.

Brandner, Peter and Klaus Neusser (1992), 'Business Cycles in Open Economies: Stylized Facts for Austria and Germany', *Weltwirtschaftliches Archiv*, Band 128, Heft 1, pp. 69–87.

Bronfenbrenner, Martin (Ed.) (1969), *Is the Business Cycle Obsolete* ?, New York: Wiley.

Brunner, Karl and Allan H. Meltzer (Eds) (1983), *Theory, Policy, Institutions: Papers from the Carnegie–Rochester Conferences on Public Policy*, Anniversary Volume, Amsterdam: North-Holland.

Bry, Gerhard and Charlotte Boschan (1971), 'Cyclical Analysis of Time Series: Selected Procedures and Computer Programs', NBER Technical paper 20, New York.

Burns, Arthur F. and Wesley C. Mitchell (1946), *Measuring Business Cycles*, New York: NBER.

CIBCR (Center for International Business Cycle Research, New York) (1995), *International Economic Indicators*, Vol. 18, No. 12, December.

—— (1993), *International Economic Indicators*, Vol. 16, No. 6, June.

Council of Economic Advisors (1999), *Economic Report of the President*, February, Washington, DC: US Government Printing Office.

Crosby, Mark and Glenn Otto (1995). 'Real Business Cycle Models: An Introduction', *Australian Economic Review*, 3rd Quarter, pp. 55–70.

Cullity, John P. and Geoffrey H. Moore (1990), 'Long-Leading and Short-Leading Indexes', in Moore (1990), Ch. 9.

—— (1988), 'Developing a Long-Leading Composite Index for the United States', in: *New Composite Indexes and Long-Term Analysis of the Business Cycle, CIRET Study 38, IFO-Institute, Munich; and Contributions of Business Cycle Surveys to Empirical Economics,* Gower Publishing, Avebury, Brookfield, Vt. being a paper presented at CIRET Conference, Zurich, Switzerland, 1987, September 10.

Danthine, Jean-Pierre and Michel Girardin (1989), 'Business Cycles in Switzerland: A Comparative Study', *European Economic Review*, Vol. 33, pp. 31–50.

Delong, J. Bradford and Lawrence H. Summers (1986), 'The Changing Cyclical Variability of Economic Activity in the United States', in Gordon (Ed.) (1986), pp. 679–734.

Dua, Pami and Anirvan Banerji (2001a), 'A Leading Index for the Indian Economy', Centre for Development Economics, Delhi School of Economics, Working Paper Series, Working Paper No. 90.

Dua, Pami and Anirvan Banerji (2001b), 'A Leading Index for India's Exports', Reserve Bank of India, Development Research Group, Study No. 23.

—— (1999), 'An Index of Coincident Economic Indicators for the Indian Economy', *Journal of Quantitative Economics*, Vol. 15, No. 2, pp.177–201.

Dua, Pami and Stephen M. Miller (1996), 'Forecasting and Analyzing Economic Activity with Coincident and Leading Indexes: The Case of Connecticut', *Journal of Forecasting*, Vol. 15, issue No. 7, pp. 509–26.

ECRI (Economic Cycle Research Institute, New York) (2001a), *US Cyclical Outlook*, Vol. vi, No. 2, February.

—— (2001b), *US Cyclical Outlook*, Vol. vi, No. 3, March.

—— (2001c), *US Cyclical Outlook*, Vol. vi, No. 4, April.

—— (2001d), *International Cyclical Outlook*, Vol. vi, No. 4, April.

—— (2001e), *ECRI Weekly Update*, 4, May.

—— (1996), *US Cyclical Outlook*, Vol. 1, No. 1, January/February (a monthly publication).

Federal Reserve Bank of Minneapolis (1991), *Quarterly Review*, Vol. 14, No. 2, Spring.

—— (1990), *Quarterly Review*, Vol.15, No. 2, Spring.

Federal Reserve Bank of New York (2001), *Economic Policy Review*, Vol. 7, No. 1, March.

Federal Reserve Bank of St. Louis (1996), *Review*, Vol. 78, No. 4, July/August.

Fisher, Lance A., Glenn Otto, and Graham M. Voss (1996), 'Australian Business Cycle Facts', *Australian Economic Papers*, Vol. 35, No. 67, December, pp. 300–20.

Green, George R. and Barry A. Beckman (1993), 'Business Cycle Indicators: Upcoming Revision of the Composite Indexes', in US Department of Commerce (1993), pp. 44–51.

Hall Robert, Martin Feldstein, Frankel Jeffrey, Robert Gordon, N. Gregory Mankiw, and Victor Zarnowitz (2002), the NBER's Recession Dating Procedure (Business Cycle Dating Committee, National Bureau of Economic Research), mimeo, 16 September, 2002, obtained from <*nber.org/cycles/recessions.html*>.

Hertzberg, Marie P. and Barry A. Beckman (1989), 'Business Cycle Indicators: Revised Composite Indexes', in US Department of Commerce (1989), pp. 97–102.

Hodrick, Robert J. and Edward C. Prescott (1997), 'Postwar US Business Cycles: An Empirical Investigation', *Journal of Money, Credit, and Banking*, Vol. 29, No. 1, February, pp. 1–16.

—— (1980), 'Post-War US Business Cycles: An Empirical Investigation',

Working Paper no. 451 (revised), November, Pittsburgh, PA: Carnegie-Mellon University.

Kaish, Stanley (1982), 'A note on dating the Canadian growth cycle', *Canadian Journal of Economics*, Vol. 15, No. 2, May, pp. 363–8.

Kim, Kunhong, R. A. Buckle, and V. B. Hall (1994), 'Key Features of New Zealand Business Cycles, *Economic Record*, Vol. 70, No. 208, March, pp. 56–72.

Klein, Philip A. (Ed.) (1990), *Analyzing Modern Business Cycles: Essays Honoring Geoffrey H. Moore*, Armonk, New York: M. E. Sharpe Inc.

—— (1981), 'Analysing Growth Cycles in Post-War Sweden', CIBCR, Rutgers University, mimeo.

—— (1976), *Business Cycles in the Postwar World:Some Reflections on Recent Experience*, Washington, DC: American Enterprise Institute.

—— and Moore, Geoffrey H. (1985), *Monitoring Growth Cycles in Market-Oriented Countries: Developing and Using International Economic Indicators*, NBER Studies in Business Cycles, No. 26, Cambridge, Mass: Ballinger Publishing Co.

—— (1979), 'A Growth Cycle Chronology for Postwar Italy', CIBCR, Rutgers University, mimeo.

Kydland, Finn E. and Edward C. Prescott (1990), 'Business Cycles: Real Facts and a Monetary Myth', in: Federal Reserve Bank of Minneapolis (1990), pp. 3–18.

—— (1982), 'Time to Build and Aggregate Fluctuations', *Econometrica*, Vol. 50, No. 6, November, pp. 1345–70.

Lahiri, Kajal and Geoffrey H. Moore (Eds) (1991), *Leading Economic Indicators: New Approaches and Forecasting Records*, New York: Cambridge University Press.

Layton, Allan P. (1987), 'Australian and US Growth Cycle Linkages, 1967–1983', *Journal of Macroeconomics*, Vol. 9, No. 1, Winter, pp. 31–44.

—— and Geoffrey H. Moore (1989), 'Leading Indicators for the Service Sector', *Journal of Business and Economic Statistics*, Vol. 7, No. 3, July, pp. 379–86.

Long, John B. and Charles I. Plosser (1983), 'Real Business Cycles', *Journal of Political Economy*, Vol. 91, No. 1, February, pp. 39–69.

Lucas, Robert E. (1981), *Studies in Business Cycle Theory*, Oxford: Blackwell.

—— (1977), 'Understanding Business Cycles', *Stabilization of the Domestic and International Economy*, Carnegie-Rochester Conference Series on Public Policy, Vol. 5, pp. 7–29; reprinted in: Lucas (1981), pp. 215–39, and in Brunner and Meltzer (Eds) (1983), pp. 1–24.

Mintz, Ilse (1974), 'Dating United States Growth Cycles', *Explorations in Economic Research*, Occasional Papers of the NBER, Vol. 1, No. 1, Summer, pp. 1–113.

Mintz, Ilse (1972), 'Dating American Growth Cycles', in Victor Zarnowitz (Ed.) (1972), pp. 39–88.

—— (1969), 'Dating Postwar Business Cycles: Methods and Their Application to Western Germany, 1950–67', Occasional Papers, No. 107, NBER, New York.

Mitchell, Wesley C. (1927), *Business Cycles: The Problem and Its Setting*, New York: NBER.

Moore, Geoffrey H. (1990), *Leading Indicators for the 1990s,* Homewood, Illinois: Dow Jones-Irwin.

—— (1987), 'The Service Industries and the Business Cycle', Business Economics, Vol. 22, No. 2, April, pp. 12–17.

—— (1983), *Business Cycles, Inflation and Forecasting*, 2nd (revised) Edn., NBER Studies in Business Cycles, No. 24, Cambridge, Mass: Ballinger Publishing Co.

—— (1980), *Business Cycles, Inflation and Forecasting*, NBER Studies in Business Cycles, No. 24, Cambridge, Mass: Ballinger Publishing Co.

—— (Ed.) (1961), *Business Cycle Indicators*: Vol. 1, *Contributions to the Analysis of Current Business Conditions;* Vol. 2, *Basic Data on Cyclical Indicators*, A Study by the NBER, Princeton: Princeton University Press.

Moore, Geoffrey H., Ernst A. Boehm and Anirvan Banerji (1994), 'Using Economic Indicators to Reduce Risk in Stock Market Investments', *International Journal of Forecasting*, Vol. 10, No. 3, November, pp. 405–17.

—— (1992), 'Using Economic Indicators to Reduce Risk in Stock Market Investment's, IAESR, Working Paper no. 2, November.

Moore, Geoffrey H., Anirvan Banerji, and Philip Y. H. Chen (1992), 'Leading and Coincident Indexes for the New York City Economy', CIBCR, Columbia University, New York, mimeo, December.

Moore, Geoffrey H. and John P. Cullity (1990), 'Leading and Coincident Indicators for Primary Metals, CIBCR, Columbia University, New York, mimeo, January.

Moore, Geoffrey H., John P. Cullity, and Ernst A. Boehm (1993), 'Forecasting Magnitudes of Economic Change with Long-Leading Indexes: Six Countries', IAESR Working Paper No. 5, December.

Moore, Geoffrey H. and Philip A. Klein (1977), *Monitoring Business Cycles at Home and Abroad: A Basic Report on the NBER International Economic Indicator System*, US Department of Commerce, Washington, DC.

Moore, Geoffrey H. and Melita H. Moore (1985), *International Economic Indicators: A Source-book*, Westport, Conn: Greenwood Press.

Niemera, Michael P. and Philip A. Klein (1994), *Forecasting Financial and Business Cycles*, New York: John Wiley.

Oppenländer, Karl H. (1994), 'Narrowing the Induction Gap: Measurement without Theory', in Oppenländer and Poser (Eds) (1994), pp. 703–26; paper presented at 21st CIRET Conference, Stellenbosch, South Africa, October, 1993.

Oppenländer, Karl H., and Günter Poser (Eds) (1994), *The Explanatory Power of Business Cycle Surveys: Papers presented at the 21st CIRET Conference Proceedings, Stellenbosch, 1993,* Avebury, Aldershot.

Orr, James, Robert Rich, and Rae Roesen (2001), 'Leading Economic Indexes for New York State and New Jersey', in Federal Reserve Bank of New York (2001), pp. 73–94.

Phillips, Keith R. (1994), 'Regional Indexes of Leading Economic Indicators', in Niemira and Klein (1994), pp. 347–61.

Plosser, Charles I. (1989), 'Understanding Real Business Cycles', *Journal of Economic Perspectives*, Vol. 3, No. 3, Summer, pp. 51–77.

Romer, Christina D. (1994), 'Remeasuring Business Cycles', *Journal of Economic History*, Vol. 54, No. 3, September, pp. 573–609.

Serletis, Apostolos and David Krause (1996), 'Nominal Stylized Facts of US Business Cycles', in Federal Reserve Bank of St. Louis (1996), pp. 49–54.

Shisken, Julius (1961), 'Signals of Recession and Recovery: An Experiment with Monthly Reporting, NBER Occasional Paper 77.

Shisken, Julius and Geoffrey H. Moore (1968), 'Composite Indexes of Leading, Coinciding, and Lagging Indicators, 1948–67', Supplement to National Bureau 1, January.

Solow, Robert M. (1970), *Growth Theory: An Exposition*, Oxford: Clarendon Press.

Stock, James H. and Mark W. Watson (1991), 'A Probability Model of the Coincident Economic Indicators', in Lahiri and Moore (Eds) (1991), ch. 4.

US Department of Commerce (1993), *Survey of Current Business*, Bureau of Economic Analysis, Washington, DC, October.

—— (1989), *Business Conditions Digest*, Bureau of Economic Analysis, Washington, DC, January.

—— (1984), *Handbook of Cyclical Indicators: a supplement to the Business Conditions Digest*, Bureau of Economic Analysis, Washington, DC.

—— (1977), *Handbook of Cyclical Indicators: A Supplement to Business Conditions Digest*, Bureau of Economic Analysis, Washington, DC, May.

Westpac-Melbourne Institute (2001), *Westpac-Melbourne Institute Indexes of Economic Activity*, Report no. 190, April, University of Melbourne.

Wolf, Holger C. (1991), 'Procyclical Prices: A Demi-Myth', in Federal Reserve Bank of Minneapolis, (1991), pp. 25–8.

Zarnowitz, Victor (1992), *Business Cycles: Theory, History, Indicators, and Forecasting,* Chicago: University of Chicago Press.

Zarnowitz, Victor (Ed.) (1972), *The Business Cycle Today: Fiftieth Anniversary Colloquim I*, New York: NBER.

Zarnowitz, Victor and Charlotte Boschan (1977), Cyclical Indicators: An Evaluation and New Leading Indexes, in: U.S. Department of Commerce (1977), pp. 170–9.

Zarnowitz, Victor and Geoffrey H. Moore, (1982), 'Sequential Signals of Recession and Recovery', *Journal of Business*, Vol. 55, No.1, January, pp. 57–85; reprinted in Moore (1983).

2

Anatomy of Recent US Growth and Business Cycles

Victor Zarnowitz

Introduction: Purposes and Plan of Study

Changes in the economy's structure are mostly gradual, those the dynamic factors and their weights tend to be relatively fast; but the structure and dynamics influence each other. These changes and interactions—along with domestic and international policies as well as outside events—explain why business cycles vary a great deal over time. Policies are reactive or proactive; they have economic, financial, and political constraints; and they can and sometimes do, benefit from learning. Outside events or shocks are represented by their presumed results, that is shifts in economic and other variables; they affect business cycles in ways that are often elusive and generally unpredictable.

This paper will look at all of these aspects of economic change as it breaks down the US business cycles of the post-World War II period into a sequence of successive expansions and contractions and their respective stages. This is done with the aid of a trend-cycle decomposition applied to a comprehensive index of aggregate economic activity. Measures relating to longer-run trends and intermediate-run fluctuations in levels, growth rates, and detrended values are examined. Combinations of monthly coincident indicators as well as quarterly aggregates from the national income and product accounts are used which allows some assessment of the relative usefulness of these two types of broadly based time series for business cycle analysis.

One purpose of these exercises is to answer the question, how can the stages of business cycles be identified and dated? Another query is, what are the dimensions of these stages and how are they related? The analysis also throws light on the common and uncommon features of individual cycles. In addressing this last question, special attention is accorded to the latest sequence of recovery–boom–slowdown–recession (1991–2001).

In broader terms, the objective of this investigation of the economy's recent evolution, continuity of movement, and innovations is eventually conventional and practical: to help distinguish signals from noise and the persistent and recurrent from the episodic and evanescent. Mechanical smoothing techniques are widely used and can help but they can also disturb and conceal. Hence, they must be used cautiously, with an understanding of their limitations and risks. Waiting for more information to accumulate, while frequently advisable, is sometimes not practical for business and government policy makers. Data about changes in the economy from one short period to the next one are now abundant but are also in large part dominated by random variations (statistical 'noise'), unstable (revised time and again), and complex (consider the aggregates in real terms from the national income and product accounts). Short-term changes in many macroeconomic time series attract great attention but are hard to interpret and are often misunderstood (mostly taken at face value and more seriously than they deserve).

The first substantive part of the paper deals with topics of broad interest, namely, how to identify successive business cycles and growth cycles and how to use the resulting trend estimates and timing measures to derive stages of business expansions and contractions. The discussion moves from levels to growth rates of the selected macroeconomic time series to consider the relative size and role of their volatility.

The second part concentrates on the latest US cycle, its common features, particularities and asks what factors and relationships help explain the recent cyclical and structural changes. This involves looking at corporate, investor, and consumer behaviour and government policies as reflected in national aggregates of expenditure and receipts. These totals, while adjusted for inflation, are affected by money, credit, and price changes as well as new developments in technology, globalization, foreign threats, and concerns about domestic security.

Patterns and Noise in Economic Change

Types, Timing, and Duration of Observed Fluctuations

A paper co-written with Ataman Ozyildirim introduced the phase average trend (PAT) and compared it with other trend estimates for the monthly US coincident index (CI) and the quarterly real US gross domestic product (GDP). The deviations of CI from its PAT serve as a good base for the dating of 'growth cycles' that is fluctuations in the detrended measure of total economic activity.[1]

In a continuation of that study, Table 2.1 shows the timing and duration of phases for 14 complete, peak-to-peak US growth cycles since 1948. The table also includes a parallel listing of the turning dates and durations for 10 complete peak-to peak US business cycles since 1948. The two chronologies have a high degree of consistency and comparability. Both are based largely on the same set of data and analogous techniques. The business cycle peaks and troughs are those selected by the National Bureau of Economic Research (NBER), which used mainly the four components of CI (industrial production, real manufacturing and trade sales, real personal income tax transfer payments, and non-farm employment). Phase average bend and growth cycles go back to the NBER work in the 1970s.[2]

Charting the Growth of the Economy

Real GDP is the most comprehensive and most widely used measure of total output or income. Thus it is reasonable to ask why it is not GDP but CI that is used to date business cycle turns, recessions, and recoveries.

Data on GDP are available only quarterly and are revised repeatedly over long periods, at times substantially. Moreover, real GDP is a very complex and imperfect measure of total economic activity. For example, national income accountants admit that their estimates of depreciation are poor, hence they prefer GDP to real net domestic product (NDP), which excludes these estimates. However,

Table 2.1: US Growth Cycles and Business Cycles, 1948–2000

Durations of Cycles and Their Phase

Growth Cycles Peaks (P) and Troughs (T)			Durations in Months of Growth Cycles and Phases			Business Cycles Peaks (P) and Throughs (T)			Durations of Months of Business Cycles and Phases		
P	T	P	P to T	T to P	P to P	P	T	P	P to T	T to P	P to P
(1)	(2)	(3)	(4)	(5)	(6)	(7)	(8)	(9)	(10)	(11)	(12)
Jul–48	Oct–49	Jan–51	15	15	30	Nov–48	Oct–49	Jul–53	11	45	56
Jan–51	Jul–52	Mar–53	18	8	26						
Mar–53	Aug–54	Feb–57	17	30	47	Jul–53	May–54	Aug–57	10	39	49
Feb–59	Apr–58	Jan–60	14	21	35	Aug–57	Apr–58	Apr–60	8	24	32
Jan–60	Feb61	Apr–62	13	14	27	Apr–60	Feb–61	Dec–69	10	106	116
Apr–62	Jan–64	Mar–66	21	26	47						
Mar–66	Oct–67	Aug–69	19	22	41						
Aug–69	Nov–70	Nov–73	15	36	51	Dec–69	Nov–70	Nov–73	11	36	47
Nov–73	Apr–75	Mar–79	17	47	64	Nov–73	Mar–75	Jan–80	16	58	74
Mar–79	Jul–80	Jul–81	16	12	28	Jan–80	Jul–80	Jul–81	6	12	18
Jul–81	Dec–82	Sep–84	17	21	38	Jul–81	Nov–82	Jul–90	16	92	108
Sep–84	Jan–87	Jan–89	28	24	52						
Jan–89	Dec–91	Jan–95	35	37	72	Jul–90	Mar–91	Mar–01	8	120	128
Mean			18.4	26.1	44.5				10.7	59.1	69.8
Median			17.0	23.0	44.0				10.0	45.0	56.0
Standard Deviation			6.2	13.2	15.0				3.4	38.0	39.1

depreciation represents the portion of capital that is worn out or becomes obsolete and needs to be replaced—an element of cost, not of output of new capital goods.

Because of a variety of conceptual and estimation problems, then, the GDP series is not as helpful in identifying and maintaining a chronology of business cycles as is the set of selected monthly indicators of current economic conditions. These data are more timely and also less affected by revisions, judgemental imputations, and accounting intricacies. The series that have proved best include non-farm employment, real personal income less transfer payments, real manufacturing, retail and wholesale trade sales, and the index of industrial production (listed in descending order in terms of comprehensiveness of coverage). The tendency of these (and other) variables to move together with limited and partly systematic timing differences constitutes a defining characteristic of business cycles.

Figure 2.1 shows the monthly CI of the Conference Board, which combines the four indicator series listed above, along with quarterly GDP (interpolated linearly between the mid-months) for the period since 1959. The recessions are shaded according to the NBER peak and trough dates identified in the figure. The dating of the recessions was, of course, based on data on coincident indicators and national income and product (NIPA) accounts available at the time. However, the CI in its present vintage, that is after all intervening revisions, misses none of the historical NBER recessions and shows no extra turning points of its own.

Real GDP, too, weakened noticeably in each of the same contraction phases and at no other time. But its cyclical changes were on several occasions less well-timed and less well-articulated than the concurrent changes in CI. This was the case during the declines in 1960, 1970, and 1981–2. Due to past revisions, GDP, in its present form shows a few leads at business cycle peaks and troughs, whereas CI turning points are most of the time exactly coincident with NBER dates.[3]

Figure 2.1 also shows, the Conference Board's leading index (LI)—the top curve drawn to the same scale as C. Its ten components represent stock prices, real money supply, interest rate spread, consumer expectations, new orders for consumer goods and for non-defence capital goods, housing permits, a speed of deliveries index, unemployment insurance claims, and average weekly hours of work in manufacturing.

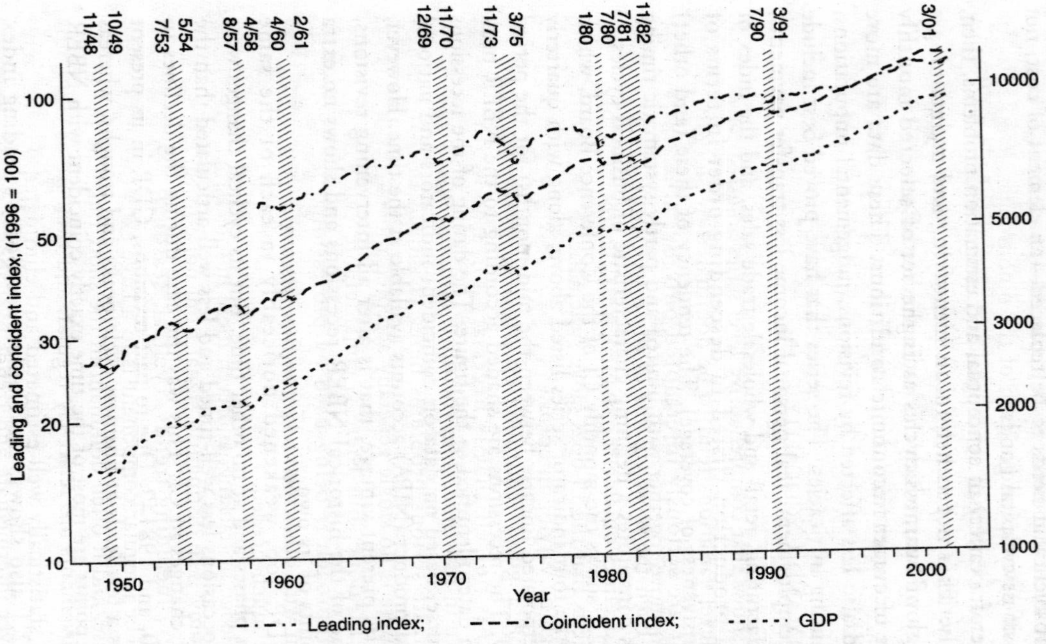

Figure 2.1: Leading and Coincident Indexes and Real GDP, United States, 1948–2002

Note: Shaded areas represent business cycle recessions.

Source: The Conference Board and BEA.

Reflecting the great sensitivity of these variables, LI shows large as well as early cyclical movements.[4] It has led at each of the ten post-war US business cycles and at each of the nine troughs. The leads are much longer at peaks than at troughs, averaging 9.4 and 5.0 months, respectively. This is because recessions were often preceded by substantial slowdowns, which the leading indicators anticipated; while most of the recoveries from the relatively short declines were prompt or 'V-shaped'.

Volatility and Cyclicality

Figure 2.1 shows that comprehensive level series adjusted for seasonal and price level variations tend to be dominated by smooth growth trends that are seriously interrupted only by rather infrequent recessions. Even the most volatile of these series, the LI, shows few significant declines outside the shaded areas. Further, the historical record suggests that the LI does move systematically ahead of CI and GDP, though by varying intervals.

However, a good record based on historical data, though important, is not all that is necessary for a good forecasting performance in real time. The volatility, tardiness, and revisions of the data create serious problems here, as indeed in many other contexts. There is no single generally accepted model or rule for the use of the LI alone. But there is considerable evidence that the indicator approach is being used by professional forecasters in combination with other methods, and that its contribution is positive and its role much needed.[5]

The challenge in tracking, and even more in forecasting, the course of the economy is to distinguish signal from noise in time series that are complex, including trends, cyclical, seasonal, and irregular variations. The irregular component is to a large extent unpredictable random noise, and it often dominant in the short run. The intra-year seasonal movements are relatively regular, and they are usually, but not always, statistically well estimated and eliminated. Cycles may dominate over intermediate and trends over longer periods, but the two influence each other.

When differenced to show changes rather than levels, even comprehensive series such as real GDP are very volatile, often swinging up and down strongly from quarter to quarter (Figure 2.2a). Even in very prosperous times, as in the mid-1950s or the mid-1960s, whether in peace or war, the growth of US output can be found to heve moved

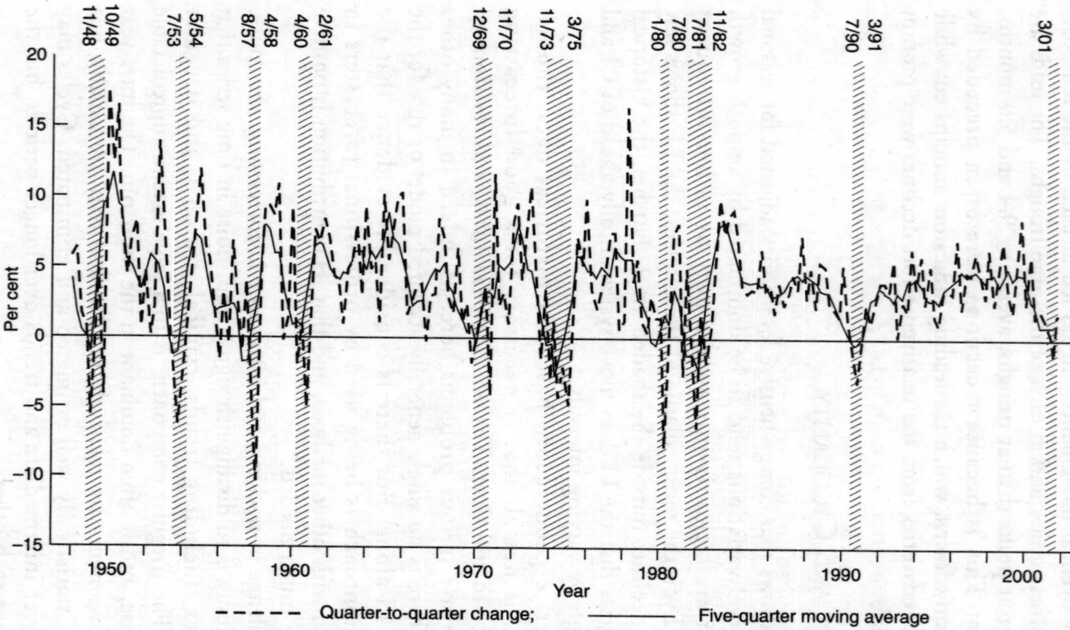

Figure 2.2a: Real GDP, Quarter-to-quarter Change and Five-Quarter Moving Average, Annual Rate, 1948–2001
Note: Shaded areas represent business cycle recessions.
Source: The Conference Board and BEA

quickly from high (as much as 7 per cent or more) to low (2 per cent or less) and *vice versa*. These jumps and falls have clearly little to do with the very much steadier growth of potential output, which proceeds in between these extremes. They are more likely related to some diverse surprise events or 'shocks' that occur frequently. Such shifts are generally poorly understood, and it should hardly be expected that they will be accurately predicted. Yet the quarterly forecasts of real GDP in fact attract a lot of attention from outside observers and the public who may expect too much of them.

Smoothing is used widely to reduce volatility and to show the cyclical component of the series (or their local trends) more clearly. But it is more helpful for analytical than forecasting purposes and must be applied with caution. Figures 2 (a–c) include five-quarter moving averages of changes centred on the third quarter. (There is a dilemma here: centering causes a loss of the critical last periods, but a 'trailing,' that is, uncentred moving average lags behind unsmoothed data.) Clearly, the moving average can reveal the tendencies of the economy's movement better than the much more erratic underlying data but at the cost of some delay and inevitable uncertainty at the end of the series. The moving average descends less below the zero line than the quarterly changes and may create artificial leads as can be seen near the downturns of 1957 and 1980.

The series of growth rates for real GDP and real NDP are very similar but the range of variation is somewhat greater for NDP (Figure 2.2b). Negative changes are concentrated in recessions, with but a few minor exceptions, but they too come in various sizes and irregular patterns. The popular rule of two consecutive declines in GDP applies in most but not all cases. It should not be regarded as a necessary feature of recessions. In five post-war contractions (1948–49, 1960, 1970, 1973–75, and 1981–82), declines in GDP (and NDP) were interrupted by rises.

The volatility of the month-to-month changes in the CI is considerable but mitigated by offsets among the four component indicators. When converted to a quarterly series for comparability, CI is much smoother than the GDP or NDP (Figure 2.2c). The declines of CI during recessions are mostly uninterrupted by rises. The CI had fewer extra declines than GDP (only four, all relatively small and short, and all in the 1950s). This is consistent with the conclusion that CI is less volatile and has clearer patterns of cyclical movement than GDP.

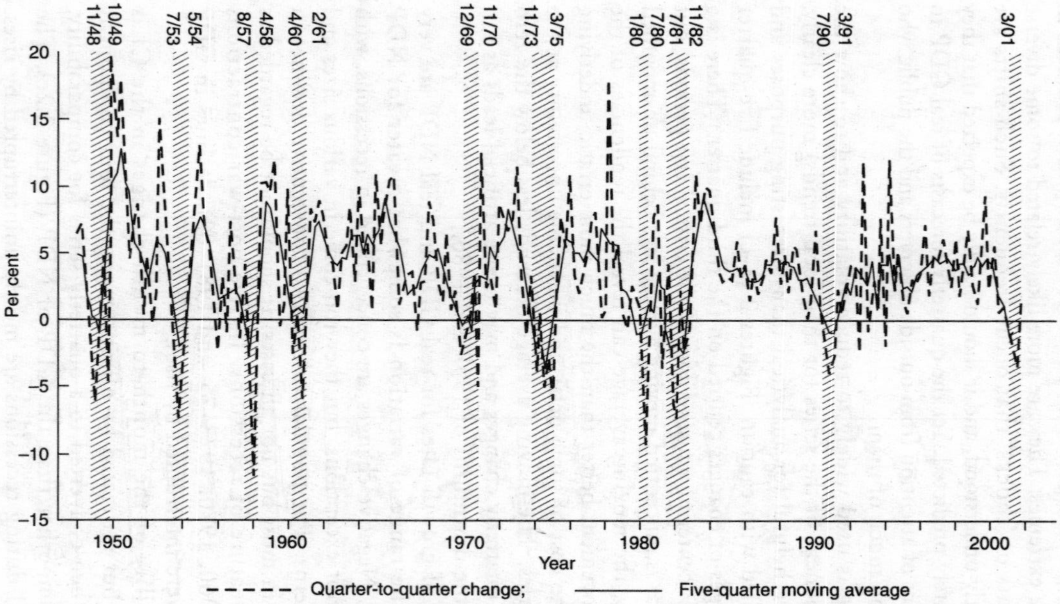

Figure 2.2b: Real NDP, Quarter-to-quarter Change, and Five-Quarter Moving Average, Annual Rate, 1948–2001
Note: Shaded areas represent business cycle recessions.
Source: The Conference Board and BEA

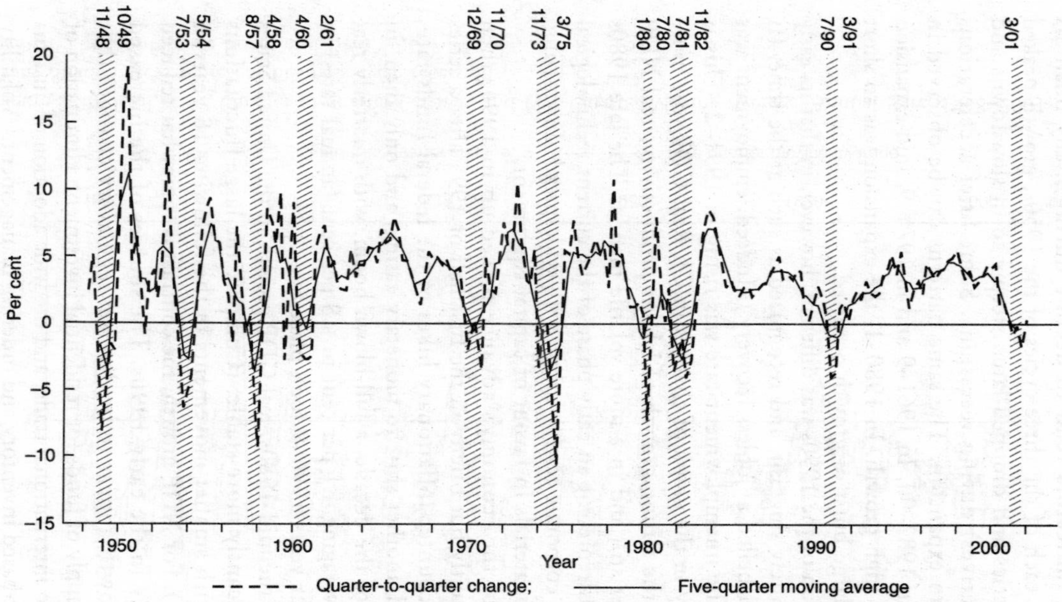

Figure 2.2c: Coincident Index, Quarter-to-quarter Change, and Five-Quarter Moving Average, Annual Rate, 1959–2001

Note: Shaded areas represent business cycle recessions.

Source: The Conference Board.

Figure 2.2 (a–c) confirm that the growth rates of comprehensive measures of economic activity such as GDP or NDP and the index of coincident indicators tend to decline during many business expansions. In each of the three cycles of the 1950s, growth peaked early in recoveries and dropped later, steeply so in slowdowns and (into the negatives) during recessions. Some brief accelerations occurred late in expansion. The same patterns can be observed in 1975–80 and in 1982–90. In 1961–9 and in 1975–9, mid-expansion stages brought high growth. In 1980–1, the expansion was so short that only one large burst of growth occurred.

The expansion of the 1990s was different, however, in that its early stage was definitely sluggish, and recognized as such at the time. (It was popularly labelled a 'jobless recovery'). Indeed, employment was stagnant and the unemployment rate was rising in 1991–2. This is reflected clearly in the graph of changes in CI. Real GDP rose more firmly due to the strong growth of labour productivity; real NDP somewhat faster still and in a more volatile manner. The late 1980s and early 1990s represent an early phase of the current technological revolution and corporate restructuring, with widespread 'downsizing' of labour and materials in favour of capital equipment.[6]

The pace of the economy's advance picked up in 1994, then slowed significantly but briefly in the first half of 1995 after a series of preventive counter-inflationary hikes of the federal funds rate. There followed another shift to monetary easing, and only then, in the latter half of the decade, a full-blown boom, with quarterly real GDP figures averaging 4.1 per cent to 4.8 per cent (annual rates) in each of the four years 1996–9 took place.

Since about the mid-1980s, real GDP growth in the United States became significantly more stable. (Compare the large fluctuations before 1984 with smaller movements in the following 18 years in Figure 2.2 a–c). For NDP growth, the contrast is somewhat reduced by its volatility in the early 1990s. The sources of the increased stability of growth appear to be diverse: regulatory changes that stabilized the supply of funds for residential investment; elimination of many barriers to international trade; and the wide adoption of 'just-in-time' computer-based inventory and ordering management.[7] Volatility may remain lower, but it has not been abolished and neither has cyclicality.

Stages of Expansion and Contraction

Business expansions vary greatly in duration, amplitude, and persistence, business contractions vary less. The shortest of the post-war expansions lasted one year, the longest ten years; the range of the recessions was from six to sixteen months (Table 2.1). Four of the ten expansions were interrupted by slowdowns, while all the contractions were essentially continuous. Given this diversity, can the cycle phases be usefully subdivided into further stages with similar characteristics?

The answer is a qualified 'yes'. Many past classifications have proved to be only temporarily valid, probably because they were overly ambitious.[8] Results that have more general validity across time and space can be obtained by using the trend–cycle decomposition applied to real time series.

One must begin with a simplified schematic representation of the underlying ideas. Consider a comprehensive time series or index measuring economic activity or its diverse interrelated aspects (for example GDP or CI). Take the prototypical cycle in economic activity to be a smoothed sinusoidal movement around its long growth trend. As depicted in Figure 2.3, the trend goes approximately through the mid-points of the cyclical declines in the so measured aggregate economic activity (like PAT does empirically for CI). Thus the series rises from trough to peak and falls from peak to trough, crossing the trend from below and from above, respectively; accordingly its troughs (peaks) lie below (above) the trend. Now divide this movement into recovery (rebound from trough to trend), boom or rise (rising above trend to the largest distance from trend, the growth cycle peak), slowdown (declining positive growth), downturn (negative growth bringing CI down to the trend) and decline (continuation of the downward movement below trend to the new trough). The first three of these steps constitute the expansion; the last two, the contraction or recession.

It is apparent that the scheme incorporates one basic assumption, namely that the economy is growing in each business cycle. Thus each peak is higher than the peak in the preceding cycle. This is normally the case, and exceptions to this rule are very rare. One can conceive of a very depressed period during which growth ceased and one or even more cycles occurred with expansions consisting only of (perhaps incomplete) recoveries. Indeed, examples of such stagnant periods exist in US and foreign economic histories. But they point to

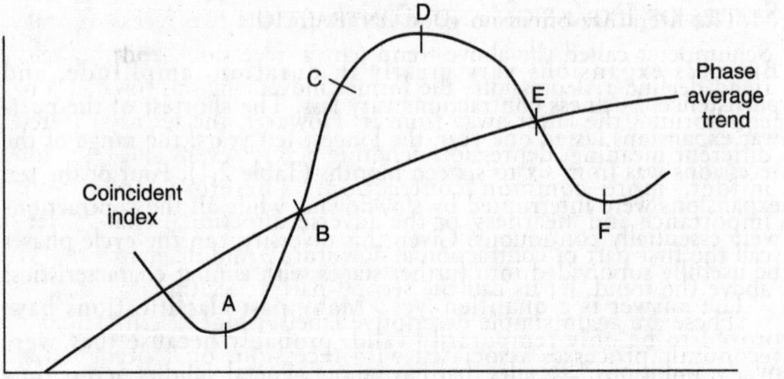

Figure 2.3: Stages of Expansion and Contraction

	Stages	Phases
A, F: Business Cycle Troughs	AB: Recovery	
B: Rising Through Trend	BC: Rise	AD: Expansion
C: Growth Cycle Peak	CD: Slowdown	
D: Business Cycle Peak	DE: Downturn	DF: Contraction (Recession)
E: Falling Through Trend	EF: Decline	

anomalous conditions that call for major reforms and/or end in major cataclysms—economic or financial crises; institutional or policy failures, and combinations thereof.[9] Such conditions have been absent in the post-war US economy. (The short expansion of July 1980–July 1981 ended just slightly higher than it began (see Figure 2.1). However, this turbulent period of high inflation and interest rates was short and initiated an era of lower and more stable prices and higher and more stable growth.)

An assumption underlying Figure 2.3 is that the last stage of expansion is a slowdown during which the gains continue but diminish. This has been true in most, but not all, recent US business cycles.

Of the stages of expansion, the first and third have the familiar and self-explanatory names of recovery and slowdown, respectively, but the second, which denotes mid-expansion growth rising above the trend, has not. If growth is strong and maintained or rising, this stage may properly be called a 'boom'. But this popular term is not always appropriate because in some cycles growth in this stage is only moderate (often less than in the recovery stage), and may also be discontinuous. 'Rise' is preferred as more neutral and more accurate. It is in this stage that economic activity rises above the highest past levels and begins to register net gains.

The literature offers no good names for the two recession stages. Schumpeter called the above-trend part a 'recession', and the below-trend decline a 'depression'; the former movement was towards a new equilibrium, the latter away from it. However, the terms acquired a different meaning; depression denoting a very severe and recession a milder, more common contraction. Therefore, to note the importance and 'nearness' of the adverse directional change, let us call the first part of contraction a 'downturn'. And, to match the 'rise' above the trend, let us call the second part a 'decline'.

These are again simple descriptive labels. Some classifications use economic processes associated with recessions or depressions and refer to stages of 'liquidation' (of excess inventories and debts) or 'absorption' (of excess capacities). These processes are real and important enough but their temporal allocation within the cycle presents difficulties: they may start in slowdowns and extend beyond contractions. Historically important, too, but more episodic, were various other processes or events such as tight money policies, financial crises and crunches, oil price shocks, and stock market bubbles—but clearly none of these is helpful here. Neither is the older emphasis on deflation, although recent developments in Japan remind us of its continued depressant power.

The nine complete business cycle contractions in 1949–91 were generally short, and the recession of 2001 now looks short too. One may well question, then, the need to divide these episodes any further. However, each recession presumably brings the economy down below its local growth trend for some time: the PAT, like most other trend estimates—that are useful for growth cycle analysis—meets this condition.[10] Hence, experimentally, two recession stages are distinguished here.

Application to US Cycles in the Post-World War II Period

Table 2.2 shows that it is possible to fit the outlined scheme to actual data representing the evolution of the US economy in the past half-century, provided this is done with sufficient flexibility in the recognition of the diversity of individual business cycles and growth cycles covered. No single multi-stage classification can fit the variety of cyclical experience without modifications. But deviations from the suggested pattern can themselves by readily identified, dated, and explained.

The Conference Board current conditions (US Coincident) index (CI) continues to serve as our database. The CI is plotted in Figure 2.4, along with its trend (PAT). As shown in Table 2.2 (column 3) and Figure 2.4, all but 2 of the 10 post-Word War II expansions in the US ended in slowing growth that turned negative. The three-year expansion of the early 1970s ended abruptly in November 1973, a month after the Organization of Petroleum Exporting Countries (OPEC) imposed an oil embargo on trade partners of Israel, starting a sharp climb in oil prices. The extremely short (one-year) expansion of 1980–1 also ended abruptly and may be attributed to the uniquely high and rising real interest rates. But such sharp downturns were exceptions in the past half-century as they were caused by special factors. (In contrast, crises were more frequent in earlier times, and some theorists perceived sharp peaks to be common.)[11]

Table 2.2 lists only the slowdowns that represent the end stages of expansions. But, as already noted, growth-cycle contractions (slowdowns) also occurred in 1951–52, 1962–63, 1966–67, 1984–86, and 1995, in each case interrupting a long rise. Figure 2.4 shows these rises and interruptions.

Recoveries, rises, and final slowdowns averaged 14, 39, and 8 months, respectively, accounting for about 22 per cent, 65 per cent, and 13 percent of the expansion durations. The corresponding standard deviations are large, matching the great dispersion of business cycle expansions (see Table 2.2 for details).

The 1990s witnessed the longest recovery as well as the longest rise of all post-war expansions. The 1960s and the 1980s had quick and short recoveries and also long but more uneven rises with longer intervening slowdowns. The developments in the 1950s, 1970s, and early 1980s show greater cyclicality: as many as six short sequences of expansion and contraction, with recoveries more pronounced relative to rises and slowdowns mostly short.

Figure 2.5 plots the deviations from the trend (PAT) of the US CI. Whereas the slowdowns that precede and accompany recessions show large and long declines below PAT, the slowdowns that merely interrupt expansions do not—they barely dip briefly below PAT. This is an important distinction analytically, which may also prove to be of some value in practical application.

The downturns ranged from 3 to 11 months in duration; so did the declines below the trend. On an average, the two stages of

Table: 2.2: Stages of Expansion and Contraction in US Economy, 1948–2001

Expansion (from BCT to BCP)					Recession (from BCP to BCT)
	Recovery	Rise	Slowdown	Downturn	Decline
	(from BCT to PAT)	(Sustained growth above PAT)	(from GCP to BCP)	(from BCP to PAT)	(from PAT to BCT)
Line	(1)	(2)	(3)	(4)	(5)
1			1/48–11/48 (10)	11/48–3/49 (4)	3/49–10/49 (7)
2	10/49–5/50 (7)	5/50–3/53 (34)	3/53–7/53 (4)	7/53–11/53 (4)	11/53–5/54 (6)
3	5/54–3/55 (10)	3/55–2/57 (23)	2/57–8/57 (6)	8/57–10/57 (3)	10/57–4/58 (5)
4	4/58–1/59 (9)	1/59–1/60 (12)	1/60–4/60 (3)	4/60–10/60 (6)	10/60–2/61 (4)
5	2/61–9/61 (7)	9/61–8/69 (95)	8/69–12/69 (3)	12/69–5/70 (5)	5/70–11/70 (6)
6	11/70–3/72 (16)	3/72–11/73 (18)	none	11/73–10/74 (11)	10/74–3/75 (5)
7	3/75–5/77 (25)	5/77–3/79 (22)	3/79–1/80 (10)	1/80–4/80 (3)	4/80–7/80 (3)
8	7/80–9/80 (2)	9/80–7/81 (10)	none	7/81–12/81 (5)	12/81–11/82 (11)
9	11/82–11/83 (12)	11/83–1/89 (62)	1/89–7/90 (18)	7/90–12/90 (5)	12/90–3/91 (3)
10	3/91–2/94 (35)	2/94–5/00 (75)	5/00–3/01 (10)	3/01–6/01 (3)[t]	6/01–11/01 (5)

Duration of Stages (in months)

		Recovery	Rise	Slowdown	Downturn	Decline
11	Mean	13.8	39.0	8.1	4.9	5.5

Contd.

		Recovery	Rise	Slowdown	Downturn	Decline
12	Median	10	23	8	4.5	5
13	St. Dev	10.5	30.7	5.0	2.4	2.3
14	Range	2–35	10–75	3–18	3–11	3–11
15	Average per cent of phase	22.7	64.0	13.3	47.1	52.9

Notes:
[a]Tentative. Based on the phase average trend (PAT) updated through April 2002 and on the assumption that the recession ended in November 2001.
BCT, business Cycle trough; BCP, business cycle peak; PAT, phase average trend; GCP, growth cycle peak; St. Dev., standard deviation.
Numbers in parenthesis represent stage durations in months.

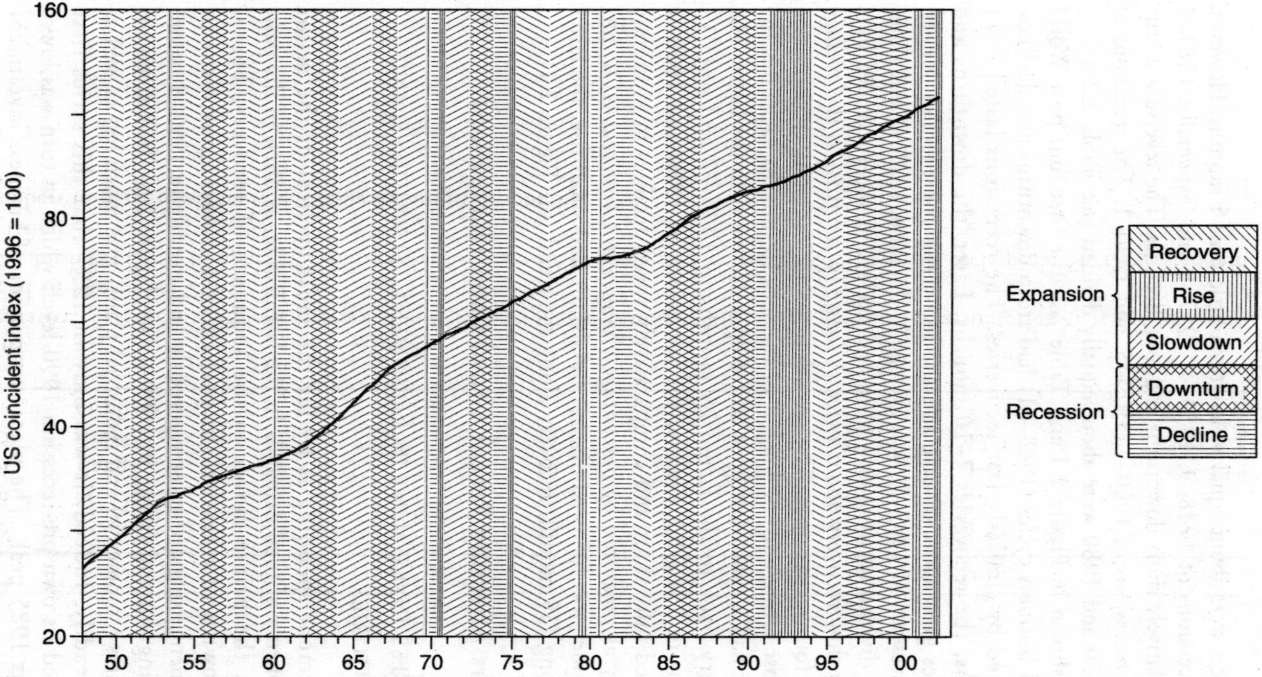

Figure 2.4: US Business Cycles—Stages of Expansion and Contraction with Growth Cycle Slowdowns, 1949–2002.

recession were about equal in length, a little over 5 months. However, the recessions of 1948–9, 1953–4, 1957–8 and, especially, 1981–2 had relatively short downturns and long declines. The reverse was true of the recessions of 1960–1, 1973–5, and 1990–1. The recessions of 1969–70 and 1980 were about equally divided (see Table 2.2).

As shown in Figure 2.4 and Table 2.2, the first four post-World War II business cycles (1948–61) had steep downturns and declines, followed by similarly fast recoveries. The recessions lasted 8–11 months, the recoveries 7–10 months. Later, the downturns and declines grew more diverse and the recoveries considerably longer. The recession of 1969–70 was average in duration, shallow, and about evenly divided between downturn and decline; it was succeeded by a mostly slow recovery about twice as long (16 months) as the average of the four earlier ones. The recessions of 1973–5 and 1981–2 were the most severe and the longest of the set (16 months each) but the former had a shorter, steeper, and deeper decline than the latter. The recovery back to the lasted 25 months in 1975-77 and only 12 months in 1982-83. Finally, the recessions of 1980 and 1990–1 involved only short and comparatively small declines in economic activity as measured by percentage changes in CI or real GDP, but the former was followed directly by a short and small rise, the latter by a long (35 month) recovery along the trend (see Figure 2.1).

Factors Affecting Recent Growth and Fluctuations

Business Investment in Equipment, Structures, and Inventories

Investment spending is by far the most cyclical of the major components of total demand. In the last decade, as often in the past, it was the prime mover in the sequence of recovery, boom, slowdown and recession. In particular, business investment in equipment expanded most vigorously and steadily in 1992–9 before flattening out and falling in 2000–1 (see Figure 2.6). Investment in structures (commercial and industrial plant) rose much less as well as less steadily. Indeed, it was only in 1997 that this series first exceeded its own pre-recession 1990 level, which in turn was lower than its 1985 peak. The plant component of business investment flattened and declined mildly in 1998 and early 1999, rebounded, and fell much more abruptly in 2001, as shown in the figure.

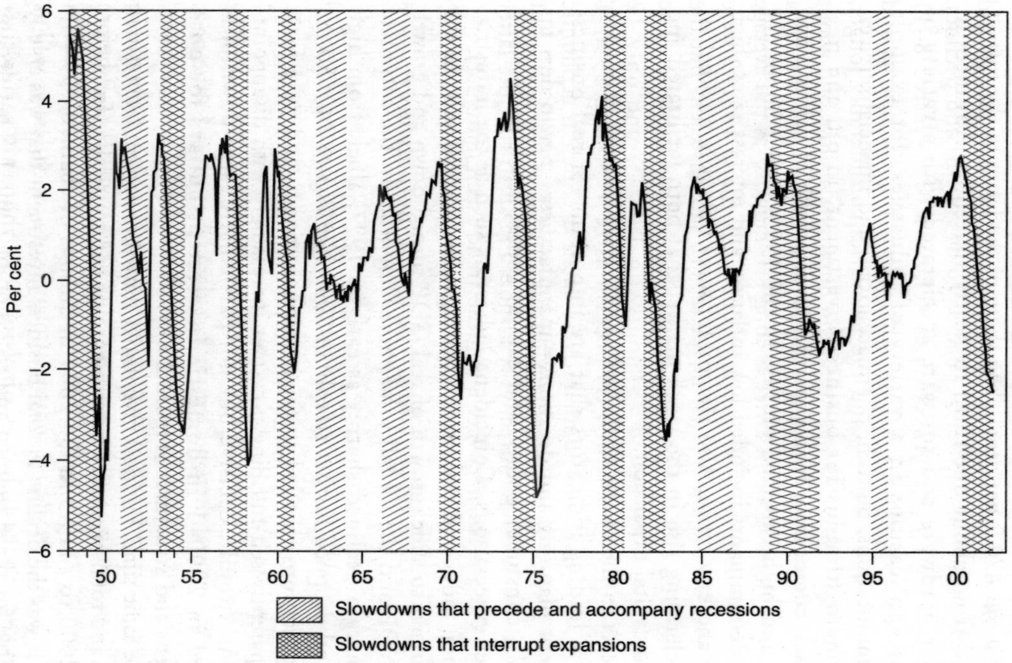

Figure 2.5: US Current Conditions Index (US Coincident Index) Deviations from Phase Average Trend.

The great rise in spending on producers' equipment reflected in large part the enormous spread of the 'new information technology'. While total investment in equipment (including software) almost tripled between its trough in Quarter (Q)1 1991 and its peak in Q1 2000, investment in information processing nearly quintupled (273.7 per cent *versus* 470.9 per cent). The share of the latter in the former increased from about one-third to nearly six-tenths. Advances in computer hardware and software accelerated with a variety of business applications in a variety of industries, for example telecommunications, biotech, pharmaceuticals, and financial services.

The main stimulus for business investment, in old and new enterprises, comes from high expectations of growth of demand and output, and high expected profits. In the 1990s, other important positive determinants included low inflation and interest rates, high liquidity and easy credit. Also Helpful for some time here was the fast and accelerating rise in the stock market that both facilitated and rewarded capital expansion.

However in the course of the year 2000, sharp declines developed in several leading indicators that are important for real business investment planning and decisions—manufacturers' new orders for materials, consumer goods, and capital goods; stock prices; and consumer expectations. Coincident indicators such as the industrial production index and real manufacturing sales followed suit. As the LI continued to slide, growth of real GDP turned down and growth of real NDP and the CI fell some more. Importantly, the corporate profit margin declined sharply as early as 1997, albeit from high levels, and dropped further steeply in 2000 (see Figure 2.6). So the high expectations that led to the investment boom, and were for a time apparently self-fulfilling now met increasingly with disappointments. As a result, decisive but not particularly large downturns occurred in 2000–1 in domestic investment outlays for both equipment and structures (Figure 2.6).[12]

At the same time, business inventories started to accumulate relative to sales, and total inventory investment was cut drastically (from 78.9 in Q2 2000 to –119.3 in Q4 2001 in billions of chained 1996 $). Clearly, it was the decline in total business investment that was chiefly responsible for the slowdown and recession of 2000–1. That decline itself was due to the rapidly spreading realization that the supply of products of the growing capital stock was at the margin, quickly outrunning the demand. As so often in the past, the boom created considerable overinvestment or malinvestment in some parts of the economy, including intangible capital such as patents, copyrights, and good will, which grew fast, especially in accounting terms.

Residential Investment and Personal Consumption

Residential investment has a long record of large cyclical fluctuations, with long leads at peaks and short leads or roughly coincident timing at troughs. This prevailing pattern shows up well in Figure 2.6 with a few minor variations (note the large extra decline of housing during the 1967 slowdown and the short lead and small decline in 1969–70). The one very unusual episode, however, is 2000–01, when housing merely flattened at very high levels and did not fall at all in the midst of rapidly slowing and then mildly declining economic activity. Thus the long and relatively steady rise in residential investment has been a source of strength for the US economy ever since 1991.

Consumer spending on furniture, fixtures, and automobiles is closely related to household formation and home building or buying. Consumption of durable goods shares some characteristics of investment in major household assets. When expressed in real terms, this series, too, has a long record of procyclical behaviour, with a tendency to lead, again primarily at peaks. Figure 2.7 illustrates this for the last four decades. It also shows that real consumer expenditures on non-durable goods have followed a much smoother, more trend-dominated path that included mild declines in some recessions and only slowing in others. The same applies more strongly to consumption expenditures on services, which showed very persistent and pronounced growth, particularly before 1980, and only some small declines more recently.

During the expansion of the 1990s, consumer spending increased approximately in step with GDP, while business investment spending increased much faster. Consumption of durable goods rose much faster than consumption of non-durable goods and services.[13]

Interestingly, in 2000–1, consumption of services and non-durables weakened more than that of durables. The latter eased slightly in the spring and fall of 2000, but actually accelerated strongly in late 2001 (see Figure 2.7). One likely reason for this lies in the large temporary sales discounts, zero interest financing and other incentives to which consumers responded. The real income gains achieved during the expansion were presumably helpful too, along with the effects of the stimulative monetary and fiscal policies.

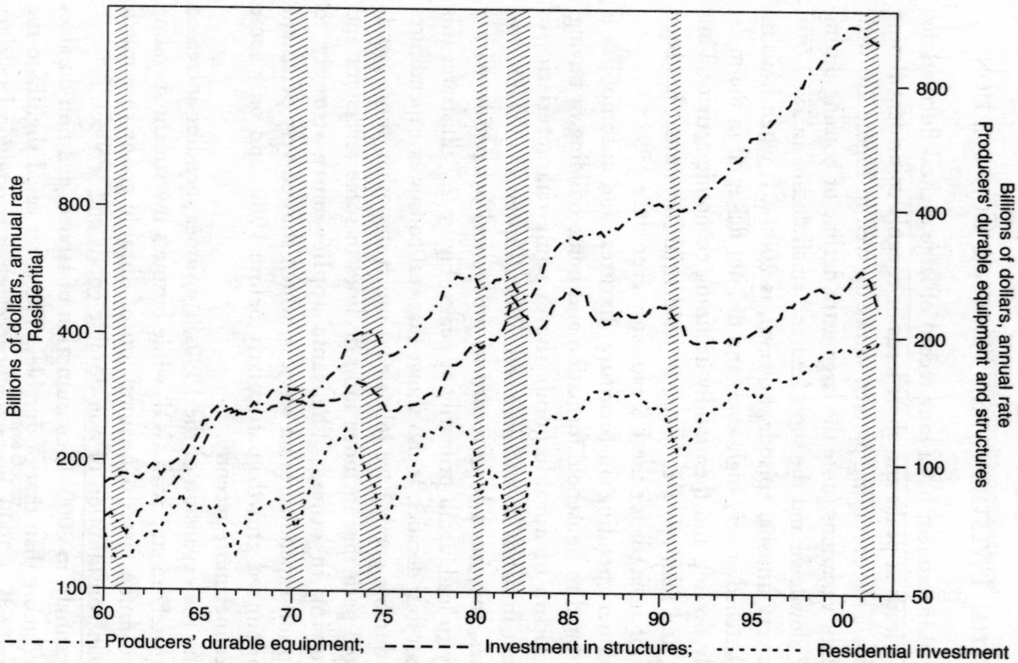

Figure 2.6: Components of Real Gross Private Fixed Investment, 1959–2002 (1996 $, Quarterly).

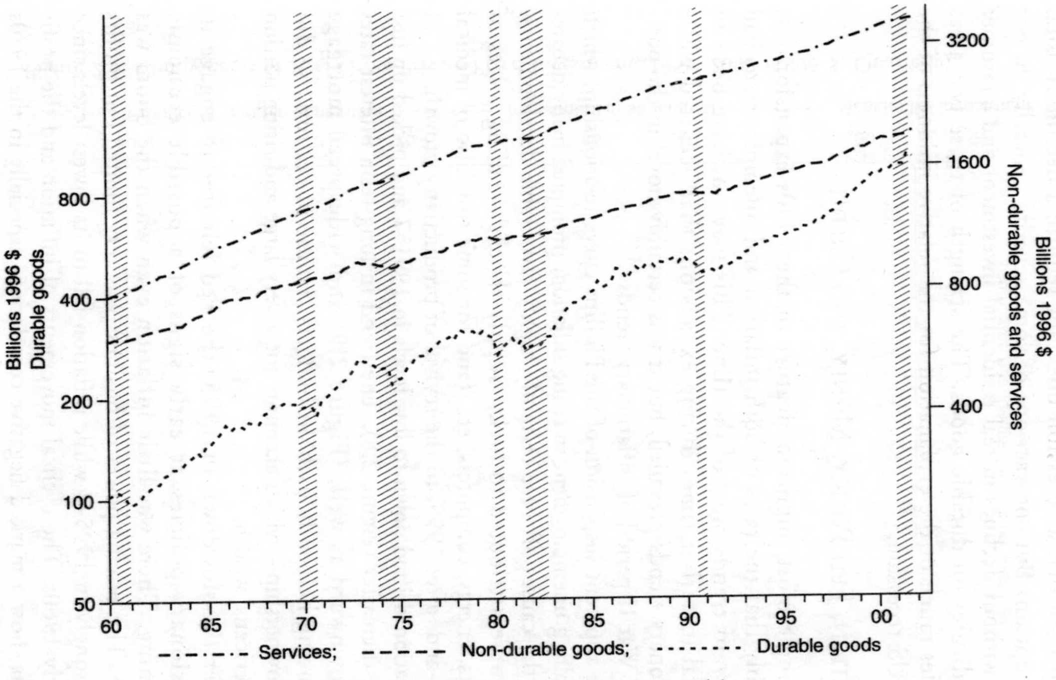

Figure 2.7: Real Personal Consumption Expenditure, 1959–2002 (quarterly).

Services and non-durables account for the bulk of total consumption, which accounts for about two-thirds of US GDP. It is well to note that a recession does not require a decline in total consumption. But contractions of some severity generally do not occur without declines in real residential investment and consumer expenditures on durable goods. The strength of these two areas provides much of the explanation for the relative mildness of the latest US recession.

Inflation, Fed Policy, Money, and Credit

The single most important feature of the 1990s expansion was probably that the rates of both inflation and unemployment had downward trends most of the time. This may not have been so unusual in earlier times during expansions that occurred while deflationary trends prevailed, but it was certainly novel in the post-World War II period of inflationary trends.[14]

The apparent suspension of the Phillips curve relationship, which links falling unemployment to rising inflation, prompted many debates about the causes of these certainly highly favourable developments. They were attributed to lucky 'supply shocks'—falling prices of imports, energy, computers, etc. (and for some time also of medical care)—and, after 1995, to the revival of productivity growth.

Inflation drifted down to low levels in 1991–7 and picked up just a little thereafter (Figure 2.8). The trend in long-term interest rates was downward as well, (Figure 2.9) and widespread mortgage refinancing helped household budgets. House prices rose, so did home ownership—which accounts for a very large and rising portion of Americans' wealth.

After the slowdown in 1995, the Fed felt free to engage in expansionary policies at early signs of a possible economic weakening. There was little inflation even when the boom was intense. The pricing power of business was very limited but profits rose strongly in 1995–7 while inflation fell to its lowest levels since the early 1960s. The cyclical movements of inflation and the profit margins show a marked negative correlation, especially in the 1970s and the 1980s (Figure 2.8).

Prompt easing by the Federal Reserve raised the growth of money supply and reduced short-term interest rates to their lowest levels in four decades; long interest rates drifted down even more and the yield spread (long minus short yields) decreased (Figure 2.9).

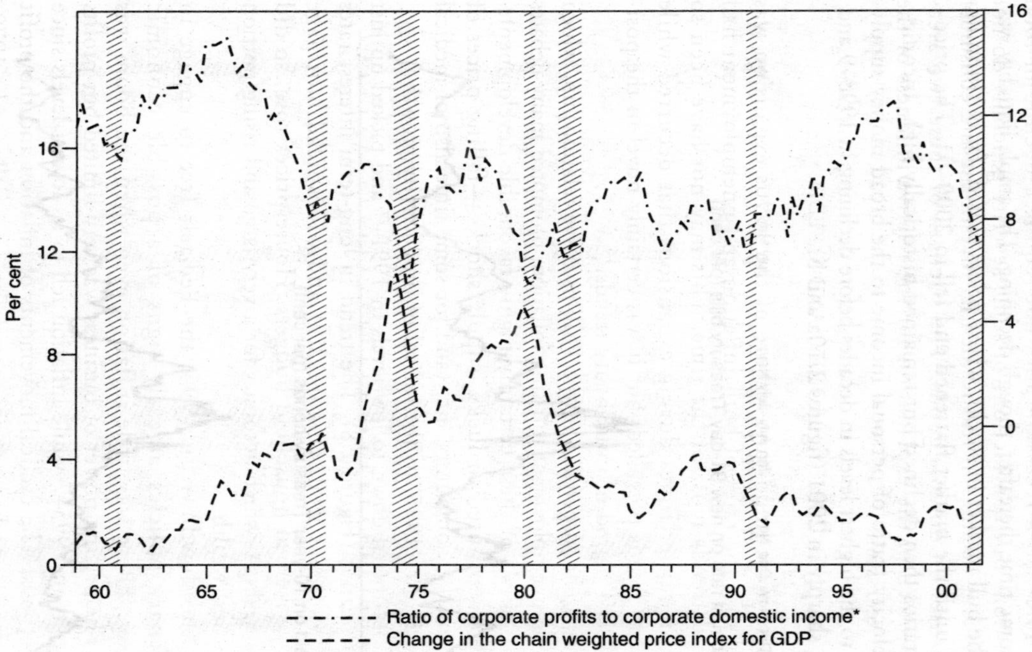

Figure 2.8: Corporate Profit Margin and Broadly Measured Inflation, 1959–2002 (quarterly).
Note: For ratio of corporate profits to corporate domestic income, changes are over four-quarter span.

Money grew slowly—less than the price level—in the relatively slack economy of the early 1990s. In 1995–8, however, growth of real money supply, broadly defined, increased strongly, and it remained high for some time thereafter, though declining. The ample liquidity was feeding the bull market in stocks, where prices soared, far outrunning earnings, until the market flattened and fell in 2000–01. The price-earnings ratios then declined but remained historically high. Income-money velocity (ratio of personal income to the broad money supply M2) rose to the highest levels in decades before declining in 1998–9 and dropping sharply in 2001 (figures 2.10a and b).

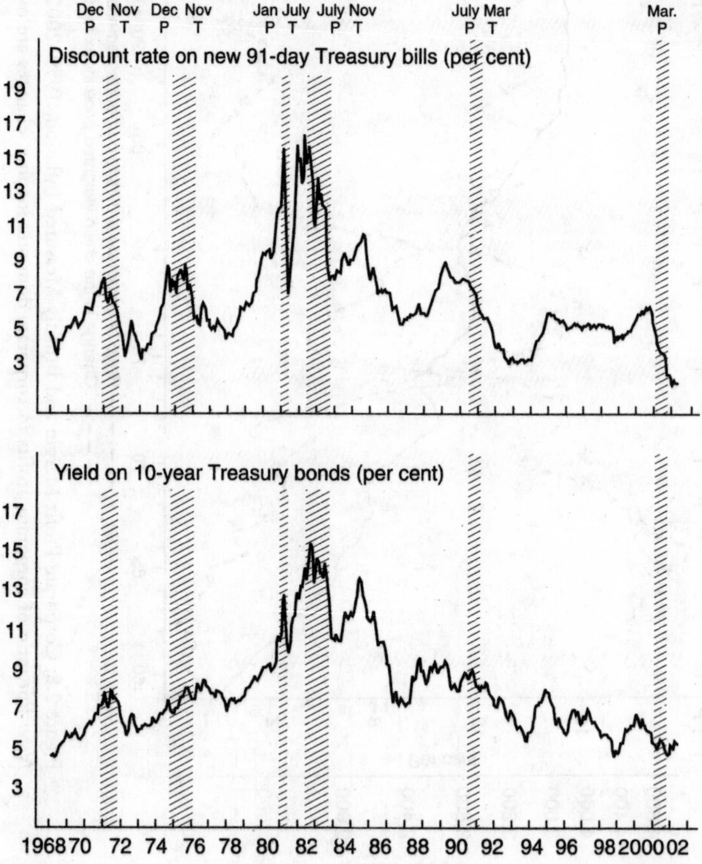

Figure 2.9: Short and Long Interest Rates, 1968–March 2002 (monthly).

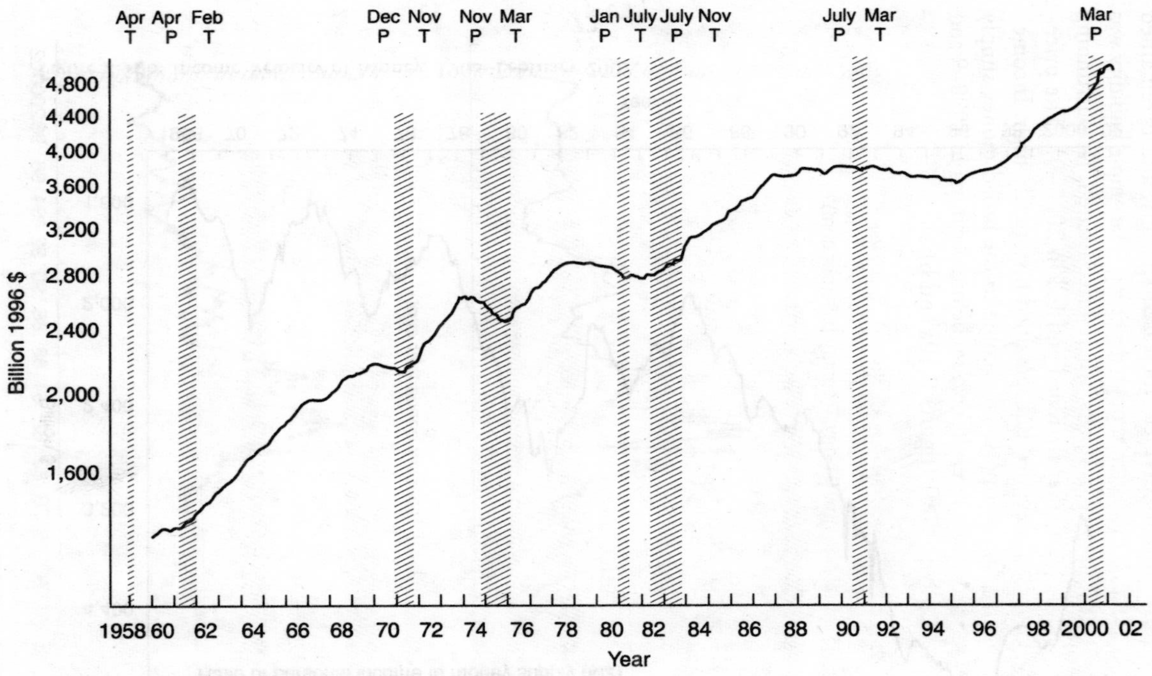

Figure 2.10a: Money Supply (M2), 1959–April 2002.

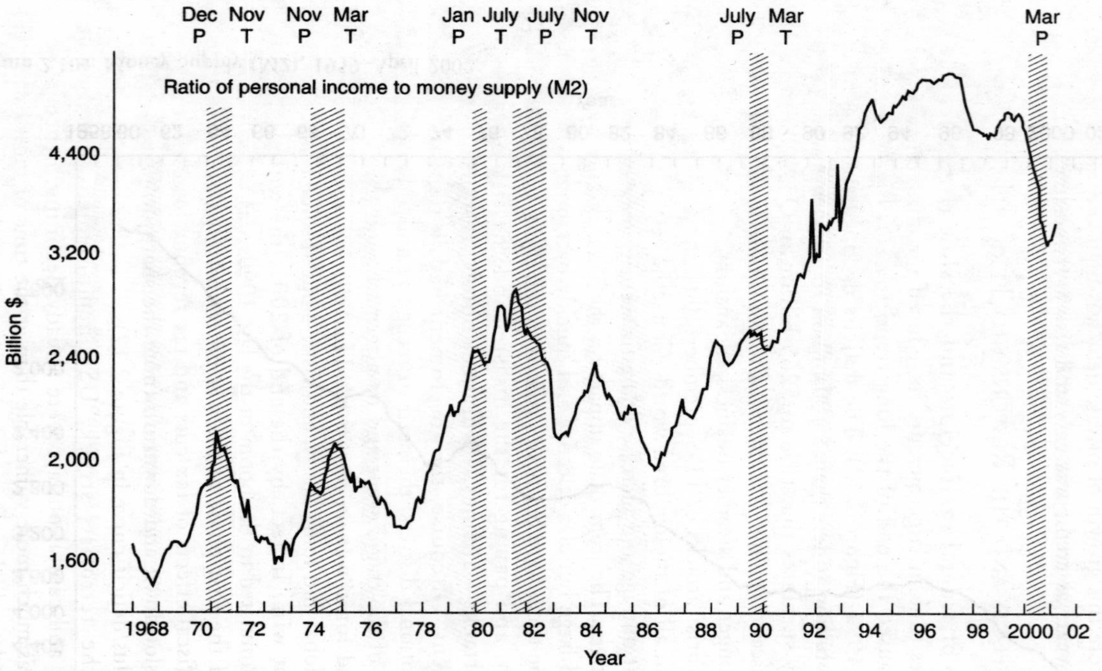

Figure 2.10b: Income Velocity of Money, 1968–February 2002.

Business loans went down at about the same time as well, but growth in consumer instalment credit merely slowed (Figures 2.11a and b). Before this growth of private debt was high and rather steady for several years as credit was easy and risk aversion low.

Fiscal Effects and the Response to Terrorism

The surge of federal tax receipts and the slow rise of federal expenditures (due in large measure to reduced spending on national defence) caused the end of the long trend towards higher budget deficits in 1992 (Figure 2.12). The deficits declined steadily from over $ 300 billion to less than $ 100 billion in 1997 and were then replaced by surpluses that rose to $265 billion in Q3 2000. This policy of 'fiscal discipline' was intended to contribute to lower interest rates and longer and steadier business expansion.

The terrorist attacks of 11 September 2001 shocked the nation and, indeed, all of the civilized world. Concerns about how best to react to that outrage and increase domestic security overshadowed all routine matters. The immediate impact on the US economy was very adverse and large but also selective and quickly overcome. The worst hit, for some time, were businesses related to travelling, going out and having fun, and paying for the disaster and the risk of future terrorist attacks—airlines, insurance, hotels, restaurants, and entertainment. Of course, the government had to respond to the general emotional distress, the need to recognize and aid the victims and heroes of the tragic event and its aftermath, and the clear need and demand for a 'war on terrorism'. That war was to be new and different, global and long, costly, and risky—but absolutely necessary and a 'must win'. In fact, by the end of 2001, the entire budget surplus accumulated in the boom of the late 1990s was wiped out by the costs of the first phase of the war on terrorism, along with the combined fiscal effects of tax cuts and tax revenue losses from the economy's slowdown and downturn (note the sharp drop at the end of the surplus/deficit curve in Figure 2.12).

When the terrorists struck, US unemployment, business operations, and capital outlays were already declining, hence, the economy was much more vulnerable than at the time of most earlier adverse shocks, which occurred during business cycle expansions.[15] The massive suicidal assault on civilians and soldiers did not cause the recession but it seriously aggravated the already deteriorating

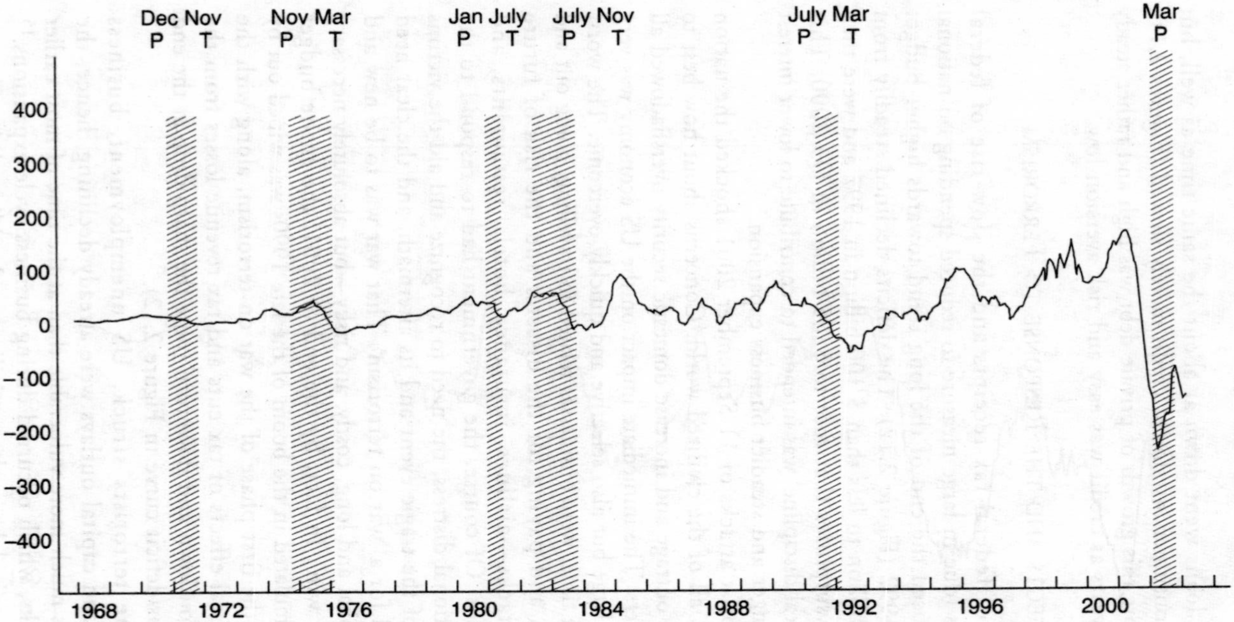

Figure 2.11a: Change in Business Credit, 1968–February 2002.
Note: Net change in business loans ann. rate, billion dol.; 6-term moving avg.

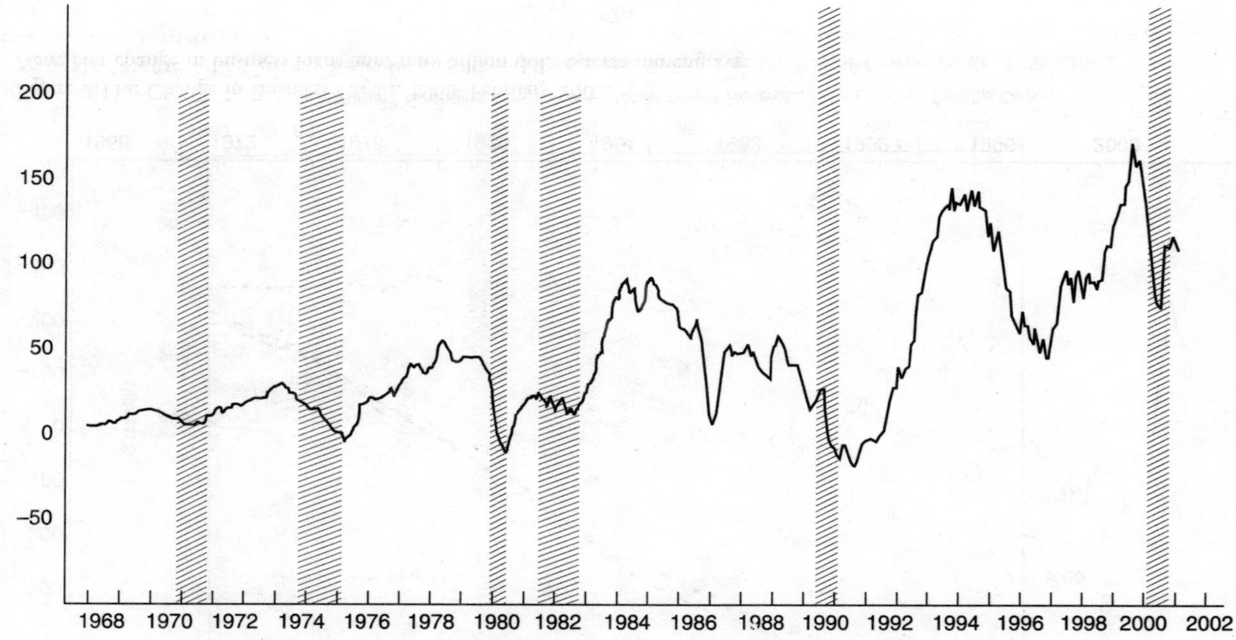

Figure 2.11b: Change in Consumer Credit, 1969–February 2002.
Note: ann. rate, billion dol.; 6-term moving avg.

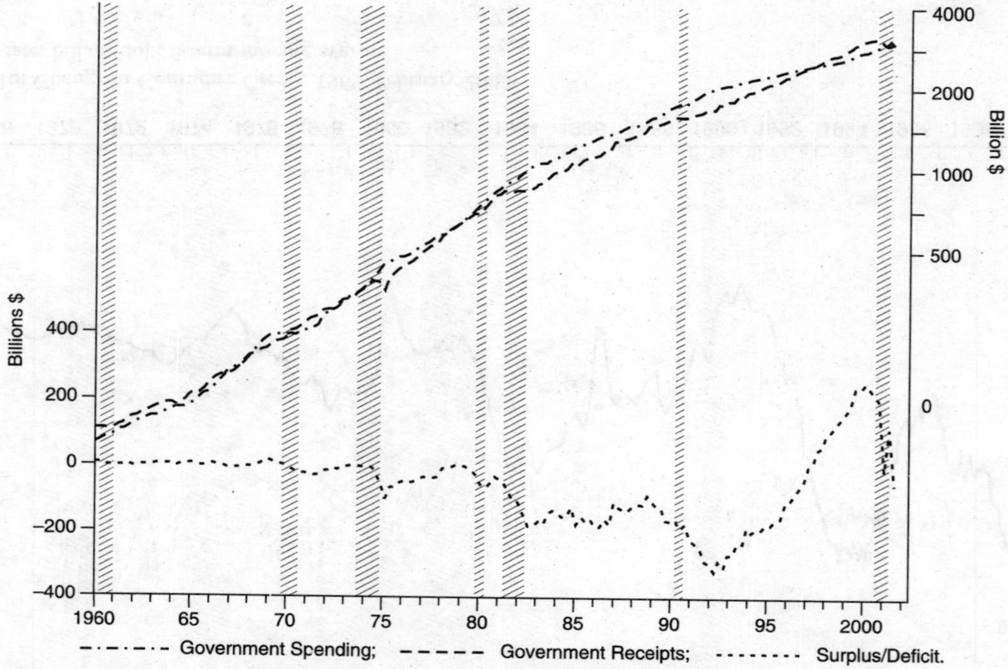

Figure 2.12 Current Receipts and Expenditures and Surplus or Deficit of Government, 1959–2002 (Quarterly).

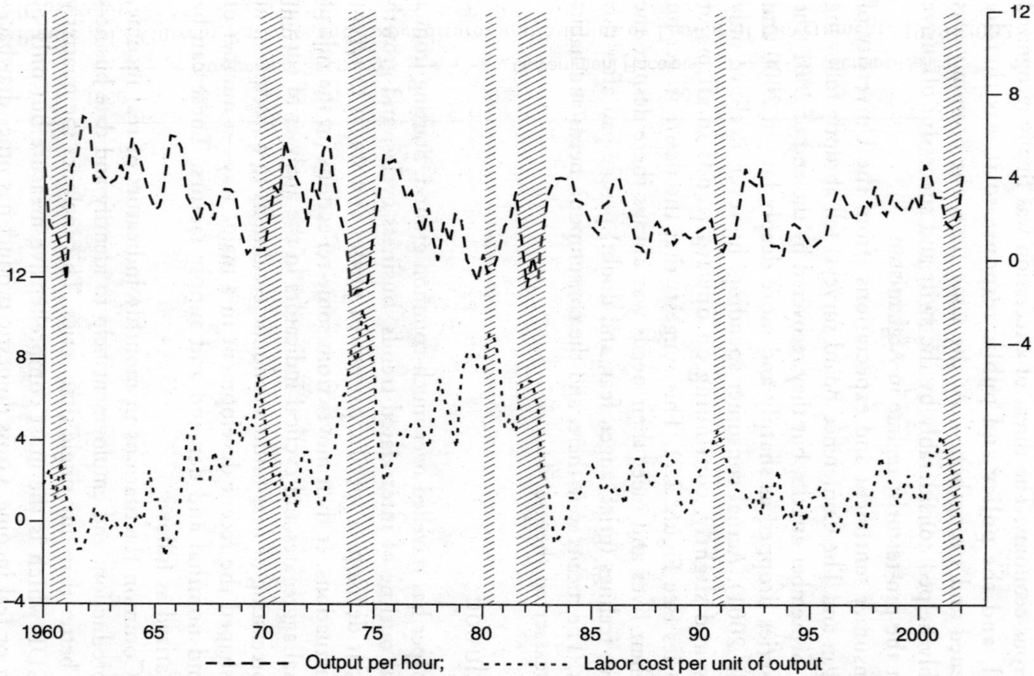

Figure 2.13: Output per Hour and Unit Labour Cost, Business Sector, Changes over 4-Quarter Spans, 1959–2002.

situation. However, it did so only temporarily. The initial shock, fear, and inertness soon gave way to a national resolve to succeed in resisting terrorism as well as returning to the normal way of life in a prosperous economy. The threat of a recession was finally recognized as real, and the policy and public response to it was thereby quickened and strengthened. At the same time, the economy was probably helped considerably by the swift and successful offensive against the pro-terrorist regime in Afghanistan.

Consumer sentiment and expectations (from the University of Michigan and The Conference Board surveys) fell abruptly following the 11 September attacks, but they recovered by the end of 2001 (the same series dropped as sharply and more deeply late in 2000 and early in 2001). Actual consumer spending, however, declined only briefly and slightly, continuing on upward trends in all major categories (see Figure 2.7). This suggests that the desire to get on with their lives and meet their needs was always there despite the negative feelings (grief, anger, fear, and doubt) people had after this attacks. The means were there, and the consumption needs and habits soon reasserted themselves.

Conclusion

This paper has travelled over much common ground. Starting from a general outline of interrelated trends, business cycles, and growth cycles, it develops a specific pattern of phases and stages in recent US fluctuations. It then moves from some reflections on the role of national aggregates and cyclical indicators in the analyses of current and forecasting of near-future economic conditions to a discussion of what shaped the recent development in a major way—a number of real and nominal and demand and supply factors. These can be summarized as follows:

1. Common fluctuations in monthly indicators of real income, sales production, and employment help to identify and date business cycles better than any single time series. This includes the quarterly real GDP which is the most comprehensive measure but only of output or real income. Gross domestic product has other drawbacks as well: it is quarterly, a product of complex accounting, and subject to long and often large revisions.

2. Smooth upward trends and shorter fluctuations dominated by the business cycle are characteristic of both the national aggregates

and the composite indexes of cyclical indicators in level form. Changes over unit periods in these series, however, show that even these comprehensive series, notably GDP, contain great short-run volatility as well as intermediate-run cyclicality.

3. Trends should be estimated so as to allow for their interaction with business cycles and, at the same time, to make them have the desired smoothness. Gains from the procedure include the derivations of reasonable measures of growth cycles (deviations from trends) and a useful division into stages of business expansions and contractions.

4. Recessions are often preceded by slowdowns or growth cycle contractions (all but two of the two post-World War II recessions were). Leading indicators anticipate these slowdowns, which accounts for their early timing at peaks.

5. All expansions start from recoveries, which extend from troughs back up to the trend. After deeper recessions, like several in the recent past, the recoveries are often relatively swift ('V-shaped'). After shallow recessions, such as those in 1990–1 and 2001, they are, or are likely to be, slow and longer. The 1990s witnessed the longest recovery and the longest boom of all post-war expansions, but the recovery was sluggish and the boom not as strong as earlier data and moods had indicated.

6. The expansion of the 1990s was driven in large measure by business investment in equipment and was associated with the rise and spread of the new technology of information and communication. The slowdown and recession of 2000–01 were similarly driven by declines in these areas and the associated inventory liquidation. Business investment in structures rose much less and much less steadily but fell more abruptly.

7. Residential investment rose strongly early in the decade, more slowly in the boom years, and just a little in the recession, so overall it was a source of strength. This is in sharp contrast to the large and early declines in housing during all previous post-war recessions. Low inflation and interest rates, and the persistent high attractiveness of home ownership explain this.

8. Real personal consumption expenditures expanded steadily in the 1990s, not only for services and non-durable goods but also for the more cyclical and more volatile durables. All these continued to rise after the downturn of early 2001 and the consumption of durables even accelerated temporarily. The continued strength of real

income, low interest rates, and various sales incentives may provide much if not all of an explanation.

9. Low and downward drifting inflation and interest rates helped greatly to keep real investment spending by firms and households high and rising. Declines in unemployment to low levels also contributed to rising consumption. The huge bull market in stocks lowered costs of capital and encouraged new investment projects (good and bad). It also raised the wealth and hence to some extent the spending of households. By the same token, the burst of the stock market bubble—by revealing the extent of corporate overinvestment and malinvestment and by inflicting big losses on investor assets—helped bring about the 2000 slowdown and the 2001 recession.

10. The monetary policy of the Federal Reserve, scored successes in stabilizing the economy after the 1987 stock market crash and after the foreign crises and recessions of the late 1990s. Despite some tough rhetoric, the Fed did little to moderate the market boom (perhaps it could not or should not have). It acted with unusual promptness and intensity in the last recession. Although it was unable to prevent declines in credit, income velocity of money, and output, it did reasonably well to keep the recession mild and short. However, the excesses of the boom increasingly show up now, in the uncertainties of and impediments to the recovery in 2002, and the Fed is limited in its capacity to respond to this latest challenge.

11. The reduction of federal government deficits in 1993–7 and the achievement of surpluses in 1998–2000 contributed to lower interest rates and longer expansion. But by the end of 2001, the surpluses disappeared and were replaced by growing deficits, reflecting the effects of the slowdown, decreasing tax revenues, and increasing military and civilian spending, partly due to the war on terrorism.

12. The main factor on the positive side over the longer term is improved actual and prospective growth of labour productivity (output per hour) due to technological innovations and progress. This factor may have already worked to reduce the recent economic weakness.

Endnotes

[1]See Zarnowitz and Ozyildilim (2001)

[2]See Mintz (1972) and Boschan and Ebanks (1978)

[3]For details, see Zarnowitz (2001a).

[4]The sensitivity is mainly to short and intermediate changes in economic and financial conditions. Only four of the ten components of the leading index—stock price, money, and the two new orders series—show strong upward trends. The others show little or no trends. Hence, as seen in Figure 2.1, LI grows more slowly than CI.

5 See Zarnowitz (1992).

[6]More on this in Zarnowitz (2000).

[7]See McConnell, Mosser, and Quiros (1999).

[8]For example, the effort to derive a chronology of business cycle stages by cross-classifying the cyclical movements of quantity and price variables suffers from the fact that 'demand-pull' and 'stagflation' phases exist only at some times and not at other times, even in the generally inflationary period of 1947–73, let alone in longer periods that include deflationary trends (see Meyer and Weinberg, 1975).

[9]In the Great Depression, the upward trend of the US economy was temporarily suspended, and the 1937 peak failed to exceed the 1929 peak by the best available measures of overall economic activity. Another contraction, shorter but deep and starting from already depressed levels, came in 1937–8. The definite end to the long economic disaster, which spread globally, arrived only with World War II. In Japan, the 1990s brought a sharp decline in the growth trend, from high to flat, and a related sharp increase in cyclicality. There were two complete recessions and a third one under way, and the economy was stagnant and plagued by deflation.

[10]See Zarnowitz and Ozyildirim (2002).

11 Keynes (1936) wrote of 'the phenomenon of the crisis—the fact that the substitution of a downward for an upward tendency often takes place suddenly and violently, whereas there is, as a rule, no such sharp turning-point when an upward is substituted for a downward tendency.' But abrupt declines occur mostly in crises that, never very frequent, have become more far and between than ever. In the post-WW II era, the downturns seem to have become more rounded, the upturns sharper.

[12]For details on what determines investment and profits, and on their roles in business cycles, see Zarnowitz (1999).

[13]Note that Figure 2.7, like Figures 2.1, 2.4, and 2.6, uses logarithmic vertical scales in which equal distances denote equal percentage in the series plotted.

[14]Declines in inflation and unemployment did occur in the mid-1980s but only briefly. For a general overview and analysis of cyclical and trend movements of prices, see Zarnowitz (1992).

[15]A Conference Board study of 15 major shock events in the past four decades shows that only two of them—the OPEC oil embargo of October 1973 and Iraq's invasion of Kuwait in August 1990—can be connected with

US business cycle recessions. All others, including several major natural disasters, bombings, assassinations, and a market crash, had only short, transitory economic effects which failed to disrupt the economic expansions during which they occurred. See Zarnowitz (2001b).

References

Walter W. Boschan, and Charlotte Ebanks (1978), 'The Phase Average Trend: A New Way of Measuring Growth', 1978 Proceedings of the Business and Economic Statistics Section American Statistical Allocation, Washington, DC.

Keynes, J. M. (1936), *The General Theory of Employment, Interest, and Money*, London: Macmillan, p. 314.

McConnell, Mosser, and Quiros (1999), 'A Decompositon of the Increased Stability of GDP Growth', Federal Reserve Bank of New York, Current Issues, Vol. 5, No. 13, September.

Meyer and Weinberg (1975), 'On the Classification of Recent Cyclical Experience, National Bureau of Economic Research', *55th Annual Report*, September, pp. 1–8.

Mintz, Ilse (1972), 'Dating American Growth in V. Zarnowitz, (Ed.) *The Business Cycle Today*, New York: NBER.

Zarnowitz ,V. (2001a), 'Coincident Indicators and the Dating of Business Cycles', in The Conference Board, *Business Cycle Indicators*, August, pp. 3–4 and Table 1.

—— (2001b), 'The US Economy Before and After the Terrorist Attacks', The Conference Board, *Business Cycle Indicators*, October, pp. 2–4.

—— (2000), 'The Old and the New in the US Economic Expansion', *The Economic Outlook for 2001*, The University of Michigan, Ann Arbor, November, pp. 85–150.

—— (1999), 'Theory and History Behind Business Cycles: Are the 1990s the Onset of a Golden Age?', *Journal of Economic Perspectives*, Vol. 13, No. 2, Spring, pp. 69–90.

—— (1992), 'Business Cycles: Theory, History, Indicators and Forecasting', *NBER Studies in Business Cycles*, Vol. 27, Chicago and London: The University of Chicago Press, Chs 11 and 13.

Zarnowitz, V. and Ataman Ozyildirim, (2002), 'Time Series Decompensation and Measurement of Business Cycles, Trends and Growth Cycles'. NBER Working Paper No. 8736, January.

—— (2001), 'On the Measurement of Business Cycles and Growth Cycles', *Indian Economic Review*, January–June 2001, Vol. XXXVI, No.1, pp. 37–54.

3

Lagging Indicators

Forgotten Aids to Forecasting

Philip A. Klein

Lagging Indicators: Forgotten Aids to Forecasting

Many of us have long argued that the reliability of indicator systems reflects Wesley Clair Mitchell's basic perspective towards the nature of business fluctuations. Indicator systems have proven their usefulness many times over in monitoring business fluctuations. They are useful over time in tracking instability in any given country. They are equally useful in monitoring business fluctuations over many industrial market countries in any given era. Indicator behaviour reflects Mitchell's answer to the question, why have all industrial market economies exhibited the kinds of instability referred to in Burns and Mitchell's well-known definition of business cycles? The basic idea of that definition is: the cycle phases merge one into the next; expansion leads to a crisis, the crisis leads to a recession, and the recession leads to recovery. Modern industrial economies are complex systems of interrelationships among many economic variables. A part of this set of relationships reflects essential sequential connections reflecting the technology that underlies modern industrial capitalist economies. There are requirements that certain

The author wishes to thank Jean Maltz, Economic Cycle Research Institute for the computer work and the charts and his secretary Nancy Cole for processing the text, preparing the tables, and completion of the charts.

economic activities must precede other types of activity: customarily increases in orders need to precede increases in the average work week and both precede increases in employment and production. Increases in employment and production in turn precede increases in inventories. In bad times, decreases in these activities unfold in roughly the same manner. Modern industrial technology is shot through with myriad essential sequences of this sort. These sequences mirror the dynamic interactive processes that are essential to capitalist industrial activity, which indicator systems try to capture and which, in turn, Mitchell's business cycle theory tries to flesh out.

The special appeal, therefore, of a system of indicators—leading, coincident, and lagging—is that the indicators reflect sequential changes in the economy. They can, therefore, be useful in forecasting subsequent cyclical developments. It is less challenging to assume that what has just happened will continue. Thus, forecasting the continuation of expansion or contraction is less difficult than forecasting the turning points when an expansion turns to contraction (at a business cycle peak) or a contraction becomes an expansion (at a business cycle trough). The development of leading, coincident, and lagging indicators has proved particularly helpful in forecasting the turning points.

Coincident indicators are the measures included in the basic notion of the business cycle, the measures of macroeconomic fluctuations included in the definition—income, output, employment, sales, etc. Leading indicators are types of economic activity which typically anticipate changes in the coincident indicators. They lead because they reflect changes in aggregate activity which must perforce precede the changes included in the coincident indicators. In a similar fashion, the lagging indicators include measures of activity which customarily follow the changes in the coincident indicators and, therefore, in a real sense, confirm the changes reflected in the coincident indicators. For example, the peak in unemployment must precede the peak in long-term unemployment because unemployment has to be, at some elevated level, for a palpably long period to produce 'long term unemployment'.

It is these dynamic imperatives which grow out of the fundamental technological nature of modern industrial processes, which indicator systems reflect, and which gives them their usefulness and their credibility. Hence, since the first set of business cycle indicators, produced by Burns and Mitchell in 1938, indicators systems have always featured all three types of indicators: leading, coincident, and lagging.

Over the years, there has been a marked tendency to give short shrift to the lagging indicators. Confirming what has happened is never as newsworthy as anticipating what is about to happen. Nevertheless, the role of the lagging index in any indicator system is an important one, because it has potentially important and distinctive properties. At the Economic Cycle Research Institute (ECRI) we have strived to improve our lagging index by producing a weekly as well as a monthly version.

From the outset Mitchell regarded business cycles as partly endogenous in origin and partly exogenous. (It is, of course, the endogenous part that an indicator system attempts to reflect.) Not only do the business cycle phases merge from one phase to the next but it is the indicator systems which can mark this journey.

Here we shall try and suggest some uses of the lagging indicators and lagging indexes which can be developed from the lagging indicators. It turns out that confirming what has happened in the past has more implications for the future than are visible at first blush.

Viewing Lagging Indicators as Long Leaders

We shall illustrate the possible uses of lagging indicators using data from two countries, the United States and Sweden. We noted earlier that few countries have developed lagging indicators, let alone kept them up to date, despite the fact that they fill a critical link in the story that indicators monitor. In our 1985 study of growth cycles in ten market-oriented economies, Geoffrey H. Moore and I invariably developed a set of lagging indicators as well as constructed lagging indexes for each country (Klein and Moore 1985).

We found that lagging indicators were indeed useful for a number of reasons including the use discussed in this section. Unfortunately, we have not been able to keep the laggers up-to-date in the past 15 years, although that is surely one of our long-run objectives. The Organization for Economic co-operation and Development (OECD) began monitoring growth cycles in member countries in 1987, but developed only leading and coincident indicators, with no attention at all to lagging indicators (OECD 1987); and continue to adhere to this policy.

In a 1950 paper, Moore looked at lagging indicators and concluded, subsequently that '...the downturns in the laggers had consistently preceded the upturns in the leaders, while upturns in the laggers had consistently preceded downturns in the leaders'.[1]

Finally, as long ago as 1971, Kathleen Moore, examined the relationship between lagging indicators and leading indicators for the US, Canada, and Japan (K. Moore 1971). As her father put it, she asked, 'do lagging indicators in other countries display the same properties *vis-a-vis* leading indicators as they do in the United States?' (Ibid., p. 363). The answer was 'yes'.

What this evidence shows is that in effect the turning point in a lagging index, for example, a peak, is the last indication that the economy has turned down before in fact it turns up again. Thus, the peak in the lagging index should precede the trough in the leading index which in fact forecasts the next expansion. It seems unnecessary to belabour the point that what all this reflects in lagging and leading indexes is exactly what the Burns–Mitchell definition of cycles suggests in asserting that one cycle phase merges into the next.

In effect, what has been suggested here is that if the lagging index is inverted so the troughs are the high points and the peaks are the low points these inverted turning points will precede the same turn in the leading index. Thus a lagging index trough (inverted to become a peak) will precede the peak in the leading index and a lagging index peak (inverted to become a trough) will precede the trough in the leading index. This means that the lagging index can be inverted to become the longest leader at both peaks and troughs.

Lagging Index Behaviour for Two Countries—A Look at the Evidence

We can illustrate these relationships with data from the United States and Sweden. They are the only major countries for which we have reasonably up-to-date findings for the lagging index. The evidence is presented in Figures 3.1 and 3.2 and in Tables 3.1 and 3.2. Consider first Figure 3.1 and Table 3.1, the behaviour of the lagging index at growth cycle turning points since 1951. Both suggest that the US lagging index in the past half century has been highly conforming to the growth rate cycle chronology and that its timing has been very consistent as well. There were three extra cycles in the index in 1963–4, 1978–9, and 1993–4. None of the growth rate cycle turning points was missed and all of the timings were lagging with the

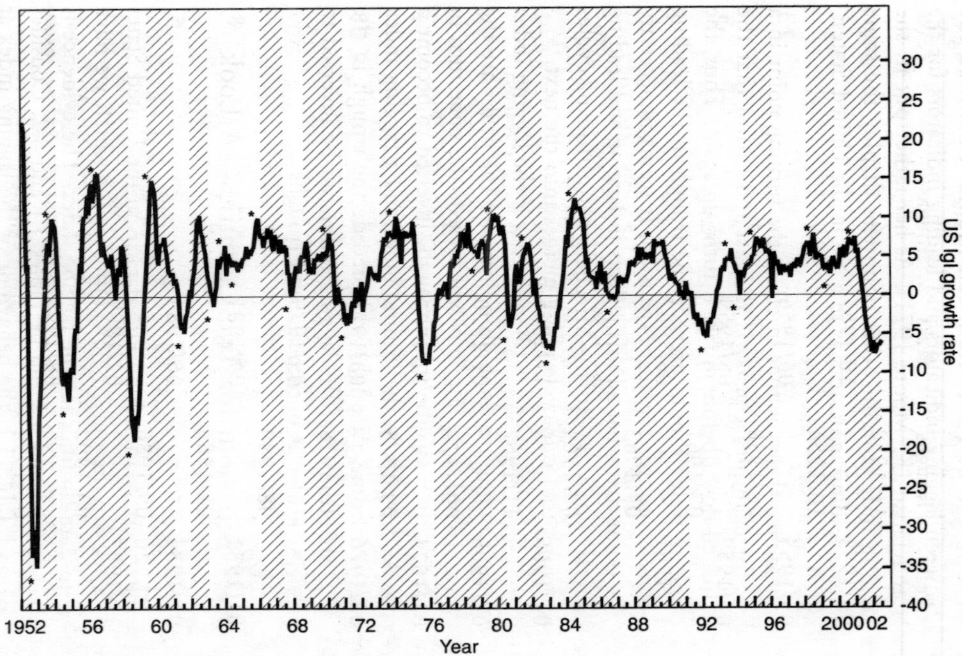

Figure 3.1: US Lagging Index, Growth Rate.
Note: Shaded areas represent Swedish growth rate cycle downturns.
Source: Economic Cycle Research Institute.

Table 3.1: US Growth Rate Cycle vs. Lagging Index Growth Rate

Growth Rate Cycle Turning Points		USLgI Growth Turning Points		USLgI Growth In Months Lead(–)	Lag(+)
Troughs	Peaks	Troughs	Peaks	Troughs	Peaks
07/1952		11/1952		4	
	03/1953		10/1953		7
01/1954		10/1954		9	
	05/1955		06/1956		13
04/1958		08/1958		4	
	05/1959		08/1959		3
12/1960		07/1961		7	
	11/1961		06/1962		7
12/1962		04/1963		4	
			12/1963		extra
		09/1964		extra	
	01/1966		11/1965		–2
05/1967		11/1967		6	
	07/1968		01/1970		18
11/1970		02/1971		3	
	01/1973		12/1973		11
03/1975		09/1975		6	
	02/1976		03/1978		25
		10/1978		extra	
			09/1979		extra
06/1980		08/1980		2	
	01/1981		09/1981		8
07/1982		02/1983		7	
	01/1984		06/1984		5
01/1987		09/1986		–4	
	12/1987		02/1989		14
02/1991		03/1992		13	
			08/1993		extra
		02/1994		extra	
	05/1994		02/1995		9
01/1996		07/1996		6	
	01/1998		06/1998		5
09/1999		06/1999		–3	
	04/2000		11/2000		7

Contd.

Growth Rate Cycle Turning Points		USLgI Growth Turning Points		USLgI Growth In Months		
				Lead(–)		Lag(+)
Troughs	Peaks	Troughs	Peaks	Troughs		Peaks
				Troughs		peaks
					Overall	
		Average		5	7	9
		Median		5.0	6.5	7.5
		Per cent lead		14	11	7
		Std. deviation		4.4	6.0	6.7

Note: US LgI Growth—US Lagging Index Growth Rate.

exception of the troughs in 1986 and 1999 and a peak in 1965. The average timing was a nine-month lag at peaks and a five-month lag at troughs for an overall average timing of seven-month lag. Recalling that the function of lagging indexes is to confirm the past turning points reflected in the coincident index and forecast by the leading index, we may say that the lagging index fulfilled its function remarkably well and gave very few false signals in the process.

If we now look at the same index in an inverted form, we find the picture shown in Figure 3.2 and Table 3.2. We underscore that this is the same index as in Figure 3.1, but inverted, so that, for example, the first turning point, which was a trough in November 1952 is now called a peak. As a trough it was related to the growth rate cycle trough in July 1952 and so is regarded as a four-month lag. The November date confirms the trough recorded in the chronology for July. When the index is inverted, the November 1952 turn is regarded as a peak and is related to the subsequent peak in the chronology, which is March 1953, for a four month lead. As Table 3.2 makes clear, the inverted lagging index regarded as a leading index exhibits five extra cycles. The leads average thirteen months at troughs, nine months at peaks, and eleven months at all turns. These leads are longer than the leads we find for the leading index over the same period and this is typically the case. The major drawback in relying on these leads from the inverted lagging index is that they are

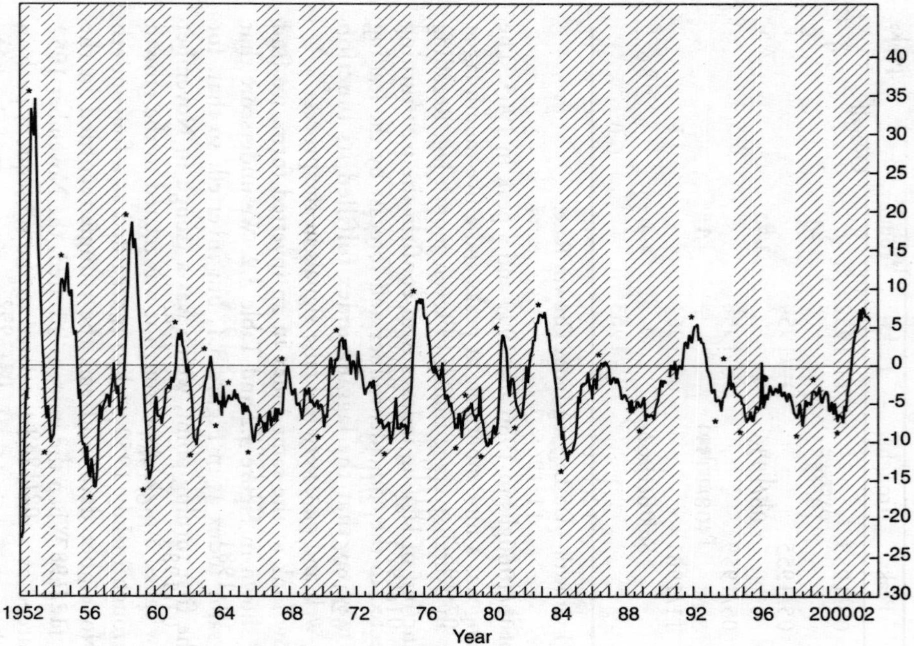

Figure 3.2: US Lagging Index, Growth Rate (Inverted).
Note: Shaded areas represent Swedish growth rate cycle downturns.
Source: Economic Cycle Research Institute.

Table 3.2: US Growth Rate Cycle vs. Lagging Index Growth Rate, Inverted

Growth Rate Cycle Turning Points		LgI, Growth Rate, (Inv.) Turning Points		LgI Growth Rate, Inverted in Months Lead(−)	Lag(+)
Troughs	Peaks	Troughs	Peaks	Troughs	Peaks
	03/1953		11/1952		−4
01/1954		10/1953		−3	
	05/1955		10/1954		−7
04/1958		06/1956		−22	
	05/1959		08/1958		−9
12/1960		08/1959		−16	
	11/1961		07/1961		−4
12/1962		06/1962		−6	
			04/1963		extra
		12/1963		extra	
			09/1964		extra
		11/1965		extra	
	01/1966				miss
05/1967				miss	
	07/1968		11/1967		−8
11/1970		01/1970		−10	
	01/1973		02/1971		−23
03/1975		12/1973		−15	
	02/1976		09/1975		−5
		03/1978		extra	
			10/1978		extra
06/1980		09/1979		−9	
	01/1981		08/1980		−5
07/1982		09/1981		−10	
	01/1984		02/1983		−11
		06/1984		extra	
			09/1986		extra
01/1987				miss	
	12/1987				miss
02/1991		02/1989		−24	
			03/1992		extra
		08/1993		extra	
	05/1994		02/1994		−3
01/1996		02/1995		−11	
	01/1998		07/1996		−18
09/1999		06/1998		−15	
	04/2000		06/1999		−10

Contd.

Growth Rate Cycle Turning Points		LgI, Growth Rate, (Inv.) Turning Points		LgI Growth Rate, Inverted in Months Lead(–)		Lag(+)
Troughs	Peaks	Troughs	Peaks	Troughs		Peaks
				Troughs	Overall	peaks
		Average		–13	–11	–9
		Median		–11.0	–10.0	–7.5
		Per cent lead		100	100	100
		Std. deviation		6.4	6.4	6.1

Note: LgI—Lagging index.
Source: Economic Cycle Research Institute.

very variable, as is shown by the standard deviation which is 6.4. In this case the variability is only slightly more than was the case in Table 3.1.

If we examine the picture which emerges from the Swedish data, the story is much the same. Figure 3.3 and Table 3.3 show the lagging index for Sweden from 1973 to early 2002. We find that for the nine growth rate cycles shown the lagging index shows two extra cycles (1976–7 and 1982–3), and the index misses one cycle (1988–9) as well. The conformity, therefore, is moderate. Inspection of the figure reveals that there was considerable instability in this period and at least two peaks were not selected by the computer programme, probably because the overall amplitude of the two episodes was smaller than all the other cycles in the period under review. In general, we may say that the series is reasonably conforming and the average lags—four months at troughs, three months at peaks, and four months overall—are clear cut. The standard deviation at 6.7 months indicates a moderate degree of variability.

Now, if we invert the Swedish lagging index, we find (Figure 3.4 and Table 3.4) we get, once again, long leads (seven months at troughs, five months at peaks, and six months overall), but here, as is typical, we also find a very high degree of variability (the standard deviation is 10.2) which reduces considerably the forecasting usefulness of the inverted lagging index. In recent cycles, the lead has not shown up.

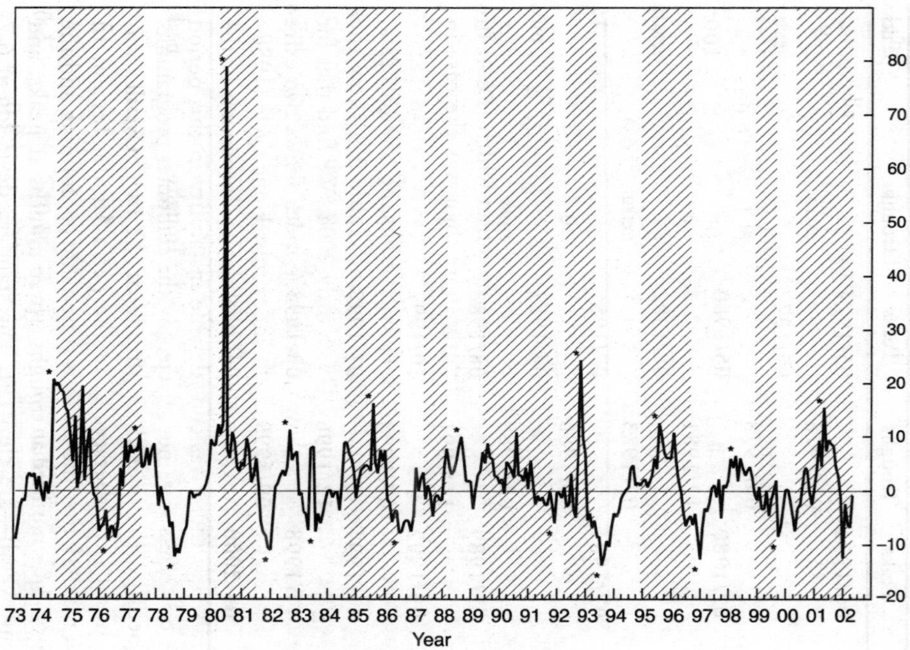

Figure 3.3: Swedish Lagging Index, Growth Rate.
Note: Shaded areas represent Swedish growth rate cycle downturns.
Source: Economic Cycle Research Institute.

Table 3.3: Swedish Growth Rate Cycle vs. Swedish Lagging Index Growth

Growth Rate Cycle Turning Points		SWLgI, Growth Turning Points		SWLgI Growth in Months		
				Lead(–)		Lag(+)
Troughs	Peaks	Troughs	Peaks	Troughs		Peaks
	06/1974		05/1974			–1
		04/1976		extra		
			05/1977			extra
06/1977		08/1978		14		
	02/1980		05/1980			3
06/1981		12/1981		6		
			08/1982			extra
		07/1983		extra		
	07/1984		07/1985			12
06/1986		06/1986		0		
			04/1987			miss
		02/1988		miss		
	05/1989		08/1988			–9
10/1991		11/1991		1		
	03/1992		10/1992			7
04/1993		07/1993		3		
	11/1994		07/1995			8
08/1996		12/1996		4		
	11/1998		03/1998			–8
08/1999		09/1999		1		
	04/2000		04/2001			12
				Troughs		peaks
					Overall	
		Average		4		3
					4	
		Median		3.0		5.0
					3.0	
		Per cent lead		7		38
					23	
		Std. deviation		4.8		8.3
					6.7	

Note: SWLgI—Swedish Lagging Index.
Source: Economic Cycle Research Institute.

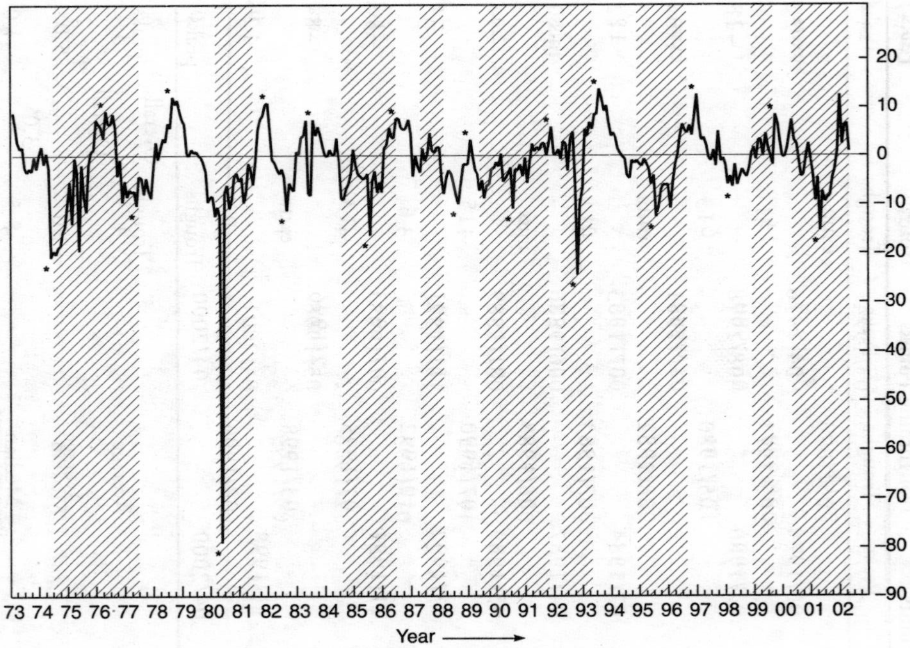

Figure 3.4: Swedish Lagging Index, Growth Rate (Inverted).
Note: Shaded areas represent Swedish growth rate cycle downturns.
Source: Economic Cycle Research Institute.

Table 3.4: Swedish Growth Rate Cycle vs. Lagging Index Growth Rate, Inverted

Growth Rate Cycle Turning Points		LgI, Growth Rate, (Inv.) Turning Points		SWLgI Growth Rate, Inverted in Months	
				Lead(−)	Lag(+)
Troughs	Peaks	Troughs	Peaks	Troughs	Peaks
		05/1974		extra	
	06/1974		04/1976		22
06/1977		05/1977		−1	
	02/1980		08/1978		−18
06/1981		05/1980		−13	
			12/1981		extra
		08/1982		extra	
	07/1984		07/1983		−12
06/1986		07/1985		−11	
	04/1987		06/1986		−10
02/1988		08/1988		6	
	05/1989		01/1989		−4
10/1991		07/1990		−15	
	03/1992		11/1991		−4
04/1993		10/1992		−6	
	11/1994		07/1993		−16
08/1996		07/1995		−13	
			12/1996		extra
		03/1998		extra	
	11/1998				0
08/1999		08/1999		0	
	04/2000		04/2000		0

	Troughs	Overall	peaks
Average	−7	−6	−5
Median	−8.5	−6.0	−4.0
Per cent lead	81	79	78
Std. deviation	7.6	9.9	12.0

Note: SWLgI—Swedish Lagging Index
Source: Economic Cycle Research Institute.

In general, however, the Swedish experience duplicates the US one and we would undoubtedly find much the same story for other modern industrial market economies, were the data available and reasonably up to date. In any case, we find that lagging indexes continue to behave much as Moore suggested they might behave, as long ago as 1951.

Lagging Indicators and Forecasting Changes in Inflation Rates

Another use of lagging indicators may be in confirming the forecasts of the leading indicators of inflation. This relationship arises out of the link between growth and inflation. Table 3.5 compares the US future inflation gauge to the US lagging index in growth rate form in an effort to answer the question, 'How well did the US lagging index forecast changes in the inflation rate in the US during the last forty years?' The results of the relationship, shown in Figure 3.5 and in Table 3.5, are clearly that the lagging index anticipated changes in the inflation rate by four months at troughs, six months at peaks, and six months overall. (For a comparison we may note that the ECRI has developed a leading index of inflation which, for roughly the same period, leads by 13 months at both peaks and troughs, hence overall.)

What is the economic logic of this relationship between turns in the lagging index and turns in the inflation rate index? Essentially, it says that customarily the economy must be well into expansion, as confirmed by a lagging index peak, before there is a likelihood of a decline in the inflation rate, and well into contraction, as confirmed by a trough in the lagging index, before inflation picks up again. The logic thus tells us that when a lagging index confirms that a business cycle trough has occurred, the expansion is customarily fairly well advanced and this is precisely the time when inflationary pressures are likely to multiply. At peaks, the reverse occurs. By the time the lagging index confirms a previous peak, the economy is likely to be well into recession.

We can tell essentially the same story for Sweden, except that we do not have a Swedish FIG. Figure 3.6 shows the Swedish lagging index against the Swedish inflation chronology. The leads and lags at the turns are shown (in months) in Table 3.6. The reasoning is, of course, precisely the same and (by chance again) we find that on an average the Swedish lagging index turns down five months before inflation eases,

Table 3.5: Two Ways to Anticipate Inflation: Future Inflation Gauge vs. Lagging Index Growth

Inflation Cycle Turning Points		USFIG1 Months		USLgI Growth Months	
		Lead(–)	Lag(+)	Lead(–)	Lag(+)
Troughs	Peaks	Troughs	Peaks	Troughs	Peaks
06/1961		–4	1		
	10/1966		–7		–11
05/1967		0		6	
	04/1970		–8		–3
08/1972		–21		–18	
	09/1974		–10		–9
04/1976		–11		–7	
	03/1980		–11		–6
03/1983		–6		–1	
	02/1984		1		4
04/1986		–13		5	
	10/1990		–39		–20
04/1994		–42		–2	
	05/1996		–17		–15
03/1998		–20		–20	
	03/2000		1		8

	USFIG1 Troughs	USFIG1 Peaks	USFIG1 Overall	USLgI Troughs	USLgI Peaks	USLgI Overall
Average	–15	–11	–13	–4.0	–6.0	–6.0
Median	–12.0	–9.0	–10.5	–1.5	–7.5	–4.5
Per cent lead	94	75	84	62.5	75	69

Note: The Future Inflation Gauge (FIG) is a monthly index developed at ECRI. It includes the growth rates in industrial prices, real estate loans, and employment; the yield spread; and the percentage of purchasing managers reporting slower deliveries.
Source: Economic Cycle Research Institute.

and the lagging index turns up three months before inflation picks up. The timing, on average is therefore, almost reduced to that in the US (–6 months in the US, –4 months in Sweden).

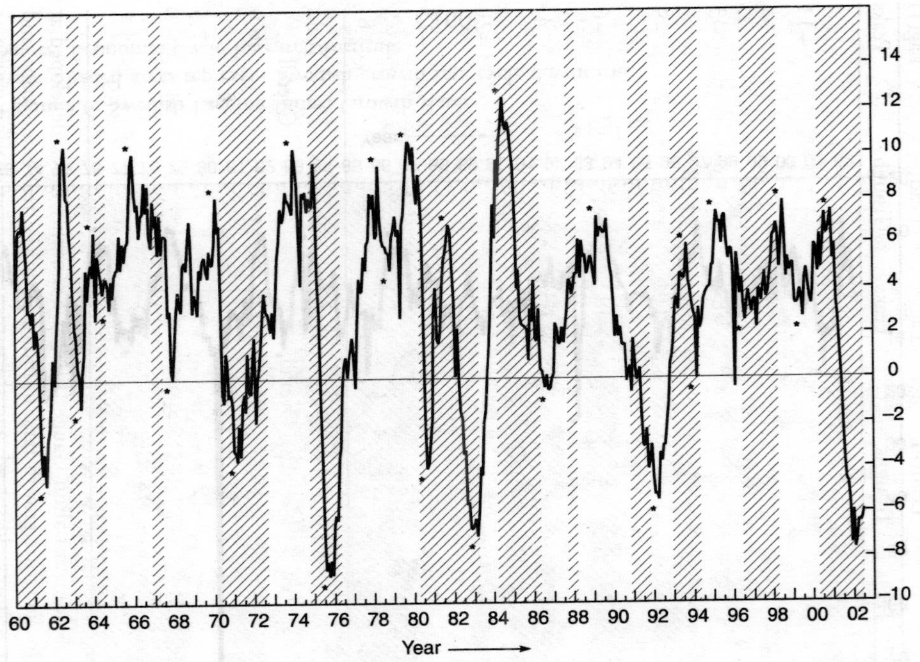

Figure 3.5: US Lagging Index, Growth Rate.
Note: Shaded areas represent Swedish growth rate cycle downturns.
Source: Economic Cycle Research Institute.

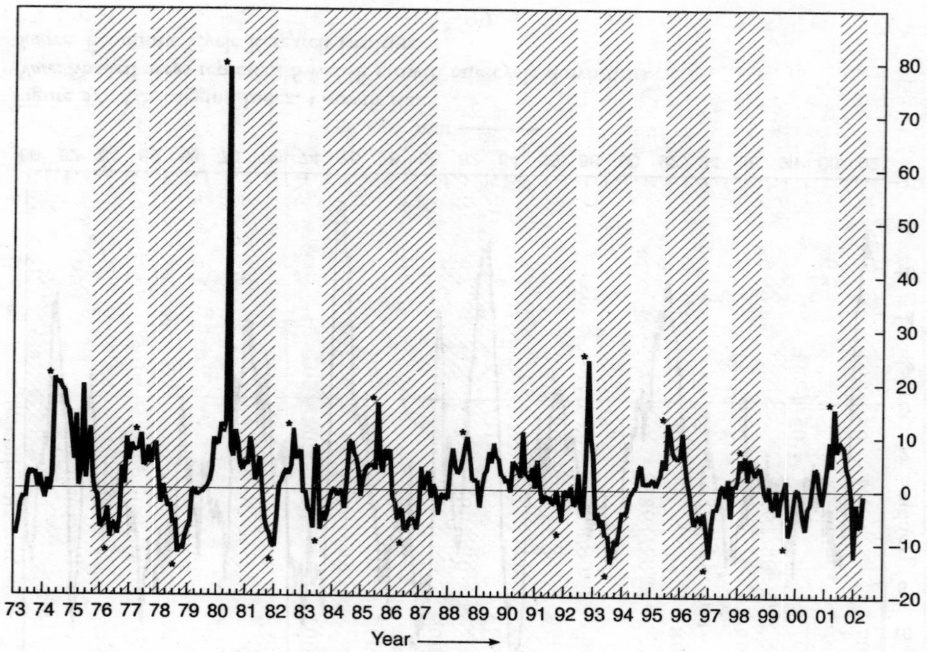

Figure 3.6: Swedish Lagging Index, Growth Rate.
Note: Shaded areas represent Swedish growth rate cycle downturns.
Source: Economic Cycle Research Institute.

Table 3.6: Swedish Inflation Cycle vs. Lagging Index Growth Rate

Inflation Cycle		SWLg1		SWLg1 Growth months	
Turning Points		Turning Points		Lead(–)	Lag(+)
Troughs	Peaks	Troughs	Peaks	Troughs	Peaks
	08/1975		05/1974		–15
01/1977		04/1976		–9	
	07/1977		05/1977		–2
02/1979		08/1978		–6	
	10/1980		05/1980		–5
12/1981		12/1981		0	
	07/1983		08/1982		–11
		07/1983		extra	
			07/1985		extra
06/1987		06/1986		–12	
	03/1990		08/1988		–19
04/1992		11/1991		–5	
	01/1993		10/1992		–3
03/1994		07/1993		–8	
	05/1995		07/1995		2
11/1996		12/1996		1	
	09/1997		03/1998		6
09/1998		09/1999		12	
	05/2001		04/2001		–1

	Troughs	Overall	Peaks
Average	–3	–4	–5
Median	–5.5	–5.0	–3.0
Per cent lead	69	74	78
Std. Deviation	7.6	7.7	8.1

Note: SWLgI—Swedish Lagging Index.
Source: Economic Cycle Research Institute.

Table 3.7: US Growth Rate Cycle vs. US CPI Growth Rate

Growth Rate Cycle Turning Points		CPI Growth Rate Turning Points		CPI Growth Rate months Lead(–)	Lag(+)
Troughs	Peaks	Troughs	Peaks	Troughs	Peaks
12/1960		06/1961		6	
	11/1961		09/1962		10
12/1962		04/1963		4	
			01/1964		extra
		07/1964		extra	
	01/1966		10/1966		9
05/1967		05/1967		0	
	07/1968		04/1970		21
11/1970		08/1972		21	
	01/1973		09/1974		20
03/1975				miss	
	02/1976				miss
		04/1976		extra	
			03/1980		extra
06/1980				miss	
	01/1981				miss
07/1982		03/1983		8	
	01/1984		02/1984		1
01/1987		04/1986		–9	
	12/1987		08/1987		–4
		02/1988		extra	
			10/1990		extra
02/1991		10/1991		8	
			11/1992		extra
		04/1994		extra	
	05/1994				miss
01/1996				miss	
	01/1998		05/1996		–20
09/1999		03/1998		–18	
	04/2000		03/2000		–1

	Troughs	Overall	Peaks
Average	3	4	5
Median	5.0	5.0	5.0
Per cent lead	31	34	38
Std. deviation	11.8	12.3	13.5

Note: CPI—Consumer Price Index.
Source: Economic Cycle Research Institute.

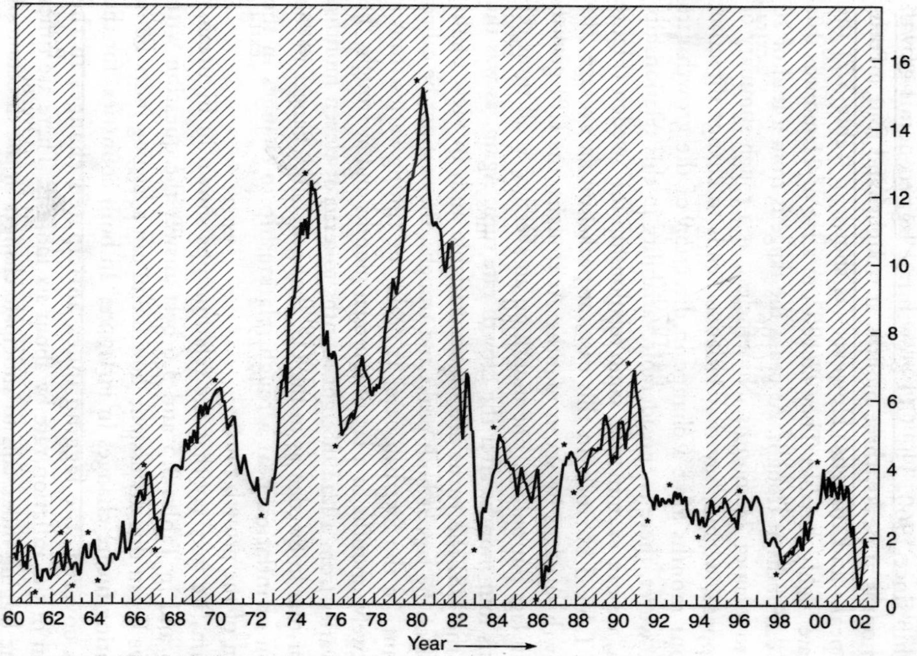

Figure 3.7: US CPI Growth Rate.
Note: Shaded areas represent Swedish growth rate cycle downturns.
Source: Economic Cycle Research Institute.

Finally, we can examine these relationships by considering the turning points in the consumer price index (CPI), as a measure of inflation, against the growth rate chronology. Figure 3.7 shows this relationship since 1960. The CPI growth rate lags economic growth by five months at peaks, three months at troughs, and four months at both peaks and troughs. However (as shown in Table 3.7) the timings are highly variable. They range from a lag of 21 months to a lead of 18 months at troughs. At peaks the range is from a lead of 20 months to a lag of 21 months. Nonetheless, as a rough summary of what happens, we may say that inflation tends to change direction about four months after a change in direction of the growth rate cycle. However, there is considerable variability in this relationship.

Again, we can examine the same relationship for Sweden (Figure 3.8 and Table 3.8) story. In this case, at peaks, on an average, the CPI growth rate lags by seven months. At troughs, the CPI growth rate again lags but only by one month on an average. At all turns the CPI turns four months after the growth rate turn. Again, as was the case in the US, the turns are highly variable and, in view of the shortness of the lags at both peaks and troughs, they cannot be called significant. In the Swedish case, at peaks the timing varies from a lead of twelve months to a lag of fourteen months and at troughs the timing varies from a lead of eight months to a lag of eleven months. It is clear that in Sweden as in the US, very generally, changes in the direction of inflation bear a rough relationship to changes in the direction of the growth rate.

In sum, we may say that the relationships shown in Figure 3.5 and 3.6 and in Tables 3.5 and 3.6 best answer the question with which we began this discussion; 'how useful can a lagging index be in anticipating future changes in inflation?' In both countries, for the periods covered, the lagging index anticipated changes in the direction of the inflation rate by about six months. There are times when the lagging index fails to anticipate changes in the direction of inflation and there is considerable variability in the length of the leads. Nevertheless, paying attention to direction changes in the lagging index is a valuable adjunct to other techniques for forecasting changes in the inflation rate.

Conclusion

We have seen that the lagging index of a country can be useful, as

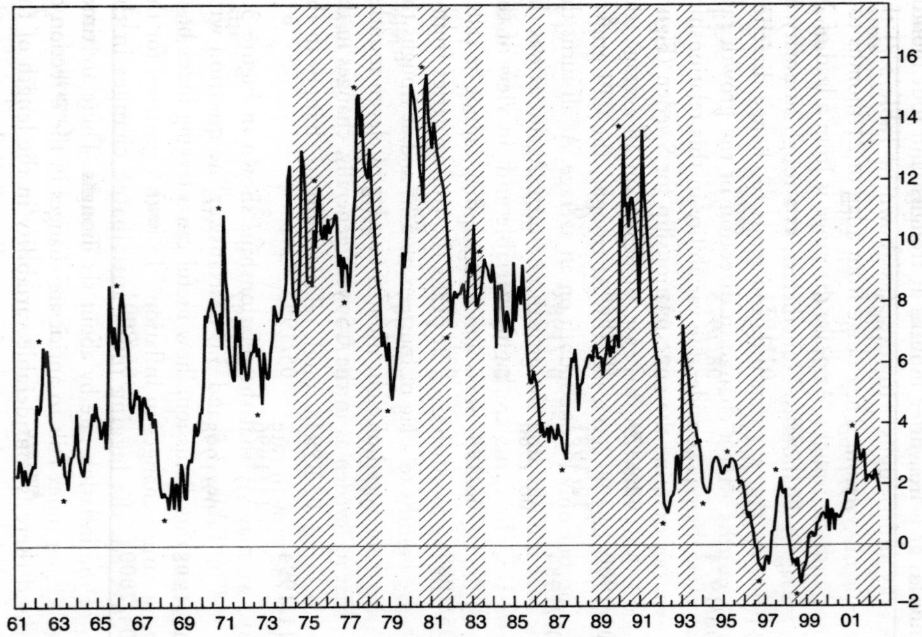

Figure 3.8: Swedish CPI Growth Rate
Note: Shaded areas represent Swedish growth rate cycle downturns.
Source: Economic Cycle Research Institute.

Table 3.8: Swedish Growth Rate Cycle vs. Swedish CPI Growth Rate

Growth Rate Cycle Turning Points		*CPI Growth Rate* Turning Points		*CPI Growth Rate* months Lead(–) Lag(+)	
Troughs	Peaks	Troughs	Peaks	Troughs	Peaks
			05/1962		extra
		07/1963		extra	
			02/1966		extra
		05/1968		extra	
			01/1971		extra
		11/1972		extra	
	06/1974		08/1975		14
06/1977		01/1977		–5	
			07/1977		extra
		02/1979		extra	
	02/1980		10/1980		8
06/1981		12/1981		6	
	07/1984		07/1983		–12
		06/1986		miss	
			04/1987		miss
02/1988		06/1987		–8	
	05/1989		03/1990		10
10/1991				miss	
			03/1992		miss
		04/1992		extra	
			01/1993		extra
04/1993		03/1994		11	
	11/1994		05/1995		6
08/1996		11/1996		3	
			09/1997		extra
		09/1998		extra	
	11/1998				miss
08/1999				miss	
	04/2000		05/2001		13

	Troughs	Overall	Peaks
Average	1	4	7
Median	3.0	6.0	9.0
Per cent lead	40	27	17
Std. deviation	7.8	8.8	9.5

Source: Economic Cycle Research Institute.

predicted by Moore and others a long time ago, in confirming changes in the direction of cyclical activity. We have also seen that the lagging index can be an aid in forecasting changes in the inflation rate. It would be useful, therefore, if more countries paid attention to the development of lagging indexes along with the attention which naturally gravitates to leading indexes. A good system of international lagging indexes would be a helpful addition to the arsenal of measures which are being developed in the ongoing pursuit of better ways to monitor instability in market economies.

Endnotes

[1]The 1950 paper was entitled 'Statistical Indicators of Cyclical Revivals and Recessions', Occasional Paper No. 31, NBER, New York. Reprinted in G. H. Moore, (Ed.), (1961) *Business Cycle Indicators*, New York: NBER. The Quotation is from 'When Lagging Indicators Lead: The History of an Idea', in G. H. Moore (1983). *Business Cycles, Inflation, and Forecasting,* Second Edition, for NBER, Cambridge, Mass: Ballinger Press, p. 362.

References

Klein, P.A. and G.H. Moore (1985), *Monitoring Growth Cycles in Market-Oriented Countries,* for the National Bureau of Economic Research, Massachusetts: Ballinger Publishing Company.

Moore, G.H. (1983), *Business Cycles, Inflation, and Forecasting,* 2nd Edn. Massachusetts: Ballinger Press.

Moore, K.H. (1971), 'The Comparative Performance of Economic Indicators for the United States, Canada, and Japan', *Western Economic Journal,* Vol. ix, No. 4, December, pp. 419–27.

OECD (1987), *OECD Leading Indicators and Business Cycles in Member Countries, 1960–1985,* Paris.

4

Tracking Turning Points in the Financial Services Industry

Lorene Hiris

Introduction

In addition to coincident and leading indexes that track turning points in the overall US economy, comparable indexes have already been developed for the major sectors of the economy; namely, services, manufacturing and construction (Banerji and Hiris 2001). Each of these sectors exhibits distinct economic cycles, marked by the co-movement of economic activities within its respective areas. It is also possible to break down each sector further and develop more focused coincident and leading indexes. This paper extends the analysis to an important industry within the service sector—the financial services industry.

In the United States, growth in the service-producing sector in general, and in the financial services sector in particular, has far outstripped growth in the goods-producing sector over the last few decades. Today, the service sector is the dominant part of the US economy, representing more than half of the gross domestic product (GDP) and over 80 per cent of employment. The financial services sector alone accounts for nearly one-fifth of the nation's gross

The author gratefully acknowledges the skilled research assistance of Dimitra Visviki and Hui-Chun Jan.

national product (GNP) (Bureau of Economic Analysis 2000). Yet, the service sector has been decidedly under-represented in available leading economic indexes. One explanation may be that many service-producing industries have not been cyclically monitored because they continue to grow during recessions, although at a slower pace, and are less sensitive to traditional cyclical contractions than are the goods-producing industries.

Although most past recessions have begun in the goods-producing sector, weakness in the growth of the increasingly important services sector can also contribute markedly to cyclical downswings in the economy. This has led to an innovative set of coincident and leading indexes being developed for the overall service sector of the US economy, providing information on the sector's current status and future prospects (Layton and Moore 1989). The growth rates of these indexes show the presence of clearly recognizable cyclical swings in service sector activity. The service sector, however, encompasses a variety of unrelated economic activities. For example, stock market activity is cyclically sensitive, but has tenuous links, at best, to personal services, which are not highly cyclical. It is advisable, therefore, to also construct leading and coincident indexes for subgroups of service activities, which are likely to move together cyclically.

Given the significant importance and the clearly cyclical nature of the financial services industry, this study focuses on identifying leading and coincident indicators for this industry, and developing leading and coincident indexes therefrom. Such a set of indexes would provide a useful tool for making turning point forecasts for the financial services industry, and would also be helpful in predicting swings in regional economies or states and cities where there is a substantial concentration of financial services activity. Comparable indexes could also be constructed for countries where the financial services industry plays a prominent role; for example the United Kingdom.

The long US expansion of the 1980s was fuelled in part by a boom in the financial services industry; its demise was hastened by a contraction in all three components of the industry—finance, insurance, and real estate, popularly known as FIRE. Symptomatic of this recession in financial services were a deterioration of loan portfolios, a downturn in real estate prices, and a jump in the unemployment rate for workers in financial companies. Since credit provided by financial companies is the lifeblood of industry, the problems of financial institutions reverberate through the entire economy. Therefore, indexes providing early warning signals of cyclical swings in the financial services industry would be important to regulators, policy makers, investors, as well as the general public.

Growth Rate Cycle Methodology

The US economy and many industries within it have experienced cyclical contractions, typically associated with recessions. However, some of the faster-growing sectors, including financial services, have not experienced many cyclical contractions in economic activity. In these cases, economic cycles assume the form of cyclical accelerations and decelerations in the growth rate of economic activity. In the financial services sector, as in the service sector as a whole, it is appropriate to concentrate on the dating of these 'growth rate cycles', rather than 'classical cycles' which involve cyclical contractions in the level of economic activity.

Growth rate cycle analysis is used in analysing the cyclical fluctuations that characterize activity in the financial services industry. The analysis of growth rate cycles provides a means of identifying slowdowns in economic activity, which may not actually become declines in the level of activity but are merely sustained low level rates of growth, called growth recessions. When growth recessions do not result in classical contractions, they are also popularly labelled 'soft landings'. Since an easing in growth precedes an actual contraction, growth rate cycle analysis also provides an 'early warning system' for cyclical episodes, which may ultimately result in actual drops in economic activity.

The components and the resulting financial services coincident and leading indexes are analysed by calculating their six month smoothed growth rates. In this smoothing procedure, the rate is obtained by dividing the current month's index number by the average index number for the previous twelve months and expressing the result as an annual rate. To obtain the annualized compound rate, the ratio is raised to the 12/6.5 power since the 12-month average is centred 6.5 months before the current month.

$$S_t = 100\left[\frac{X_t}{\sum_{i=1}^{12} X_{t-1}}\right]^{\left(\frac{12}{6.5}\right)} - 100$$

A smoother series results because a single month's number in the denominator is replaced by the average of twelve observations. Thus, the random element in the base from which the change is measured is reduced. This six month smoothed change answers the question 'How much higher (lower) is the index now than it was on average during the past year?' The more traditional 12-month change calculation answers the question, 'how much higher (lower) is the index than it was a year ago?' This method is consistent with the idea of growth rate cycle analysis already described here, wherein it is the growth rate, rather than the level, of financial services activity that best reveals its cyclical performance, just as in the case of total services (Hiris 1992).

Coincident Indicators

Traditionally, turning points in certain series have been identified as being roughly concurrent with turning points in aggregate economic activity. These include measures of employment, output, income, and trade. After investigating coincident candidates for the financial services sector, four corresponding measures have been identified as components for the coincident index.

Two series capture growth rate cycle swings in employment conditions in the financial services industry. They are FIRE's aggregate employee-hours and its unemployment rate. Aggregate hours are a more accurate and cycle-sensitive measure of labour input than the number employed, especially with an increasing number of persons employed part-time in service industry jobs. Changes in overtime hours are also captured by this series. Also, the aggregate hours series avoids the double counting of persons on more than one payroll, since only the hours worked are reported. The unemployment rate is, of course, a fundamental comprehensive measure of employment conditions that is known to be roughly coincident. This holds for the US economy as a whole, as well as for financial services.

A third coincident component is real national income for FIRE. This quarterly series is a comprehensive measure of income, and is, therefore, an important coincident indicator for this industry. Finally, the fourth component of the coincident index tracks personal consumption expenditures on financial services. Figure 4.1 displays the growth rates of the coincident components comprising the financial services coincident index (FSCI).

The Composite Index and Reference Chronology

Individually, the coincident indicators are measures of economic activity in the financial services sector, but they do not all have the same cyclical turning points. Thus, a method is needed to construct a composite index combining the movements of a number of heterogeneous time series that cannot be combined by quantity, price, or any other similar units (Boschan and Banerji 1990). This is necessary because some series would 'prove more useful in one set of conditions, others in a different set. To increase the chances of getting true signals and reduce those of getting false ones, it is advisable to rely on all such potentially useful (series) as a group' (Zarnowitz and Boschan 1975). This is the rationale for combining the chosen coincident indicators into a composite index, which then serves as a summary measure of aggregate activity. 'Because of (their) diversified and comprehensive coverage, composite indexes are more reliable as cyclical indicators and less subject to measurement error and erratic behaviour than any of their components taken singly' (Bureau of Economic Analysis 1977).

Constructing the Composite Index

There are several possible ways of constructing composite indexes (Boschan and Banerji 1990). The method used for constructing the financial services coincident and leading indexes is similar, but not identical, to that based on the traditional National Bureau of Economic Research (NBER) methodology. This method was also used by the US Department of Commerce (Bureau of Economic Analysis 1984), when it constructed its well-known leading, coincident, and lagging indexes. Basically, the procedure includes the transformation of each series to ensure symmetrical treatment; component standardization to prevent the more volatile series from dominating the index; accumulation of the standardized series into a raw index;

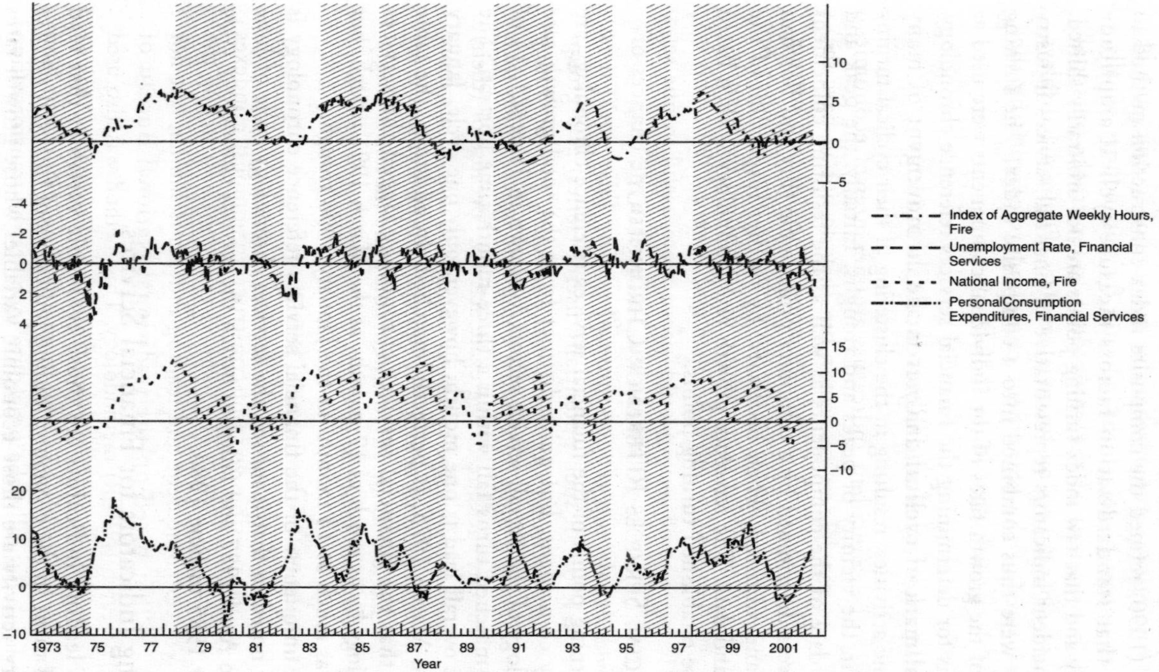

Figure 4.1: Financial Services Coincident Index Components, Annualized Growth Rate (per cent).
Note: Shaded areas represent cyclical downturns in the growth rate of US financial services.

trend adjustment; and, establishment of a base year. Boschan and Banerji (1990) refined the composite index construction method to ensure that standardization factors measure cyclical amplitude correctly and that raw index turning points are not arbitrarily shifted.

Coincident indicators representative of financial services industry activity were thus combined into a composite index. The turning points of the growth rates of the individual components were used as the basis for determining the financial services reference chronology. The hallmark of cyclical analysis is the co-movement of many economic activities, resulting in the clustering of their cyclical turning points in the vicinity of peaks and troughs. Initially, the peak and trough date of the components as well as the resulting coincident index were determined by a computer programme (Bry and Boschan 1971) and adjusted, when necessary, by further inspection of the charts and data. The reference growth rate chronology is then based on these established turning points.

Financial Services Reference Chronology

The turning points of the financial services reference chronology are roughly coincident, but quite distinct from the total growth rate chronology of the overall service sector. As shown in Table 4.1, 14 of the 21 matched turns fall within a three-month time horizon. The average overall lead is one month; however, only one cycle, January 1973 to March 1975, is perfectly matched. In addition, the table shows that the financial services chronology lagged the services chronology by as much as 17 months at the March 1991 trough, but led by as much as 14 months at the January 1996 trough.

The uniqueness of the financial services reference chronology is further noted in that it missed the services chronology cycle of June 1986 to April 1987 and failed to match the services chronology cycle of May 1985 to June 1986.

Leading Indicators for Financial Services

Just as leading indicators are those economic variables that lead cyclical turns in the economy, leading indicators of financial services industry activity are those economic variables whose growth rates lead cyclical peaks and troughs in the growth rate of financial services activity.

Table 4.1 Lead/Lag Record of Services vs. Financial Services Growth Rate, Reference Chronologies

Services Growth Rate Reference Chronology		Financial Services Growth Rate Reference Chronology		Lead (–) / Lag (+) in months	
Troughs	Peaks	Troughs	Peaks	Troughs	Peaks
Dec.–60		Nov–60		–1	
	Apr–62		Jun–62		2
Mar-63		May–63		2	
	Jan–64		Nov–63		–2
Feb.–65		Jan–65		–1	
	Oct–65		Feb–66		4
Nov.–67		Nov–66		–12	
	Oct–68		Jul–68		–3
Nov.–70		Feb–70		–9	
	Jan–73		Jan–73		0
Mar.–75		Mar–75		0	
	Apr–78		Apr–78		0
May–80		Aug–80		3	
	Dec–80		Mar–81		3
May–82		Jun–82		1	
	Oct–83		Oct–83		0
		May–85		extra	
			Jan–86		extra
Jun.–86				miss	
	Apr–87				miss
Jun.–89		Aug–88		–10	
	Apr–90		May–90		1
Mar.–91		Aug–92		17	
	Oct–94		Oct–93		–12
Jan.–96		Nov–94		–14	
			Feb–96		extra
		Jan–97		extra	
	May–98		Nov–97		–6

	Troughs	Overall	Peaks
Average	–2	–2	–1
Media	–1	0	0
Per cent lead	59	55	50

Source: Economic Cycle Research Institute.

The potential leading indicators considered are conceptually similar to those included in leading indexes of overall economic activity. Theoretical justification, as well as the consistency with which the growth rates of these indicators lead turning points in the financial services growth rate chronology, were the primary bases for their selection. Except for the series on corporate profits, which is available quarterly, the remaining four series are available monthly. The monthly series include stock prices for financial services, BAA corporate bond yields, deflated M2 money supply, and building permits. As Figure 4.2 shows, each of these series generally lead the peaks and troughs in the financial services growth rate reference chronology.

The Financial Services Leading Index

The growth rates in the five series described have been identified as providing advance warning of changes in activity in the financial services industry. Hence, when these leading indicators are combined into a composite index, they serve as a comprehensive measure of expected activity in the financial services industry. As shown in Table 4.2, the growth rate of the financial services leading index (FSLI) leads the financial services growth rate chronology by average and median overall leads of five months. Of the 26 turns monitored since 1960, the FSLI leads its growth rate chronology 88 per cent of the time. Since 1960, the FSLI leads at 100 per cent of all 13 turns at troughs, and at 77 per cent of the 13 peak turns. At FSLI peaks, two 3-month lags and two coincident turns are noted. The LSLI growth rate also records an extra cycle during the 1990–1 US business cycle recession.

The correspondence between the cycles in the FSLI and the financial services growth rate reference chronology is apparent (see Figure 4.3). The figure shows that when the FSCI growth fell below zero, as in 1994, 1990–1, 1988, 1981–2, 1980, 1974–5, 1970, and 1966, it was generally anticipated by growth falling below zero in the FSLI. Other downturns in financial services growth were milder, such as the one in 1996, and were preceded by milder downturns in FSLI growth.

Table 4.2: Lead/Lag Record Financial Services Leading Index vs. Financial Services Growth Rate Reference Chronologies

Financial Services (Growth Rate) Reference Chronology		Financial Services Leading Index Growth Rate Reference Chronology		Lead (–) / Lag (+) in months	
Troughs	Peaks	Troughs	Peaks	Troughs	Peaks
Nov–60		Mar–60		–8	
	Jun–62		Apr–62		–2
May–63		Oct–62		–7	
	Nov–63		Sep–63		–2
Jan–65		Dec–64		–1	
	Feb–66		Oct–65		–4
Nov–66		Sep–66		–2	
	Jul–68		Oct–68		3
Feb–70		Jan–70		–1	
	Jan–73		Apr–71		–21
Mar–75		Sep–74		–6	
	Apr–78		Sep–76		–19
Aug–80		Mar–80		–5	
	Mar–81		Mar–81		0
Jun–82		Jan–82		–5	
	Oct–83		Apr–83		–6
May–85		Jul–84		–10	
	Jan–86		Apr–86		3
Aug–88		Dec–87		–8	
	May–90		Oct–89		–7
		Oct–90		extra	
			Aug–91		extra
Aug–92		Jul–92		–1	
	Oct–93		Oct–93		0
Nov–94		Mar–94		–8	
	Feb–96		Sep–95		–5
Jan–97		Jul–96		–6	
	Nov–97		Jul–97		–4
			Troughs	Overall	Peaks
		Average	–5	–5	–5
		Media	–6	5	–4
		Per cent Lead	100	88	77

Source: Economic Cycle Research Institute.

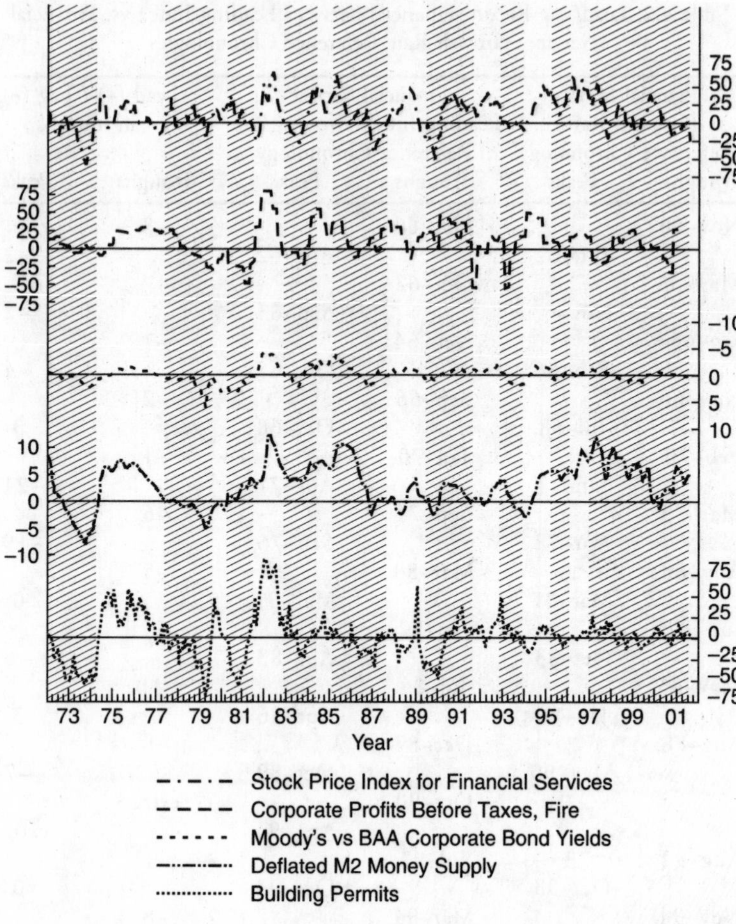

Figure 4.2: Financial Services Leading Index Components, Annualized Growth Rate (%).

Note: Shaded areas represent cyclical downturns in the growth rate of US financial services.

Applications and Conclusions

The primary purpose of the FSLI is to predict cyclical swings in the growth rate of financial services activity, thus providing a useful tool for making turning point forecasts for the finance, insurance and real estate sectors. This index would also be helpful in predicting cyclical

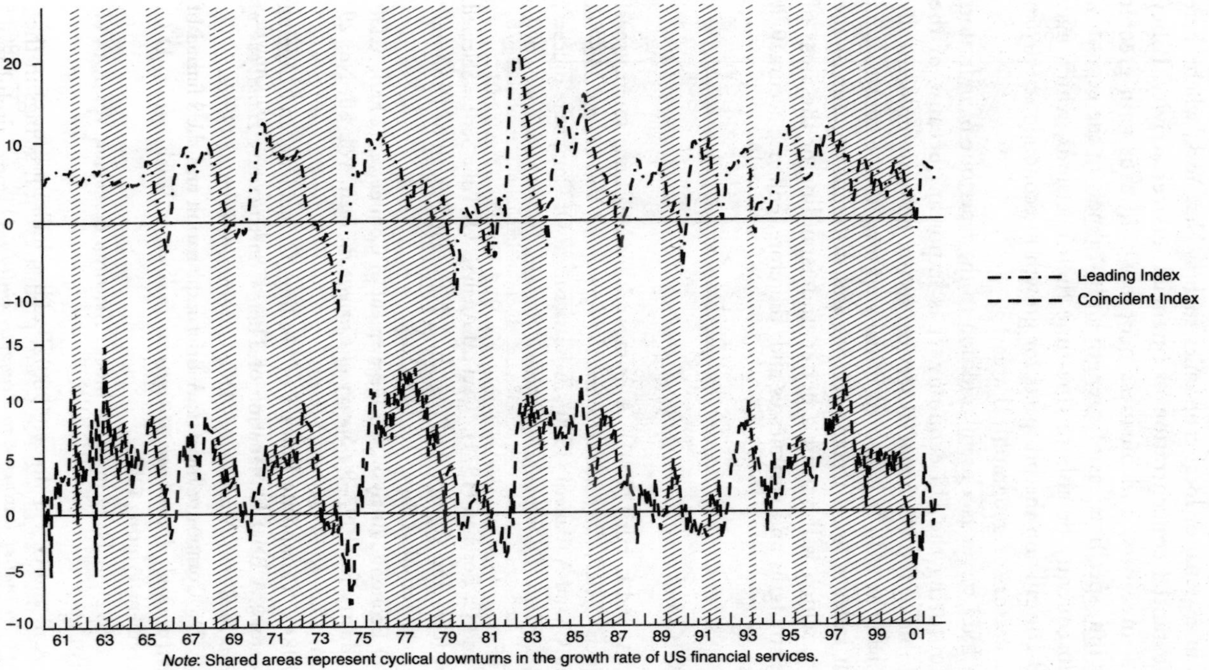

Figure 4.3. Leading and Coincident Indexes of Financial Services, Growth Rate (%).
Note: Shaded areas represent cyclical down turns in the growth rate of US financial services.

swings in regional or local economies such as New York, where there is a substantial concentration of financial services activity. Policy makers, investors, and business people would thus gain greater insight into specific areas of strength and weakness in the economy, and subsequently be able to fine-tune their decisions, which may depend critically on the prospects for growth in economic activity in specific sectors or geographical areas.

The FSLI serves as a useful addition to the repertoire of indicators for monitoring the US economy. It is important because of the central role of the US financial services sector, not only domestically but globally as well. It is also an initial step towards the construction of such indexes for different sectors and different regions of the country, which will permit a better understanding of the areas of relative strengths and weaknesses and, therefore, enhance accuracy in forecasting.

References

Banerji, A. and L. Hiris (2001), 'A Framework for Measuring International Business Cycles', *International Journal of Forecasting*, Vol. 17, pp. 333–48.

Boschan, C. and A. Banerji (1990), 'A Reassessment Of Composite Indexes', in P.A. Klein (Ed.) *Analyzing Modern Business Cycles*, New York: M. E. Sharpe.

Bry, G. and C. Boschan (1971), 'Cyclical Analysis Of Time Series: Selected Procedures and Computer Programs', National Bureau of Economic Research, Technical Paper 20, New York.

Bureau of Economic Analysis, US Department of Commerce. (2000), 'GDP By Industry for 1997–9', *Survey of Current Business*, Vol. 80, No. 29, pp. 24–35.

—— (1984), 'Composite Indexes of Leading, Coincident, and Lagging Indicators: A Brief Explanation of Their Construction', *Handbook of Cyclical Indicators*, Washington, DC: Government Printing Office.

—— (1977), 'Composite Indexes: A Brief Explanation and the Method of Construction', *Handbook of Cyclical Indicators*, Washington, D.C: Government Printing Office.

Hiris, L. (1992), 'A Daily Inflation Index', *American Economist*, Vol. XXXVI, pp. 19–29.

Layton, A. P. and G. H. Moore (1989), 'Leading Indicators for the Service Sector', *Journal of Business and Economic Statistics*, Vol. 7, pp. 379–86.

Zarnowitz, V. and C. Boschan (1975), Cyclical Indicators: An Evaluation and New Leading Indexes', *Handbook of Cyclical Indicators*, Washington, D.C: Government Printing Office.

5

Time-Variant Component Weighting in Business Cycle Indicators

Michael P. Niemira

Introduction

One of Geoffrey H. Moore's many contributions to the empirical side of macroeconomics was the development of a diffusion index to summarize cyclical economic activity and to answer the question, how widespread was the cyclical disturbance or improvement? At the National Bureau of Economic Research (NBER), Moore (1950) also developed the basic methods to form composite indicators from baskets of indicators having common timing characteristics with turning points in the business cycle. Along with the efforts of Julius Shiskin (1961), Moore's work led to the establishment of composite cyclical indicators of the US Department of Commerce in the 1960s, which were transferred to the Conference Board, a private sector trade group in the late 1990s. However, the basic methods pioneered by Moore in the 1950s, improved upon by Zarnowitz and Vaccara in the 1970s, and corrected by Stock and Watson in the 1990s continue to form the basis of the US composite cyclical indicators project at the Conference Board. These traditional NBER techniques are also used around the world by government statistical offices, educational institutions, and private sector research groups, including the one founded by Geoffrey Moore—the Economic Cycle Research Institute (ECRI) in New York.

The logic for compiling composite indexes to monitor and forecast business activity was stated succinctly by Zarnowitz (1992, p. 316). He observed, 'to increase the chances of getting true signals and reduce those of getting false signals, it is... advisable to rely on a reasonably diversified group of... series with demonstrated predictive potential'. However, econometrically, it can be difficult to include a broad-based set of indicators that have similar movement,[1] so the index formulation still has appeal to capture that diversification requirement for economic forecasting.

One of the crucial characteristics of composite cyclical indicators is component weighting. However, since the influential paper by Auerbach (1982), most applications of the cyclical indicator methodology simply use equal component weighting to average the change in the components, after the component standardization is applied.[2] In that paper, Auerbach demonstrated that there was no empirical improvement to the US composite index of leading indicators when the component weights were fixed and close to each other (essentially unity) *versus* the situation when they were set equal to one.

Equal weighting, however, may not be the optimal structure for compiling composite indicators at cyclical turning points when seemingly volatile observations may contain considerably more information than just noise. If, as John Maynard Keynes observed, economic activity experiences an abrupt change at a cyclical turning point, then those indicators undergoing that change first should be given more importance in the cyclical indicator. Keynes wrote, '[T]he substitution of a downward for an upward tendency often takes place suddenly and violently'. But even if that change is not abrupt, changes in specific indicators that lie in the tails of the historical time series distribution may contain potential information about broader adjustment. This is the logic for the Goldstein, Kaminsky and Reinhart (2000) threshold 'signalling technique'. To capture these concepts in a composite indicator, a new methodology must be embedded into the traditional index compilation process that allows for adjustable time-varying weights conditioned upon some indicator distribution property.

Methods for Determining Component Weighting

Weighting of components in a composite indicator can be implemented using different methods. The traditional NBER method first used an indicator scoring system to determine those weights by assigning a 'score' to each component of the index based on the characteristics of the data, including their quality and quantity. The indicator scores were derived following Moore and Shiskin (1967). Indicators were given a judgmental point score after evaluating their economic significance (their importance in business cycle theory or broadness of coverage), statistical adequacy (how good the indicators were from a technical standpoint), conformity to the business cycle, consistency in their timing relationship with business cycle turning points, promptness of data reporting by the source, and smoothness of the series. Then the sum of these Moore–Shiskin factor scores (W_i) for each indicator was used to derive the component's composite weight (w_i) for the ith indicator, where $w_i = W_i/\Sigma W_j$ for all components, $j = 1,\dots, n$. In practice, the resulting weights for the US composite index of leading indicators were all close to one, because the components were selected from among the set of best performing indicators available, based on those same criteria. Holmes (1986) offered a different approach where he used relative correlation of the components with its target series to derive weights. However, these techniques are static or time invariant.

Alternatively, the analytic hierarchy process (AHP) is a direct method for deriving component weights based on predetermined criteria, such as a magnitude-of-move criterion. The AHP was developed by Saaty (1990, 1994a, 1994b) as a decision making or judgemental forecasting framework whereby tangible and intangible characteristics of a decision were compared and ranked in terms of their importance to the objective of the problem. Work by Frei and Harker (1999) demonstrated the use of AHP to develop a performance indicator for the banking industry, which loosely provides the motivation for blending the AHP methodology with the traditional NBER indicator methods.

AHP Methodology—An Overview

Analytic hierarchy process is a well-established mathematical theory for measurement 'concerned with deriving dominance priorities from paired comparisons of homogeneous elements with respect to a common criterion or attribute' (Saaty 1994b). This pairwise coupling technique yields a matrix of comparisons $A = (a_{ij})$ which is positive and reciprocal, meaning that $a_{ij} = 1/a_{ji}$ for $i, j = 1, 2,\dots, n$. If the pairwise comparisons are consistent, then $a_{ik} a_{kj} = a_{ij}$ for $i, j, k = 1, 2, \ldots, n$ and $a_{ij} = w_i / w_j$. To compute the vector of weights, $w = (w_1, w_2, \ldots, w_n)$, solve the linear equation: $A w = \lambda_{max} w$, which can be written as $(A - \lambda_{max} I) w = 0$. If this equation has a non-zero solution for w, then λmax (which is a scalar) is an eigenvalue or characteristic value of A (which is an $n \times n$ matrix of pairwise comparisons) and w (which is an $n \times 1$ matrix) is an eigenvector belonging to I, the identity matrix, which is a diagonal matrix with the main diagonal terms equal to 1 and zero elsewhere. The resulting weights would be period dependent.

Component Weighting Through Distributional Filtering

Using the AHP structure, it is possible to condition the component weights on various indicator distributional characteristics to yield a time-sensitive rule for evolving weights. For example, it is possible to condition the indicator-weight selection based on Keynes' view that an abrupt change is a significant factor for signalling a turning point in the cyclical process. Similarly, the opposite view could be conditioned that all sharp moves are 'noise' and at distributional weighting can downplay the significance of that type of fluctuation. But extremes are not that only way to condition the weights. If the data distribution is bi- or multi-modal, that conditioning is equally possible to incorporate through the AHP structure. In this manner, time-varying weights can be implemented easily based on component amplitude change. Of course, the criterion for conditioning can be extended in many ways to include, among other possibilities, a weighting structure that increases a component's importance based on whether it has passed its recent peak or trough (a level criterion).

Application to US Business Conditions

To demonstrate conditional weighting based on distributional characteristics of the data, two examples are shown. The Conference Board's composite indexes of US coincident and leading indicators are reformulated as AHP-based indicators using the same components and standardized component changes that are embedded in the Conference Board measures. In doing so, three simplifying assumptions are made: (i) the component data distributions are approximated by normal distributions with the mean of μ_i and the variance of σ_i^2 for each 'i' component; (ii) the extreme values of each distribution are assumed to be, potentially, an 'abrupt' turning point signal and not just noise. In essence, this also tests the economic significance of Keynes' view; (iii) The values of Saaty's standard nine-point evaluation scale (1, 2, …, 9) were assigned to the distributional thresholds as follows: (μ_i +/– 0.25σ_i) = 1 on the Saaty scale, (μ_i +/– 0.50σ_i) = 2, (μ_i +/– 0.75σ_i) = 3, (μ_i +/– 1.0σ_i) = 4, (μ_i +/– 2.0σ_i) = 5, (μ_i +/– 3.0σ_i) = 6, (μ_i +/– 4.0σ_i) = 7, (μ_i +/– 5.0σ_i) = 8, and (μ_i +/– 6.0σ_i) = 9 for each component i.

All pairwise combinations of the components in the indicator were evaluated for each period. For the ten components of the composite index of leading indicators, this necessitated 100 comparisons (including comparison with the same component) per period, while the four components of the composite index of coincident indicators necessitated 16 pairwise comparisons per period. Based on how far the indicator's current period reading was from the mean, a score of 1 through 9 was assigned to the first component of the indicator. A similar calculation was done for the second component and so forth. Then the pairwise combination of component i and component j scores ($a_{ij} = w_i/w_j$) was calculated per period for the entire set of component couplets. Finally, the system was solved for current period weights, which were time variant. For example, the January 2001 weight for payroll employment in the AHP-based composite coincident indicator was 0.170, which jumped to 0.333 in February 2001 even though the monthly change in that component itself was roughly the same in January and February. By March 2002, the payroll employment weight in the index rose to a relatively high 0.494.

The US composite index of coincident indicators formulated as a traditional or AHP-based measure shared common turning point dates in specific cycles without exception, as shown in Figure 5.1. Table 5.1 shows the range for component weights using the AHP methodology; it is clear that AHP-based weights can be volatile. However, the AHP-based long-term average weights for the four components of the US composite index of coincident indicators were similar to those of the fixed equal weights of the traditional formula.

Prior to January 2001, the Conference Board's leading indicator and the AHP based leading indicator showed more noticeable differences due to index methodology. However, subsequent to the Conference Board's data and methodology revisions in January 2001,

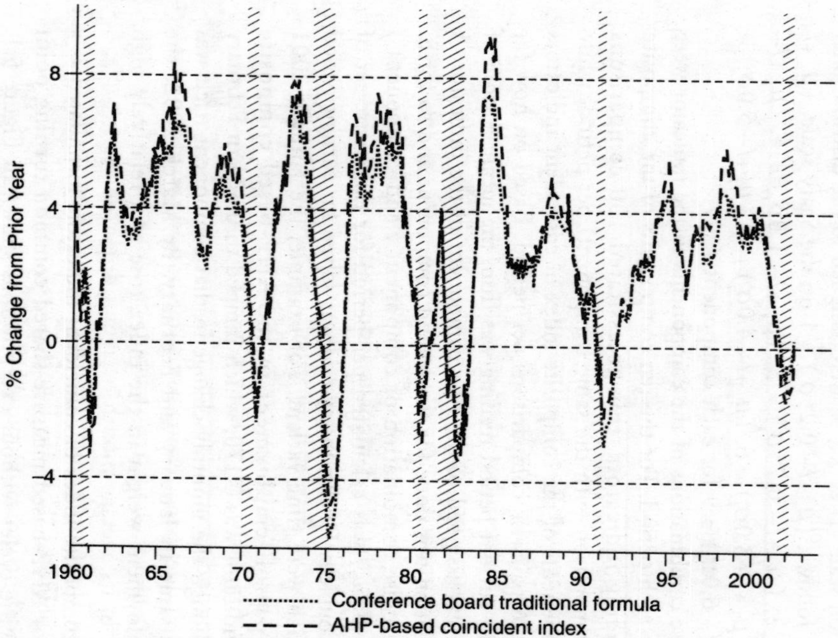

Figure 5.1: Comparison of Coincident Indicator Growth Rates (Traditional Method vs AHP-based Method).

Note: Shaded areas represent recessions.

Table 5.1: Comparison of AHP–Weights and Fixed Equal Weighting for the US Composite Index of Coincident Indicators, 1959–June 2002

Weights	Employees on non-agricultural payrolls	Personal incomes less transfer payments	Industrial production	Manufacturing and trade sales
Maximum	0.612	0.625	0.453	0.672
Minimum	0.063	0.056	0.091	0.055
Average	0.247	0.257	0.230	0.265
Equal	0.250	0.250	0.250	0.250

Source: Computed by the author.

the performance of the leading indexes based on the two methodologies largely converged. In January 2001, the Conference Board removed the index standardization process used with the leading indicator composite to peg it to the coincident index's variance and updated their data set to account for the North American Industrial Classification System (NAICS) .

Nonetheless, the US composite index of ten leading indicators, which was formulated using the AHP-weighting method provided somewhat crisper or sharper turning point recognition, in level terms, than was exhibited by the Conference Board index as demonstrated in Figure 5.2. Similarly, the year-over-year percentage change of the AHP leading indicator, as shown in Figure 5.3, had slightly larger cyclical amplitude swings owing to the methodology that accentuated large relative moves, while the standard deviation between 1959 and June 2002 in its average month-over-month percentage change was larger than the Conference Board's counterpart (0.87 vs 0.61 percentage points as shown in Figure 5.4). As was true for the AHP-based coincident indicator, the AHP-based weights derived for the leading indicator composite averaged, over the long run, to nearly the same value as the fixed equal weights of the traditional index. Yet the ten-component weights of the AHP formulation ranged between 0.02 and 0.35 as a group (Table 5.2).

Additionally, when the cyclical turning points differed by more than a month between the AHP-based and traditional leading formulations, the AHP formulation tended to have a longer lead time at peaks (for the 1980 and 1990 recessions).

Finally, the AHP-index formulation provided support for Keynes'

Table 5.2: Comparison of AHP Weights and Fixed Weight Equal Weighting for the US Composite Index of Leading Indicators, 1959–June 2002

	Components of the Leading Indicator									
Weights	Average Weekly Hours of Production Workers in Manufacturing	Average weekly initial claims for unemployment insurance	Vendor performance, Slower deliveries Diffusion Index	Manufacturers' New Orders, Consumer Goods and Materials	Building permits for new private housing units	Standard and Poor's 500 Stock Price Index	Money Supply, M2, Inflation-adjusted	Interest Rate Spread, 10-Year Treasury Bonds less Federal funds	Value of Manufacturers' New Orders for Capital Goods Non-defence Industries	Index of consumer expectations
Maximum	0.350	0.286	0.304	0.313	0.267	0.316	0.313	0.250	0.333	0.333
Minimum	0.024	0.023	0.024	0.024	0.024	0.021	0.025	0.024	0.020	0.023
Average	0.091	0.104	0.093	0.108	0.096	0.107	0.118	0.082	0.107	0.094
Equal	0.100	0.100	0.100	0.100	0.100	0.100	0.100	0.100	0.100	0.100

Source: Computed by the author.

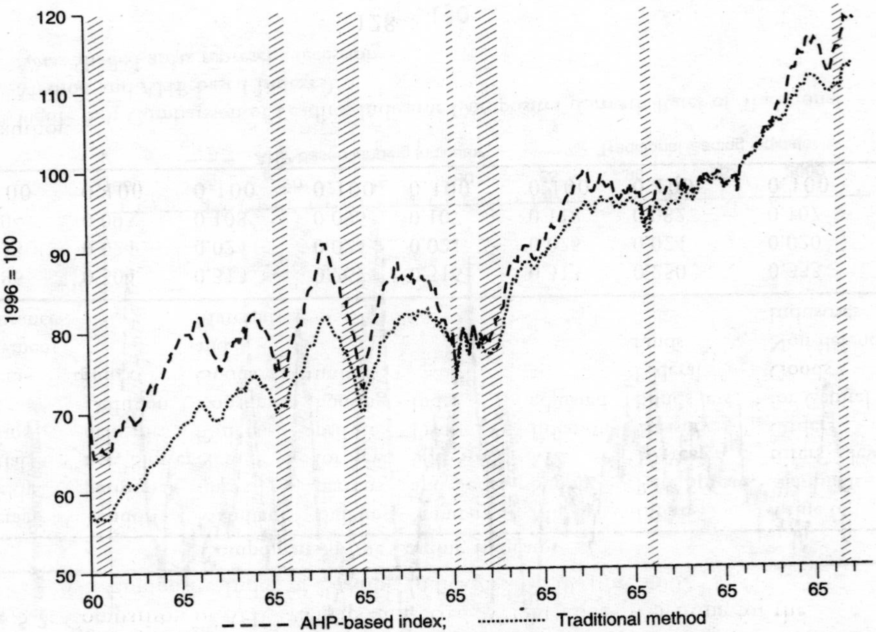

Figure 5.2: Comparison of Leading Indicator Composites (Traditional Method vs AHP-based Method).

Note: Shaded areas represent recessions.

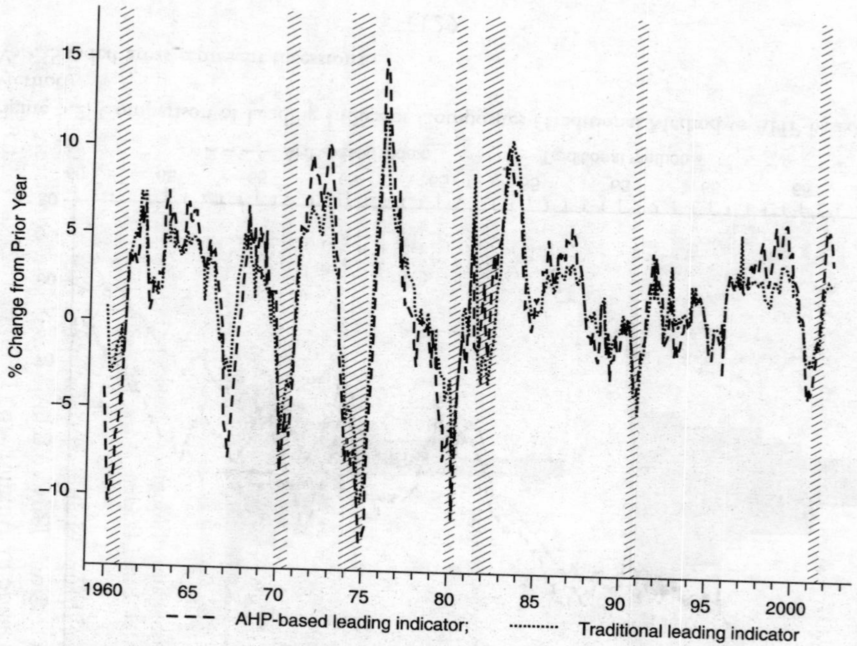

Figure 5.3: Comparison of Leading Indicator Composites (Growth Rates of Traditional Method and AHP-based Indexes).
Note: Shaded areas represent recessions.

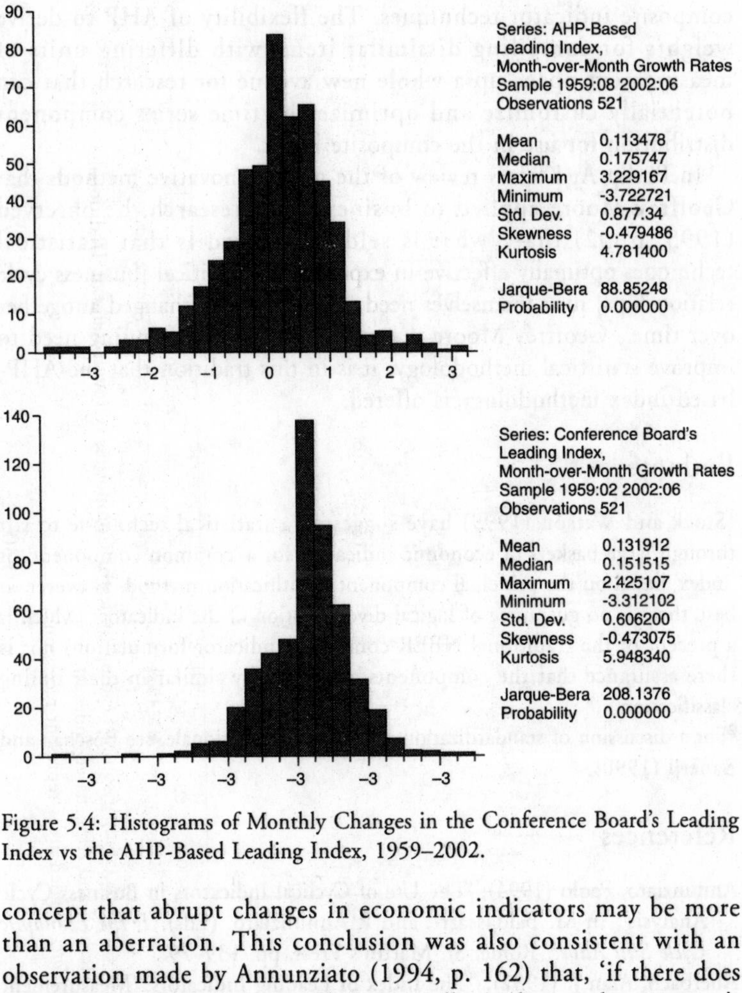

Figure 5.4: Histograms of Monthly Changes in the Conference Board's Leading Index vs the AHP-Based Leading Index, 1959–2002.

concept that abrupt changes in economic indicators may be more than an aberration. This conclusion was also consistent with an observation made by Annunziato (1994, p. 162) that, 'if there does ... exist a synthetic indicator [for] optimally predicting the economy's cyclical fluctuations, it is probable that it is considerably more unstable [over] time'. This underscores a conceptual need to further explore variable weighting of the composite indicator components.

Conclusion

The simplicity of the AHP-based methodology blended with the traditional NBER indicator formulation is a powerful advancement in composite indicator techniques. The flexibility of AHP to derive weights for compiling dissimilar items with differing units of measurement opens up a whole new avenue for research that can potentially customize and optimize the time series component distribution for use in the composite index.

In Philip A. Klein's review of the many innovative methods that Geoffrey Moore applied to business cycle research, he observed (1993, p. 32) that, 'what is seldom realized is that statistical techniques optimally effective in exposing these critical [business cycle relationships] may themselves need to be varied or changed altogether over time'. Geoffrey Moore was mindful of the continuing need to improve statistical methodology; it is in this tradition that the AHP-based index methodology is offered.

Endnotes

[1]Stock and Watson (1999) have suggested a statistical technique to sift through large baskets of economic indicators for a 'common component' or 'index' based on the principal component identification method. However, at best, there is no guarantee of logical diversification of the indicators (which is a precept of the traditional NBER composite indicator formulation) nor is there assurance that the components are cyclically similar in their timing classification.

[2]For a discussion of standardization techniques and rationale, see Boschan and Banerji (1990).

References

Annunziato, Paolo (1994), 'The Use of Cyclical Indicators in Business Cycle Analysis', in M. Baldassarri, and P. Annunziato, (Eds), *Is the Economic Cycle Still Alive?,* Rome: St. Martin's Press, pp. 139–79.

Auerbach, Alan J. (1982), "The Index of Leading Indicators: 'Measurement Without Theory', Thirty-Five Years Later", *Review of Economics and Statistics*, November, Vol. 64, pp. 584–95.

Boschan, Charlotte and Anirvan Banerji (1990), 'A Reassessment of Composite Indexes', in P. A. Klein, (Ed.), *Analyzing Modern Business Cycles: Essays Honoring Geoffrey H. Moore,* Sharpe, Armonk, New York: pp. 206–25.

Frei, Frances X. and Patrick T. Harker (1999), 'Measuring Aggregate Process Performance Using AHP', *European Journal of Operational Research*, Vol.

116, pp. 436–42.

Golden, B. L., E. A. Wasil, and P. T. Harker, (Eds) (1989), *The Analytic Hierarchy Process: Applications and Studies,* New York: Springer-Verlag.

Goldstein, M., G. Kaminsky, and C. Reinhart (2000), *Assessing Financial Vulnerability: An Early Warning System for Emerging Markets,* Institute for International Economics, Washington, DC.

Holmes, R. A. (1986), 'Leading Indicators of Industrial Employment in British Columbia', *International Journal of Forecasting,* Vol. 2, No. 1, pp. 87–100.

Klein, Philip A. (1993), 'Geoffrey H. Moore and Dynamic Statistical Methods', *International Journal of Forecasting,* Vol. 9, pp. 31–7.

Moore, Geoffrey H. (1950), 'A Technique for Summarizing the Current Behavior of Groups of Indicators', reprinted in: G. Moore, (Ed), *Business Cycle Indicators,* Princeton, NJ: pp. 653–65, NBER.

Moore, Geoffrey H. and Julius Shiskin (1967), *Indicators of Business Expansions and Contractions,* New York: NBER.

Saaty, Thomas L. (1994a), *Fundamental of Decision Making and Priority Theory,* Vol. VI, RWS, Pittsburgh, PA.

—— (1994b), Highlights and Critical Points in the Theory and Application of the Analytic Hierarchy Process, *European Journal of Operational Research,* Vol . 74, pp. 426–47.

—— (1990), *Multicriteria Decision Making: The Analytic Hierarchy Process,* Vol. 1, RWS, Pittsburgh, PA.

Shiskin, Julius (1961), *Signals of Recession and Recovery: An Experiment with Monthly Reporting,* New York: NBER.

Stock, James and Mark Watson (1999), 'Forecasting Inflation', *Journal of Monetary Economics,* Vol. 44, No. 2, pp. 293–335.

Zarnowitz, Victor (1992), *Business Cycles: Theory, History, Indicators, and Forecasting,* Chicago: The University of Chicago Press.

6

The 2001 US Recession What Did Recession Prediction Models Tell Us?

Andrew J. Filardo

Introduction

Geoffrey Moore (1963) in his essay on 'What is a recession?' chose to answer this question by focusing on the famous description of the business cycle from Burns and Mitchell (1963):

Business cycles are a type of fluctuation found in the aggregate economic activity of nations that organize their work mainly in business enterprises: a cycle consists of expansions occurring at about the same time in many economic activities, followed by similarly general recessions, contractions, and revivals which merge into the expansion phase of the next cycle; this sequence of changes is recurrent but not periodic; in duration business cycles vary from more than one year to ten or twelve years; they are not divisible into shorter cycles of similar character with amplitude approximately their own.

The views expressed are those of the author and not necessarily the views of the Bank for International Settlements. The author thanks Bob McGuckin and Ataman Ozyildirim of the Conference Board, and Jim Stock and Mark Watson for providing data on their respective business cycle measures. The author also thanks Palle Andersen, Bill English, and Steve Landefeld for helpful discussions.

The National Bureau of Economic Research (NBER)—considered by many to be the official arbiter of business cycle peaks and troughs—continues to use this guidance to define the phases of business cycles in the twenty-first century.

The choice of this description then, as well as now, was not motivated by its precision and irrefutable quality. As economic definitions go, it is quite inexact and vague. But, the description is apt now for the same reason that it has been circulating largely unchanged for nearly 80 years—it has resonated with those who study the recurrent ups and downs in US economic activity.

There has been far less success in translating this qualitative description into quantitative models to predict recessions. Various models have been offered over time with varying degrees of econometric sophistication to capture the salient features of the business cycle. Some are simple, maybe too simple. Some are quite sophisticated, reflecting state-of-the-art econometric modeling methods. Simple or sophisticated, at the proverbial end of the day, the yardstick with which to measure the performance of any recession prediction model is its ability to provide reliable, advanced warning of a recession.

The recent downturn in the US offers another, though increasingly rare, opportunity to examine the 'out-of-sample' reliability of recession prediction models. According to the NBER business cycle dating committee, the US entered recession in March 2001. Prior to this date, economy showed tangible signs that the risk of recession had risen. After surging in the late 1990s, economic activity began its rapid deceleration in the second half of 2000 as many economic factors weighed heavily on the expansion. Key economic factors included a dramatic decline in the stock market—especially the collapse of high-tech stock prices, a jump in oil and gas prices to very high levels, an increase in interest rates, a significant drop in industrial activity, and a build-up of what proved to be excessive inventories. Despite expansionary monetary and fiscal policies in 2001, the economy continued to decelerate with consumption moderating and capital spending contracting. This recession was somewhat atypical in several dimensions. It was one of the mildest on record with the housing sector remaining remarkably healthy, durable goods consumption faring relatively well when compared to non-durable consumption spending, and the brunt of the recession disproportionately hitting the industrial sector.

How well did recession models predict the end of the longest US expansion in the record books? This chapter examines the empirical performance of four popular recession prediction models. The next section describes the alternative models. The third section evaluates their empirical performance in the late 1990s and early 2000s using revised and 'real-time' data. The final section concludes that the superior performance of several 'old-fashioned' recession prediction models highlights the continuing need to reconcile modern econometric methods with the insights and valuable intellectual contributions to our understanding of the business cycle by Geoffrey Moore and other early business cycle pioneers associated with the NBER.

The Four Recession Prediction Models

This section briefly describes four recession prediction models considered by Filardo (1999). They include a simple rule-of-thumb model using the Conference Board's composite index of leading indicators (CLI), Neftçi's sequential probability model, a Probit model, and Stock and Watson's experimental recession indexes.

Simple Rules of Thumb Using the CLI

The CLI has played a central role in the long history of business cycle prediction at the NBER (Moore 1961; Zarnowitz 1992). The composite index methodology was developed in the mid-twentieth century as a means to provide a summary of economic series that exhibited a leading relationship with the business cycle. Designing an index was no simple task, especially in an era when computers were rare. The question was how to best summarize information about the state of the business cycle contained in potentially hundreds of time series.[1] Moore, who some consider the father of the leading indicators, argued that a small set of leading indicator series could be combined to provide a useful quantitative index that would provide early signals of changing economic activity (Moore 1961; Banerji and Klein 2000). In addition, it was recognized at that time that a simple average of the various leading indicator series would put too much weight on series with high volatility relative to those with low volatility. Moore, therefore, advocated a volatility adjustment, which till today is the basis for averaging the component series of the composite index. In terms of modern econometric modelling methods, the weighting scheme is crude. Nonetheless, the CLI continues to attract considerable attention, especially at times thought to be turning points in the economy.

By construction, declines in the CLI are supposed to provide an advance warning of an economic downturn, and hence should provide useful information as a signal of a future recession. In this sense, the rules of thumb are non-parametric models of recession prediction. The rules of thumb in this chapter are restricted to those using consecutive declines in the CLI as an indicator of imminent recession. For example, a *k*-month rule of thumb would signal an imminent recession if there were k consecutive declines in the CLI:

If $\{CLI_t < 0, ..., CLI_{t-k} < 0)\}$, then a recession signal is sent.

In general, multi-month rules of thumb that require consecutive declines are considered to be more reliable predictors of imminent recession than the month-to-month changes in the CLI (Hyman 1973; Vaccara and Zarnowitz 1978; Wecker 1979; and Zarnowitz and Moore 1982). This is because month-to-month changes in the CLI often produce false signals. To further filter out false signals, it is necessary to consider rules of thumb that include a constraint that the consecutive CLI decline must be sufficiently large to send a valid signal of imminent recession.[2]

Neftçi's Sequential Probability Model

Neftçi's sequential probability model is a non-linear method that provides an inference about a regime shift in the data generating process of the CLI data, which then can be used to infer a turning point in economy-wide activity. The theory behind this model comes from the literature on optimal stopping time and provides algorithms to assess the likelihood of a regime shift within a particular time-series data subsample. To use this model to predict recessions, several assumptions are required. First, a downturn in CLI data can be accurately and reliably characterized as a shift in the distribution of CLI data from an expansion distribution to a recession distribution. Second, because the method provides information only about a regime shift somewhere in the data subsample but not at an exact date, the lag between a downturn in the data and its detection via the model is short. Third, a turning point in CLI data provides reliable information about an imminent turning point in general economic activity.

With these assumptions, Neftçi (1982) and Diebold and Rudebusch (1989) provide a method to draw inferences about the likelihood of an imminent recession. Technically, the model is a Bayesian recursion that uses CLI data to update the probability at time t-1 that a turning point in the CLI data had occurred at some point in the subsample of data and can be calculated by the following equation:

$$P_t\,(t-\tau < Z \leq t \mid CLI_{t-\tau}, \ldots, CLI_t) = \frac{[P_{t-1} + \pi^r(1-P_{t-1})]F^r}{[P_{t-1} + \pi^r(1-P_{t-1})]F^r + (1-P_{t-1})(1-\pi^r)F^e}$$

where P_t is the conditional probability at time t of a turning point (represented by the integer-values random variable Z that is a time index for the first period after a regime switch from an expansion distribution to a recession distribution) having occurred in the data subsample $\{CLI_{t-\tau}, \ldots, CLI_t\}$; P_{t-1} is the analogous probability at time $t-1$; π^r is the unconditional transition probability of the economy entering a recession under the assumption that the economy is in expansion; and F^e and F^r are the density functions of *CLI* data under the assumption that they came from an expansion distribution or a recession distribution, respectively.[3] This equation highlights the feature of the model that the exact time of the turning point is not estimated. Rather, the method only provides an inference on whether a turning point occurred at some time between $t-\tau$ and t.

To use this model to predict recessions, the estimated probability of a turning point, P_t, is compared to a pre-specified threshold level of confidence which is intentionally set to allow a small probability of type I error. This level of confidence reflects two types of inferences: (i) confidence of a statistically significant regime shift in *CLI* data and (ii) confidence that such a shift portends a turning point in general economic activity. Following Diebold and Rudebusch (1989), this threshold is assumed to be 95 per cent that represents a conventional burden of proof for this type of model, that is a small probability of type I error. Operationally, soon after the model's probability, P_t, exceeds the threshold level of confidence, the recursion is reinitialized to search for another turning point over a subsequent subsample of *CLI* data.[4]

Probit Model

Consistent with previous research by Estrella and Mishkin (1998) and Lamy (1997), the Probit model is a (non-linear) regression model that translates information contained in leading indicators into a probability of recession at a particular time horizon:

$$P\ (\text{recession}/X_{t-k}) = F\,(\beta_0 + \beta_1 TS_{t-k} + \beta_2 CS_{t-k} + \beta_3 SP500_{t-k} + \beta_4 CLI_{t-k})$$

The variables that are assumed to help to predict a recession are the change in the term spread (*TS*), change in the corporate spread (*CS*), *S* and *P* 500 return (*SP 500*), and growth rate of the *CLI*. To predict a recession k-months ahead, the model is estimated using lagged information as represented in the vector X_{t-k}, = {TS_{t-k}, CS_{t-k}, $SP500_{t-k}$, CLI_{t-k}). The threshold criterion for this model is 50 per cent. If the probability is less than 50 per cent, the model signals an expansion because an expansion is more likely than a recession; if the probability is above 50 per cent, a recession is more likely.[5]

Stock and Watson's Experimental Recession Indexes

Stock and Watson (1989, 1991, and 1993) built a sophisticated econometric time-series model to infer the probability of recession, which is estimated in two steps. First, business fluctuations are viewed through the lens of a multi-equation unobserved variable model. The unobserved component is assumed to represent the common business cycle factor shared by four cyclically-sensitive variables. The cyclically-sensitive variables are industrial production, real personal income less transfer payments, real trade sales, and employment hours in non-agricultural establishments. The model has the following structure:

$$\begin{aligned}
\Delta X_t &= \beta + \gamma(L)\Delta C_t + u_t \\
D(L)\, u_t &= \varepsilon_t \\
\Delta C_t &= \mu_c + \lambda_{cc}\, \Delta C_{t-1} + \lambda_{CY}\,(L)\, Y_{t-1} + \nu_{Ct} \\
Y_t &= \mu_Y + \lambda_{YC}\,(L)\,\Delta C_{t-1} + \lambda_{YY}\,(L)\, Y_{t-1} + \nu_{Yt}
\end{aligned}$$

The growth rates of the cyclically-sensitive variables are stacked in the vector ΔX_t, the growth rate in the unobserved coincident indicator of economic activity is ΔC_t, ε is an uncorrelated error term, and $\gamma(L)$, $D(L)$, and $\phi(L)$ are standard lag polynomials. The lag polynomials, λ_{ij}, are estimated using statistical criteria and the error terms (v_{Ct}, v_{Yt}) are assumed to be uncorrelated and independent of ε_t. The last two equations in the model provide a link between the leading indicator series and the coincident index of economic activity, where leading indicators, Y, are used to help predict the growth rate of the unobserved coincident indicator ΔC_t.[6] With this model, Stock and Watson define a leading index, not as the simple volatility-weighted sum of the leading indicator variables, but as a weighted average of the indicators that have weights chosen to minimize the mean squared forecast error of the coincident indicator ΔC_t six months ahead.[7]

In the second step, Stock and Watson use the estimated model in the first step to generate forecasts of C_{t+k}. Defining a multi-period pattern for C_{t+k} consistent with past recessionary episodes, a probability index of recession six months ahead, XRI, is constructed. This second step is called the pattern recognition step.

How Well did the Models Predict the 2001 Turning Point?

The NBER Dating Committee announced that the recent recession began in March 2001, but as is usual, dating the initial month of the recession is subject to considerable uncertainty. While there is little controversy that the US economy contracted in 2001, there are some questions about when the contraction began. For example, industrial production peaked in June 2000 as did real manufacturing and wholesale–retail sales, real personal income less transfers peaked in November 2000, and total non-agricultural payroll employment peaked in March 2001.[8] The large benchmark revision to real GDP in July 2002 raised further questions about the starting date of the recession. Prior to the benchmark revisions, the Bureau of Economic Analysis estimated that real GDP contracted only once during the year, in the third quarter. This new snapshot of the data showed that the US economy contracted during three consecutive quarters starting in the second quarter. The revised picture also showed an economy that experienced a deeper and longer recession than previously estimated.

Given the uncertainty about the starting date of the recession, it should not be surprising that the extent of the advance warning from different recession prediction models could vary considerably. Nor should it be surprising that, for a given model, differences between the results using real-time data and recent data vintages (that is, subsequently revised data) could be significant. This section reviews the performance of the four recession prediction models in the light of these possibilities.[9]

Did the Recession Prediction Models Predict the Start of the 2001 Recession?

The CLI rules of thumb performed fairly well in predicting the March 2001 business cycle peak. Table 6.1 shows that the 2-month rule signalled an imminent recession 8 months prior to the NBER-denoted starting date. The performance, however, may be somewhat suspect because the 2-month rule has had the tendency to send frequent false signals. For example, over the past four decades, the 2-month rule produced 19 false signals.

In contrast, the 2-month rule with threshold and the 3-month rules provided an early warning of imminent recession in November 2000, four months ahead of the official starting date. These rules were also subject to many false signals in the period 1960–2002. What do the false signals indicate about the performance of these rules? The false signal tally for these rules appears high at first examination but it is important to note that most of the misses were influenced by the economic slowdown in 1966. This episode accounts for 7, 7, and 6 of the false signals for the 2-month rule with threshold, the 3-month rule, and the 3-month rule with threshold, respectively. Excluding the 1966 episode, for example, the 3-month rule of thumb produced only two false signals: one at the end of 1991 when the economy was experiencing anaemic economic activity and one in the spring of 1995 when the economy experienced a mild slowdown due in part to the rise in commodity prices and interest rates. The 4-month rules sent no advance warning of an imminent recession. These rules, however, may be too stringent. The post-1960 record shows that the power of these rules to predict recessions was spotty.

The usual complaint about the rules of thumb is that their predictive power may be overstated when using the latest vintage of data. This happens because of the sensitivity of the rules' performance to revisions in the CLI data. Figure 6.1 shows the number of false

Table 6.1: CLI Thumb Rules and the start of the 2001 recession; Timeliness and Accuracy of Various CLI Rules of Thumb

	Advanced warning of the start of a recession (in months)					
	2-month rule	2-month rule with threshold	3-month rule	3-month rule with threshold	4-month rule	4-month rule with threshold
Start of recession						
May 1960	10	9	9	9	8	7
January 1970	7	7	6	6	no signal	no signal
December 1973	8	8	7	7	6	6
February 1980	14	14	13	13	no signal	no signal
August 1981	7	7	6	6	no signal	no signal
August 1990	3	3	–3	–3	1	–1
Mean (lead time)	8	8	7	7	5	5
April 2001	8	4	4	4	no signal	no signal
	Number of signals of recession without an imminent onset of recession					
False signals	19	13	9	8	6	5

Note: False signals are defined as those signals that fall outside a one-year period before or after a peak date.

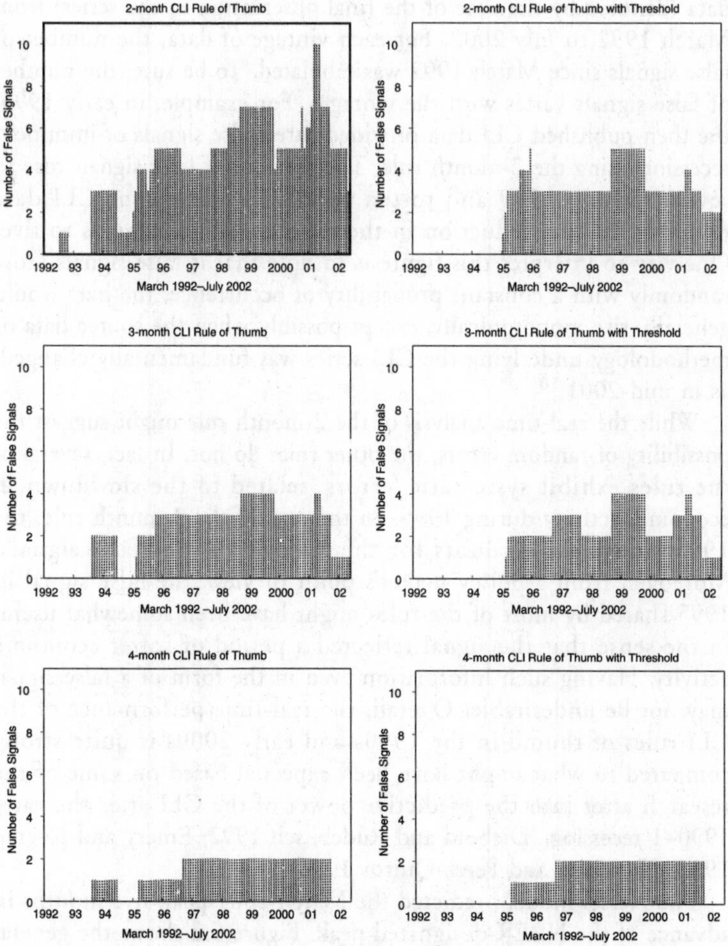

Figure 6.1: Variation in the Number of False Signals by Data Vintage.
Note: The height of narrow vertical bars represent the number of false signals from the respective rules of thumb for each of the real-time data vintages (vintages from March 1992 to July 2002).

signals from the rules using different vintages of CLI data. In this figure, the number of false signals is calculated for each vintage of data (denoted by the date of the final observation in the series) from March 1992 to July 2002. For each vintage of data, the number of false signals since March 1992 was tabulated. To be sure, the number of false signals varies with the vintages. For example, in early 1994, the then-published CLI data provided three false signals of imminent recession using the 2-month rule. The number of false signals rose to seven by early 1999 and to ten by 2001. Subsequent CLI data revisions led to a reduction in the number of false signals to five. One way to interpret this figure is to note that if false signals arose randomly with a constant probability of occurrence, the bars would generally rise monotonically, except possibly when the source data or methodology underlying the CLI series was fundamentally changed, as in mid-2001.[10]

While the real-time analysis of the 2-month rule might suggest the possibility of random errors, the other rules do not. In fact, several of the rules exhibit systematic 'errors' related to the slowdown in economic activity during 1995. In the case of the 3-month rule, the 1995 slowdown accounts for the majority of the false signals. Moreover, from a policy maker's point of view, the false signal in 1995 shared by most of the rules might have been somewhat useful in the sense that the signal reflected a period of softer economic activity. Having such information even in the form of a false signal may not be undesirable. Overall, the real-time performance of the CLI rules of thumb in the 1990s and early 2000s is quite strong compared to what might have been expected based on some of the research after into the predictive power of the CLI after the early 1990–1 recession (Diebold and Rudebusch 1992; Emery and Koenig 1993; Hamilton and Perez-Quiros 1996).

The Neftçi model predicted the March 2001 peak five months in advance of the NBER-designated peak. Figure 6.2 shows the general performance of the Neftçi model since late 1959. The model, using the CLI, has provided a median lead time of seven months using the 95 per cent threshold. However, it provided false signals in the mid-1960s during the dramatic industrial slowdown. As already discussed, such a false signal should not necessarily be interpreted as a failure of the model. There were also two false signals in the first half of the 1990s. Although these false signals coincide with slower economic activity, the findings certainly raise questions about the sensitivity of the model.

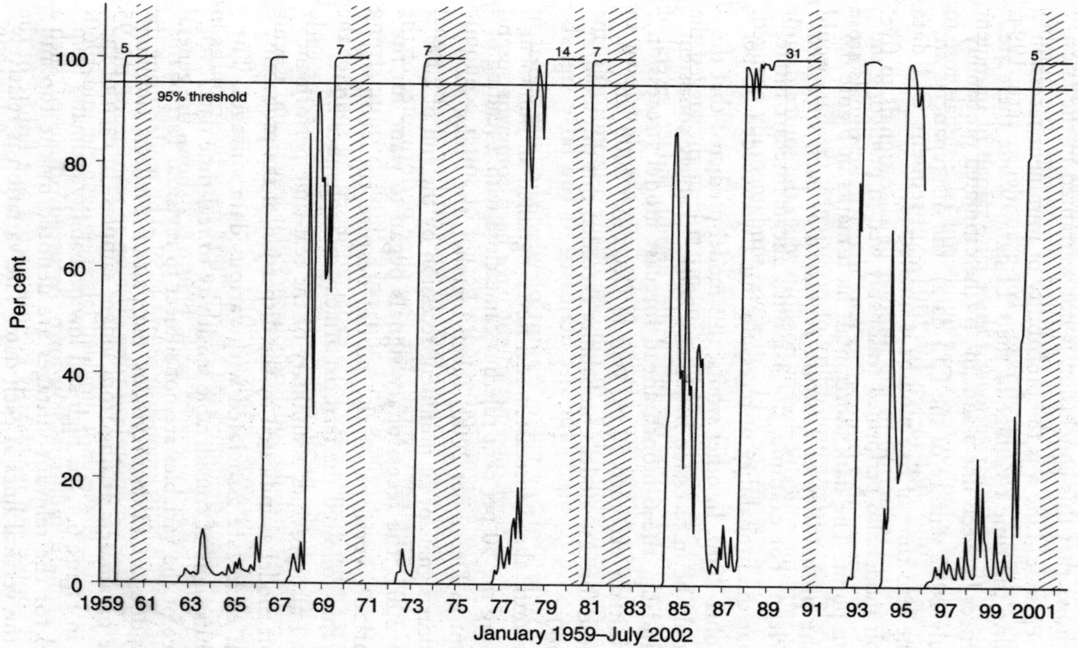

Figure 6.2: Probability of Imminent Recession Using Neftçi's Model.
Note: NBER recessions are represented by the shaded bars. The numbers next to the bars indicate the number of months prior to the peak when the probability is above the 95 per cent threshold level of confidence.

This model also has been subject to complaints that its signals of recession often look much better in retrospect because of revisions to the CLI data (Diebold and Rudebusch 1992; Filardo 1999). Figure 6.3 shows that this conclusion is not warranted in the latest recessionary episode. Line a is the probability of imminent recession at time t using the time t vintage of the CLI data. While there are some differences between line a and line b (the estimated probability using the July 2002 vintage of the CLI data), the discrepancies are small and the lead time of five months is unaffected.

The Probit model also performed reasonably well in predicting the 2001 turning point. The dark (horizontal) hash marks in Figure 6.4 represent the probability of a future recession at each specified forecast horizon. For example, the 3-month ahead forecast model indicates that the probability of recession initially exceeded 50 per cent in October 2000. In other words, this model predicted that the economy would be in recession in January 2001.[11] Largely consistent with this finding, the 6-month ahead forecast model's recession probability initially exceeded 50 per cent in December 2000, and the 9-month ahead forecast model's probability exceeded this threshold in October 2000.

The 12-month ahead forecast model never signalled an imminent recession using the 50 per cent rule but came close with a reading of 49.1 per cent in December 2000. Taken together, the Probit model sent fairly clear signals of an imminent recession by the end of 2000. By autumn 2001, the recessionary signals began to wane for the shorter horizon versions of the model despite the economic disruptions that followed the terrorist attacks in September 2001.[12]

Figure 6.4 also provides a summary of the real-time performance of the Probit model as indicated by the dispersion of the probability estimates at each date associated with various data vintages. The model exhibits signs of considerable sensitivity to real-time data, even though three of the variables are not subject to revision. Part of this sensitivity is due to CLI data revisions, but part of it reflects sampling error of the parameters arising from longer samples. In each of the four panels in Figure 6.4, the high and low probability estimates from each model for the relevant vintages are denoted by the top and bottom of the vertical lines at each date. The variation is relatively large near the NBER-designated turning point and generally larger for the longer forecast horizons. The variation is so high in the 12-month ahead forecast model that it began sending false signals in late 1998

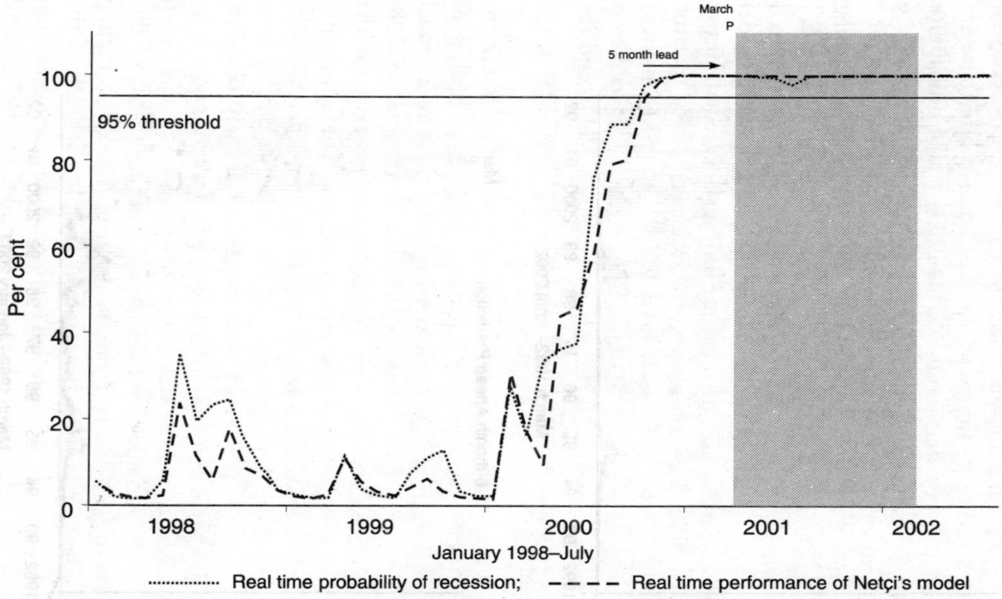

Figure 6.3: Real-time Performance of Neftçi's Model

Note: The NBER Business Cycle Dating Committee determined the latest recession began in March. As of November 2002, the NBER had not called the trough date. For illustrative purposes, the length of the recession is arbitrarily set to the average 1945–91 recession duration (11 month).

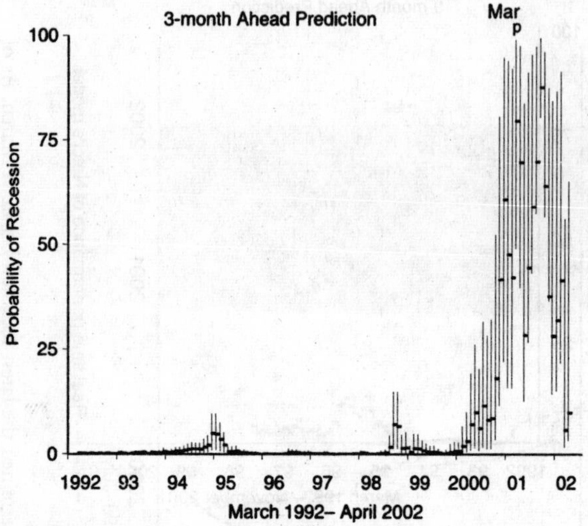
3-month Ahead Prediction
Mar
p
Probability of Recession
100
75
50
25
0
1992
93
94
95
96
97
98
99
2000
01
02
March 1992– April 2002

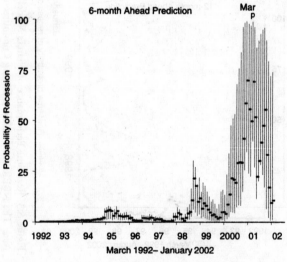

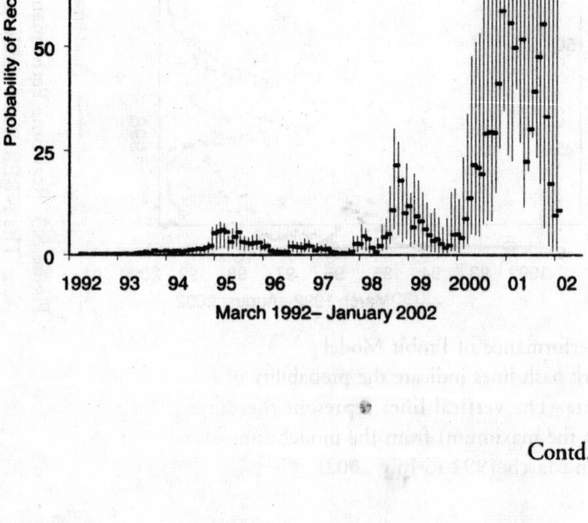
6-month Ahead Prediction
Mar
p
Probability of Recession
100
75
50
25
0
1992
93
94
95
96
97
98
99
2000
01
02
March 1992– January 2002

Contd. Fig. 6.4

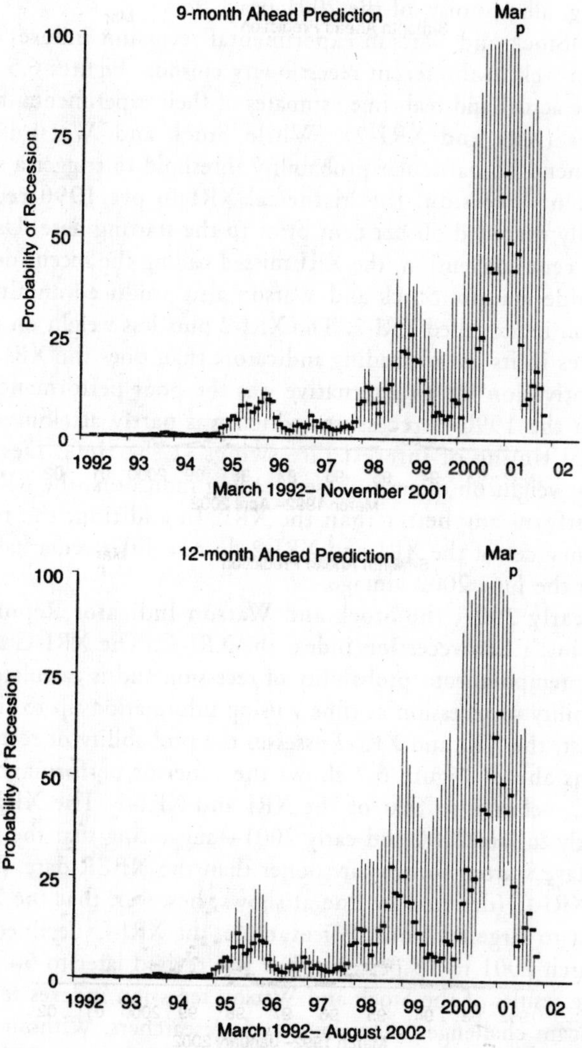

Figure 6.4: Performance of Probit Model
Note: The dark hash lines indicate the probability of recession using the July 2002 vintage of data. The vertical lines represent the range of probability estimates (minimum to the maximum) from the model using all relevant real-time vintages (vintages from March 1992 to July 2002).

with an earlier vintage of data. Overall, the Probit model appears to be sensitive to real-time data but it nonetheless sent advanced warning, albeit noisy, of the 2001 peak.

The Stock and Watson experimental recession indexes did not perform well in the recent recessionary episode. Figures 6.5 and 6.6 plot the actual and real-time estimates of their experimental recession indexes (XRI and XRI-2). While Stock and Watson (1993) recommend no particular probability threshold to trigger a signal of imminent recession, the historical XRI in pre-1990 recessions generally exceeded 50 per cent prior to the starting date. Using this 50 per cent convention, the XRI missed calling the recent downturn by a wide margin. Stock and Watson also produced an alternative recession index called XRI-2. The XRI-2 puts less weight on financial variables in its list of leading indicators than does the XRI. Part of the motivation for an alternative was the poor performance of the XRI in the 1990–1 recession, which was partly attributed to the atypical timing of interest rate swings at the time. Despite the heavier weight on quantity-based leading indicators, the XRI-2 does not perform any better than the XRI. In addition, the real-time performances of the XRI and XRI-2 do not differ remarkably from that of the June 2002 vintage.

In early 2001, the Stock and Watson Indicator Report began including a new recession index, the XRI-C. The XRI-C measures the contemporaneous probability of recession and is calculated as the probability of recession at time *t* using information up to time *t*. In contrast, the XRI and XRI-2 assesses the probability of recession six months ahead. Figure 6.7 shows the superior performance of the XRI-C, relative to that of the XRI and XRI-2. The XRI-C rises abruptly in late 2000 and early 2001—suggesting that the recession may have started somewhat sooner than the NBER date. The real-time XRI-C (denoted by line a) shows, however, that the XRI-C is subject to large revisions. For example, the XRI-C declined sharply in March 2001 to 13 per cent, but was revised later to 56 per cent.

The results of the Stock and Watson recession indexes represent a significant challenge for business cycle researchers. Without a doubt, the Stock and Watson experimental recession indexes are built on one of the strongest scientific foundations in this literature. To be sure, missing a turning point (or two) by itself does not necessarily reveal a fatal flaw in a recession prediction model. Recessions are complex

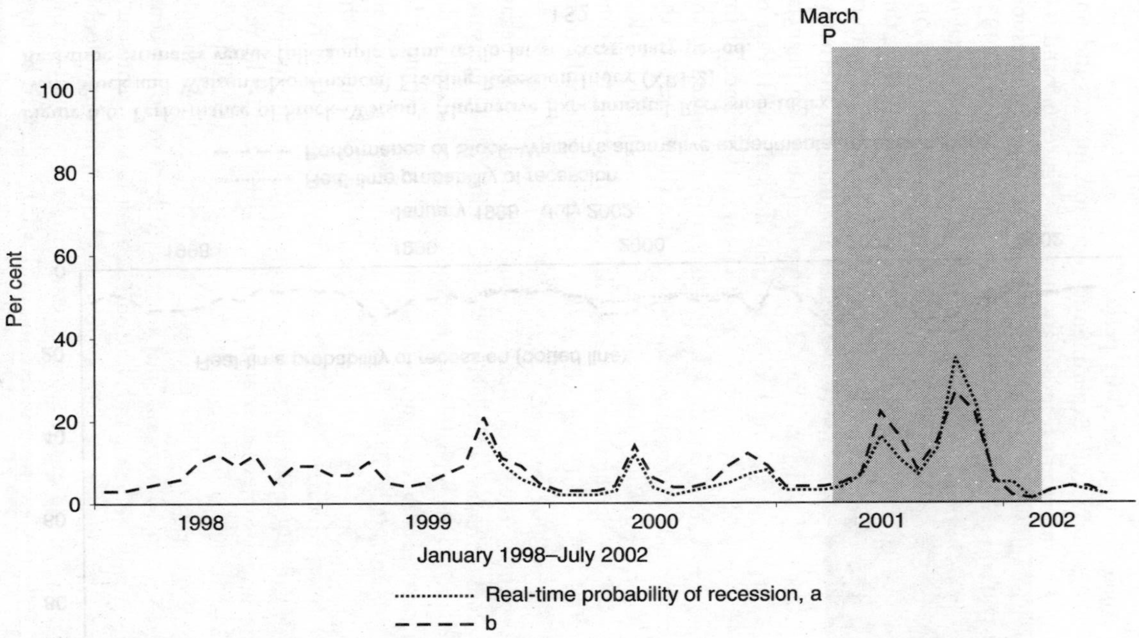

Figure 6.5: Performance of Stock–Watson's Experimental Recession Index.
Stock and Watson's Leading Recession Index (XRI)
Real-time estimates versus full-sample estimates in latest recessionary period.

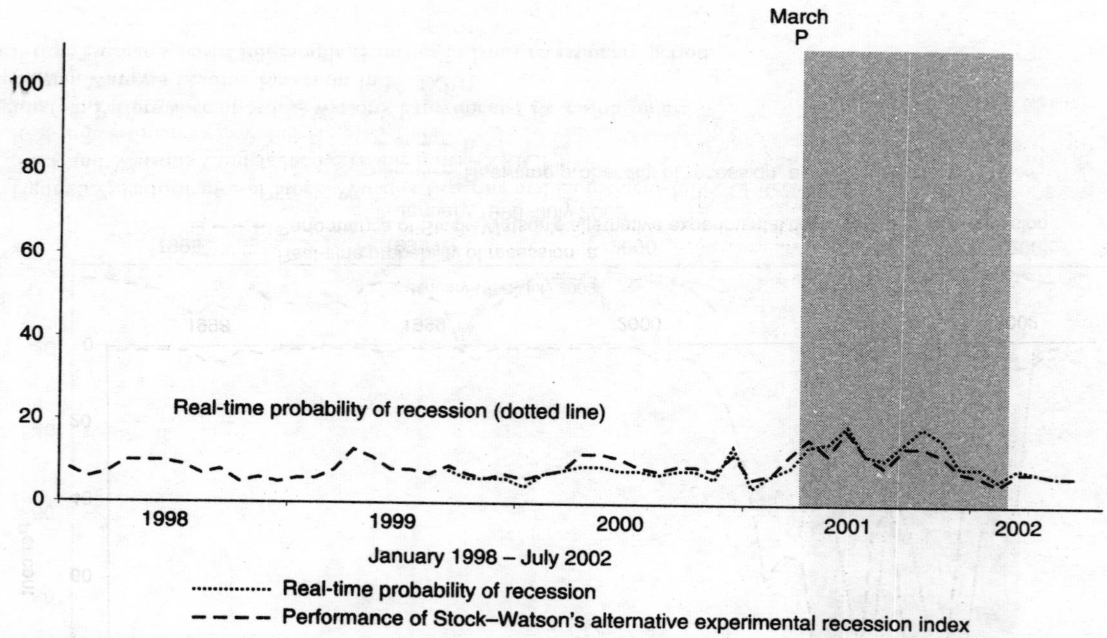

Figure 6.6: Performance of Stock–Watson's Alternative Experimental Recession Index.
Note: Stock and Watson's Nonfinancial Leading Recession Index (XRI-2)
Real-time estimates versus full-sample estimates in latest recessionary period.

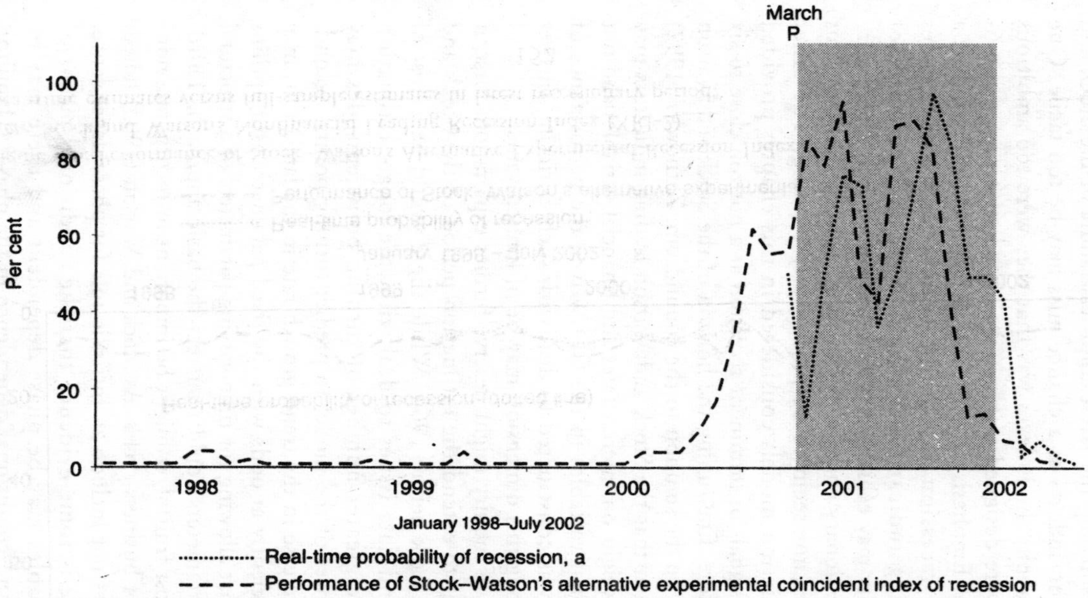

Figure 6.7: Performance of Stock–Watson's Experimental Coincident Index of Recession.
Stock and Watson's Coincident Recession Index (XRIC)
Real-time estimates versus full sample estimates in latest recessionary period.
Note: The real-time Coincident Recession Index (XRI-C) was first published in the February 2001 Stock-Watson Indicator Report.

economic phenomena that are sufficiently different from episode to episode to humble even the best built recession prediction models.

However, dismissing the latest empirical failure of the Stock and Watson recession indexes as a chance miss may be too facile. One early concern about the indexes was that they were too ambitious because they were designed to focus their predictive power at a 6-month horizon. Emphasis on a fixed lead might be too stringent a constraint for recession prediction models because lead times between leading indicator series and coincident measures of economic activity may exhibit substantial variability from recessionary episode to recessionary episode. In the latest episode, however, this constraint does not seem to be particularly binding. The other recession prediction models considered in this chapter provided relatively clear signals of imminent recession at a horizon close to six months. Therefore, fine-tuning the horizon of the Stock and Watson model may not be the solution to the conundrum. Zarnowitz (1992) has also suggested that the Stock and Watson leading indicators may put too much weight on interest rates and financial variables and not on the traditional variables in the CLI. Given the performance of XRI-2, which was constructed to deal with such criticism, further data-mining along this dimension may be of limited value.

Several lines of inquiry might deserve further exploration. First, it might be useful to extend the estimation period of the Stock and Watson model back before 1960. While there would be a host of econometric and data issues to deal with, the longer estimation period and the greater number of turning point episodes may increase the power of the model to predict turning points. Second, the apparent increase in the trend growth rate in the late 1990s may have been sufficiently at odds with the fixed parameter assumptions of this model that allowing for time-varying parameters or a structural break in the parameters could resurrect the basic approach. Third, and possibly most fruitful, it might be important to incorporate non-linear features of business cycles. As Stock and Watson (1993) noted, their model does not include an intrinsic role for phase dependence. However, there is some evidence that the conditional means of economic variables may be phase dependent and there may be unconditional and conditional dependence in the phases (Hamilton 1989; Filardo and Gordon 1998). If a data generating process underlying business cycle fluctuations is highly non-linear, then Stock and Watson's linear model with pattern recognition may be missing important features that could help increase the predictive power for turning points. Whatever the solution, further investigation into the 2001 recession may shed more light on the appropriate modern econometric approach to modelling business cycles fluctuations.

Conclusion

The various recession prediction models had mixed success in predicting the start of the 2001 recession. The non-parametric CLI rules of thumb provided a four to eight month early warning of the peak. The advance warning from the Neftçi model was also consistent with this range. It is not always true that these two models send similar lead times, but in this recent recessionary episode the fluctuations in the CLI data were strong enough to affect both models in a similar way. Moreover, the results from these two models were relatively robust to the use of real-time data. Even though the Probit model does not provide a perfectly comparable lead-time calculation, it too generated probabilities of recession that rose significantly prior to March 2001, but the sensitivity of the results to the use of real-time data might raise some concerns about the model's reliability and deserves further research. The Stock and Watson experimental recession probability indexes performed less well.

In light of recent history, the superior performance of the CLI-based models may help to resurrect their perceived usefulness. At the very least, those who track the economy—and attempt to predict turning points—may renew their interest in the value of the CLI data and the traditional analysis of business cycle fluctuations that has sometimes been belittled as 'measurement without theory'. For business cycle researchers, the results stand as a challenge to those who have had reservations, if not doubts, about the marginal predictive content of the CLI. While predictions about the future are always subject to considerable risk, it seems reasonable to expect with some confidence, that the impressive contributions of Geoffrey Moore to the theory and construction of the CLI and to our understanding of business cycles will help lead to a better synthesis of traditional business cycle analysis and modern econometric practice of recession prediction.

Endnotes

[1]Moore (1950) chronicles the early efforts of the NBER to sift through hundreds of economic series available at the time to find the important statistical indicators of business cycle expansions and recessions. Burns and Mitchell used roughly 500 series and identified 71 as useful. Moore winnowed the list further and found eight series that provided good leading properties. They included business failures, stock prices, new orders for durable goods, residential building contracts, commercial and industrial building contracts, average hours worked per week, new incorporations, and wholesale prices.

[2]Other rules might include more elaborate sequences of the CLI (Moore, and Zarnowitz 1982) to help filter out the false signals. In addition, Klein and Moore (1985) have pointed out that the CLI also provides information about growth cycle rather than business cycle turning points, and hence the fluctuations in the series can send false signals about imminent business cycle recessions.

[3]The probability distribution functions of the CLI data, F^e and F^r, are modelled as being normally distributed around mean growth rates of the 3-month moving average of the CLI during expansionary and recessionary periods. The 3-month moving average of the CLI smooths the wiggles, or noise, in the CLI data. Following Diebold and Rudebusch (1989), the transition probability from expansion to recession, π^r, is assumed to be independent of the time elapsed in the phase and is set to 0.02 which is consistent with results from Hamilton (1989). Alternatively, the transition probabilities could be modeled as being time-varying as in Filardo (1994).

[4] In practice, the recursion was reinitialized 18 months after the trough and a year after a false signal. The exception to this rule occurred during the 1980 recession because it was followed so closely in time by the 1981–2 recession. In this case, the recursion was reinitialized 3 months after the July 1980 trough.

[5]The 50 per cent threshold is different from the threshold level in the Neftçi model because of the different type of model inference about the business cycle. In particular, the Probit model assesses the probability of being in a recession *k* periods ahead rather than assessing the probability that sufficient information has become available to infer that the CLI distribution had switched and that the switch is accurately signalling an imminent regime switch in economic activity. In the Probit model, the state of the economy *k* periods ahead is assumed to be in only one of two states: either recession or expansion. Hence, for example, the inferred probability of recession less than 50 per cent indicates that the inferred probability of expansion is greater than the probability of recession. With a symmetric loss function, the best

assessment of the state of the economy *k* periods ahead is expansion. It should be noted, however, that the 50 per cent threshold may be considered somewhat arbitrary because in an optimal decision-making setting, the optimal threshold would depend on the nature of the loss function. If the loss function is not symmetric, the optimal threshold would generally not be 50 per cent. Other loss functions might justify a neutral range where it might be optimal not to call a turning point.

[6]The components of their leading index are building permits, real manufacturers unfilled orders (smoothed), the trade-weighted index of the nominal exchange rate, part-time work because of slack, the 10-year treasury bond yield, and the yield spread between the 10-year bond and the 1-year Treasury bill.

[7]Technically, the parameters are estimated by minimizing the mean of the squared errors over the sample period. It is well-known that a good in-sample fit may not guarantee a good out-of-sample fit, that is, a good predictor of turning points. Conversely, a good model of turning points may not do well at forecasting economic activity during 'normal' economic times—those periods not subject to turning points in the business cycle. See also Kling (1987) and Wecker (1979).

[8]In addition, the Federal Reserve's aggressive easing actions in early 2001, especially the one at the unscheduled January meeting, suggested a certain urgency to act at the time. These actions also support the view that there was evidence of a significant downdraft in economic activity prior to the NBER-designated turning point date.

[9]The concern about using real-time data is well established in the literature on leading indicators. Moore (1950, 1961) and Moore and Shiskin (1967) performed some of the original out-of-sample studies of the CLI. Moore and Zarnowitz (1982) compare the performance of the CLI in real-time and propose robust criteria (that is the 'band approach') to deal with data uncertainty.

[10]In August 2001, the US Department of Commerce's Census Bureau and Bureau of Economic Analysis converted its industrial classification scheme from a SIC classification system to the NAICS classification system. This change significantly affected some component series of the CLI (see Conference Board).

[11]It is interesting to note that the last signal of recession at the 3-month horizon occurred in October 2001, indicating that the last month of recession was likely to be January 2002.

[12] In general, the three financial variables in the model are statistically significant. The CLI tends to be statistically significant at the shorter horizons.

References

Auerbach, Alan (1982), 'The Index of Leading Economic Indicators: Measurement Without Theory, Thirty-Five Years Later'. *Review of Economics and Statistics*, November, Vol. 64, pp. 589–95.

Banerji, Anirvan, and Philip A. Klein (2000), 'Father of Leading Indicators: The Legacy of Geoffrey H. Moore', *International Journal of Forecasting*, April–June, Vol. 16, pp. 227–82

Braun, Philip and Victor Zarnowitz (1989), 'Comment on Stock and Watson', *NBER Macroeconomics Annual*, Cambridge: The MIT Press.

The Conference Board, Various Issues, *Business Cycle Indicators*.

Dueker, Michael J. (2002), 'Regime-Dependent Recession Forecasts and the 2001 Recession', *Federal Reserve Bank of St. Louis Review*, November/ December.

Diebold, Francis X., and Glenn D. Rudebusch (1992), 'Turning Point Prediction with the Composite Leading Index: An Ex Ante Analysis', in Kajal Lahiri and Geoffrey H. Moore, (Eds), *Leading Economic Indicators*, Cambridge: Cambridge University Press.

—— (1991), 'Forecasting Output with the Composite Index of Leading Indicators: A Real-Time Analysis', *Journal of American Statistical Association*, September.

—— (1989), 'Scoring the Leading Indicators', *Journal of Business*, July.

Emery, Kenneth M., and Evan F. Koenig (1993), 'Why the Composite Index of Leading Indicators Doesn't Lead', Federal Reserve Bank of Dallas, Research Paper No. 9318, May.

Estrella, Arturo, and Frederic S. Mishkin (1998), 'Predicting US Recessions: Financial Variables as Leading Indicators', *Review of Economics and Statistics*, February.

Filardo, Andrew J. (1999), 'How Reliable Are Recession Prediction Models?', Federal Reserve Bank of Kansas City, *Economic Review*, second quarter.

—— (1994), 'Business Cycles and Their Transitions', *Journal of Business and Economic Statistics*, July.

—— and Stephen F. Gordon (1998), 'Business Cycle Durations', *Journal of Econometrics*, July.

—— (1999), 'Business Cycle Turning Point: Two Empirical Business Cycle Model Approaches', in Philip Rothman, (Ed), *Nonlinear Time Series Analysis of Economic and Financial Data*, Boston: Kluwer Academic Publishers.

Fredman, Giela T. and Michael Niemira (1991), 'An Evaluation of the Composite Index of Leading Indicators for Signaling Turning Points in Business and Growth Cycles, *Business Economics*, October, Vol. 26, No. 4, pp. 49–55.

Hamilton, James D. (1989), 'A New Approach to the Economic Analysis of Nonstationary Time Series and the Business Cycle', *Econometrica*, March, Vol. 57, No. 2, pp. 357–84.

—— and Gabriel Perez-Quiros (1996), 'What Do the Leading Indicators Lead?' *Journal of Business*, January, Vol. 69, No. 1, pp. 27–49.

Hyman (1973), *Brookings Paper on Economic Activity*, Vol. 2, pp. 339–75.

Klein, P.A., and G. H. Moore (1985), 'Monetring Growth Cycles in Market-oriented countries: Developing and using International Economic indicators, for NBER, Combridge, MA: Ballinger.

Klein, Philip A. and Michael P. Niemira (1994), *Forecasting Financial and Economic Cycles*, New York: John Wiley and Sons, Inc.

Kling, John L. (1987), 'Predicting the Turning Points of Business and Economic Time Series', *Journal of Business*, Apri, Vol. 60, No. 2, pp. 201–38.

Lamy, Robert (1997), 'Forecasting US Recessions: Some Further Results from Probit Models', *Finance Canada*, working paper, May.

McGuckin, Robert H., Ataman Ozyildirim, and Victor Zarnowitz (2001), 'The Composite Index of Leading Economic Indicators: How to Make It More Timely', NBER working paper 8430, August, Combridge, MA.

Moore, Geoffrey H. (1983), *Business Cycles, Inflation, and Forecasting*, Cambridge: Ballinger Publishing Company.

—— (1979), 'The Forty-second Anniversary of the Leading Indicators', in W. Fellner, (Ed), *Contemporary Economic Problems, 1979*, Washington, DC: American Enterprise Institute.

—— (1978), 'Why the Leading Indicators Lead?' *Across the Board*, May.

—— (1963), 'What is a Recession', *The American Statistician*, October.

—— (1961), 'Business Cycle Indicators', for NBER Princeton, NJ: Princeton University Press.

—— (1950), 'Statistical Indicators of Cyclical Revivals and Recessions', NBER Occasional paper 31, New York.

Moore, Geoffrey H., and Julius Shiskin (1967), 'Indicators of Business Cycle Expansions and Contractions', NBER Occasional paper 103, New York.

Moore, Geoffrey H., Julues Sheskin, and Victor Zarnowitz (1992), 'Forecasting Recessions Under the Gramm-Hollings Law', in Kajal Lahiri and Geoffrey H. Moore, (Eds), *Leading Economic Indicators*, Cambridge: Cambridge University Press.

—— (1986), 'Major Changes in Cyclical Behavior', in Robert Gordon, (Ed), *The American Business Cycle: Continuity and Change*, Chicago: The University of Chicago Press.

—— (1982), 'Sequential Signals of Recession and Recovery', *Journal of Business*, January, Vol. 55, No. 1, pp. 57–85.

Neftçi, Salih (1982), 'Optimal Prediction of Cyclical Downturns', *Journal of Economic Dynamics and Control*, August.

Sims, Christopher A. (1989), 'Comment on Stock and Watson', NBER *Macroeconomics Annual*, Cambridge: The MIT Press.

Stock, James H., and Mark W. Watson (1993), 'A Procedure for Predicting Recessions with Leading Indicators: Econometric Issues and Recent Experience', in James H. Stock and Mark W. Watson, (Eds), *Business Cycles, Indicators, and Forecasting*, Chicago: The University of Chicago Press.

—— (1991), 'Turning Point Prediction with the Composite Leading Index: An Ex Ante Analysis', in Kajal Lahiri and Geoffrey H. Moore, (Eds), *Leading Economic Indicators*, Cambridge: Cambridge University Press.

—— (1989), 'New Indexes of Coincident and Leading Economic Indicators', *NBER Macroeconomics Annual*, Cambridge: The MIT Press.

—— Various Issues. Stock and Watson Indicator Report.

Wecker, William E. (1979), 'Predicting the Turning Point of a Time Series', *Journal of Business*, January, Vol. 52, No. 1, pp. 35–50.

Zarnowitz, Victor (2000), The Old and the New in US Economic Expansion of the 1990s', NBER working paper 7721, May, Combridge, massachusetts.

—— (1999), 'Theory and History Behind Business Cycles: Are the 1990s the Onset of a Golden Age?' NBER working paper 7010, March, Combridge, Massachusetts.

—— (1998), 'Has the Business Cycle Been Abolished?', *Business Economics*, October, Vol. 33, No. 4, pp. 39–45.

—— (1992), Business *Cycles*: *Theory, History, Indicators, and Forecasting*, Chicago: University of Chicago Press.

Zarnotwitz, Victor and G.H. Moore (1982), *Journal of Business* January, Vol. 55, No. 1, pp. 57–85.

7

The Performance of the New US Composite Leading Economic Indicators and Predicting the 2001 Recession

Mehdi Mostaghimi

Introduction

In December 1996, the Conference Board—the developer of the composite leading economic indicators (CLI) in the United States—completed a major restructuring of the components of CLI and their weightings. In another move in January 2001, the Board introduced a new procedure for calculating CLI using the data more efficiently. The reason mentioned for these actions is to improve CLI's predictability of the business cycle in a more timely manner. One purpose of the current research is to investigate this claim. Another purpose is to check the ability of the new CLI in predicting the 2001 recession.

The US CLI is an index originally developed by the US Department of Commerce by combining several major leading economic indicators, with the objective of maximizing the predictability of a turning point in the business cycle from an expansion to a recession and *vice versa*. The development of the CLI was transferred to the Conference Board, a private non-profit economics research organization, at the beginning of the 1996. In December 1996, the Conference Board decided that a major restructuring of this index would improve its performance.

Despite frequent revisions of the weights assigned to its components, a restructuring of the components of the CLI is rare, and it happens whenever a structural change occurs in the economy causing one or more of the leading indicators to lose their predictability and other leading indicators to emerge with better performance. The Board concluded that this had happened when a restructuring decision was made in 1996. Table 7.1 shows the components of CLI, along with the changes from pre-1996 to post-1996. Examples of the weights assigned to the components for each design are also provided in Table 7.1 (BCI-December 1996, BCI-January 1997).

Table 7.1: Components of the composite leading indicators and their weights: pre- and post-1996

Leading Indicators	Weight 1996 (%)	Weight 2001 (%)
Average weekly hours, manufacturing	15.6	18.3
Average weekly initial claims for unemployment insurance	1.5	2.5
Manufacturers' new orders, consumer goods, and materials	3.3	5.0
Vendor performance	1.5	2.8
contracts and orders for plant and equipment	1.2	0.0
Building permits, new private housing units	1.2	1.9
change in manufacturers' unfilled orders, durable goods	15.8	0.0
change in sensitive materials prices	40.5	0.0
Index of stock prices, 500 common stocks	2.3	3.1
Money supply M2	15.8	30.1
Index of consumer expectations	1.3	1.8
+ Interest rate spread, 10-year treasury bonds less federal funds	0.0	32.2
+ Manufacturers' new orders for non-defence capital goods and materials	0.0	1.3
Total	100.0	100.0

Note: Arrow indicates that about 50 per cent weights are shifted from the real economy to the money economy

Sources: The Conference Board Business Cycle Indicators, February 1996; The Conference Board Business Cycle Indicators, January 2001: Standardization Factors.

In the 1996 restructuring, three components were removed from CLI and two new ones were added, resulting in a net total of ten components. The major reasons indicated for the removal of the series 'change in manufacturer's unfilled orders, durable goods' and 'change in sensitive material prices' are that they tended to give false signals in recent years prior to the change and that the performance CLI was improved without them. The replacement series 'interest rate spread, 10-year treasury bonds less federal funds', was selected because of its widespread use as a forecasting variable. The series 'contracts and orders for plant and equipment' was replaced by 'manufacturers' new orders for non-defence capital goods and materials'. A series consists of about 90 per cent information of the prior series. The added series is considered to be a more reliable leading indicator for its purpose.

There have also been some changes in the technical process used to assign weights to the components. The weights of the new process are called standardization factors. The objective of this process is to give each series a similar opportunity to contribute to a change in CLI and to equalize volatility across the composite indices. The latter objective, and the process leading to it, were dropped beginning in January 2001 due to their unimportance to the analysis (BCI-November 2000).

By comparing the two examples of weight distributions given in Table 7.1, we see that as a result of this restructuring, over 55 per cent of the total weight of the deleted series has been almost entirely distributed between the two series of interest rate spread and money supply. Thus, the leading monetary and finance indictors have about 67 per cent of the total weight in the post-1996 CLI, an increase of about 50 per cent from the pre-1996 CLI. This is a reflection that in recent years the US structure of the economy has been less manufacturing oriented and has been dominated by monetary policy. Since the interest rate spread and money supply are two monetary policy tools, this also means that the Federal Reserve directly controls over 63 per cent of the weights assigned in the new CLI.

In a move in January 2001 the Conference Board decided to make CLI more timely by using the latest information on its components. In this process, the most up-to-date data for some variables such as stock and bond prices and interest rate spread are used along with the best estimates of the other variables. This is in contrast to the existing process, which used old data on financial variables. The new process has made it possible to make CLI available about four weeks earlier, with practically no loss of reliability and accuracy (BCI-September 2000).

The Conference Board has used the post-1996 the CLI design to back-calculate CLI to 1959, the first year in which the information for all the component series became available. It is claimed that the new series' predictability of the US economy is improved.

In spite of containing a good amount of information about the near future state of the US economy, the CLI by itself cannot make a prediction. Its information must be inferred and a decision rule must be developed. The Conference Board has used an ad hoc method of combining a 2 per cent drop in annualized CLI and information from the CLI diffusion index to conclude that CLI predictability has improved in detecting a down turning point, going back to 1984.

This research uses a normative approach to evaluate the performance of the post-1996 CLI in predicting a down turning point and to compare it with the one for the pre-1996 CLI. Specifically, I will employ a Bayesian methodology developed in Mostaghimi (1997) to estimate the probability of a downturn from the post-1996 CLI. These probabilities are used to compare the performance of the post-1996 CLI with the ones for the pre-1996 version.

The next section briefly describes the methodology used for estimating the Bayesian probability of a turning point. The third section evaluates and compares the performance of the post-1996 CLI *versus* the pre-1996 CLI in predicting a downturn in the US economy using the Bayesian methodology. The fourth section extends the prediction of the post-1996 CLI to the out-of-sample period of 2000-01 with the purpose of checking its ability to predict the 2001 recession. The last section gives a summary and future research directions.

Bayesian Probability Forecast of a Downturn: Methodology

The Bayesian methodology used for estimating the probability of a down turning point using information theory is developed in Mostaghimi (1997). A similar analysis based on the classical statistical decision theory using information theory, is developed in Mostaghimi and Rezayat (1996).

In a Bayesian paradigm for estimating the posterior probability of a down turn, in addition to the prior probabilities, there is a need to assess two likelihood functions from CLI: one for an upturn and one for a downturn. Information theory is used to assess these two likelihood functions. The final result for assessing the likelihood of a downturn is given here. The likelihood function of an upturn is similar.

The likelihood function of a downturn is:

$$Pr_d\,(\theta_K, \theta_{(K-1)}, \ldots, \theta_1 \mid q_d)$$

$$\approx \kappa \exp\; -\left[\sum_{k=1}^{k} I_d^k + I_d^{K,(K-1),\ldots,1}\right], \qquad \ldots(7.1)$$

where θ_k is the percentage change in CLI observed at time k, $q_d = (q_{d0}, q_{d1}, \ldots, q_{dM})$ is the probability mass function of a percentage in CLI during a downturn, $I_d^{\,k}$ is a relative entropy measuring the amount of information in θk relative to q_d, and $I_d^{K,\,(K-1),\,\ldots,\,1}$ is a measure of the joint information in θ_k; for $k = 1, 2, \ldots, K$. Under a normality assumption, this joint information measure is a function of the θk autocorrelation.

This result relates the likelihood function of a downturn to the amount of information that the percentage changes in CLI provide. The nice part is the additive form of the information measure. For example, for this case, it tell us that the total information about a downturn in CLI is the sum of two parts:

1. Information related to the closeness of θ_k; for $k = 1, 2, \ldots, K$ to the downturn distribution q_d ($I_d^{\,k}$; k = 1, 2, …, K, $I_d^{\,k} = 0$ if the information of θ_k is the same as q_d, and $I_d^{\,k} > 0$ and is monotonically increasing with an increase in the deviation of the amount of θ_k information from q_d).

2. Information related to the autocorrelation of θ_k; for $k = 1, 2, \ldots, K$ ($I_d^{K,\,(K-1),\,\ldots,\,1}$); the higher the autocorrelation, the greater the value of this, function. For zero autocorrelation this function has a value of zero.) The likelihood of a downturn increases with a decrease in the values of one or both of $I_d^{\,k}$; $k = 1, 2, \ldots$, K, and $I_d^{K,\,(K-1),\,\ldots,\,1}$.

(For the steps used to estimate the Bayesian probability of a downturn, see appendix in Mostaghimi 2001a).

Performance Evaluation: Post-1996 CLI and PRE-1996 CLI

The question we will entertain is whether the post-1996 CLI has more predictability information about a downturn in the US economy than the pre-1996 CLI. Predictability is defined in terms of the ability to accurately detect or predict a recession and to avoid false alarms.

First, two sets of probability distributions of the expansion periods and of the recession periods are produced: one set for pre-1996 CLI the other set for post-1996 CLI. For the pre-1996 CLI distributions, we use those derived in Mostaghimi (1997) and Mostaghimi and Rezayat (1996) using CLI for the period 1948–1970. The same information is used in several other studies cited in these references. For the post-1996 CLI distributions, data for 1959–99 are used. These two sets of probability distributions, along with their summary statistics, are shown in Figure 7.1.

A quick comparison of the two sets clearly indicates that there is a greater contrast between the expansion and recession periods for the pre-1996 CLI than for the post-1996 CLI. This is supported by a comparison of their summary statistics; for example, the pre-1996 CLI has a wider gap between its mean percentage changes. The information divergence (Kullback 1959; Mostaghimi 2001b) between the recession and expansion distributions for the pre-1996 CLI is substantially greater than that for the post-1996 CLI. The information divergence measures dissimilarity between two probability distributions; its value increases with an increase in dissimilarity in the range of (0, + ∞). Thus, if the contrast between the expansion probability distribution and the recession probability distribution is used to measure the business cycle predictability of a design, the pre-1996 CLI has more information. However, the true performance of a design must be measured in its real time predictability of a downturn.

Suppose the actual probabilities of expansion and recession for the pre-1996 and post-1996 measures are the ones given in Figure 7.1. The Bayesian probability forecast of a downturn methodology for using *K* consecutive CLI values (BPFDK) is applied to both pre-1996 CLI and post-1996 CLI for $K = 1, 2, \ldots$. The best forecasts for both sets of data turned out to be using K=2 consecutive CLIs (BPFD2). Figures 7.2a and 7.2b show the time series graphs of BPFD2 for pre-1996 CLI and for post-1996 CLI, respectively. The NBER recession periods are also identified in these two figures. BPFD2 for both the sets is considered to be optimum because using a 95 per cent probability level, it has been able to perform the best

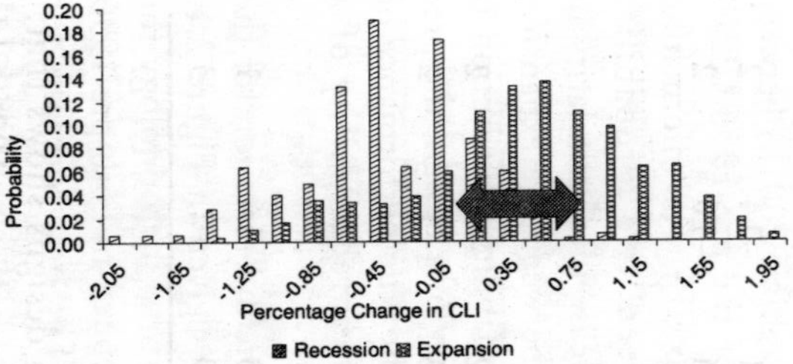

Distributions of Percentage Change in CLI — 1948–70
(CLI 1982 = 100)

	Recession	Expansion
Mean	–0.375	0.464
Standard deviation	0.537	0.681

Information Divergence = 2.28

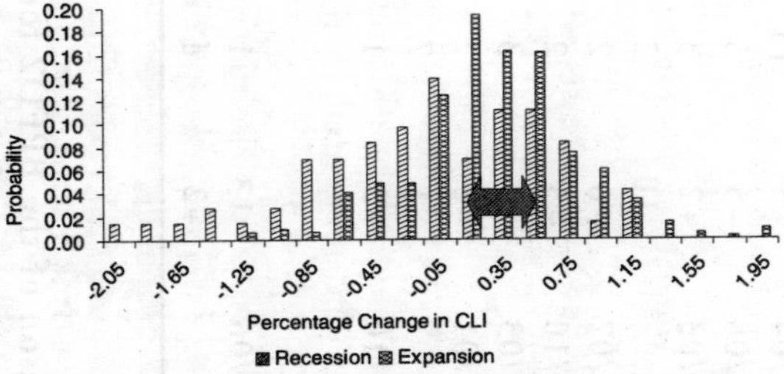

Distributions of Percentage Change in CLI—1959–99
(CLI 1996 = 100)

	Recession	Expansion
Mean	0.103	0.283
Standard deviation	0.714	0.520

Information Divergence = 0.72

Figure 7.1: Contrast between recession and expansion distributions of percentage changes in CLI in pre- and post-1996.

in detecting or predicting a recession in terms of accuracy and false alarms.

Table 7.2 shows the performance of BPFD2 ≥ 95 per cent for both pre-1996 CLI and post-1996 CLI in signalling a downturn for 1973–90, the period of time for which we have information for both data sets. For each NBER peak date, the official peak date, this table shows the month a downturn signal is made, the lead or lag number of months of each signal relative to the NBER peak date, and the number of consecutive times this signal is repeated (NCDS).

Table 7.2: Evaluation of BPFD2 95% downturn signals, pre- and post-1996 CLI, 1973–90

NBER	Pre-1996 CLI			Post-1996 CLI		
Peaks	Signal Dates	Lead (–) Lag (+)	NCD	Signal Dates	Lead (–) Lag (+)	NCD
73/11	73/09	−1	2	73/12	+ 1	2
	73/12	+1	1	74/04	+ 5	10
	74/04	+5	11			
80/01	79/08	−5	5	78/11	−14	2
	80/03	+2	3	79/04	−10	2
79/07		−10	2			
	79/07	−6	2			
	79/10	−3	2			
	80/03	+2	3			
81/07	81/01	−6	2	80/12	−7	2
81/06		−1	7	81/06	−1	2
	81/10	+3	1			
84/07	–	2				
87/11	–	2				
90/07	89/06	−13	1	89/03	−16	1
90/08		+2	4	90/09	+2	3

Source: Author.

A comparison of the BPFD2 for the two designs shows that, assuming a minimum probability of 95 per cent, the pre-1996 CLI has been perfect in signalling a recession with NCDS ≥ 3 and no false alarm. At NCDS ≥ 2, pre-1996 CLI had two false alarms, in 1984 and 1987. The post-1996 CLI has also been perfect in signalling a recession with no false alarm, but with NCDS ≥ 1. In other

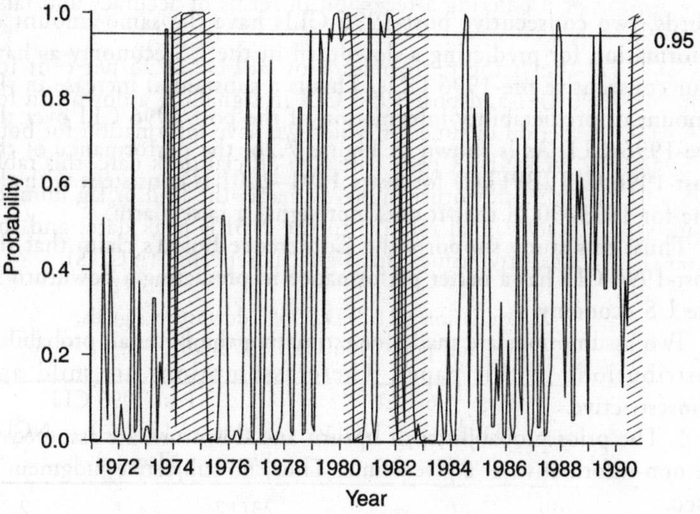

Figure 7.2a: BPFD2: Bayesian Probability Forecast of a Downturn Using Two Consecutive CLI.
Note: CLI 1982=100

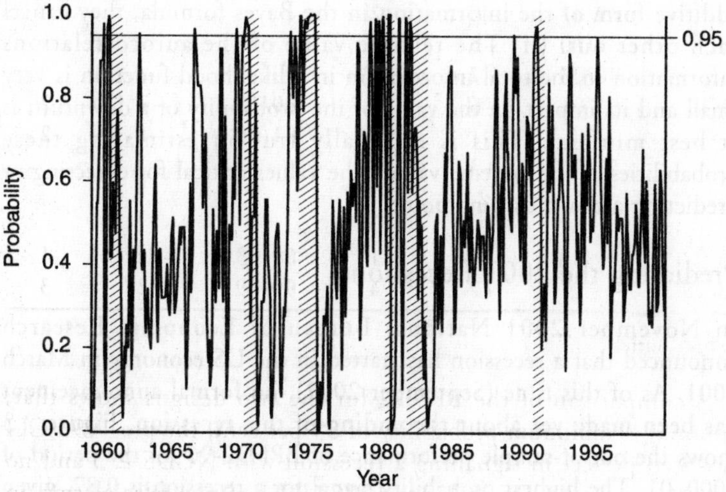

Figure 7.2b: BPFD2–1996: Bayesian Probability Forecast of a Downturn Using Two Consecutive CLI.
Note: CLI 1996 = 100

words, two consecutive post-1996 CLIs have the same amount of information for predicting a downturn in the US economy as have four consecutive pre-1996 CLIs. This is a substantial increase in the amount of predictability information of the post-1996 CLI over the pre-1996 CLI. As is shown in Figure 7.2b, the performance of the post-1996 CLI (BPFD2) for years 1991–2001 is consistent with the one for 1973–90 in that it does not signal a false alarm.

Thus, this study supports the Conference Board's claim that the post-1996 CLI has a better performance in predicting a downturn in the US economy.

Two assumptions are made for estimating the Bayesian probability distributions in this paper. These assumptions are mild and nonrestrictive.

1. The prior probabilities of upturn and downturn are assumed to be non-informative at a given time. Thus, no subjective judgment is used.

2. Zero autocorrelation is assumed for estimating the expansion and recession likelihood functions. This is because of the following findings in Mostaghimi (1997) and Mostaghimi (2001a): (i) For the pre-1996 CLI, the information content of the autocorrelations for the expansion and recession periods are relatively close and, given the additive form of the information in the Bayes formula, they cancel each other out. (ii) The relative value of the autocorrelations information to the total information in a likelihood function is very small and its impact on the value of the probability of a downturn is at best minimal. This is especially true in estimating these probabilities at the extreme values, the values critical for detecting or predicting a down turning point.

Predicting the 2001 Recession

In November 2001 National Bureau of Economic Research announced that a recession has started in the US economy in March 2001. As of this time (September 2002), no formal announcement has been made yet about the ending of this recession. Figure 7.3 shows the out-of-sample performance of BPFD2-96 for the period of 2000–01. The highest probability signal for a recession is 0.87, given in December 2000. This value is short of the threshold probability value of 0.95 historically observed to accurately signal a recession.

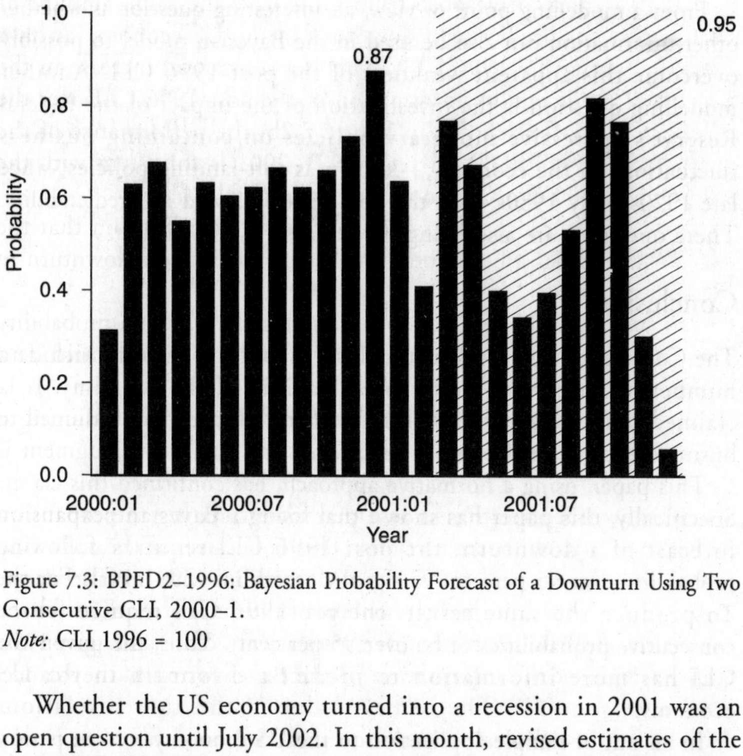

Figure 7.3: BPFD2–1996: Bayesian Probability Forecast of a Downturn Using Two Consecutive CLI, 2000–1.
Note: CLI 1996 = 100

Whether the US economy turned into a recession in 2001 was an open question until July 2002. In this month, revised estimates of the real GDP for 2001 showed negative growth rates for the first three quarters. This is a clear indication of a recession. The real GDP growth rates for the first two quarters of 2001 were positive prior to the July 2002 revisions. As a result, a large number of economists had believed that it was a slowdown than in a recession.

Missing this recession has prompted many questions about the post-1996 CLI's predictive quality information. It that seems problems for the CLI started from January 2001, when the Federal Reserve suddenly turned to an aggressive expansionary monetary policy. When the economy was moving into a deeper recession, as BPFD2-96 probabilities for 2001 (figure 7.3) show, CLI information was painting a rosy picture for the near future. With about 64 per cent of the total new CLI weight assigned the monetary policy indicators, is the predictive quality information of CLI compromised by the Federal Reserve's aggressive policies? This question is currently being studied by the author.

From a modelling point of view, an interesting question is whether other information can also be used in the Bayesian model to possibly overcome this apparent weakness of the post-1996 CLI? Another modelling question is the investigation of the impact of the Federal Reserve's aggressive monetary policies on containing business fluctuations in the economy,—known as soft-landing policies, since late 1970s–early 1980s,—on the post-1996 CLI and its predictability. These questions are also being investigated by the author.

Conclusion

The Conference Board restructured the US CLI in 1996 to include a number of series with better predictability of the economy. It is claimed that the post-1996 CLI performs better in predicting a business cycle than the one it replaced.

This paper, using a normative approach, has confirmed this claim. Specifically, this paper has shown that using a Bayesian probability forecast of a downturn, the post-1996 CLI requires only one probability over 95 per cent to signal a recession, with no false alarm. To produce the same result, the pre-1996 CLI requires three consecutive probabilities to be over 95 per cent . Thus, the post-1996 CLI has more information to predict a downturn in the US economy.

In an out-of-sample application to the US economy for the period 2000–01, the post-1996 CLI, has, however, failed to predict accurately the 2001 recession. There are modelling questions as also questions about the impact of monetary policies on the post-1996 CLI quality predictive information that are currently being investigated.

References

BCI Nov. 2000, 'Removing the Standardization Process from the Leading and Lagging Indexes', *Business Cycle Indicators*, Vol. 5, No. 11, November.

BCI Sept. 2000, 'How to Make the Composite Index of Leading Economic Indicators More Timely', *Business Cycle Indicators*, Vol. 5, No. 9, September.

BCI Jan. 1997, 'Cyclical Indicator Approach', *Business Cycle Indicators*, Vol. 2, No. 1, January.

BCI Dec. 1996, 'Cyclical Indicator Approach', *Business Cycle Indicators*, Vol. 1, No. 11, December.

Kullback, S. (1959), *Information Theory and Statistics*, New York: Wiley, reprsented in 1968 by Dover Publications Inc.

Mostaghimi, M. (2001a), 'Are the New US Composite Leading Economic Indicators More Informative?' *Indian Economic Review*: *Special Issue on Analysis of Business Cycles*, Vol. XXXVI, No. 1, pp. 205–13 January–June.

—— (2001b), 'Information Collection Strategic Design in Experts-assisted Decision Making Paradigm', to appear in *Group Decision and Negotiation*.

—— (1997), 'An Information-Theoretic Methodology for Estimating Bayesian Probability of a Turning Point', Working Paper, Department of Economics and Finance, Southern Connecticut State University, New Haven.

Mostaghimi, M. and F. Rezayat (1996), 'Probability Forecast of Downturn in US Economy Using Classical Statistical Decision Theory', *Empirical Economics*, Vol. 21, pp. 255–79.

8

The Forecasting Effectiveness of US Leading Economic Indicators

Further Evidence and Initial Results for G7 Countries

John B. Guerard, Jr.

Introduction

In this study, the author examines the forecasting effectiveness of the composite index of leading economic indicators (LEI). The leading indicators can be as an input to a transfer function model of real gross domestic product (GDP). The transfer function model forecasts are compared to several naïve models test which model produces the most accurate forecast of real GDP. No-change forecasts of real GDP

The author acknowledges the assistance of the Conference Board for providing its database of leading economic indicators and Related Composite Indexes and the Foundation of Business and Economic Research. The author is grateful for the financial support of the Centre for Innovation Management Studies (CIMS) at North Carolina State University, for funds to acquire the various leading economic indicators. The author was an adjunct faculty member at Lehigh University, when the original analysis was developed. The author appreciates the comments and suggestions of Victor Zarnowitz of the Conference Board, Richard Ashley, and Pami Dua. The author is solely responsible for the contents of this paper and any remaining errors.

and random walk with drift models may be useful as a forecasting benchmark (Mincer and Zarnowitz 1969; and Granger and Newbold 1977). Economists have constructed leading economic indicator series to serve as a business barometer of the changing US economy since the time of Wesley C. Mitchell (1913). The purpose of this study is to examine the time series forecasts of composite economic indexes produced by the Conference Board (TCB) and the Foundation for International Business and Economic Research (FIBER), and to test the hypothesis that leading indicators are useful as an input to a time series model to forecast real output in the US.

Economic indicators are descriptive and anticipatory time-series data used to analyse and forecast changing business conditions. Cyclical indicators are comprehensive series that are systemically related to the business cycle. Business cycles are recurrent sequences of expansions and contractions in aggregate economic activity. Coincident indicators have cyclical movements that approximately correspond with the overall business cycle expansions and contractions. Leading indicators reach their turning points before the corresponding business cycle turns. While lagging indicators reach their turning points after the corresponding turns in the business cycle.

An example of business cycles can be found in the analysis of Irving Fisher (1911), who discussed how changes in the money supply lead to rising prices and an initial fall in the rate of interest, and how this results in raising profits, thus creating a boom. The interest rate rises later, reducing profits, and ending the boom. A financial crisis ensues when businessmen, whose loan collateral is falling as the interest rates rise, run to cash and banks fail.

In the next section, the author presents an introduction to the models that are estimated and tested in our analysis of the forecasting effectiveness of the leading indicators. In the third section, the author presents the empirical evidence to support the time series models and why the models adequately describe the data. Out-of-sample forecasting results are shown in the fourth section 4 for the United States (US) and the G7 nations. Conclusions are reported in the last section.

An Introduction to Time Series Modelling

In the world of business, one often speaks of autoregressive, moving average, and random walk with drift (RWD) models, or processes. Let us briefly define these time series terms, in the tradition of Box and Jenkins (1970). One often speaks of the current value of the series, Z, as a deviation from the mean of the series:

$$\widetilde{Z}_t = Z_t - m \qquad \text{...(8.1)}$$

In an autoregressive (AR) model, the current value of the series is a linear aggregate function of previous (p terms) values of the series and a shock, *a*, the white noise term.

$$\widetilde{Z}_t = \phi_1 \widetilde{Z}_{t-1} + \phi_2 \widetilde{Z}_{t-2} + \ldots + f_p \widetilde{Z}_{t-p} + a_t \qquad \text{...(8.2)}$$

$$\phi(B) = 1 - \phi_1 B - \phi_2 B^2 - \ldots - \phi p B p \qquad \text{...(8.3)}$$

or

$$\phi(\mathrm{B}) \widetilde{Z}_t = a_t \qquad \text{...(8.4)}$$

In a moving average (MA) model, the current value of the series is a function of a finite number (*q* terms) of previous shocks, '*a*'.

$$\widetilde{Z}_t = a_t - \theta_1 a_{t-1} - \theta_2 a_{t-2} - \ldots - \theta_q a_t$$

$$\theta(B) = 1 - \theta_1 \mathrm{B} - \theta_2 \mathrm{B}_2 - \ldots - \theta_q B_q$$

or

$$\widetilde{Z}_t = \theta(b) a_t \qquad \text{...(8.5)}$$

It is well known that the majority of economic series follow a random walk with drift, and are represented with autoregressive integrated moving average (ARIMA) model with a first-order moving average operator applied to the first-difference of the data (Granger and Newbold (1977). The data is differenced to a produce series stationary, where a process has a (finite) mean and variance that do not change over time and the covariance between data points of two series depends upon the distance between the data points, not on the time itself. The ARIMA model is said to be of order (*p*, *d*, *q*) where p is the order of the autoregressive operator, d is the order of differencing of the data, and q is the moving average operator. A first-order autoregressive operator implies that the current value of the series is a function only of the previous value of the series and a white noise error term. The moving average model implies that the current value of the series is a function of the current (original) white noise value of the series and the previous value of the white noise term, implying a smoothing process. The RWD process, estimated with an ARIMA (0, 1, 1) model, is approximately equal to a first-order exponential smoothing model (Cogger 1974).

$$\widetilde{W}_t = V^d Z_t \qquad \text{...(8.6)}$$

$$\phi(\mathrm{B}) \widetilde{W}_t = \theta(B) a_t \qquad \text{...(8.7)}$$

The random walk with drift model has been supported by the work of Nelson and Plosser (1982), who found that the first-differenced models of 14 US macroeconomic series, including real gross national product (GNP), Nominal GNP, and common stock prices, are characterized by difference-stationarity (DS). The long-run models were characterized by as opposed to trend-stationarity (TS). That is, the first-difference of the series had a constant (finite) mean and variance. The assumption of a random walk with drift framework for univariate modelling does not imply that we assume that the ARIMA (0, 1, 1) framework is the only correct estimation technique; it is a statistically adequate representation of the data generating process. The author is aware of the Diebold and Rudebusch (1990, ch. 9) presentation that for the 14 Nelson and Plosser series a larger appropriate confidence interval exists for the TS model than for the DS model alone. Diebold and Rudebusch (1999) found that neither the TS nor the DS models dominated in forecasting accuracy.

In a transfer function model, one models the dynamic relationship between the deviations of input *X* and output *Y*. One is concerned with estimating the delay between the input and output. The set of weights is often referred to as the impulse response function.

$$Y_t = V_0 X_t + V_1 X_{t-1} + V_2 X_{t-2} \qquad \ldots(8.10)$$

$$= V(B) X_t \qquad \ldots(8.11)$$

We introduce the time series modelling process in this study as we will use The Conference Board's US composite leading economic indicator as an input to a transfer function model of US real GDP, both series being first-differenced and logarithmic-transformed. We will test the null hypothesis that there is no statistical association between changes in the logged LEIs and changes in logged real GDP in the US, UK, Germany (GR), Japan (JP), Italy (IT), and France (FR) during the period 1970–2002. A positive and statistically significant coefficient indicates that the leading indicator composite series is associated with rising real output, which leads to the rejection of the null hypothesis.

The Conference Board's components of the composite leading index for 2002 reflect the work and variables shown in the Zarnowitz (1992) list, which continued the work of Mitchell (1913, 1951), Burns and Mitchell (1946), and Moore (1961). The Conference Board index of leading indicators comprises:

1. average weekly hours (mfg.);
2. average weekly initial claims for unemployment insurance;
3. manufacturers' new orders for consumer goods and materials;
4. vendor performance;
5. manufacturers' new orders of non-defence capital goods;
6. building permits of new private housing units;
7. index of stock prices;
8. money supply;
9. interest rate spread; and
10. index of consumer expectations.

Leading Economic Indicators and Real GDP Analysis: The Statistical Evidence, 1970–2002

Zarnowitz (1992) examined the determinants of Real GDP, (1953–82), using VAR models. In this analysis, we test the statistical significance of the Conference Boards (LEI by adding the lags of the variable to an AR(1) model. In a recent study of univariate and time series model post-sample forecasting, Thomakos and Guerard (2001) compared RWD and transfer-function models with no-change forecasts using rolling one-period ahead post-sample periods. Guerard (2001) found that the AR (1) and random walk with drift processes are adequate representations of the time series process of real GDP, given the lags of the autocorrelation and partial autocorrelation functions. He reported the estimated cross-correlation functions between the LEI and real GDP of the G7 countries for the 1970–2000, and found that the resulting transfer function models were statistically significant in forecasting real GDP in the G7 nations.

In this study, the author reports the estimated autocorrelation and partial autocorrelation functions of US real GDP, 1978–March 2002, shown in Table 8.1. The estimated functions substantiate the estimation of the first-order AR model of the first-differenced, logarithmic-transformed US real GDP series, denoted AARIMA, shown in Table 8.2. The AARIMA model is a variation of the random walk with drift model. Guerard (2001) used the AARIMA estimation as a forecasting benchmark. The residuals of this model show few deviations from normality. Thus, it is statistically an adequately fitted model.

The author estimates the cross-correlation function of the LEI and real GDP for an initial 32 quarters estimation period, following

Table 8.1: Estimated Correlogram Function of Real US GDP 1978–March 2002

Lags	AC	PAC	Q-Stat	Prob.
1	0.282	0.282	10.420	0.001
2	0.204	0.135	15.928	0.000
3	0.077	–0.012	16.722	0.001
4	0.040	–0.004	16.940	0.002
5	–0.076	–0.103	17.720	0.003
6	–0.102	–0.072	19.137	0.004
7	–0.127	–0.064	21.367	0.003
8	–0.246	–0.189	29.748	0.000
9	–0.025	0.129	29.835	0.000
10	–0.029	0.022	29.955	0.001
11	0.002	–0.007	29.956	0.002
12	–0.203	–0.248	35.876	0.000
13	–0.067	–0.020	36.517	0.000
14	–0.169	–0.137	40.665	0.000
15	–0.186	–0.147	45.763	0.000
16	–0.056	0.048	46.227	0.000
17	–0.093	–0.045	47.534	0.000
18	–0.005	0.027	47.537	0.000
19	–0.026	–0.075	47.643	0.000
20	0.096	–0.041	49.050	0.000
21	0.041	–0.009	49.309	0.000
22	0.109	–0.001	51.158	0.000
23	0.017	–0.077	51.206	0.001
24	0.029	–0.020	51.338	0.001

Thomakos and Guerard (2001), and uses the period 1978–March 2002 for initial US, UK, German, Japanese, and French LEI post-sample evaluation. The changes in the logarithmic-transformed LEI are statistically significantly associated with changes in logarithmic-transformed real GDP in the respective countries during this 1978–2002 period, (shown in the respective GDP regressions in Table 8.3). (The lag structures of the models were discussed in Guerard (2001), and we refer the reader to the initial modelling and forecasting analysis). The statistical significance of the transfer functions in table 8.3 leads one to reject the null hypothesis of no statistical association changes in the LEI and changes in real GDP. The

Table 8.2: Autoregressive Time Series Model of Real US GDP

Variable	Coef	Std Error	t-Statistic	Prob
C	0.007	0.0011	7.210	0.0000
AR(1)	0.283	0.0857	3.300	0.0013
R-squared	0.079			
Adjusted R-squared	0.072			
S.E. of regression	0.0085	Akaike info criterion		−6.6730
Sum squared resid	0.0091	Schwarz criterion		−6.6282
Log likelihood	425.74	F-statistic		10.8631
Durbin-Watson stat	2.07	Prob(F-statistic)		0.0012

Note: Dependent Variable: DLUSGDP

Table 8.3: Post-Sample Regression Coefficients of Leading Economic Indicators, 1978–March 2002

Country	Const	LEI (−1)	LEI (−2)	LEI (−3)	LEI (−4)	AR (1)	Adj R-sq	F-Stat
US	0.005	0.337	0.060	0.141		0.053	0.2831	0.400
(t)	7.200	4.800	0.890	2.130		0.480		
UK	0.005			0.214		−0.166	0.088	5.600
	7.500			2.610		−2.300		
Germany	0.004	0.242		0.211		−0.250	0.102	4.610
	5.750	2.610		2.370		−2.300		
France	0.004		0.140	0.133	-0.064	0.038	0.058	2.470
	7.960		1.930	1.870	-0.910	0.360		
Japan	0.005	0.217				−0.437	0.174	11.030
	5.860	2.900				−4.660		
Canada	0.008		0.306	0.036	-0.263	0.150	0.240	3.290
	4.880		2.340	0.270	−2.100	0.640		
Italy	0.004		0.132	−0.089	−0.009	−0.050	0.059	1.460
	4.670		2.260	−1.480	−1.490	−0.240		

statistically significant lags in the cross-correlation functions show how the past values of the LEI series are associated with the current values of real GDP. That is, the LEI series lead their respective real GDP series and can be used as inputs to transfer function models of real GDP. The multiple regressions of the post-sample period are generally statistically significant at the 1 per cent level, as shown by the respective F-statistics of the regressions. The exception to this result is the French real GDP estimate, which is significant at approximately 5 per cent level. Thus, the estimation of the transfer function is statistically significant relative to the use of an AR (1) time series model. The author performed similar analysis with the FIBER index of short-term leading indicators, (LDs), with virtually identical results. (these multiple regression results are available upon request from the author). The results of this section are up-to-date and consistent with the results reported in Guerard (2001).

US and G7 Post-Sample Real GDP Forecasting Analysis

In this analysis, we estimate several time series models for the US leading indicators and real GDP, and corresponding models for the G7 nations. A simple autoregressive variation on the random walk model, an ARIMA (1, 1, 0), is estimated to serve as a naïve forecasting model. The ARIMA model is referred to as the AARIMA Model. The transfer function model uses the LEI series as the input to the real GDP (output) series. We evaluate the forecasting performances of the models with respect to their root mean square error (RMSE), defined as the square root of the sum of the individual observation forecast errors squared. The most accurate forecast will have the smallest forecast error squared and hence the smallest RMSE. The RMSE criteria are proportional to the average squared error criteria used in Granger and Newbold (1977). We can estimate models using date for 32 quarters and forecast one-step-ahead. We compare the forecasting accuracy of four models of US real GDP. The models tested are: (i) the transfer function model in which the Conference Board's composite index of LEIs is lagged three quarters, (denoted as TF); (ii) a no-change (NoCH) forecast; (iii) the simple AARIMA model; and (iv) a simple transfer function model in which The Conference Board's composite index of LEIs is lagged one period, (denoted TF1). One finds that the three-quarter lagged LEI transfer function is the most accurate out-of-sample forecasting model for US real GDP; although there is no statistically significant difference in the rolling one-period-ahead root mean square forecasting errors of the AARIMA, TF, and TF1 models. The one-period ahead quarterly RMSE of real GDP for the 1978– March 2002 are shown in Table 8.4.

Table 8.4: Post-Sample Accuracy of US Real GDP Models Using the Conference Board LEI in the Transfer Function Model

Model	RMSE
No-change	0.0117
AARIMA	0.0086
TF1	0.0080
TF	0.0079

Thus, the US leading indicators lead real GDP, as one should expect, and the transfer function model produces lower forecast errors than the univariate model, and a naive benchmark, the no-change model. The transfer function model that uses a one-quarter lag produces forecasts that are not statistically different from the three-quarter lags suggested by the estimated cross-correlation function.

The use of the FIBER short-term leading economic indicators, shown in Table 8.5, produces the result that the RMSE of the three-quarter lagged leading indicators is lower than that for the univariate model. The RMSE of the FIBER data are computed relative to the raw data, whereas the RMSE of the Conference Board data is computed relative to the first-differenced, logarithmic-transformed data. One is only concerned with the respective model RMSE rankings.

The model forecast errors are not statistically different (the t-value of the paired differences of the univariate and TF models is 0.91). An analysis of the rolling one-period ahead RMSE produces somewhat different results for post-sample modelling than the use of one long period of post-sample period. The multiple regression models indicate statistical significance in the US composite index of leading economic indicators for the 1978-March 2002 period. One does not find that the transfer function model forecast errors are (statistically) significantly lower than univariate ARIMA model (AARIMA) errors in a rolling one-period ahead analysis. We prefer to measure forecasting performance in the rolling period manner (as we often live in a one-period ahead forecasting regime).

The RMSE for the G7 nations cast doubt on the effectiveness of the leading economic indicators as statistically significant inputs in the transfer function models that forecast real GDP. Transfer function

Table 8.5: Post-sample Accuracy of Real GDP Models Using TCB LEIs and FIBER LDs in the Transfer Function Model

Nation	Model	Input Source	RMSE
US	NoCH		66.711
	AARIMA		47.398
	TFFIBER	45.289	
CA	NoCH		7270.49
	AARIMA		5476.58
	TFFIBER	5102.10	
GR	NoCH		0.0106
	AARIMA		0.0090
	TFFIBER	0.0106	
	TFTCB	0.0106	
FR	NoCH		0.0081
	AARIMA		0.0065
	TFFIBER	0.0075	
	TFTCB	0.0070	
JP	NoCH		0.0177
	AARIMA		0.0152
	TFFIBER		
	TFTCB	0.0163	
UK	NoCH		0.0106
	AARIMA		0.0090
	TFFIBER	0.0084	
	TFTCB	0.0089	
IT	NoCH		0.0098
	AARIMA		0.0085
	TFFIBER	0.0090	

model forecasts of real GDP, using the Conference Board (TB) and FIBER LDs as inputs, do not significantly reduce RMSE relative to the AARIMA model forecasts during the 1978–March 2002 (Table 8.5).

A final statistical test of LDs is undertaken for the period 1970–2002. The FIBER data used in this section. Does the US LD lead the G7 LDs? A 32-quarter period is used to estimate the cross-correlation functions. We report forecasting comparisons of four models for each country's composite index of LEIs: (i) a no-change model; (ii) the AARIMA model; (iii) a transfer function model for each country's LD assuming a one-quarter lag in the US leading index; and (iv) transfer function models with lags in the US leading index determined by examining the cross-correlation function estimates of the respective country and the US leading economic indicator series. The four forecasts are compared on a one-step-ahead forecasting RMSE. There is no statistically significant RMSE reduction when we use the US LEI in a transfer function model to forecast G7 leading economic indicators compared to an autoregressive model. This is consistent with earlier reported real GDP forecasting results.

Table 8.6: RMSE of FIBER Leading Economic Indicators (LDs)

Nation	Coef on USLD (–1) (t)	USLD lags	Model NoCH	AARIMA	TF1	TF
CA	0.056 (0.86)	1, 4	1.154	1.082	1.123	1.139
GR	0.129 (1.89)	1, 2	1.283	1.259	1.263	1.278
FR	0.209 (2.43)	1,2	1.772	1.767	1.849	1.884
IT	0.172 (2.27)	1,4	1.450	1.402	1.443	1.503
JP	0.200 (1.60)	3,4	2.368	2.343	2.347	2.459
UK	0.126 (2.64)	1	0.909	0.897	0.933	0.933

Despite the positive and statistically significant correlations between the US LD and the G7 LDs during the 1978–March 2002 post-sample period, the one-step ahead forecasting errors are not statistically different. The US composite index of LEIs does not significantly lead the G7 leading economic indicators. Recent work by Krolzig (2001) and Batchelor (2001) suggests traditional time series models are not sufficient for business cycle analysis, and that one should test the Hamilton models of regime switching should be tested.

Conclusion

In this study, we have examined the predictive information in the Conference Board's LEIs for the US, UK, Japan, and France and FIBER's LDs. We find that the Conference Board's LEI and FIBER's LDs are statistically significant in modelling the respective real GDP changes during 1970–2000. One rejects the null hypothesis of no association between changes in the LEIs and changes in real GDP in the US, and the G7 nations. If one uses a rolling 32 quarter estimation period and a one-period ahead forecasting RMSE calculation, the LEI forecasting errors are not significantly lower than those for the univariate ARIMA model forecasts. One might well conjecture that the transfer function estimates are quite variable during the rolling post-sample estimation period. One rejects the will hypothesis of no association between changes in the LEI and changes in real US GDP, and changes in the G7 LEIs and changes in real GDP in the G7 nations.

References

Ansley, C.F. (1979), 'An Algorithm for the Exact Likelihood of a Mixed Autoregressive Moving Average Process', *Biometrika*, Vol. 66, pp. 59–65.

Ashley, R. (1998), 'A New Technique for Postsample Model Selection and Validation', *Journal of Economic Dynamics and Control*, Vol. 22, pp. 647–65.

Ashley, R., C.W.J. Granger, and R. Schmalensee. (1980), 'Advertising and Aggregate Consumption: An Analysis of Causality', *Econometrica*, Vol. 48, No. 5, pp. 1149–67.

Batchelor, Roy (2001), 'Confidence Indexes and the Probability of Recession: A Markov Switching Model', *Indian Economic Review*, Vol. 36, pp. 107–24.

Box, G.E.P. and G.M. Jenkins. (1970), *Time Series Analysis: Forecasting and Control*, San Francisco: Holden-Day.

Burns, A. F. and W.C. Mitchell (1946), *Measuring Business Cycles*, New York: NBER.

Clemen, R.T. and J.B. Guerard. (1989), 'Econometric GNP Forecasts: Incremental Information Relative to Naive Extrapolation', *International Journal of Forecasting*, Vol. 5, pp. 417–26.

Cogger, K. (1974, 'The optimality of general order exponential smoothing', *Operations Research*, Vol. 22.

Diebold, F.X. and G.D. Rudebusch (1999), *Business Cycles: Durations, Dynamics and Forecasting*, Princeton: Princeton University Press.

Diebold, F.X. and R.S. Mariano (1995), 'Comparing Predictive Accuracy', *Journal of Business and Economic Statistics*, Vol. 13, No. 3, pp. 253–63.

Fisher, Irving (1911), *The Purchasing Power of Money*, New York: Macmillan.

Friedman, M. and A. Schwartz. (1963), 'Money and Business Cycles', *Review of Economics and Statistics*, Vol. 45, pp. 32–64.

Gordon, R.J. (1986), 'The American Business Cycle', Chicago: University of Chicago Press.

Granger, C.W.J. (1980), 'Testing for Causality: a personal viewpoint, *Journal of Economic Dynamics and Control*, Vol. 2, pp. 329–52.

Granger, C.W.J. and P. Newbold (1977), *Forecasting Economic Time Series*, New York: Academic Press.

Guerard, John B., Jr. (2001), 'A Note on the Forecasting Effectiveness of the US Leading Economic Indicators', *Indian Economic Review*, Vol. 36, pp. 251–68.

Hamilton, J.R. (1994), *Time Series Analysis*, Princeton: Princeton University Press.

Koopmans, T.C. (1947), 'Measure without Theory', *The Review of Economic Statistics*, reprinted in R. Gordon and L. Klein, *Readings in Business Cycles*, Homewood, Illinois: Richard A. Irwin, Inc., 1965.

Krolzig, Hans-Martin (2001), 'Business Cycle Measurement in the Presence of Structural Change: International Evidence', *International Journal of Forecasting*, Vol. 17, pp. 349–68.

Lahiri, K. and G.H. Moore (1991), *Leading Economic Indicators*, Cambridge: Cambridge University Press.

Ljung, G.M. and G.E.P. Box. (1978), 'On a measure of lack of fit in time series models', *Biometrika*, Vol. 65, pp. 297–303.

Maddala, G.S. and I.M. Kim. (1998), *Unit Roots, Cointegration and Structural Change*, Cambridge: Cambridge University Press.

Makridakis, S. and M. Hibon (2000), 'The M3-Competition: results, conclusions and implications', *International Journal of Forecasting*, Vol. 16, pp. 451–76.

McCracken, M. (2000), 'Robust out-of-sample inference', *Journal of Econometrics*, Vol. 99, pp. 195–223.

McLeod, A.I. and W.K. Li (1983), 'Diagnostic checking ARMA time series models using squared residual autocorrelations', *Journal of Time Series Analysis*, Vol. 4, pp. 269–73.

Mincer, J. and V. Zarnowitz (1969), 'The Evaluation of Economic Forecasts', J. Mincer (Ed.), *Economic Forecasts and Expectations*, New York: Columbia University Press.

Mitchell, W.C. (1951), *What Happens During Business Cycles: A Progress Report*, New York: NBER.

—— (1913), *Business Cycles*, New York: Burt Franklin (reprint).

Moore, G.H. (1961), *Business Cycle Indicators*, 2 volumes, Princeton: Princeton University Press.

Nelson, C.R. and C.I. Plosser (1982), 'Trends and Random Walks in Macroeconomic Time Series', *Journal of Monetary Economics*, Vol. 10, pp. 139–62.

Montgomery, A.L., V. Zarnowitz, R.S. Tsay, and G.C. Tiao (1998), 'Forecasting the US Unemployment Rate', *Journal of the American Statistical Association*, Vol. 93, pp. 478–93.

Tashman, L. (2000), 'Out-of-sample tests of forecasting accuracy: an analysis and review', *International Journal of Forecasting*, Vol. 16, pp. 437–50.

Theil, H. (1966), *Applied Economic Forecasting*, Amsterdam: North-Holland.

Thomakos, D. and J. Guerard (2001), 'Naïve, ARIMA, Transfer Function, and VAR Models: A Comparison of Forecasting Performance', *The International Journal of Forecasting* (forthcoming).

Vining, R. (1949), 'Koopmans on the Choice of Variables to be Studied and on Methods of Measurement', *The Review of Economics and Statistics*, reprinted in R. Gorgon and L. Klein, *Readings in Business Cycles*, Homewood, Illinois: Richard A. Irwin, Inc. 1965.

West, K. and M. McCracken. (1998), 'Regression-based tests of predictive ability', *International Economic Review*, Vol. 39, pp. 817–40.

Zarnowitz, V. (2001), 'The Old and the New in the U.S. Economic Expansion, The Conference Board. EPWP # 01 – 01.

—— (1992), *Business Cycles: Theory, History, Indicators, and Forecasting*, Chicago: University of Chicago Press.

Zarnowitz, V and A. Ozyildirim, (2001), 'On the Measurement of Business Cycles and Growth Cycles', *Indian Economic Review*, Vol. 36, pp. 34–54.

9

Measuring the Onset of the Great Depression

Then and Now

Bryan L. Boulier, H.O. Stekler, and Jeremy Dutra

Introduction

Economic historians frequently base their analyses of what happened to manufacturing output in the early years of the Great Depression on *recent* versions of the Federal Reserve Board's index of industrial production. (see Romer 1993). On the assumption that the currently available series (based on the 1940 revisions of the index) accurately portrays the economy's movements in that period, it is the one that is most appropriate for determining what *actually* happened during that period.[1] However, if one wanted to explain why economic agents acted in a particular way during that period, it is necessary to examine the data that were actually available at that time. The behaviour of these agents may appear inconsistent with the data that are available currently but entirely plausible when viewed in the context of the information that was available contemporaneously.[2] This topic is of particular interest because economists are still trying

We wish to thank Carol Corrado and Charles Gilbert of the Board of Governors for their valuable assistance and comments on an earlier draft of this paper. Any errors are our responsibility.

to explain the behaviour of the US economy in 1930. For example, an important question is whether or not the deflation of 1930 was anticipated (see Cecchetti 1992; Hamilton 1992; Nelson 1991).

In this paper, we show that the Federal Reserve's index of industrial production available contemporaneously in 1929–30 differed from the revised index for the same period that was published in 1940 and is the basis of recent analyses of the onset of the Great Depression (for example, Romer 1993). We first describe the differences between contemporaneous measures of industrial production and the later revised series. We then try to reconcile the differences in the series. We explore how revisions in the index might have contributed to measured differences in the economy's movements and identify seasonal adjustment as an important source of the difference. Next, we investigate the seasonal patterns that were reported and analyse whether the use of modern seasonal adjustment programmes would have yielded the same pattern as was observed in the 1940 version of the index. This is tantamount to asking whether the seasonal pattern of that version of the index is the 'true' one. We also examine whether applying a modern seasonal adjustment procedure to the data that were available in 1929–30 would have shown a pattern that was closer to the 'true' one. We conclude by relating the views of economic agents who were making decisions in 1929–30 with the data that were actually available to them.

The Differences in the indexes

Differences in Magnitude—1929

The difference in the magnitude of the economic movements actually reported during this period and what has been used in current analyses may be substantial. Romer (1993, p. 26), for example reports that '(s)easonally adjusted industrial production peaked in July 1929 and declined slowly between July and October 1929 (falling 3 per cent over three months)'. She then adds that between October and December 1929, industrial production declined nearly 10 per cent,... (p. 29). This analysis was based on the 1977 version of the index of industrial production, which is merely a rescaled version of the index that was revised in 1940.

Although this 12 per cent decline in production from the peak to the end of 1929 is substantial, in Table 9.1 (column 1), which

Table 9.1: Percentage changes in the index of industrial production for various sub periods, 1929–30

Column	(1)	(2)	(3)	(4)	(5)	(6)	(7)
	Seasonally Adjusted					Seasonally Unadjusted	
Date Data Available in Federal Reserve Bulletin	Feb 30	Apr 30	Aug 30	Aug 40	1986	Aug 30	Aug 40
Date of 1929 Peak	June	June	June	June, July, August	July	June	September
Percentage Change:							
Peak–Oct 1929	–7.4	–7.4	–7.9	–3.5	–3.0	–4.0	–2.6
Oct 1929–Dec 1929	–15.4	–15.4	–15.4	–9.1	–9.3	–20.8	–18.4
Peak–Dec 1929	–21.4	–21.4	–22.0	–12.3	–12.0	–24.0	–20.5
Dec 1929–Feb 1930	+7.1	+8.1	0.0	–0.7	+14.7	+7.5	
Feb 1930–June 1930	–5.6	–7.0	–6.8	–8.3	–5.0		
Base Year of Index	1923–5	1923–5	1923–5	1935–9	1977	1923–5	1935–9

presents the data that were available contemporaneously, paints a picture of an even weaker economy during this early period of the Great Depression. According to the numbers available at the end of January 1930, the peak in production occurred in June (not July) and the decline from the peak through October was over 7 per cent, and there was an additional decline of 15.4 per cent from October through the end of 1929. Thus the total decline from the peak in June through the end of the year was over 21 per cent.[3] No matter which version of the industrial production index is used, one obtains the same qualitative result: the peak to October 1929 decline was small relative to the October–December plunge. The magnitude of the quantitative decline does, however, differ substantially and depends on the version of the index that is analysed.

Difference in Trends—1930

The data for early 1930 show a different kind of disparity. Whereas the contemporaneous figures show that industrial production, on a seasonally adjusted basis, had increased 7 per cent between December 1929 and February 1930, the data revised in 1940 show no increase whatsoever. (Table 9.1 columns 2 and 4). The revised version of the index shows that the levels of production in both January and February 1930 were identical to the December 1929 level, and that the decline began again in March.

Revisions in the index

Why do the figures of index of industrial production for 1929 and 1930 that were published contemporaneously differ qualitatively or quantitatively from those that were published in later years? To determine why these differences occurred, it is necessary to explain how the Federal Reserve constructs and revises its index.

The index has reported the level of production for every month since January 1919 and continues to do so today. The numbers in this index that refer to past periods are, however, revised occasionally. When those revisions are made, the index still remains descriptive of past periods because the weights that are used in constructing the overall index are the ones that are relevant to each of those past periods. In other words there is not a single set of weights that is applied to the entire period, 1919–2000; rather 1923 weights are used for the years 1923–9, etc. In every revision the index is then chain-linked with prior time periods in chronological segments, and the Laspeyre's method is usually used in this procedure. After it has been revised for a particular period, there usually are no further revisions. The data available at a later time that refer to a particular time period are merely figures expressed as units of the new base year levels.

The data in Table 9.1 (columns 4 and 5) indicate that using either the 1935–9 or 1977 base years yields virtually identical results. The results are the same because there was a major revision in 1940, and the data for to 1929–30 have not been revised since that time. We, therefore, focus our attention on the effects of the 1940 revision of the index. In that revision, 1923 weights were used for the period 1923–9, while 1937 weights were used to construct the index starting with 1930. In addition, the index revised in 1940 displayed a different seasonal pattern than that of the earlier contemporaneous version of the index.

There are at least three reasons why the revision process could have produced the differences between the contemporaneous and later data referring to 1929–30. First, the version of the index of industrial production that was available contemporaneously in 1929–30 was based on only 60 series, with some of these series also representing activity in allied industries. For example, the output of steel ingots was used to estimate the level of production of all steel-consuming industries with the exception of automobiles (Garfield 1940, p. 499). The 1940 revision expanded the coverage to 81 series and revised a substantial number of the series that were common to both versions of the index.[4] Second, the base period was changed from 1923–5 to 1935–9 with 1923 weights for the period ending in 1929 and 1937 weights for the years beginning 1930. Finally, the pattern of seasonal adjustment differs between the two versions of the index. The change in seasonal adjustment factors can be attributed either to a change in the procedure for estimation of seasonality or to the inclusion of additional series which had seasonal patterns different from those exhibited by the previously included series.

Revisions for 1929

The revised index for 1929 (and prior years), published in 1940, is based on 81 component series and 1923 weights.[5] The index had originally been based on only 60 series and the same weights. If the two versions of the index using (seasonally) unadjusted data are compared, any differences would be entirely due to the expanded number of series. The February 1930 issue of the *Federal Reserve Bulletin* did not include the unadjusted index. However, values of the unadjusted index for 1929 were published in March 1930. Since subsequent monthly issues published in 1930 reported values of the unadjusted index that were identical to those released in March, we presume that the data reported in August 1930 accurately reflect the unadjusted series that would have been available in February 1930. Table 9.1 (columns 6 and 7) compares the (seasonally) unadjusted data for the contemporaneous and revised indexes. The revised version shows that production on an unadjusted basis reached a peak in September rather than in June as had been originally reported. The decline from the peak to end of the year is 20.5 per cent, that is (117–93) /117, for the revised version of the index versus the 24 per cent, (125–95)/125, decline that was reported contemporaneously, a difference of about 3.5 per cent.

In Table 9.1 it was shown that the seasonally adjusted decline from the peak to the end of 1929 was over 21 per cent based on the contemporaneous version of the index but only 12.3 per cent when it was derived from the revised version, a difference in magnitude of measured decline of nearly 10 per cent. Since the difference in the measured decline using seasonally unadjusted figures is only 3.5 per cent, only about one-third of the discrepancy between the contemporaneous index and the 1940 revised index can be attributed to the change in composition of the index. Consequently, the change in the seasonal pattern of the index must also account for a large portion of the discrepancy. We explore seasonal adjustment issues further in this paper.

Revisions for Early 1930

There are three reasons why the revised index's figures for 1930 may differ from those that had been published contemporaneously. The revised index not only includes more component series and different seasonal adjustment factors, but the weights were also changed. The 1930 figures were originally based on 1923 weights and starting from 1940 were reported using 1937 weights.[6] A comparison of the seasonally unadjusted versions of the index would reveal whether the combination of the additional series and the newer weights produced the differences in the reported trends for early 1930.[7] The unadjusted version of the contemporaneous index published in August 1930 shows an increase in the index by 14.7 per cent from December 1929 to February 1930 before a decline sets in. The unadjusted version of the 1940 revisions to the index for the same period shows a much smaller increase of 7.5 per cent. Consequently, the inclusion of additional series and updating the weights in the revised index materially affect differences in reported trends for early 1930. Since the seasonally adjusted version of the contemporaneous index shows a rise in industrial production from December 1929 to February 1930 of 8.1 per cent compared to no change for the revised index, it would appear that the addition of new series and change in weights account for most of the disparity between the differences in measured trends in economic activity in the early 1930s.

Seasonal Adjustment: Then and Now

Introduction

We have noted that there were a number of reasons why the contemporaneous and revised versions of the index could have produced differences in measured economic activity for the period 1929–30 and have concluded that seasonal adjustment factors appeared to have played an important role in 1929. In this section, we show how changes in the measured seasonal patterns affected both the quantitative and qualitative movements of the index of industrial production. The results obtained from this analysis have wider applicability because, in the 1930s, most time series were adjusted in a similar fashion.

Table 9.2 presents both the unadjusted and seasonally adjusted versions of the index for the period May 1929–June 1930. Columns 1 and 2 show the unadjusted indexes published in August 1930 and 1940, respectively. The corresponding seasonally adjusted indices are shown in Columns 4 and 6.[8] To obtain an approximation of the effect of the changes in the seasonal pattern, we derive seasonal adjustment factors for 1929 and 1930 by dividing the unadjusted values of the total index by the adjusted numbers (and multiplying by 100). This method is different from the procedure by which the Federal Reserve actually constructs the seasonally adjusted index. It weighs components

Table 9.2: Unadjusted and Seasonally Adjusted index of industrial production

Column		(1)	(2)	(3)	(4)	(5)	(6)
		Unadjusted		Seasonally Adjusted (Original Data and X-11 Estimates)			
Date Available		8/30	8/40	August 1930		August 1940	
Description*		I(30)	I(40)	Original IS (30)	X–11 ARIMA IXA (30)	Original IS (40)	X–11 IX (40)
1929	May	125	115	123	122	112	111
	June	125	115	127	124	114	113
	July	119	112	124	123	114	114
	Aug	121	114	123	121	114	113
	Sept	123	117	122	119	113	112
	Oct	120	114	117	116	110	110
	Nov	108	103	106	111	105	105
	Dec	95	93	99	104	100	101
1930	Jan	103	96	104	106	100	102
	Feb	109	100	107	106	100	101
	Mar	106	98	104	104	98	98
	April	107	100	106	104	98	98
	May	105	99	104	102	96	95
	June	100	95	101	99	93	93

*Note:** $I(t)$ is the seasonally unadjusted index published at time t; $IS(t)$ is the seasonally adjusted index published at time t; $IX(t)$ is a seasonally adjusted index based on the unadjusted data published at time t and adjusted using *X*-11; and $IXA(t)$ is a seasonally adjusted index based on the unadjusted data published at time t and adjusted using *X*-11ARIMA.

that have separately been seasonally adjusted. However, the Federal Reserve calculated the ratios of the unadjusted and adjusted Indices to illustrate that the seasonal pattern of its index had changed (Board of Governors 1940).

Based on the ratios of the unadjusted and adjusted values of the index, columns 1 and 3 of Table 9.3 show that the change in the seasonal patterns was substantial. Using the 1940 seasonal adjustment factors, the level of production in the summer months of 1929, when the peak occurred, was reduced and the level for December, when the lowest level of 1929 output occurred, was raised. Both changes reduced the observed seasonally adjusted rates of decline. These results indicate that changes in the seasonal pattern were a major factor accounting for the differences observed in the two sets of data.

These seasonal adjustment factors were obtained in the 1930s and 1940s using techniques that were state of the art at that time. Suppose a modern technique such as X-11 had been used to derive the seasonal adjustment factors, what seasonal pattern would have been observed in 1929 and 1930? We, thus, pose two questions that are of interest to both statisticians and economic historians.

1. Compared to current best practice methods of seasonally adjusting data, how good were the statistical practices of the 1930s?
2. If current best practice methods of seasonally adjusting data had been available in the 1930s, would the contemporaneous (real-time) interpretation of 1929–30 data have been altered?

We first describe the methodology that is used to address those two questions and then explain the seasonal adjustment procedures that were used in the 1930s and modern procedures embodied in the X-11 seasonally adjustment programme. The subsequent section compares the various published versions of the seasonally adjusted index with those obtained by using X–11.

Methodology

In order to describe our methodology, it is necessary to define the symbols that we use:

I (*t*) is the seasonally unadjusted index that was published at time *t*,

IS (*t*) is the seasonally adjusted index that was published at time *t*,

IX (*t*) is a seasonally adjusted index based on unadjusted data published at time t and adjusted using *X*–11,

IXA (*t*) is a seasonally adjusted index based on unadjusted data published at time *t* and adjusted using *X*–11ARIMA,

TABLE 9.3: Seasonal Adjustment Factors, Contemporaneous, and X–11 Estimates

	Column	(1)	(2)	(3)	(4)
	Date Available	August 1930		August 1940	
Year	Month	Original	X-11 ARIMA	Original	X–11
1929	May	101.6	102.5	102.7	103.6
	Jun	8.4	100.8	100.9	101.8
	Jul	96.0	96.7	98.2	98.2
	Aug	98.4	100.0	100.0	100.9
	Sep	100.8	103.4	103.5	104.5
	Oct	102.6	103.4	103.6	103.6
	Nov	101.9	97.3	98.1	98.1
	Dec	96.0	91.3	93.0	92.1
1930	Jan	99.0	97.2	96.0	94.1
	Feb	101.9	102.8	100.0	99.0
	Mar	101.9	101.9	100.0	100.0
	Apr	100.9	102.9	102.0	102.0
	May	101.0	102.9	103.1	104.2
	June	99.0	101.0	102.2	102.2

The first question is, in essence, a question of whether historical data provide an accurate description of what actually occurred in the 1930s. For the period 1923–38, I (40) was published in 1940 and has not been revised substantially since then except to take into the account rescaling of data when the base year was changed.[9] That is why these data can still be used to analyse the economic patterns of the 1930s. These data are assumed to reflect the conditions, including the seasonal pattern, that actually prevailed in that period. We want to determine whether the seasonal adjustment procedures of the 1930s that were used to generate this index were appropriate and whether, in fact, the index does reflect the conditions that prevailed in 1929–30. We do this by comparing IS (40) with IX (40). In other words, we are comparing the seasonally adjusted data that were actually published in 1940 with seasonally adjusted numbers derived applying X–11 to the seasonally unadjusted numbers that are published in 1940. If the two sets of seasonally adjusted numbers are similar, we would conclude that the Federal Reserve statisticians, who produced the seasonally adjusted data in 1940—without the benefit of modern statistical techniques and computers—had done an excellent job. In addition, we would conclude that IS(40) was a good representation of the time path of output.

The second question is concerned with the real time use and interpretation of the index. We have already noted that for 1929–30, the time paths reported by IS(30) and IS(40) differed. If a modern seasonal adjustment programme had been used to adjust the data in 1930, would the time path of output in 1929–30 have been closer to the numbers that are now accepted as reflecting the state of the economy? This involves a comparison of IS(30) and IXA(30) to determine which time path is closer to that of IS(40).

Seasonal Adjustment Methods

The 1930s

Until 1938, the seasonal adjustment procedure that the Federal Reserve used was 'the ratio-to-twelve-month-moving average method'. (*Federal Reserve Bulletin*, December 1936, p. 952). Although this procedure was not explained in any of the Bulletins, forecasting and statistical texts published in 1931 describe this method (Haney 1931, p. 353; Macaulay 1931).[10] Haney indicated that the seasonal adjustment involved seven steps: (i) compute a twelve-month moving average; (ii) Compute a two-month moving average of the twelve-month moving average; (iii) smooth this moving average for accidental fluctuations; (iv) compute the deviations of the monthly data from the moving average; (v) calculate the mean and median deviations for each month; (vi) adjust the medians arbitrarily; and (vii) express the adjusted medians as relatives.

Using modern time series terminology, Newbold and Bos (1994, pp. 160–5) analysed an identical problem. Combining the two moving average processes yields a 2 x 12 moving average expressed as Equation 9.1.

$$X_t^{**} = (X_{t-6} + 2X_{t-5} + 2X_{t-4} + \ldots + 2X_t + \ldots + 2X_{t+4} + 2X_{t+5} + X_{t+6})/24 \qquad \ldots(9.1)$$

The deviation for the ith month is obtained by calculating the ratio of the actual observation to the double smoothed value, this is X_i / X_t^{**}. The median of all of the ith month deviations is then used as the seasonal adjustment factor for the ith month of every year.

In 1938, the Federal Reserve placed more emphasis on a different approach for seasonally adjusting data. Instead of relying exclusively on twelve-month moving averages, there was 'a more extensive use of freehand curves as the base from which to measure seasonal variation…' (*Bulletin*, October 1938, p. 836). These curves were used to represent the business cycles whenever it was felt that the moving averages did not do an adequate job. The Bulletin stated that these freehand curves were compared with the moving average processes, but no specific details or examples were provided. This method was used in making the 1940 revisions of the index.

Modern Methods

Our estimates of seasonally adjusted indexes are derived using the X–11 and X–11–ARIMA procedures as embodied in the US Census Bureau's X–12–ARIMA seasonal adjustment programme (US Census Bureau 2000).

The default version of X-11 for a multiplicative model is applied to the unadjusted monthly index as revised in 1940 to obtain the 'modern' estimates of the seasonally adjusted data. (The procedure is described in Section A of Appendix 9.1).

In order to answer the first question, the aforementioned approach of comparing IS(40) with IX(40) is appropriate. The default version of X-11 is, however, not fully satisfactory for analysing the second question which is whether the contemporaneous data represented by IS(30) would have been altered had a modern statistical procedure been available in 1930. The reason is that trend adjustment at the end (or beginning of a series) is problematical,[11] and asymmetrical moving average procedures must be used to derive the seasonal adjustment factors (see US Census Bureau 2000, p. 1.) Consequently, we have used the X–11–ARIMA procedure for identifying the seasonal adjustment factors with contemporaneous data. Thus, to answer the second question we compare IS(30) with IXA(30), the data available in 1930 that have been adjusted using X–11–ARIMA. (The procedure is described in Section B of the Appendix 9.1).

Results

Seasonal Adjustment of Currently Available index (1940)

Columns 5 and 6 of Table 9.2 and Figure 9.1 present IS(40) and IX(40).

The differences in the two series are minor. The date of the 1929 peak differs slightly, that is it is clearly July using the X-11 procedure, but June, July and August in the other case.[12] Both methods identify July 1932 as the trough. The declines from the peak in the summer of 1929 to the end of the year are similar in the two cases, but the X–11 version shows a one point uptick in January 1930 that is not observed in the other version of the index. Given these results, we conclude that the historically available data referring to the Depression based on 'freehand' curve seasonal adjustment procedures of the late 1930s reflect a pattern similar to the one that would have been observed had X–11 been available and been used to make the adjustments.[13] Since the use of a modern seasonal adjustment procedure does not change the pattern of the economy's movements, we conclude that the historical data represented by IS(40) reflects the 'true' situation in the economy and that the contemporaneous data published in the 1930s provide incorrect information.

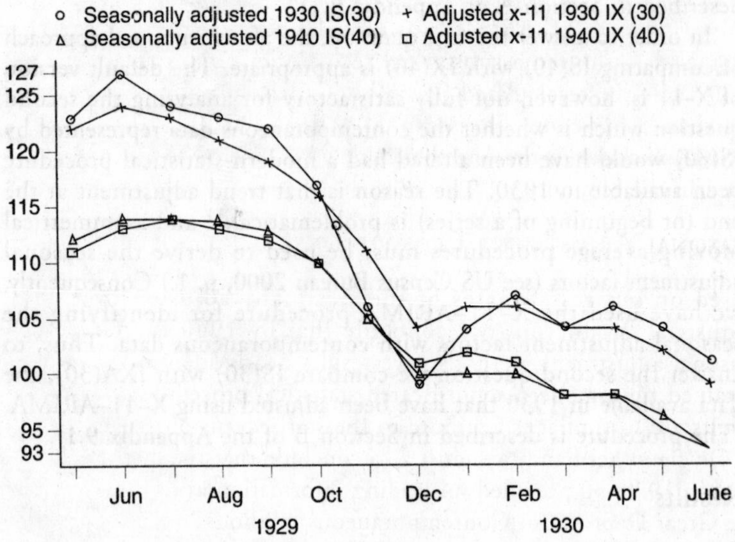

Figure 9.1: Comparison of Seasonally Adjusted Indexes of Industrial Production, August 1930 and August 1940 with X-11 Estimates.

Seasonal Adjustment of Contemporaneous Data

As a counterfactual, however, it is important to determine whether the accuracy of the contemporaneous data would have improved had X–11 been available in real time during the Depression.

In order to determine whether X–11 might have changed the seasonal pattern from that which was reported contemporaneously in 1930 that is I (30), we assume that we are in real time and only use data that were available then. We, therefore, use X–11–ARIMA to seasonally adjust the published unadjusted data that were available through June 1930.[14] The contemporaneous and X–11–ARIMA estimates of the seasonally adjusted series are given in columns 3 and 4 of Table 9.2. Figure 9.1 compares the seasonally adjusted movements of the index as it was reported in August 1930 and as calculated using X–11–ARIMA.

Using data through June 1930, both methods identify the peak as occurring in June 1929, but the quantitative movements in the two seasonally adjusted versions of the index, IS (30) and IXA (30) are different. The contemporaneous data indicated that the decline from the peak to the end of 1929 was over 22 per cent while the pattern derived from X–11–ARIMA was only 16 per cent. Moreover, the original data showed a substantial recovery in production in early 1930 while the recalculated figures show that output had increased less than 2 per cent. The seasonal pattern derived from X–11–ARIMA is closer to the one that is now considered to be the 'true' trend in the economy.

Seasonal Adjustment Conclusions

Based on our re-estimates of the seasonally adjusted index of Industrial Production, we conclude that by 1940 the freehand seasonal adjustment methods gave results nearly identical to those obtained from modern sophisticated statistical procedures. That the results are so similar is a tribute to the statisticians of that era.

On the other hand, we must also conclude that the methodology used in 1929–30 provided misleading information as to the onset of the Great Depression. Contemporaneous methods indicated (as do modern methods) that a contraction began in mid-1929. However, while contemporaneous methods also imply that a substantial recovery from the initial contraction was underway from December 1929 to February 1930, modern techniques do not imply this recovery.

Conclusion

Economic forecasters were optimistic in early 1930. They expressed the view that the recession had bottomed out and that a slow recovery could be expected.[15] Moreover, the stock market also had a substantial recovery in early 1930. This optimism cannot be reconciled with information that is available today which shows that there had been no increase in production in early 1930. This optimism is, however, consistent with the information that was published at that time.

In a historical context, analyses of the forecasts and actions of economic agents must be related to the information that was available at the time the decisions were made. Evidence indicates that most economic agents making decisions in early 1930 made forecasts and decisions based on the numbers that were available then. Unfortunately, our analysis shows that those data were misleading and what was being reported in 1929 and early 1930 was not what was actually occurring. This finding may explain why, if Hamilton (1992) is correct, the deflation of 1930 was not anticipated. The 'apparent' recovery in early 1930 may have convinced investors and speculators that a deflation was not a likely occurrence.[16]

Endnotes

[1]Except for the scaling required when the base years are changed, the numbers referring to 1929–30 have not been revised since 1940. (See Board of Governors, *Industrial Production—1986 Edition.*) That is why the trends observed in Table 9.1 (columns 4 and 5) are virtually the same regardless of whether the indexes use 1935–39 or 1977 base years. Any differences in the observed movements in the indexes would be attributable to rounding errors. This analysis can, therefore, focus on the changes that occurred when the index was revised in 1940.

[2]While there have been a number of studies that have analysed the magnitude of GNP data revisions, they have not examined the impact that the revisions might have had on interpretations of historical events such as the Great Depression. The earliest studies of data revisions include Cole (1969), Stekler (1967), and Zellner (1958).

[3]These data were published in the *Federal Reserve Bulletin*, February 1930, p. 67. During this period, the industrial production numbers for a particular month were published close to the end of the subsequent month. Thus the figures for September 1929 were released in late October during the period

when the stock market was becoming very volatile and then finally crashed. The data for September show that industrial production was down nearly 4 per cent from the June peak and had declined 1.6 per cent in the month. (*Federal Reserve Bulletin*, November 1929, p. 729). It is possible that the release of these data was a contributing factor to the stock market crash.

[4]Information about the revisions that were made in 1940 can be found in Garfield (1940), Thomas and Conklin (1940), and Board of Governors (1940, 1986).

[5]The new series represent industries that were newer, were growing faster, and had been given insufficient weight in the original version of the index.

[6]This was the only time that the index was not constructed by the Laspeyres method. Rather the weights were closer to Paasche weights (Board of Governors 1986, p. 63) that might not have been appropriate for 1930.

[7]It is not possible to disentangle the two effects from the published data.

[8]Unadjusted figures for 1929 were not published in the Febrary 1930 issue of the *Federal Reserve Bulletin*. However, the unadjusted figures for 1929 published in March 1930 (p. 107) are identical to those published in August 1930 (p. 494). The seasonally adjusted figures for 1929 published in Febrary 1930 differ slightly from those published in August 1930 for the months of June and September. The Febrary 1930 values for June and September 1929 are 126 and 121, respectively, while the comparable figures published in August 1930 are 127 and 122.

[9]There was only a minor revision in 1941. (See Board of Governors 1986.)

[10]In fact, McCaulay (1931, pp. 121–2) indicates that he had suggested this approach to 'the statistical department of a government agency' in the 1920s.

[11]Macaulay (1931, p. 25–6 and pp. 113–17) had suggested that seasonal adjustments at the end of a series be made by extrapolating the unadjusted series backward and forward in time.

[12]June had been identified as the peak based on the data available contemporaneously.

[13] Macaulay (1931, pp. 20–2) cautioned against freehand methods. He noted that 'the' investigator may easily describe the same data by distinctly different smooth curves if he does the fitting twice—with a month's time between operations. Most persons are incapable of good freehand smoothing. I do not hesitate to say, after having worked with many hundreds of students, that any fairly good mathematical method will, in at least nine cases out of ten, give better results than any method which requires much judgment... .Theoretically, freehand smoothing is ideal. Practically, it is a little like the faith of a mystic. It is conclusive evidence to the recipient of the vision alone.

[14]The data are from the Federal Reserve Bulletin August 1930, p. 494.

[15]Other indexes, such as the one published contemporaneously as the Annalist in The Commercial and Financial Chronicle, also showed a seasonally adjusted upswing in production, but there were some observers who questioned whether the observed increases were greater than the expected seasonal movements.

[16]There is direct evidence that the reported upturn influenced economic forecasts. The Foreman–State National Bank of Chicago indicated that the reported recovery of early 1930 was a factor that it had taken into account in preparing its forecasts for late 1930 and for 1931. This was reported in *The Commercial and Financial Chronicle, 25, October 1930*, p. 2598.

APPENDIX 9.1

SEASONAL ADJUSTMENT PROCEDURES OF X–11 AND X–11–ARIMA

A. The Default Version of X–11: Multiplicative Model

In the X–11 multiplicative model, a monthly series (Y_t) is decomposed into trend (T_t), seasonal (S_t), and irregular components (I_t).:

$$Y_t = T_t S_t I_t \qquad \text{... (9.1)}$$

As described by Findley, *et al.* (1998), the decomposition of Y_t is done in two stages. In the first stage, preliminary estimates are obtained by using the following steps:

1. The initial trend estimate ($T_t^{(1)}$) is obtained by a centred 13-term moving average, with weights of 1/12 for terms Y_{t-5} through Y_{t+5} and 1/24 for terms Y_{t-6} and Y_{t+6}.

2. An initial 'seasonal-irregular' ($SI_t^{(1)}$) is obtained by dividing the monthly series by the initial trend estimate.

3. An initial preliminary seasonal factor is estimated using a '3 × 3' seasonal moving average:

$$SP_t = \frac{1}{9} SI^1_{t-24} + \frac{2}{9} SI^1_{t-12} + \frac{3}{9} SI^1_t + \frac{2}{9} SI^1_{t+12} + \frac{1}{9} SI^1_{t+24} \qquad \text{... (9.2)}$$

4. An initial seasonal factor ($S_t^{(1)}$) is obtained by dividing the preliminary seasonal factor by a centred 13-term moving average of the preliminary seasonal factor, using the weights described in step 1.

5. An initial seasonally adjusted series is obtained by dividing the values in the series by the initial seasonal factors:

$$A_t^{(1)} = \frac{Y_t}{S_t^{(1)}} \qquad \text{... (9.3)}$$

In the second stage, the initial seasonal adjustment factors are smoothed with a Henderson filter to form an intermediate trend. The original values of the series are divided by the intermediate trend to obtain the second-stage 'seasonal-irregular' factor ($SI_t^{(2)}$). A preliminary seasonal factor is obtained by applying a '3 × 5' seasonal moving average to these values:

$$SP2_t = \frac{1}{15}SI^2_{t-36} + \frac{2}{15}SI^2_{t-24} + \frac{3}{15}SI^2_{t-12}$$

$$+ \frac{3}{15}SI^2_{t+12} + \frac{2}{15}SI^2_{t+24} + \frac{1}{15}SI^2_{t+36} \qquad \text{... (9.4)}$$

A final seasonal factor ($S_t^{(2)}$) is computed by dividing the preliminary seasonal factor by a centred 13-term moving average of the preliminary seasonal factor, using the weights described in step 4 of stage 1, and the final seasonally adjusted series is obtained by dividing the original series by the final seasonal factor:

$$A_t^{(2)} = \frac{Y_t}{S_t^{(2)}} \qquad \text{... (9.5)}$$

B. The X–11–ARIMA Procedure

The first stage of this procedure is to fit an ARIMA model to the original unadjusted series and then to use the forecasted (and 'backcasted') values of the series derived from the ARIMA model, to extend the original series for use by X–11. In order to provide an objective estimate of the ARIMA model untainted by knowledge of future events, we use the AUTOMDL procedure to select the seasonal ARMA model. The AUTOMDL procedure selects the model with the lowest average forecast error that meets acceptable criteria: A (i) the absolute average percentage error of the extrapolated values within the last three years of the data is less than 15 per cent, (ii) the p-value associated with the fitted model's Box–Ljung Q-statistic testing the uncorrelatedness of the model's residuals must be greater than 5 per cent, and (iii) there are no signs of overdifferencing. (Bureau of the Census 2000, p. 135). Using the data available through June 1930, the AUTMODL procedure chose an ARIMA model of the form (0 1 2) (0 1 1)$_s$, where the subscript$_s$ denotes the seasonal period.

References

Board of Governors (1986), *Industrial Production—1986 Edition*, Board of Governors of the Federal Reserve System, Washington, DC.

—— (1940), 'New Federal Reserve index of Industrial Production', *Federal Reserve Bulletin*, Vol. 26, August, 753–60.

Cecchetti, S.G. (1992), 'Prices During the Great Depression: Was the Deflation of 1930-1932 Really Unanticipated?', *American Economic Review*, Vol. 82, pp. 141–56.

Cole, R. (1969), *Errors in Provisional Estimates of Gross National Product*, New York: National Bureau of Economic Research.

Findley, D.F., B.C. Monsell, W. Bell, M. Otto, B. Chen (1998), 'New Capabilities and Methods of the X-12-ARIMA Seasonal Adjustment Programme, *Journal of Business and Economic Statistics*, Vol. 16, pp. 127–52.

Garfield, F.R. (1940), 'General indexes of Business Activity', *Federal Reserve Bulletin*, Vol. 26, June, pp. 495–501.

Hamilton, J.D. (1992), 'Was the Deflation During the Great Depression Anticipated? Evidence from the Commodity Futures Market', *American Economic Review*, Vol. 82, pp. 157–78.

Haney, L.H. (1931), *Business Forecasting*, New York: Ginn and Company.

Macaulay, F.R. (1931), *The Smoothing of Time Series*, New York: National Bureau of Economic Research.

Nelson, D.B. (1991), 'Was the Deflation of 1929–1930 Anticipated? The Monetary Regime as Viewed by the Business Press', *Research in Economic History*, Vol. 13, pp. 1–65.

Newbold, P. and T. Bos (1994), *Introductory Business and Economic Forecasting*, Cincinnati: South-Western Publishing Company.

Romer, C. (1993), 'The Nation in Depression', *Journal of Economic Perspectives*, Vol. 78 No. 2, pp. 19–39.

Stekler, H.O. (1967), 'Data Revisions and Economic Forecasting', *Journal of the American Statistical Association*, Vol. 62, pp. 470–83.

Thomas, W. and M.R. Conklin (1940), 'Measurement of Production', *Federal Reserve Bulletin*, Vol. 26, September 912–23.

US Census Bureau (2000), *X-12-ARIMA Reference Manual, Version* 0, 2.6, Washington, DC: US Census Bureau.

Zellner, A. (1958), 'A Statistical Analysis of Provisional Estimates of Gross National Product and its Components, of Selected National Income Components, and of Personal Saving', *Journal of the American Statistical Association*, Vol. 53, pp. 54–65.

10

Confidence Indexes and the Probability of Recession

A Markov Switching Model

Roy Batchelor

Introduction

This paper asks whether there is a relationship between what people really feel about the economy, as summarized in responses to surveys of consumer and business confidence, and one measure of economic performance that people really care about—the likelihood of recession. We examine whether indexes of consumer and business confidence are useful in predicting turning points in the United States (US) and the United Kingdom (UK). The paper is an extension of the studies of Moore and Cullity (1989) and Klein and Moore (1991).

These studies analysed in an informal way the timing relationships between the US business cycle and, respectively, the US Conference Board and University of Michigan consumer confidence indexes, and the US National Association of Purchasing Managers survey of business conditions. Our study is different in three respects.

First, we use more recent data, which in itself is of interest for two reasons. Consumer confidence is recognized to have played a key role in triggering the US recession of the early 1990s (Blanchard 1993; Hall 1993). And as this paper is being written in mid-2001, the US economy has enjoyed a decade of sustained healthy growth, but with a background of steadily weakening consumer and business confidence.

Second, we look at indexes of economic activity and confidence in the UK and the US. These are under-researched relative to their US counterparts, and prove to have rather different properties. Thus, the US findings are unlikely to generalize to even a single other G8 economy.

Third, we use a more formal econometric technique, which allows us to test the statistical significance of some of the relationships observed in the data. Turning points in coincident economic indicator series and confidence indexes are identified using a two-state Markov switching model, with time-varying transition probabilities. The predictive value of the indexes is assessed by examining whether their turning points consistently lead those in the coincident index, and whether the level of confidence significantly affects the probability that the coincident index will switch states.

The second section of the paper describes the switching model, and summarizes what we have learnt from its application in the US. The third section introduces the data. The fourth section analyses timing relationships in the US and the UK, between the state of the economy and the state of consumer and business confidence. The final section discusses implications of the study for empirical modelling, and for the leading indicator properties of confidence indexes.

The Markov approach turns out to be a mixed blessing. On the one hand, the estimated models show that confidence indicators play a statistically significant role in determining the probability of recovery from recessions. On the other hand, the visualization of this relationship, which is generally one of the strengths of the model, is not successful. Phases of low and high growth are not well defined in the UK, for example. In the US, the business cycle chronology is more obvious. But it is hard to argue that switches in the confidence indexes lead switches in the state of the US economy in an operationally meaningful way.

The Markov Switching Model

The Markov model assumes that there are two or more 'states' or 'regimes' which might characterize the variable we are interested in modelling. For example, gross domestic product (GDP) growth might be in a 'normal' state or in a 'recession' state, interest rates might be at 'low', 'moderate', or 'high' levels. The state of the variable at any time is not deterministic, but depends on its previous state and on the probability that the variable will switch states in the current time period. These transition probabilities, in turn, may be fixed or may depend on other variables. For example, the probability of GDP growth switching out of recession into the normal state might depend on the length of time the economy has already been in recession—the hypothesis of 'duration dependence'.

In this paper, we use a two-regime Markov switching model with time-varying transition probabilities. For variable y_t this model can be written as:

$$y_t = S_t \mu_1 + (1 - S_t)\mu_2 + u_t \qquad \text{...(10.1)}$$

$$u_t \sim \text{i.i.d. } N(0, \sigma^2) \qquad \text{...(10.2)}$$

$$p_{kt} = \Phi\left(\alpha_{k0} + \sum_i \alpha_{ki} X_{it-1}\right), \; k = 1, 2 \qquad \text{...(10.3)}$$

where S_t is a variable which takes the value 1 or 0 depending on whether as y_t is in state 1 or state 2, μ_1 and μ_2 are the expected values of y in the two states; p_{1t} and p_{2t} are the probabilities that y will persist in state 1 or 2 at time t given that it was in that state at time $t - 1$; x_{it-1} are the variables determining these transition probabilities; and Φ[.] is the normal cumulative density function which constrains the probabilities to lie between 0 and 1. The probability of switching from state 1 to state 2 in period t is, therefore $(1 - p_{1t})$, and the probability of switching from state 2 to state 1 is $(1 - p_{2t})$. The expected durations of the states at t are consequently $1/(1 - p_{1t})$ and $1/(1 - p_{2t})$ periods respectively.

The parameters α_{ki} measure the impact effects of the values of predetermined variables x_i at time $t - 1$ on the probabilities that y will persist in the same state between $t - 1$ and t. However, because the state of the system is path-dependent, changes in x_{it-1} will have effects beyond period t, and in particular will change the expected duration of the current regime.

This basic structure above can be generalized in various ways. There may be more than two states. Sichel (1993), for example, argues convincingly for a three-state description of the US business cycle. The regime means μ_1 and μ_2 may vary over time (as in Raymond and Rich 1997). The residual u_t may follow an autoregressive process (Hamilton 1989, 1990). The variance σ^2 need not be the same in all states. The density function Φ need not be normal, and so on.

Algorithms for finding maximum likelihood estimates for the parameters of simple and time-varying probability models are discussed in Hamilton (1989, 1990); Diebold, Lee, and Weinbach (1994); Kim (1994); Filardo (1994); and Durland and McCurdy (1994). These are now incorporated in some specialised econometrics packages such as RATS, though we use GAUSS programmes for the implementations.

Given estimates of the parameters $\theta = (\mu_1, \mu_2, \sigma_2, \alpha_{ki})$, probabilistic inferences can be made about the state of the system at time t. The exact inferences made will, however, depend crucially on the information set used.

Suppose there are n observations on y_t and the x_{it} available for estimation, and we write the parameter vector conditional on the full sample Ω_n as θ_n, and the parameter vector conditional on sample observations $\Omega_{t-1} = (y_1, y_2, \ldots, y_{t-1}; x_1, x_2, \ldots, x_{t-1})$ up to period $t-1$ as θ_{t-1}. One possibility is to use the whole data set to estimate the parameters and make inferences about the probability that the variable is in state 1 at time t. This full-sample smoother can be written as:

$$\pi^s_t = \text{Prob}\{\, y_t \in \text{State } 1 \mid \Omega_n, \theta_n\},\quad t = 1, 2, \ldots, n. \qquad \ldots(10.4)$$

An alternative is to estimate these probabilities period by period using only data available up to that period. This recursive filtered estimator can be written as:

$$\pi^r_t = \text{Prob}\{\, y_t \in \text{State } 1 \mid \Omega_{t-1}, \theta_{t-1}\},\quad t = 1, 2, \ldots, n. \qquad \ldots(10.5)$$

The full-sample smoothed estimates use all the observations to interpret the history of the whole time series. The recursive filtered estimator gives an interpretation based only on past data and, in that sense, reflects the conditions faced by a forecaster at time t who could not use later observations.

The recursive filter requires an extremely time-consuming iterative computation of the system parameters, and Hamilton (1989) and Kim

(1994) propose the compromise statistics Prob $\{ y_t \in \text{State } 1 \mid \Omega_{t-1}, \theta_n \}$, which use the full sample to estimate the parameters, but update the probabilities period by period conditional on these parameters and data up to period t only. If the parameters can be assumed to be stable, this is a convenient procedure, but Lahiri and Wang (1994) show that this assumption is not always warranted in business cycle applications. We use only full-sample and recursive filtered models in this paper.

The benefit of the Markov switching approach is that, if the underlying data can be approximated by a two-regime model, these filters will transform sample data into visually striking representations of the regimes. The model squashes observations which clearly lie in one or other regime close to probabilities of 1 or 0, and highlights the brief periods when there are transitions from one regime to the other.

The basic two-regime model has been used extensively in empirical analysis of the US business cycle. These applied studies fall into three categories. Some studies take y_t to be the index of the current state of the economy (for example, real gross national product (GNP), industrial production, the index of coincident indicators), assume fixed transition probabilities, and use the filter to determine the dates of recessions and recoveries. Examples are Hamilton (1989) and Boldin (1994) for the US, and the cross-country study of Goodwin (1993). The filter mimics closely the National Bureau of Economic Research (NBER) dating of the US business cycle. This is of value since it uses only past data, and hence provides more timely signals than conventional heuristic methods such as that of Bry and Boschan (1971), which are typically based on long centered moving averages.

Other studies assume that the state of the economy is already given, for example, by the official NBER dating of recessions and recoveries in the US; and take y_t to be a possible predictor of the state of the economy. An example is Lahiri and Wang (1994), who use the Hamilton filter to establish turning points in the US Department of Commerce index of leading indicators, and compare these with the NBER peaks and troughs. By construction, switches in the leading indicators anticipate peaks and troughs in economic activity. But the frequent revisions to the leading indicators series makes their value as genuine ex ante forecasting tools extremely dubious (see Koenig and Emery 1991; Diebold and Rudebusch 1991).

Finally, several recent studies have taken y_t to be the current state of the economy, and here tested the value of various possible determinants x_{it-1} of the transition probabilities. Filardo (1994) tests whether leading indicators, interest rates, and stock prices affect transition probabilities in a model of US industrial production. Durland and McCurdy (1994) test whether the duration of recessions and recoveries is important. Raymond and Rich (1997) measure the effects of oil price shocks on transition probabilities and on mean GNP growth rates in recovery and recession.

In this paper, we perform all three types of exercise. First, the full-sample smoother, applied to a model with constant transition probabilities, is used to identify what in retrospect appear to have been regime shifts in the coincident indicator.

Second, the recursive filtered estimator is applied to constant transition probability models of consumer and industrial confidence. The objective is to establish whether regime shifts in these series, which could have been identified at the time, consistently anticipate regime shifts in the coincident index.

Third, we apply the recursive filtered estimator to the more general time-varying probability model of the coincident indicator, to formally test the significance of changes in confidence for changes in the coincident indicator regime. Based on this model, we propose an 'early warning' indicator for regime switches—the difference between the recursive conditional probability of being in one regime and the corresponding full-sample unconditional probability.

Data

We use the US Department of Commerce (DOC) index of coincident indicators to track the state of the US economy, and the Office for National Statistics (ONS) coincident indicator for the UK economy. These indexes are somewhat different. The DOC index is based on industrial production, real personal income, manufacturing and trade sales, and non-agricultural employment. The ONS index is based on series for real GDP, industrial production, retail sales, the real value of the monetary base, and capacity utilization and raw materials stocks as reported by the Confederation of British Industry (CBI). The ONS series is published with time-varying trends in the components removed, and we also use the trend-removed version of the DOC series. Both series are monthly for the period January 1956 to April 2001.

Our measure of business confidence in the US is the overall index published by the National Association of Purchasing Managers (NAPM), and our measure of consumer confidence is the index of consumer confidence published by the Conference Board. The NAPM purchasing manager's index is a weighted average of the balances of responses by members of the NAPM to monthly questions about changes in new orders, production, supply deliveries, inventories, and employment. It is constructed with the intention that a high level of the index means that the economy is growing fast. The Conference Board's index is, similarly, an average of responses of a panel of households to questions about changes in their past and prospective financial well-being, and the general well-being of the economy. The NAPM survey is available from 1956 onwards (and earlier), while the Conference Board monthly survey starts only in April 1969.

The UK business and consumer confidence series are taken from the harmonized surveys co-ordinated among European Union (EU) member countries by the European Commission. The business survey data are available since January 1976, and the consumer survey since January 1974. The business surveys ask (mainly manufacturing) firms about past and expected production trends, expected price trends, and current orders and stocks. In the UK, the survey is conducted by the (BI), so some of the responses are incorporated directly into the coincident indicator. The consumer surveys exactly parallel the Conference Board surveys in constructing the consumer confidence index from the balances of responses to questions about past and future own and general economic conditions, and about the advisability purchases of major durables. Again, if these businesses and households have rational perceptions and expectations, high levels of these indexes should be associated with fast economic growth.

Figures 10.1 and 10.2 show the raw data on US and UK coincident indicators and confidence indexes. The UK coincident series is smoother and more cyclical than the corresponding US series. This is in part due to differences in the objectives of the constructors of the indexes. The US series is constructed to dip only in officially recognized major recessions, and ride out less dramatic downturns. The UK does not have an official recession chronology, and there are more troughs in the UK coincident indicator than there

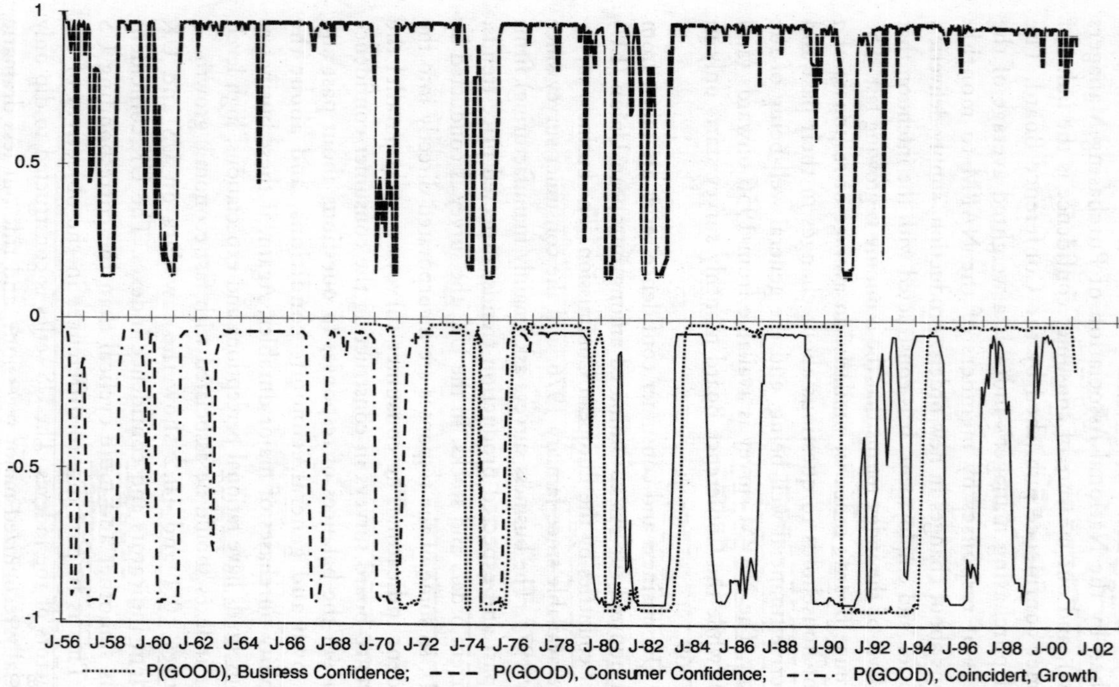

Figure 10.1: P (GOOD) from Simple Markov Switching Models, US.

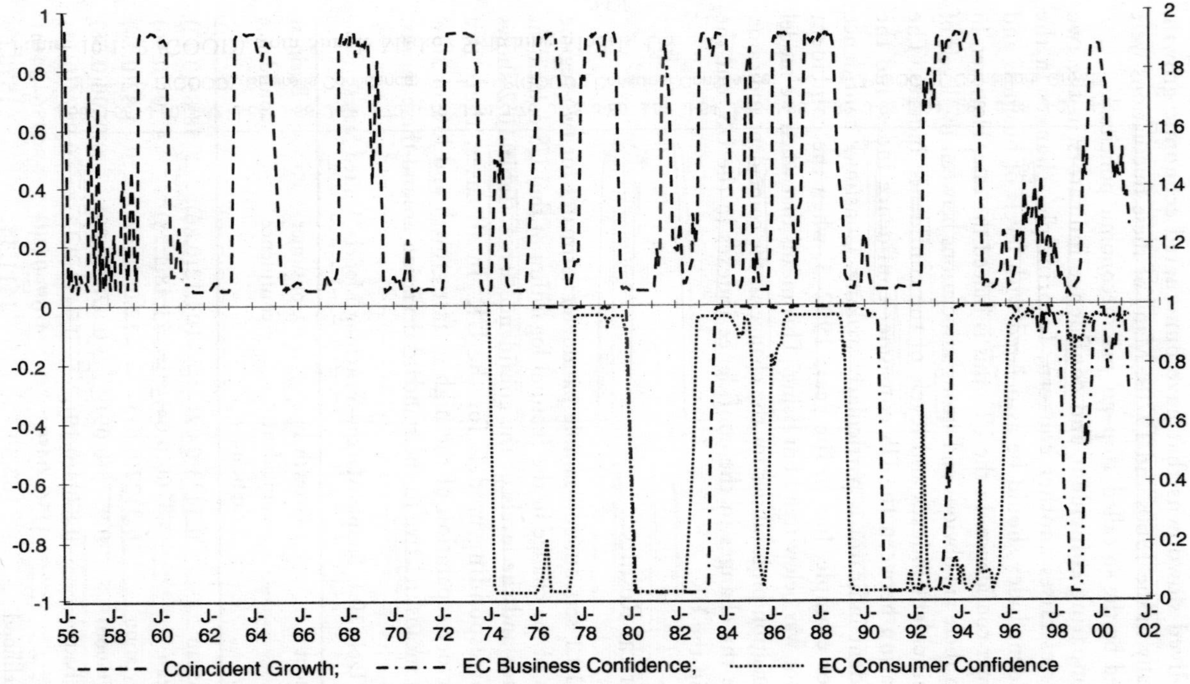

Figure 10.2: P (Good) from Simple Markov Switching Models, UK.

are truly recessionary periods. The UK index instead records the short-lived slowdowns that have punctuated economic growth, especially in the 1960s and 1970s. Many of these fluctuations were induced by the so-called 'stop–go' macroeconomic policies.

Comparing coincident and confidence indicators in the two countries raises another concern. In principle, changes in the coincident index should be associated with levels of business and consumer confidence. In the UK, this is indeed the case. However, in the US there are obvious and strong associations between the levels of the coincident indexes and levels of the confidence indexes. The correlation between the US consumer confidence index and the coincident indicator is particularly striking. Consumer confidence was, for example, low in the years 1992–3, when the coincident indicator was below trend but rising. This means that when we model the transition probabilities for the change in the coincident indicator, we use the changes in the confidence indexes in the US, but the levels in the UK.

Empirical Results

Table 10.1 sets out full-sample parameter estimates for two-regime models of the change in the (natural logarithm of the) US coincident indicator and the levels of the confidence series. Table 10.2 shows the corresponding models for the UK. In all cases, there is a satisfactory separation of the high or fast growth and low or slow growth means, relative to the standard deviation around these means.

Table 10.1: Simple Markov Switching Models, United States

Coefficient	Growth in coincident indicator	Consumer confidence	Business confidence
Good Mean	0.3433(0.02)	103.12(0.86)	58.85(0.42)
Bad Mean	–0.3100(0.04)	71.48(1.28)	47.01(0.56)
Std. Deviation	0.3127(0.01)	12.03(0.47)	4.82(0.14)
P (Stay Good)	0.9775(0.09)	0.9763(0.09)	0.9600(0.08)
P (Stay Bad)	0.8704(0.19)	0.9411(0.12)	0.9474(0.11)
Sample	1/56–04/01	4/69–04/01	1/56–04/01
Log-Likelihood	162.39	1411.34	1570.69

Note: Figures in parentheses are standard errors.
Source: Computed by author.

Table 10.2: Simple Markov Switching Models, United Kingdom

Coefficient	Growth in coincident indicator	Consumer confidence	Business confidence
Good Mean	0.6014(0.05)	–1.7022(0.52)	1.4426(0.84)
Bad Mean	–0.5447(0.05)	–18.0505(0.64)	–28.4922(1.42)
Std. Deviation	0.5419(0.02)	6.8517(22.57)	9.4977(0.52)
P (Stay Good)	0.9333(0.09)	0.9693(0.11)	0.9747(0.14)
P (Stay in Bad)	0.9487(0.09)	0.9770(0.11)	0.9751(0.15)
Sample	1/56–04/016	1/74–04/01	1/76–04/01
Log-Likelihood	467.2	1014.1	1025.6

Note: Figures in parentheses are standard errors.
Source: Computed by author.

For the level models, the probabilities of staying in state 1 (good) and state 2 (bad) are similar, with the bad state persistence probability only slightly lower. For the US growth rate model, there is a significantly lower probability of staying in the low growth state, reflecting the well-known phenomenon that US recessions tend to be much shorter-lived than expansions. The UK growth rate model shows the exact opposite effect, with the bad regime more persistent than the good, reflecting the tendency of the UK coincident indicator to show sharp recoveries and long slow declines.

Figures 10.3 and 10.4 compare the full-sample smoothed estimates of the probability that the growth of the coincident index indicator was in the fast growth regime month by month, with the filtered probabilities that the confidence indicators were in their good states. The figures show some tendency for both consumer and business confidence to lead the switches between low and high levels of the coincident index. Looking at the US experience, the confidence indexes both dip ahead of the recessions of the early 1980s and 1990s. However, they do not lead fluctuations in growth in the 1970s, perhaps because these fluctuations were caused by external forces. And the business confidence index series produces a number of false alarms—dips in confidence which are not associated with any fluctuations in the state of the economy.

We have established a chronology of switches in these variables for the US, using switching points for π^s_t = Prob (good) of 0.9 and 0.1 to identify transitions into and out of good to bad states. The

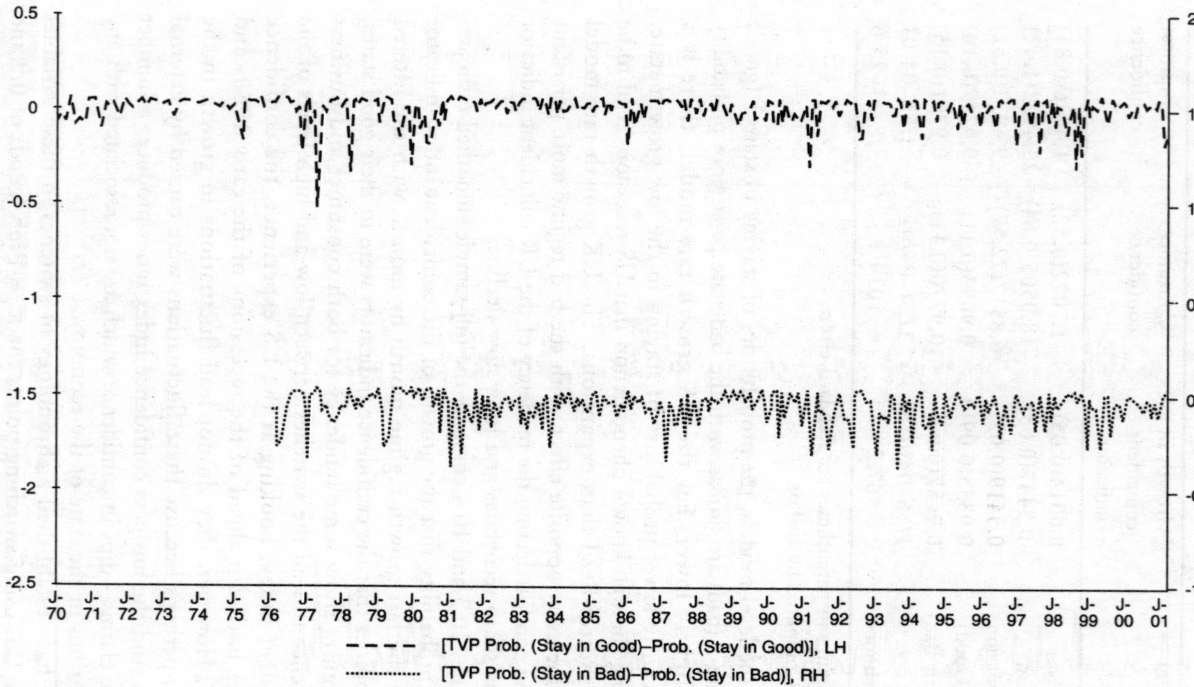

Figure 10.3: Marginal Contribution of Confidence Indexes; Probabilities of Regime Persistence, US Coincident Growth.

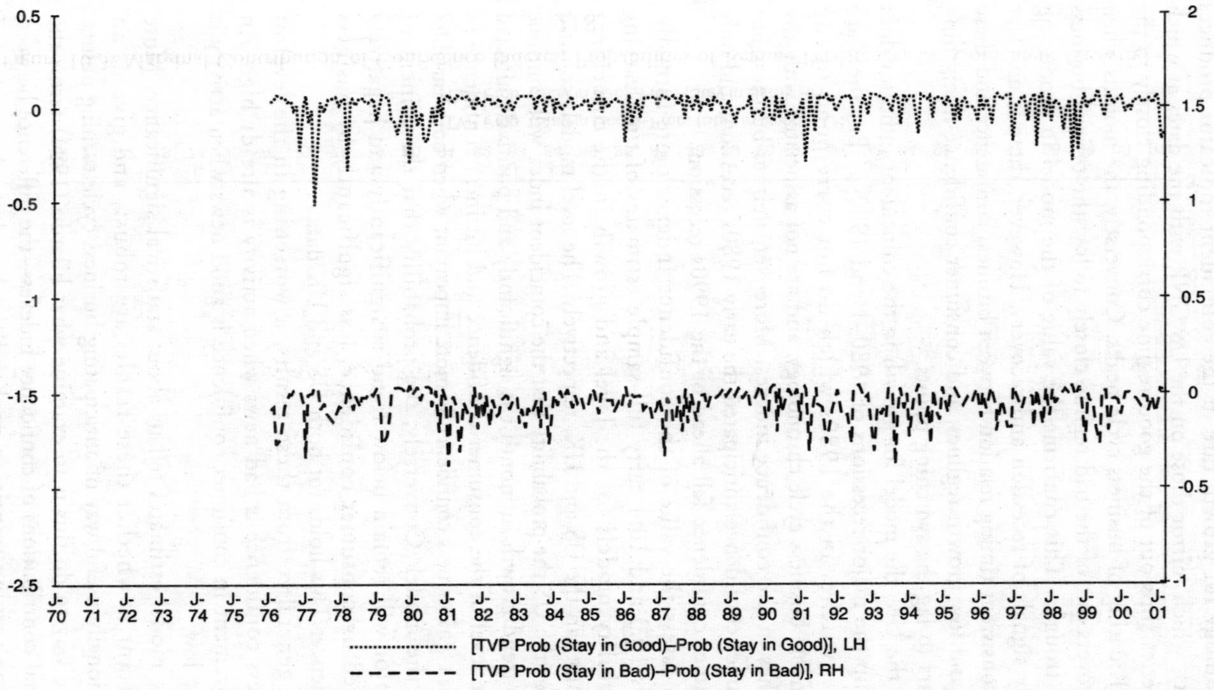

Figure 10.4: Marginal Contribution of Confidence Indexes; Probabilities of Regime Persistence, UK Coincident Growth.

chronology for growth rate in the coincident indicator produces results, which mirror those on the US GNP, with the dates at which the series slips out of the good regime corresponding closely to the NBER dating of business cycle peaks. Conversely, the months when it recovers out of the bad regime closely follow the official business cycle troughs. This confirms the value of the model in producing timely signals of recession and recovery. However, there is no clear and consistent timing relation between business confidence and these high and low growth regimes, and consumer confidence if anything appears to lag the switching points.

In the UK, the model for growth in the coincident indicator does pick up the major recessions of 1980–1 and 1990–1. But there are many switches in the 1980s which do not correspond to any reasonable business cycle chronology, and are not associated with any switches in the confidence indexes. Moreover, neither business nor consumer confidence anticipated the early 1980s recession, and only consumer confidence fell ahead of the 1990s recession.

To assess the value of the confidence indexes more formally, Tables 10.3 and 10.4 carry full-sample estimates of time-varying probability models for the level and growth in the coincident indicators in the US and UK, respectively. The level models confirm that for the US the probability that the coincident index will continue above trend growth in month t is significantly and positively affected by the level of the consumer confidence and business confidence in month t-1. Business confidence is more important when both variables enter the model. Conversely, the probability that the coincident indicator will remain below trend is significantly and negatively affected by consumer confidence, less significantly by business confidence. This holds for both US and UK data.

To generalize from these results, a worsening in the level of business confidence is bad news when activity is already high. An improvement in consumer confidence is good news when activity is already low.

The model estimates tell us about statistical significance. More important is whether these results are robust, and give us an operationally useful way of anticipating business cycle turning points.

One way to do this is to examine what Filardo (1994) terms the marginal contributions of confidence indexes—the difference between the time-varying transition probabilities based on the models of Tables 10.3 and 10.4, and the fixed probabilities from Tables 10.1

Table 10.3: Time Varying Probability Markov Switching Models for growth in US Coincident Indicator

Coefficient	Consumer confidence	Business confidence	Both
Good Mean			0.3230
Bad Mean			−0.3225
Std. Deviation			0.2966
P (Stay in Good):			
Constant	−2.5661(1.84)	−11.3547(4.17)	11.5540(2.32)
Δ Consumer Confidence, *t*−1	0.0492(3.42)	0.0329(1.53)	
Δ Business Confidence, *t*−1	0.2718(3.01)	0.2105(1.98)	
P (Stay in Bad):			
Constant	6.1011(2.02)	5.9733(2.01)	8.1168(2.34)
Δ Consumer Confidence, *t*−1	−0.0722(3.50))	−0.0616(3.13)	
Δ Business Confidence, *t*−1	−0.0677(2.91)	−0.0581(1.88)	
Sample	4/69–04/01	1/56–04/01	4/69–04/01
Log-Likelihood	552.13	810.89	647.05

Note: Figures in parentheses are *t*-statistics.
Source: Computed by author.

and 10.2. Figure 10.5 shows that in the US, confidence indexes have little visible impact on the probability of staying in the high growth regime, but they do have an impact on the probability of staying in, and hence recovering from, the low growth regime. Specifically, the indexes contributed to the probability of continuing low growth in 1980–1 and 1990–1. In spite of the low statistical significance of these models, then, it appears that on important occasions, notably in 1975, 1980, 1983, and 1991, rising confidence appreciably reduced the probability that the economy would stay in recession. Similar, but weaker, patterns appear in the UK marginal significance plots in Figure 10.6.

Another way to assess operational significance is to compute what Batchelor (1998) termed the 'early warning signal'. In the notation of equations (10.4) and (10.5), the early warning signal is:

$$\text{Early warning} = \pi^{v}_{t}\,(\text{TVP}) - \pi^{s}_{t}\,(\text{Simple}) \qquad \ldots(10.6)$$

Table 10.4: Time Varying Probability Markov Switching Models for growth in UK Coincident Indicator

Coefficient	Consumer confidence	Business confidence	Both
Good Mean			0.3206
Bad Mean			–0.7642
Std. Deviation			0.4424
P (Stay in Good):			
Constant	3.0226(5.09)	2.6022(6.96)	2.6236(4.41)
Consumer Confidence, *t*–1	0.0777(2.81)		0.0208(1.53)
Business Confidence, *t*–1		0.0652(3.10)	0.0624(2.61)
P (Stay in Bad):			
Constant	0.9722(2.18)	1.8445(6.49)	0.7952(1.74)
Consume Confidence, *t*–1	–0.0702(2.63)		–0.1331(3.18)
Busines Confidence, *t*–1	–0.0204(1.66)		–0.0209(0.85)
Sample	1/74–04/01	1/76–04/01	1/76–04/01
Log Likelihood	743.7	702.9	729.2

Note: Figures in parentheses are *t*-statistics.
Source: Computed by author.

This is the probability, conditional on the values of the confidence indexes, of being in the state other than that which would be predicted from the simple two-regime model for the coincident indicator. So, if the estimate from the simple two-regime model of Table 10.1 suggests that the US economy is in a normal positive growth state, the early warning signal is the probability of recession from the time varying parameter (TVP) model of Table 10.3. If the US economy is assessed to be in the recession state, the early warning signal is the probability of recovery from Table 10.3.

This has been calculated in Figure 10.7 only for US data, since the dating of UK recessions is less reliable. Looking first at the months preceding recessions, the early warning signal goes progressively more negative in all the cases—that is, in 1973, 1974, 1980, 1981, and 1990. Conversely, once in recession, increasing confidence has been an important factor that progressively increases the probability of a return to the normal state. Both these are desirable properties of an early warning system. As this paper is written in 2001, confidence indexes have been weak for two years, the probability of the negative growth state according to our model is rising sharply, and the US economy shows signs of slipping into outright recession.

However, the model generates several false alarms. For example, in 1984–5, 1987, 1989, and 1995, consumer and business confidence fell in the US and the probability of the negative growth state increased as much as in the years preceding recessions. But the economy did not subsequently fall into recession. This is decidedly not a desirable property of an early warning system.

Conclusion

The aim of this paper has been to evaluate the usefulness of consumer and business confidence indexes in anticipating turning points in economic activity in the US and UK. We use a Markov switching model to provide an objective criterion for determining points at which the series changed their character.

We have been partially successful, but the exercise has raised as many problems as it has solved. One problem is that the characterization of the business cycle as alternate phases of high and low (negative) growth works well for the US, but not for the UK. Another is that the consumer and business confidence indexes appear cointegrated with the level of activity in the US, but with growth in the UK. Thus, our models show significant relationship between changes in confidence and activity in the US, but between the levels of the confidence indexes and growth in the UK. This is consistent with the results of Batchelor (1998), where it was found that in the US, switches in the level of confidence were more closely associated with switches from above-to-below trend levels of activity, rather than switches from high to low growth rates.

Subject to this caveat we have uncovered statistically significant relationships between confidence indexes and economic growth, even in the US. Broadly, a fall in business confidence leads to a fall in the probability of staying in the good, high-growth state. A rise in consumer confidence lowers the probability of staying in the bad, recession, state. These findings, to some extent, justify the preoccupation of the press with confidence indicators at times when the state of the economy is uncertain.

However, statistical significance does not necessarily translate into a reliable rule for forecasting recessions and recoveries. Transition probabilities are affected progressively by changes in confidence in the months before turning points occur. However, weakening confidence on its own does not necessarily lead to recession, and many false alarms would be generated by a mechanical forecasting rule based on the Markov model.

References

Batchelor, R. A. (1998), 'Confidence and the macroeconomy: a Markov switching model', in G. Poser and H. Oppenlander (Eds), *Social and Structural Change*, London and Sydney: Ashgate.

Blanchard, O (1993), 'Consumption and the recession of 1990–1991, *American Economic Review*, Papers and Proceedings, pp. 270–4.

Boldin, M. D. (1994), 'Dating turning points in the business cycle', *Journal of Business*, Vol. 67, pp. 97–131.

Bry, G. and C. Boschan (1971), *Cyclical analysis of time series: selected procedures and computer programs*, Technical Paper 20, National Bureau of Economic Research, Columbia University Press. New York.

Diebold, F. X, J.–H. Lee, and G. C. Weinbach (1995), 'Regime-switching with time-varying transition probabilities', in C. Hargreaves (Ed.), *Nonstationary time series analysis and cointegration*, Oxford: Oxford University Press.

Diebold, F. X. and G. D. Rudebusch (1991), 'Turning point prediction with the composite leading index: an ex ante analysis', in K. Lahiri and G. H. Moore (Eds), *Leading Economic Indicators: New Approaches and Forecasting Records*, Cambridge: Cambridge University Press.

Durland, J. M. and T. H. McCurdy, (1994), 'Duration-dependent transitions in a Markov model of US GNP growth', *Journal of Business Economics and Statistics*, Vol. 12, pp. 279–88.

Filardo, A. J. (1994), 'Business-cycle phases and their transitional dynamics', *Journal of Business and Economic Statistics*, Vol. 12, pp. 299–308.

Goodwin, T. H. (1993), 'Business cycle analysis with a Markov switching model', *Journal of Business Economics and Statistics*, Vol. 11, pp. 331–9.

Hall, R. E. (1993), 'Macro theory and the recession of 1990–1991', *American Economic Review, Papers and Proceedings*, pp. 275–9.

Hamilton, J. D. (1990), 'Analysis of time series subject to changes in regime', *Journal of Econometrics*, Vol. 45, pp. 39–70.

Hamilton, J. D. (1989), 'A new approach to the econometric analysis of nonstationary time series and the business cycle', *Econometrica*, Vol. 57, pp. 357–84.

Kim, C. J. (1994), 'Dynamic linear models with Markov switching', *Journal of Econometrics*, Vol. 60, pp. 1–22.

Klein, P. A. and G. H. Moore (1991), 'Purchasing management survey data: their value as leading indicators', in K. Lahiri and G. H. Moore (Eds), *Leading Economic Indicators: New Approaches and Forecasting Records*, Cambridge: Cambridge University Press.

Koenig, E. F. and K. M. Emery (1991), 'Misleading indicators? Using the composite leading indicators to predict cyclical turning points', *Federal Reserve Bank of Dallas Economic Review*, July, pp. 1–14.

Lahiri, K. and J. G. Wang (1994), 'Predicting cyclical turning points with leading index in a Markov switching model', *Journal of Forecasting*, Vol. 13, No. 3, pp. 245–63.

Moore, G. H. and J. P. Cullity (1989), *An evaluation of consumer confidence surveys as leading indicators*, Centre for International Business Cycle Research, Columbia Graduate School of Business, Discussion Paper, May, p. 29.

Raymond, J. E. and R. Rich (1997), 'Oil and the macroeconomy: a Markov state-switching approach', *Journal of Money, Credit, and Banking*.

Sichel, D. E. (1993), 'Inventories and the three phases of the business cycle', *Journal of Business Economics and Statistics*, Vol. 12, pp. 269–77.

11

When Should We Care About Consumer Sentiment?

Evidence From Linear and Markov-Switching Models

Detelina Ivanova and Kajal Lahiri

Introduction

The last decade has witnessed a renewed interest in the power of consumer sentiment to forecast aggregate consumption and the overall state of the economy. The 1990–1 recession in the US was largely blamed on a drop in consumer sentiment during the Gulf War. Despite media popularity of sentiment measures, the econometric evidence regarding their predictive value is still inconclusive. Existing research has focused on two broad questions: does consumer sentiment really help predict consumption? and if so, why? Empirical studies have reached differing conclusions. Throop (1992), Fuhrer (1993), Carroll *et.al* (1994), and Eppright *et.al* (1998) find a small but significant effect of sentiment on consumption growth, even when other variables such as income growth are accounted for. Bram and Ludvigson (1998) also find that both measures of US consumer sentiment—the University of Michigan's index of consumer sentiment (ICS) and the Conference Board's index of consumer confidence—have significant predictive power for several categories of consumer spending even after controlling for economic fundamentals. In other studies, however, sentiment proved redundant in the presence of variables such as income, interest rates, and financial variables. Mishkin (1978) points out that the presence of financial asset and liability measures typically reduces consumer sentiment effects to insignificance. Garner (1991) also reports that, regardless of what other variables are included, spending on consumer durables is not affected by the Michigan ICS.

One possible reason why studies disagree is that the effect of sentiment on consumption may be regime-dependent and non-linear. Throop (1992) finds that a structural model for the ICS including inflation, unemployment, and short-term interest rates as explanatory variables explains sentiment fairly well in times of usual political and economic activity but collapses around points of extraordinary events such as the Persian Gulf War. It is possible then that the explanatory power of the ICS in models of consumption is most significant in such periods. If this is the case, results of empirical studies will differ depending on the sample period and model used.

The question of why consumer sentiment helps predict consumption is not the subject of this paper. Most researchers have assumed that consumer sentiment reflects consumers' changing attitudes about the economy and job prospects, which ultimately determine their future income. Indeed, the analysis in Ivanova and Lahiri (1998) using household data provides substantial evidence that consumer sentiment proxies consumers' expectations of change in their personal financial situation over the near term.

The purpose of this paper is two-fold. First, utilizing more recent data, we revisit the question of whether consumer sentiment carries useful information for predicting consumption on its own and when added to other macroeconomic aggregates using the methodology of Granger-causality. We then extend the analysis by allowing sentiment to affect consumption differently in different states of the economy. For this purpose, we use a Markov-switching model in which consumption growth depends on past consumption growth as well as past changes in sentiment, and this relationship differs across states of the economy. Our results show that the sample period can be divided into periods characterized by a strong relationship between sentiment and consumption, and periods where past sentiment matters little when added to past consumption. However, the independent predictive power of sentiment becomes statistically insignificant in the presence of certain forward-looking financial variables such as stock prices and interest rate spreads.

Explanatory Power of ICS in Linear Models Revisited

To address the issue of whether the ICS helps predict consumption, we first use Granger-causality tests in bivariate VARs for various measures of household spending and the ICS to test whether ICS helps predict the change in consumption expenditures. We then use multivariate VARs to test whether the ICS adds to the predictive power of these models once other macroeconomic indicators such as personal disposable income, inflation rate, unemployment rate, stock market returns, and interest rate differentials have been included.

Data

We use monthly data for the sample period January 1978–December 1996. The ICS series was obtained from the University of Michigan's Survey Research Centre. The data on personal consumption expenditures (viz., total, durables, non-durables, and services), unemployment rate, Standard & Poors (S&P) 500 index, and the Conference Board's index of coincident indicators were obtained from Datastream. Data on consumer price index (CPI) inflation came from the Bureau of Labour Statistics, and data on the 6-month T-bill rate, 6-month commercial paper rate, 1-year T-bill rate, and 10-year T-bond rate from the Federal Reserve Board of Governors. The definitions of the variables used in this paper are displayed in Appendix 11.1.

We use the augmented Dickey–Fuller test to detect the presence of unit root in all data series. Stationarity is rejected at the 5% level of significance for all variables defined in Appendix 11.1 except for the two interest rate differentials and the return on S&P 500. We also apply a residual test for cointegration to the regression:

$$C_t = \alpha + \beta' X_t + u_t \tag{11.1}$$

where C_t is one of the consumption variables, and the variables included in X_t for each model are described in Appendix 11.2. For each model, a test for cointegration among the X_t variables and each of the consumption measures—PCE (total), PCED (durable), PCEN (non-durable), and PCES (services)—is carried out. Cointegration is rejected at the 5% level of significance for all models for each of the consumption expenditure measures.

Granger-causality Tests

Since the tests reject the hypothesis of cointegration for all models and all measures of consumption, we examine the Granger-causality relationship between consumption and sentiment in a first-difference framework. We first test for the causal effects of ICS on the various measures of consumption in a bivariate model. We use the following autoregressive distributed lag model to test for Granger-causality:

$$\Delta C_t = \alpha + \beta_1 \Delta C_{t-1} + ... + \beta_p \Delta C_{t-p}$$
$$+ \gamma_1 \Delta ICS_{t-1} + ... + \gamma_p \Delta ICS_{t-p} + \varepsilon_t \qquad (11.2)$$

where C_t is one of PCE_t, $PCED_t$, $PCEN_t$, or $PCES_t$.[2] The results of the test of the hypothesis:

$$H_0: \gamma_1 = \gamma_2 = ... = \gamma_p = 0$$

show sentiment to be Granger-causal to the consumption of durables and services. The addition of lags of the ICS to the regression for growth of durables consumption brings an increase of 0.03 in R^2. For the growth of services consumption the increase is only 0.01. Other components of consumption (that is, total and non-durable) are not affected by ICS.

The Granger-causal relationship of sentiment to consumption of durables and services may be due to the omission of other important factors, which affect the consumption decision. If sentiment is a reflection of only widely-known macroeconomic conditions, then the omission of key macroeconomic indicators such as aggregate disposable income, inflation rate, and interest rate differentials would lead us to falsely conclude that sentiment contains independent information useful for the prediction of consumption growth. To test whether sentiment contains information useful for forecasting consumption growth over and above what is contained in other available macroeconomic indicators, we test the hypothesis that sentiment Granger-causes the growth in each of the four types of consumption spending in the presence of other macroeconomic variables. This amounts to testing the restrictions:

$$H_0 : \gamma_1 = \gamma_2 = ... = \gamma_p = 0$$

in the model:

$$\Delta C_t = \alpha + \beta_1 \Delta C_{t-1} + ... + \beta_p \Delta C_{t-p} + \delta_1' \Delta X_{t-1}$$
$$+ ... + \delta_p' \Delta X_{t-p} + \gamma_1 \Delta ICS_{t-1} + \; + \gamma_p \Delta ICS_{t-p} + \varepsilon_t \qquad (11.3)$$

where the macroeconomic indicators included in the matrix X_t for each model are as described in Appendix 11.2 (interest rate differentials and the return on the S&P 500 are included as levels), and C_t is one of PCE_t, $PCED_t$, $PCEN_t$, or $PCES_t$. Results from these tests are show the Granger-causality effect of ICS on the growth in consumption of durables persists in the presence of lags of inflation rate, unemployment rate, real disposable income, and the index of coincident indicators—implying that sentiment, indeed, captures factors other than the present state of the economy. However, in the presence of the two interest rate differentials and return on the stock market this effect disappears. One possibility is that the information contained in sentiment is also contained in earlier lags of interest rate differentials and the stock market return and, therefore they are all Granger-causal to sentiment and consumption growth, and the effect of sentiment in the bivariate models is due to the omission of these variables. Table 11.1 presents the results of the test of:

$$H_0 : g_1 = g_2 = ... = g_p = 0$$

in the model

$$\Delta ICS_t = \alpha + \beta_1 \, \Delta ICS_{t-1} + ... + \beta_p \, \Delta ICS_{t-p}$$
$$+ \gamma_1 \, y_{t-1} + ... + \gamma_p \, y_{t-p} + \varepsilon_t \qquad (11.4)$$

where y_t is one of 6MCP_6MTB, 10YB_1YTB, or S&P500. The null is rejected for each model at the 5 per cent level of significance. This result strongly supports the hypothesis that sentiment reflects forward-looking information rather than the current state of the economy. The ability of the interest rate spreads to predict business cycle fluctuations with a lead of about 6 months has been well documented in the literature.[3] Although sentiment anticipates some changes in consumption growth as indicated by our bivariate Granger-causality tests, it does so with a shorter lead, thus earlier values of the interest rate differentials already anticipate the information contained in

Table 11.1 Causality Tests of Interest Rate Differentials and Stock Market Returns to ICS

Factor	VAR lag	χ^2 statistic	5% criterion value	F-statistic	5% criterion value
6MCP_6MTB	6	13.55	12.60	2.12	2.14
10YTB_1YTB	5	15.13	11.10	2.88	2.26
S&P500	1	12.53	3.84	12.36	3.89

Source: Computed by authors.

sentiment. The information about expected future real interest rates and the expected path of inflation contained in the term structure seems to be reflected in consumer sentiment.

The result for the stock market return offers some more support for the idea that sentiment reflects consumer optimism. Financial theory postulates that a stock's price reflects the expected future path of dividends on the stock, hence the stock market indexes can be perceived as reflecting expectations on the future path of the stock market return. This information proves useful in predicting consumer sentiment, and with a lead of only 1-month, suggesting that sentiment reflects forward-looking behaviour, rather than current conditions.

Consumption and Sentiment in a Markov-Switching Model

Throop's (1992) finding that sentiment can be explained fairly well at the aggregate level in normal times, but not in times of economic or political uncertainty suggests that the extent of independent information contained in sentiment may differ depending on the general uncertainty of the socio-economic and political environment. As a result, the value of sentiment as a predictor of consumption growth may also vary over time. Therefore, a linear framework would not be the best choice for utilizing this information. A framework, which allows for non-linearities in the effect of sentiment on consumption, such as the Markov switch (MS) models of Hamilton (1990), would allow us to examine this hypothesis.[4]

We start off by extending our linear framework in (11.6) to a two-regime MS model. We specifically focus on models for durables consumption $PCED_t$ and total consumption PCE_t, the latter because of general interest, and the former because our earlier analysis showed it to be most sensitive to sentiment changes. We estimate five different models as shown below:

Model 1

$$\Delta C_t = \alpha_{s_t} + \beta_1 s_t \, \Delta C_{t-1} + \ldots + \beta_p \, s_t \, \Delta C_{t-p} + \gamma_1 \, s_t \, \Delta ICS_{t-1} + \ldots + \gamma_p \, s_t \, \Delta ICS_{t-p} + u_t \quad (11.5)$$

Model 2

$$\Delta C_t = \alpha_{s_t} + \beta_1 s_t \, \Delta C_{t-1} + \ldots + \beta_p \, s_t \, \Delta C_{t-p} + u_t \quad (11.6)$$

Model 3

$$\Delta C_t = \alpha_{s_t} + u_t \tag{11.7}$$

Model 4

$$\Delta C_t = \alpha_{s_t} + \gamma_{1 s_t} \Delta ICS_{t-1} + \ldots + \gamma_{p s_t} \Delta ICS_{t-p} + u_t \tag{11.8}$$

Model 5

$$\Delta C_t = \alpha_{s_t} + \gamma_{1 s_t} \Delta ICS_{t-1} + \ldots + \gamma_{p s_t} \Delta ICS_{t-p} + u_t$$

$$\gamma_{12} = \ldots = \gamma_{p2} = 0 \tag{11.9}$$

In all models $u_t \sim N(0, \sigma_{st}^2)$, $s_t = 1, 2$. For PCE_t^2 the lag length is $p = 1$, and for $PCED_t$ we have $p = 2$.[5] The aim of Model 1 is to differentiate between regimes in which consumption is affected differently by sentiment. Model 2 is used to test the hypothesis that sentiment does not help predict consumption even in a regime-switching framework. Model 3 is a benchmark model of consumption as a random walk with a state-dependent drift. Models 4 and 5 will be used to test the restriction that sentiment helps predict consumption only in certain periods but not in others.[6] Tables 11.2 to 11.4 show the parameter estimates for models 1–3 for PCE_t and $PCED_t$.[7] For both variables, the models distinguish between two distinct regimes. The benchmark model 3 distinguishes between two regimes of the same mean growth but different volatility. The test statistics for testing the hypotheses of equal means and equal variances across states, based on model 3 estimates, are shown in Table 11.5. The hypothesis of equal means cannot be rejected at conventional levels of significance, but the hypothesis of equal variances is rejected even at the 1 per cent level.[8] The rest of the models preserve this differentiation between regimes of low and high volatility of consumption growth.

Models 1 and 2 allow us to conduct a 'Granger-causality' test of sentiment on consumption in an MS framework. The test consists of a likelihood ratio test of the null hypothesis:

$$H_0 = \gamma_{11} = \ldots = \gamma_{p1} = 0, \gamma_{12} = \ldots = \gamma_{p2} = 0 \tag{11.10}$$

As noted in Krolzig (1997), hypothesis testing in MS models can be performed using the usual t, F, and χ^2 tests, as long as the number of regimes remains unchanged under the null and the alternative. Then the test of (11.10) can be carried out using an LR test based on:

$$LR = 2\left[\ln L\left(\hat{\theta}\right) - \ln L\left(\hat{\theta}_r\right)\right] \sim \chi^2(r)$$

Table 11.2: Estimates for Markov-Switch Model 1

	Consumption		Durable	
Coefficients	Regime 1	Regime 2	Regime 1	Regime 2
α	15.430	25.976	3.176	–37.549
	(1.985)	(2.038)	(0.643)	(24.813)
β_1	–0.064	–0.378	–0.366	–2.191
	(0.116)	(0.074)	(0.059)	(0.732)
β_2	–	–	–0.259	0.398
			(0.055)	(0.632)
γ_1	0.801	–0.154	0.279	–30.50
	(0.245)	(0.398)	(0.159)	(13.113)
γ_2	–	–	0.138	–9.877
			(0.157)	(7.384)
σ^2	74.141	358.765	78.597	795.591
	(12.916)	(40.800)	(8.422)	(418.578)
p_{11}	0.993		0.981	
	(0.009)		(0.010)	
p_{22}	0.995		0.570	
	(0.005)		(0.174)	
Log (L)	–726.065		–630.080	

Note: Standard errors shown in parentheses.
Source: Computed by authors.

Table 11.3: Estimates for Markov-Switch Model 2

	Consumption		Durable	
Coefficients	Regime 1	Regime 2	Regime 1	Regime 2
α	14.183	26.405	2.756	16.027
	(1.926)	(2.044)	(0.648)	(17.445)
β_1	0.031	–0.385	–0.247	–1.019
	(0.105)	(0.074)	(0.089)	(0.475)
β_2	–	–	–0.218	–0.638
			(0.059)	(0.352)
σ^2	85.766	359.195	72.527	757.727
	(15.150)	(41.316)	(10.219)	(523.61)
p_{11}	0.992		0.971	
	(0.010)		(0.018)	
p_{22}	0.995		0.678	
	(0.005)		(0.161)	
Log (L)	–733.736		–636.472	

Note: Standard errors shown in parentheses.
Source: Computed by authors.

Table 11.4: Estimates for Markov-Switch Model 3

	Total Consumption		Durable Consumption	
Coefficients	Regime 1	Regime 2	Regime 1	Regime 2
α	17.130	17.550	2.209	1.365
	(0.983)	(4.173)	(0.608)	(2.744)
σ^2	125.885	886.925	53.661	470.678
	(24.108)	(249–136)	(11.326)	(123.539)
p_{11}	0.906		0.964	
	(0.045)		(0.019)	
p_{22}	0.720		0.907	
	(0.112)		(0.055)	
Log (L)	–739.361		–648.950	

Note: Standard errors shown in parentheses.
Source: Computed by authors.

Table 11.5: Tests of Equality of Means and Variances in MS Model 3

Hypothesis	PCE_t	$PCED_t$
$\alpha_1 = \alpha_2$	0.009	0.087
$\sigma_{12} = \sigma_{22}$	10.102	12.579

Note: $\chi^2_{1,0.05} = 3.84$; $\chi^2_{1,010} = 2.71$
Source: Computed by authors.

where $\hat{\theta}$ is the maximum likelihood estimate (MLE) of the model parameters, $\hat{\theta}_r$ is the constrained MLE, and r is the number of restrictions. Table 11.6 shows that the restriction in (11.10) is rejected for both total consumption and durables consumption. Therefore, sentiment does help predict $PCED_t$ and even PCE_t in this regime-switching framework.

A related question is whether sentiment has a differential impact on $PCED_t$ and PCE_t in the two regimes. In the interest of parsimony we omit lagged consumption terms and estimate model 4 for both consumption measures, and carry out a test of:

$$H_0 : \gamma_{i1} = \gamma_{i2}, i = 1, \dots, p \tag{11.11}$$

Table 11.7 shows the Wald test statistics and critical values. The hypothesis of equal sentiment coefficients in both regimes is rejected at

Table 11.6: Test of Causality of Sentiment of Consumption in MS Model 1

Model 1	χ^2 statistic	d.f.	5% criterion value
PCE_t	15.342	2	5.99
$PCED_t$	12.784	4	9.49

Source: Computed by authors.

the 5% level for total consumption. For durables, the hypothesis of equal coefficients on lag 1 is not rejected, but the equality of lag 2 coefficients is rejected at the 10% level.

Table 11.7: Wald Test Statistics for H0 : $\gamma_{i1} = \gamma_{i2}$, $i = 1, \ldots, p$

Hypothesis	PCE_t	$PCED_t$
$\gamma_{11} = \gamma_{12}$	4.261	1.826
$\gamma_{21} = \gamma_{22}$	–	2.813

Note: $\chi^2_{1,005} = 3.84$; $\chi^2_{1,0.10} = 2.71$
Source: Computed by authors.

Since the coefficients on sentiment lags in the low-volatility regime are insignificant for both total consumption and durables consumption, we impose this restriction explicitly as:

$$H_0 : \gamma_{11} = \ldots = \gamma_{p1} = 0 \qquad (11.12)$$

and estimate model 5. To test the restriction (11.12) we again use a LR test. Table 11.8 shows the test statistics. For both $PCED_t$ and PCE_t the restrictions are rejected at the 5% level. Interestingly, regime 2 coefficients of sentiment on durables are much larger in magnitude

Table 11.8 LR Statistics for Testing $\gamma_{11} = \ldots = \gamma_{p1} = 1$

Hypothesis	PCE_t	$PCED_t$
$\gamma_{11} = 0$	4.284	–
$\gamma_{11} = \gamma_{21} = 0$	–	11.152

Note: $\chi^2_{1,005} = 3.84$; $\chi^2_{2,0.05} = 5.99$
Source: Computed by authors.

than those in regime 1, and are of opposite signs possibly due to lagged adjustment (see Table 11.2).

The dates for the two regimes were determined using the probabilities from the MS filter. Since we only discriminate between two regimes, we take the process to be in regime j if

$$P\{S_t = j|\Psi_{t-1}\} > 0.5$$

where $\Psi_{t-1} = \{\Delta C_{t-1}, \Delta C_{t-2}, \ldots, \Delta ICS_{t-1}, \Delta ICS_{t-2}, \ldots\}$. For the benchmark model 3, the probability that state 2 (high volatility) will persist is $p_{22} = 0.671$ for PCE_t and $p_{22} = 0.679$ for $PCED_t$, which implies an average length of regime 2 periods of three months. Indeed, for both consumption measures, regime 2 comes in several short spurts. Since the consumption of durables is the most volatile component of total consumption expenditures, and much of the volatility in ΔPCE_t is due to volatility in $\Delta PCDE_t$, of special interest are periods when both processes appear to be in the high volatility, and the effect of sentiment is strong. Through our MS model, those periods are identified as September 1986–March 1987, December 1989–February 1990, February 1991–April 1991, and December 1995–February 1996. It is interesting to note that using dummy variables, Throop (1992) also identified a few short periods (for example, Nixon wage-price controls, Arab oil embargo, Carter credit controls, 1986 stock market crash, and the Gulf war) when the relationship between ICS and its determinants became temporarily unstable. Note that with quarterly data, the identification of high volatility regime 2 would be impossible. We should, however, point out that the *ex ante* predictive ability of sentiment in the high volatility regime is rather limited in view of the fact that the average length of this regime where sentiment seems to be most potent is just three months. Nevertheless, without the MS model, the impact of ICS on components of consumption during Regime 1 will be miscalculated as well.

The period September 1986–March 1987 in the US was not preceded or marked by unusual political events, but was characterized by a number of conflicting economic factors which caused significant volatility in durables consumption growth. Following Oil Producing and Exporting Countries (OPEC) members' formal abandonment of production quotas in late 1985, petroleum prices plunged to their lowest levels in a decade during the third quarter of 1986, and the energy prices followed. Interest rates also declined throughout the year, reaching their lowest levels in nearly a decade. This was accompanied by extensive sales-incentive programmes for motor vehicles, and as a result durable consumption surged. When these programmes were terminated at the beginning of the last quarter of 1986, durable expenditures fell sharply. However, in October 1986 the Tax Reform Act was signed into law. This caused an upsurge in consumer durables spending in December 1986 in response to provisions of the act which affected deductions for sales taxes and loan interest payments. Although sentiment was not marked by any unusual volatility during this period, its movements were closely related to those of durables consumption.

A number of conflicting factors caused consumption volatility in the February 1989–February 1990 episode. Rising consumer prices caused a 25 per cent drop in $PCED_t$ at the end of 1989. Inflation rose to its highest level in eight years at the beginning of 1990. However, generous sales incentives programmes boosted auto and durables sales, and spending increased nearly as much as it had dropped at the end of 1989. Consumer sentiment declined steadily in the last four months of 1989, which possibly reflected increasing consumer prices.

The period February 1991–April 1991 coincides with the beginning of the recovery after the last US recession. After a considerable drop in ICS during August 1990–October 1990, which was reflected in a consistent decline in consumption spending, it surged to its pre-recession levels after the successful completion of the Gulf War. Durables consumption also surged sharply, reflecting mostly motor vehicle sales increase. Throop (1992) showed that during this period the relationship between ICS and its determinants changed abruptly, and that during the Gulf war period, ICS had a very significant impact on consumption of durables.

The period December 1995–February 1996 exhibits entirely different characteristics. It was preceded by a drop in the ICS to its lowest level in two years in November 1995. Considering the sensitivity of sentiment to the public's perception of government economic policy, the likely culprits for the drop are the shutdowns of Federal Government in the fourth quarter of 1995. The drop in sentiment was translated into a drop in motor vehicle consumption in the period January 1996–February 1996.

We cannot generalize the strong relationship between sentiment and consumption to recessions, or even recession turning points. There are two other recession periods in the early 1980's in our sample which fall entirely in the low volatility, weak consumption-sentiment regime. However, what we find is that past changes in consumer sentiment can forecast consumption changes when a multitude of political and socio-economic factors generate wide swings in consumption. This relationship is stronger for durables consumption. Such periods appear to be sporadic and of short duration in our sample. Therefore, it is useful to compare the forecasting performance of the linear models described at the beginning of this paper, and the MS model 1 based on past consumption and sentiment changes. We compute the in-sample predictions for ΔC_t based on filter probabilities from the MS model 1 as:

$$f_t^{MS} = E(\Delta C_t \mid \Psi_{t-1}) = P(s_t = 1 \mid \Psi_{t-1}) E(\Delta C_t \mid s_t = 1, \Psi_{t-1})$$
$$+ P(s_t = 2 \mid \Psi_{t-1}) E(\Delta C_t \mid s_t = 2, \Psi_{t-1})$$

For the linear model, the projection is simply $f_t^L = E(\Delta C_t \mid \Psi_{t-1})$. We compute the root mean squared error (RMSE) of these projections as

$$\text{RMSE} = \sqrt{\frac{(\Delta C_t - f_t)2}{T}}$$

where f_t is one of f_t^{MS} or f_t^L and T is the actual number of observations used to estimate the models and compute the projections. Table 11.9 shows the RMSE for both models and both consumption measures. As expected, the improvement in forecasting power is greater for durables, and more modest for total consumption.

Table 11.9: RMSE for Linear and MS Models for PCEt and PCEDt

Model	PCE_t	$PCED_t$
Linear	16.869	11.559
MS	16.474	10.088

Source: Computed by authors.

It is reasonable, however, at this point to revisit the question whether the significance of sentiment in the Markov-switching models is due to omitted third factors. We previously discovered that sentiment was reduced to insignificance in the VAR models by the inclusion of interest rate term spreads and stock market returns. We now test whether sentiment Granger-causes consumption and durables growth in the presence of l0YTB_1YTB, 6MCP_6MTB, or S&P500. This amounts to testing the null:

$$H_0 : \gamma_{11} = \ldots = \gamma_{p1} = 0, \gamma_{12} = \ldots = \gamma_{p2} = 0 \qquad (11.13)$$

in the model:

$$\Delta C_t = \alpha_{s_t} + \beta_1 s_t \, \Delta C_{t-1} + \ldots + \beta_p \, s_t \, \Delta C_{t-p} + \gamma_1 s_t \, \Delta ICS_{t-1}$$

$$+ \ldots + \gamma_p s_t \Delta_t \left(CS_{t-p} \right) + \delta_1 s_t X_{t-1} + \ldots + \delta_p s_t X_{t-p} + u_t$$

where $u_t \sim N(0, \sigma_{st}^2)$, $s_t = 1, 2$; X_t is one of 10YTB_1YTB, 6MCP_6MTB, or SP500, and ΔC_t is one of $\Delta PCED_t$ or ΔPCE_t.[9] A small chi-square value suggests evidence in favour of the null that the ICS has no independent predictive power in the presence of the particular X_t variable. The likelihood ratio statistics for testing the hypothesis in (11.13) are shown in Table 11.10. The hypothesis of no Granger causality of sentiment to consumption in the presence of interest rate spreads is accepted at the 1% level (5% for durables). Stock market returns also reduce sentiment to insignificance at the 1% level in the consumption model, but not for durables. For our purpose, it is sufficient to note that in the presence of S&P500 in the PCE equation and the two spreads in the PCED, equation ICS loses its independent explanatory power in predicting consumption. Thus, the finding that both spreads and stock returns eliminate the usefulness of sentiment as predictor of consumption can be generalized to the class of Markov-switching models as well.

Table 11.10: Test of Granger Causality of Sentiment on Consumption in the Presence of X_t

		PCE_t		$PCED_t$
X_t	d.f.	χ^2	d.f.	χ^2
10YTB_1YTB	2	7.802	4	3.740
6MCP_6MTB	2	8.782	4	4.406
SP500	2	0.514	4	17.572

Note: $\chi^2_{2,0.05} = 5.99$; $\chi^2_{4,0.05} = 9.49$; $\chi^2_{2,0.01} = 9.21$; $\chi^2_{4,1.01} = 13.28$.
Source: Computed by authors.

Conclusion

Our time series analysis suggests that the confidence index reflects forward-looking expectations, rather than current and past states of the economy. This evidence is consistent with the findings in Ivanova and Lahiri (1998) which are based on cross-sectional data analysis. We found a modest 3 per cent increase in R^2 resulting from the addition of sentiment to the linear model for consumption durables, and no discernible improvement in the models for total consumption and non-durables. Extending the models to allow for two regimes, in which the relationship between sentiment and consumption differs, we found that ICS causes an improvement in the forecasting performance for both total and durables consumption. The regime-switching models differentiate between two regimes of high and low volatility of consumption growth. The high volatility regime is also marked by a very strong relationship between consumption expenditures and sentiment. We conclude that the benefits from including consumer sentiment in models of consumption are the largest in periods when conflicting economics and socio-political factors cause high overall uncertainty and wide swings in near-term expectations of real personal income, and hence wide changes in discretionary consumer spending. However, the *ex ante* ability of sentiment to predict future consumption even in the high volatility regime is rather limited in view of the fact that the average length of this regime where sentiment seems to be most potent is about three months. More importantly, the predictive power of sentiment is reduced almost to the point of insignificance when we include certain forward-looking variables such as interest rate spreads and stock returns in linear as well as Markov-switching models.

Endnotes

1. For a recent contribution on the subject, see Lovell and Tien (2000).

2. The lag length p is determined by an appropriate F-test as described in Hamilton (1994).

3. See for example Estrella and Mishkin (1998), Friendman and Kuttner (1998), and Lahiri and Wang (1996).

4. The Markov-switching (MS) regression framework has been discussed fairly extensively in the literature. Comprehensive sources include Hamilton (1994) for general single-equation models, and Krolzig (1997) for a treatment of MS–VARs. The use of this econometric framework for consumption, however, is new to the literature.

5. In our linear analysis we had 4 lags of sentiment (in first difference) in the model for $PCED_t$. However, due to the large number of regime-dependent parameters when $p = 4$, we could not obtain a global maximum. Therefore,

here we constrain the lag length to 2.

6. It has been noted in the literature that even if the relationship between sentiment and consumption is contemporaneous it may still be useful, since current sentiment is available almost immediately, while consumption is available only with a lag.

7. We do not report estimates for all estimated models for conservation of space.

8. The test statistics for these Wald tests are described in Engel and Hamilton (1990).

9. A large number of regime-dependent parameters tend to create convergence problems, so here we use the same lag length as in models 1–5, and not the lag length established in the linear VAR models.

Appendix 11.1: Variable Definitions

ICS	Index of Consumer Sentiment
PCE	Consumption expenditures, in 1978 dollars (log)
PCED	Consumption expenditures, durables, in 1978 dollars (log)
PCEN	Consumption expenditures, nondurables, in 1978 dollars (log)
PCES	Consumption expenditures, services, in 1978 dollars (log)
DI	Personal disposable income, in 1978 dollars (log)
UNEMP	Unemployment rate
INFL	Inflation rate (monthly rate of change of urban CPI)
ICI	Index of Coincident Indicators
SP500	Return on the S&P 500 index, monthly rate of change
6MCP_6MTB	Spread between 6-month commercial paper and T-Bill rates
10YB_1YTB	Spread between 10-year T-Bond and 1-year T-Bill rates

Appendix 11.2

Explanatory Variables in Models (1) to (8)

Model #	Explanatory variables (*X*)
(1)	ICS
(2)	ICS, UNEMP, INFL
(3)	ICS, UNEMP, INFL, ICI
(4)	ICS, UNEMP, INFL, DI
(5)	ICS, UNEMP, INFL, DI, ICI
(6)	ICS, DI, 6MCP-6MTB
(7)	ICS, DI, 10YB-1YTB
(8)	ICS, UNEMP, INFL, S&P500

References

Bram, L. and S. Ludvigson (1998), 'Does Consumer Confidence Forecast Household Expenditure? A Sentiment Index Horse Race', *Federal Reserve Bank of New York Economic Policy Review*, Vol. 4, pp. 59–78.

Carroll, Christopher D., J. Fuhrer, and D. Wilcox (1994), 'Does Consumer Sentiment Forecast Household Spending? If So, Why?', *American Economic Review*, Vol. 84, pp. 1397–1408.

Engel, C. and J.D. Hamilton (1990), 'Long Swings in the Dollar: Are They in the Data and Do Markets Know It?', *American Economic Review*, Vol. 80, pp. 689–712.

Eppright, D., N. Arguea, and W. Huth (1998), Aggregate Consumer Expectation Indexes as Indicators of Future Consumption Expenditures', *Journal of Economic Psychology*, Vol. 19, pp. 215–35.

Estrella, A. and F.S. Mishkin (1998), 'Predicting US Recessions: Financial Variables as Leading Indicators', *Review of Economics and Statistics*, Vol. 80, pp. 45–61.

Friedman, B.M. and K. N. Kuttner (1998), 'Indicator Properties of the Paper-Bill Spread: Lessons from Recent Experience', *Review of Economics and Statistics*, Vol. 80, pp. 34–44.

Fuhrer, J.C. (1993), 'What Role Does Consumer Sentiment Play in the U.S. Economy?', *New England Economic Review*, January/February, pp. 32–44.

Garner, A. (1991), 'Forecasting Consumer Spending: Should Economists Pay Attention to Consumer Confidence Surveys?', *Federal Reserve Bank of Kansas City Economic Review*, May/June, pp. 57–71.

Hamilton, J.D. (1994), *Time Series Analysis*, Princeton: Princeton University Press.

—— (1990), 'Analysis of Time Series Subject to Changes in Regime', *Journal of Econometrics*, Vol. 45, pp. 39–70.

Ivanova, D. and K. Lahiri (1998), 'A Time Series and Cross Sectional Analysis of the Index of Consumer Sentiment and Its Components', in K.H. Oppenlander and G. Poser (Eds), *Social Structural Change—Consequences for Business Cycle Surveys* (pp. 337–62), Aldershot England: Ashgate Publishing.

Krolzig, H.M. (1997), *Markov-switching Vector Autoregressions*, Berlin: Springer.

Lahiri, K. and J.G. Wang (1996), 'Interest Rate Spreads as Predictors of Business Cycles', in G. S. Maddala and C. R. Rao (Eds), *Handbook of Statistics*, Vol. 14, pp. 297–315, Amsterdam: Elsevier Science.

Lovell, M. C. and P. Tien (2000), 'Economic Discomfort and Consumer Sentiment', *Eastern Economic Journal*, Vol. 26, pp. 1–8.

Mishkin, F.S. (1978), 'Consumer Sentiment and Spending on Durable Goods', *Brookings Papers on Economic Activity*, 1978, Vol. 1, pp. 217–31.

Throop, A.W. (1992), 'Consumer Sentiment: Its Causes and Effects', *Federal Reserve Bank of San Francisco Economic Review*, 1992, Vol. 1, pp. 35–59.

12

Some Possibilities for Indicator Analysis in Economic Forecasting

Lawrence R. Klein and
Suleyman Ozmucur

Structural Models and Indicator Analysis

Our long-standing conviction remains intact that detailed structural model building is the best kind of system for understanding the macro economy through its causal dynamic relationships, specified by received economic analysis. There are, however, some related approaches, based on indicator analysis that are complementary for use in high frequency analysis. For most economies, the necessary database for structural model building, guided by consistent social accounting systems (national income and product accounts (NIPA), input–output accounts (IO), national balance sheets) are, at best, available only at annual frequencies. Many advanced industrial countries can provide the accounts at quarterly frequencies, but few, if any, can provide them at monthly frequencies.

A more complete understanding of cyclical and other turbulent dynamic movements might need even higher frequency observation, that is, weekly, daily, or real time. It would not be impossible to construct a structural model from monthly data, but a great deal of interpolation and use of short cut procedures would be needed; so we have turned to a specific kind of indicator method to construct econometric models at this high frequency. No doubt, systems of monthly accounts of national income and product will become available, in due course, for construction of complete structural models, and indicator analysis will probably then be used for even higher frequency, say, for a weekly model.

In a festschrift volume, honouring the business cycle indicator research of Geoffrey H. Moore, there is already a chapter that shows how leading indicators, that he found to be useful, already appear in some form or other in quarterly structural models.[1] This represents an ex-post treatment, in the sense that many forward-looking variables were quite naturally and understandably used in quarterly model construction and some turned out to be among the leading indicators that Geoffrey Moore had developed, quite independently.

In step with new technological developments in the information sector of modern economies, attention has been paid to the use of newly available computer power, data resources, telecommunication facilities and other technical changes that make higher frequency analysis of economic statistics possible.

In a few countries, new methods of high frequency analysis (monthly or higher) have already been applied and are entirely plausible for India, where data collection and thriving 'new economy' activities have been firmly established.[2] There are excellent structural models available for India, and these have been applied on an annual basis for economic analysis (forecasting, policy implementation, and quantitative historical analysis).[3] There have also been studies that use indicators (as in the present volume). It remains to examine how these two approaches may be used in a complementary way.

A Suggested Indicator Approach

The emphasis on leading, coincident, and lagging indicators for spotting or interpreting cyclical phases is very interesting, but this methodology seems to extract less from the data than is plausible, certainly less than can be sought with the new technologies. It is not purely a matter of the contribution of each individual series, examined one at a time, in trying to unfold the cyclical story, but more a matter of trying to interpret the collective message (or signal) of the group as a whole. Much of macroeconometric model building focuses attention on the final adding-up to obtain total gross domestic product (GDP) or some related aggregates from the system as a whole, at the same time that the parts are examined.

The phases of the cycle that are generated by a combination of specific shocks, together with aggregate signals, may be due to shifting forces, sometimes on the demand side, sometimes on the supply side, sometimes from pressures in market-clearing, sometimes from natural cause; sometimes from geo-political causes, sometimes from cumulative effects of small random errors, and so on. It seems to be too narrow to base ultimate decision making on 10-15 sensitive leaders, particularly for their timing.

Short of building the ultimate high-frequency model with many potential inlets of disturbance to the economy, our approach is to measure the collective impact of several high frequency indicators at many closely spaced time intervals—weekly or even daily in this high, interconnected global environment, and let their aggregate measured impact show where the economy is going. Both timing and magnitude will matter, and the specific indicators that account for observed change need not always be the same. We are looking for a generalization of the traditional indicator approach. To be specific, we collect and combine the joint effects of 20 to 30 (or even more) high frequency indicators. Each is separately measured, but the signal evolves from an aggregative measure.

We propose to form principal components of the monthly indicators whose periodic values appear at either different or similar time points of each month. An indicator will be denoted as:

I_{it} = the i–th indicator value at month t where $i = 1, 2, \ldots, 30$

The actual number of indicators will depend on the status of the data files of the economy being studied, and 30 need not be the limit of what can be used.

Another kind of variable will be an anticipatory or expectational variable, giving some subjective impression in advance, based on sampling human populations. Surveys of ordinary households, investing households, business executives, or possibly public officials may be used. These will be written as:

S_{it} = sample survey response of the i–th economic agent at month t. The agents are asked to respond to future intentions or judgments, to contemporary or recent feelings or intentions.

The outcome of the economic decision will be X_{it} = i–th economic measurement or outcome such as consumer spending by households, business production or capital formation by firms, or financial market price averages by investors.

Having formed principal components of relevant indicators, we plan to regress important substantive variables jointly on sample survey indexes, allowing lagged (carry-over) effects from earlier sample results, generally of the most recent past months, as well as the current month, and also upon those principal components that show significant relationships with the chosen substantive variables (consumer spending, industrial production, capital formation, or financial market averages).

It is noteworthy that these substantive variables constitute some of the important coincident indicators of the US economy, while consumer surveys are one of the leading indicators of the US economy, as are the financial market (that is, the stock market) averages.

Principal components is a well-known technique often used in social and psychological measurement.[4] If we write the i–th principal component

$$PC_{it} = \sum_{i=1}^{30} \gamma_i I_{it}$$

our procedure can be stated as one that estimates regression relationships between the specific economic variables that we want to project and the principal components, which, in turn, are based on the primary indicators.

$$PC_{it} = \sum_{j=1}^{n_i} \alpha_{ij} PC_{jt} + \beta_{iq} S_{t-q} + e_{it}$$

$n_i < 30$, is the subset of principal components that are found to be significantly related to X_{it}, a magnitude that we are trying to project. S_{q-t} is the coefficient of a relevant survey index referring to the q–th period (lag). In many cases we distribute the lag in St over a few recent months. And e_{it} is random error.

Simultaneously, in estimating the coefficients in the above relationship we also represent eit as an ARIMA process:

$$e_{it} = \sum_{j=1}^{3} \rho_{ij} e_{it-j} + \sum_{j=1}^{3} \mu_{ij} u_{it-j}$$

where both e_{it} and u_{it} are independent random variables. The 'noise' in this process comes from e_{it}.

There is much data processing and analysis in these various steps, but the structure of the system also pays a lot of attention to the underlying structure of the social accounts. It is not a purely empirical approach. In particular, it depends very much on the structure of a social accounting system, involving NIPA, IO, and flow-of-funds accounts (F/F). It should be noticed that appropriate accounting balance among these three accounts requires that GDP, which is close to, but not directly identified as the end result of aggregate economic activity, is a very important summary statistic, which is the objective of much economic analysis. It is well-known that GDP can be expressed as the sum of all final expenditures, as shown in the NIPA system. This represents the demand side of the economy. But GDP can also be expressed as the sum of all payments to the primary factors of production that are responsible for aggregate output. The primary factors are labor, capital, land, and public services. This represents the supply side of the economy. The sum of all primary factor payments can also be evaluated for each sector of the economy as the sum, sector-by-sector, of gross sector output less intermediate sector output, to obtain sectoral value-added. These totals can be computed from a full IO table. By double entry accounting principles, the independent computation of these three estimates of GDP should be identical, but errors and omissions of observations infiltrate each method in practice, so that the three sums do not necessarily agree. They may differ from each other by at least as much as one or two per cent, and this can be important, especially since it does not turn out to be a random variable; therefore in choosing indicator variables, there must be strong representation from the demand side of the accounts, from the supply side, and from sectoral production flows. Also there should be consistency with the F/F accounts, dealing with saving and investment balances, from which indicators can be extracted.

The accounting balances arise from double-entry book keeping and even from quadruple-entry book keeping in the F/F accounts, which are important for financial market clearing. Hence, the indicator list should contain interest rates, inflation rates, exchange rates, and prices of factor inputs. In the applications, described here, the diversification of indicators follows these principles very carefully.

Also, since the objectives are forecasting, there should be indicators for the future, in the form of forward and futures market variables in addition to the anticipatory components of sample surveys. In this sense, a great deal of economic analysis goes into the selection of indicators.

We form principal components of indicators by extracting the characteristic root of correlation matrices among indicator values. The normalized variables in correlation analysis avoid sensitivity to units of measurement.

We choose dependent variables that are jointly associated with the indicator variables and with sample survey structures; thus we determine which principal components are significantly related, for example, to (i) real consumer expenditures, (ii) industrial production, (iii) employment, and (iv) stock market averages. These are shown in the examples, presented below, but we could equally well have used other dependent variables. The four that are selected above are clearly identified with the traditional indicator analysis of the National Bureau of Economic Research (NBER) and are available at monthly (or higher) frequency in the US. Since the terrorist attacks of 11 September, 2001 in the US, it has been widely noted that these variables have all had key roles in supporting the US economy in an entirely new environmental situation, and we have been following their patterns, month-by-month, in regularly updated studies of their movement on the basis of equations that affect the general economy, people's attitudes, and stochastic, dynamic (ARIMA) error terms.

It should be noted that the use of principal components by Nagar and his associates has been related to latent variables, that are not directly measured. In our work, we use objective estimates of variables, such as those listed above and are not forced to define what the principal components express, such as 'quality of life'. That type of study is, of course, equally important, but it is different.

An important early use of principal components, though not expressly for indicator analysis, was introduced by Richard Stone, more than 50 years ago. He regressed objective measured variables on components, for his purposes of analysis.[5]

Some Examples

Each of the four relationships noted in the previous section have been estimated using principal components of economy-wide indicators and a corresponding sample survey. The first relates real consumer expenditures to selected principal components (selected on the basis of statistical significance), to the University of Michigan monthly survey of consumer sentiment and an ARIMA of the error term. The Michigan Survey has been available monthly since the

1970s. Following the regression of the designated series to be explained, we present diagnostic test statistics for serial correlation and normality of distribution of residuals. These are followed by extrapolation of the dependent variable from equations that are re-estimated every month, up to the last month prior to extrapolation. Each re-estimated equation is extrapolated one-month ahead. The regression that is presented is only the last case in the sequence of re-estimates. The specification remains unchanged in this sequence.

The consumption equation estimated most recently is given in Appendix 12.1. We are reporting results on consumption only for sake of brevity. The equation is estimated with 295 monthly observations from May 1978 to November 2002 (Equation A 12.1). The equation includes thirteen principal components, which account for over 75 per cent of the variation in 27 indicators, a polynomial distributed lag of the Michigan index of consumer sentiment, and a moving average process of residuals.

Indicators used for personal consumption expenditures are: new orders, housing starts, real value of construction put in place, number of building permits, average hourly earnings, average hours worked, consumer price index, producer price index, real retail sales, trade-weighted real exchange rate, real money supply, real consumer credit, S and P 500 index, Dow-Jones index, real personal income, index of industrial production, non-agricultural employment, manufacturing and trade sales (all variables considered in terms of percentage change); inventory/sales ratio, ratio of budget revenues to budget expenditures, unemployment rate, federal funds rate, prime rate, corporate bond rate, 3-month treasury bill rate, 1-year bond yield, 10-year bond yield (all variable considered in terms of change).

The determination coefficient (R^2) for the equation is 0.71, and all parameters associated with the principal components are significant at the 5% level, most of them at the 1% level. The Michigan index of consumer sentiment is significant at the 6% level. The actual, fitted and residual diagram indicates the degree of closeness of fit. In addition, the Durbin–Watson statistics (1.97), Ljung–Box–Pierce *Q* statistics (6.04 for 12 lags) and Breusch–Godfrey Lagrange multiplier tests for 12 lags ($\chi^2 = 6.68$) indicate that there is no serial correlation in residuals. Engle's ARCH test indicates that there is no autoregressive conditional heteroscedasticity ($\chi^2 = 0.4$). Residuals are not only random, but they also are normally distributed, as indicated by the low Jarque-Bera statistic ($\chi^2 = 4.48$).

These tests are based on the final equation estimated (the longest sample). In order to test the forecasting power of the model, the equation is first estimated using data from May 1978 to July 2001, and the real consumption expenditure is extrapolated for August 2001. The equation is then estimated using data from May 1978 to August 2001, and the real consumption expenditure is extrapolated for September 2001. The process has been continued up to the latest data point available (November 2002). This is as close as one can get to the test of the one-period ahead ex-ante forecasting power of the model. There is a close relationship between actual and extrapolated real consumption expenditures (Table A 12.1). Correlation between the actual and extrapolated values exceeds 0.9 (Figure A1). One-period ahead forecast errors are well below one per cent, with the exception of April 2002. Mean absolute per cent error (MAPE) is 0.41.

Twenty-six indicators are used to calculate principal components to be used in the prediction of the monthly index of industrial production. These indicators are: new orders, housing starts, real value of construction put in place, number of building permits, average hourly earnings, average hours worked, consumer price index, producer price index, real retail sales, trade-weighted real exchange rate, real money supply, real consumer credit, S and P 500 index, Dow-Jones index, real personal income, non-agricultural employment, manufacturing and trade sales (all variables in terms of percentage change); inventory/sales ratio, ratio of budget revenues to budget expenditures, unemployment rate, federal funds rate, prime rate, corporate bond rate, 3-month treasury bill rate, 1-year bond yield, 10-year bond yield (all variables in terms of change).

The final equation estimated using 349 observations (November 1973–November 2002) includes ten principal components, which account for over 50 per cent of the variation in 26 monthly indicators, the composite index of the Institute for Supply Management (ISM), and autoregressive processes of residuals. The R^2 for the equation is 0.69, and all parameters associated with the principal components and the index are significant at the 5% level, most of them at the 1% level (Equation A 12.2). Residuals are normally distributed, with no serial correlation. One-period ahead forecast errors are well below one per cent, with the exception of July 2002. MAPE is 0.42.

Twenty-six indicators are used to calculate principal components to be used in the prediction of monthly employment. These indicators are: new orders, housing starts, real value of construction put in place, number of building permits, average hourly earnings, average hours worked, consumer price index, producer price index, real retail sales, trade-weighted real exchange rate, real money supply, real consumer credit S and P 500 index, Dow-Jones index, real personal income, manufacturing and trade sales (all variables in terms of percentage change) inventory/sales ratio, ratio of budger revenues to budget expenditures, federal funds rate, prime rate, corporate bond rate, 3-month treasury bill rate, 1-year bond yield, 10-year bond yield, 20-year bond yield, and new claims for unemployment insurance (all variables in terms of change).

The final equation estimated using 357 observations (March 1973–November 2002) includes seven principal components, which account for over 55 per cent of the variation in twenty-six monthly indicators, the employment index of the ISM, and autoregressive and moving average processes of residuals (Equation A 12.3). The R^2 for the equation is 0.64, and all parameters associated with principal components and the index are significant at the 5% level, most of them at the 1% level. There is no serial correlation in residuals, but the Jarque-Bera test indicates that they are not normally distributed, and Engle's test indicates that there is autoregressive-conditional heteroscedasticity. One-period ahead forecast errors are quite low. The MAPE is 0.075 which corresponds to an employment of 100,000.

Thirty indicators are used to calculate principal components to be used in the prediction of the monthly average of the stock market index (the S and P Index). These indicators are: new orders, unfilled orders, housing starts, real value of construction put in place, number of building permits, average hourly earnings, average hours worked, consumer price index, producer price index, real retail sales, trade-weighted real exchange rate, export/import ratio, real money supply, real consumer credit, real personal income, index of industrial production, non-agricultural employment, manufacturing and trade sales, expected inflation, measured as the difference between the yields of indexed and non-indexed treasury notes (all variables considered in terms of percentage change); inventory/sales ratio, ratio of budget revenues to budget expenditures, unemployment rate, federal funds rate, prime rate, corporate bond rate, 3-month treasury bill rate, 1-year bond yield, 10-year bond yield, 20-year bond yield, mortgage rate (all variables considered in terms of change).

The final equation estimated using 65 observations (July 1997–November 2002) includes seven principal components, which account for over 50 per cent of the variation in 30 monthly indicators, the UBS index of investor optimism, and autoregressive and moving average processes of residuals (Equation A 12.4). The R^2 for the equation is 0.77, and all parameters associated with the principal components and the index are significant at the 1% level, with the exception of P10 which is significant only at the 13% level. Residuals are normally distributed, but there is serial correlation according to the LM statistic. One-period ahead forecast errors are below five per cent, with two exceptions: September 2001 (15.89 per cent), and January 2002 (8.73 per cent). The MAPE is 4.1.

Conclusion

Many indicators are helpful in improving statistical performance for forecasting and policy analysis. We do believe, however, that no single indicator (or type of indicator) can do the necessary work by itself. The principal components—which are estimated linear functions of the whole set of indicators that we choose to represent the movement of the economy as a whole—methodology is used as a short-cut and quick method to a full scale structural econometric model.

Timeliness, flexibility, and foresight are important properties of indicators, and we are especially interested in information that reflects the subjective feelings of participants in the economy. Results of surveys covering consumers, producers or managers are useful in forecasting major macroeconomic variables, such as personal consumption expenditures, industrial production, employment, and financial market averages. Our results indicate that models including survey results perform better than those that do not include survey results.

In the US, there was extreme uncertainty following the terrorist attack of 11 September, 2001. Many conflicting judgements were expressed in the financial media concerning consumption, the largest single expenditure component in GDP. Our use of the model presented here has enabled sensible, objective forecasts to be made in advance of each month since then.

Endnotes

[1]See Klein (1990).
[2]Klein (2000).
[3]Mammen (1999) and Palanivel and Klein (2002).
[4]See Nagar and Basu (1999).
[5]See Stone (1947).

APPENDIX 12.1

Equation A 12.1

DLOG(CONSUMPTION) *100 = 0.255 + 0.136 I2 – 0.062 I3
(26.06) (15.10) (– 5.71)
+ 0.029 I4 + 0.060 I6 + 0.038 I8 – 0.067 I9 + 0.087 I12 + 0.238 I13
(2.12) (2.98) (2.34) (-3.64) (4.54) (9.52)
+ 0.062 I14 + 0.148 I15 – 0.088 I17 + 0.094 I18 – 0.134 I19
(3.25) (5.10) (–3.14) (2.91) (–3.95)
+ 0.00631 D (MICHIGAN) + 0.00473 D (MICHIGAN (–1)) + 0.00315
(1.89) (1.89) (1.89)
D (MICHIGAN(–2)) + 0.00158 D (MICHIGAN (–3)) – 0.437 MA (1)
(1.89) (–7.72)

R^2 = 0.709, SEE = 0.303, F = 45.22, D.W. = 1.973, Jarque-Bera = 4.48, Ljyung-Box Q (2) = 0.05, Q (12) = 6.04, Breusch-Godfrey LM (2) = 1.51, LM (12) = 6.68, ARCH (1) = 0.40, n = 295 (May 1978-November 2002)

Notes: I2, I3, …I19 are the selected principal components, and MA(1) the moving average error term.

Equation A 12.2

DLOG(INDPRODUCTION) *100 = 0.20 + 0.129 A1 + 0.145 A2
(3.74) (14.91) (9.94)
– 0.111 A3 – 0.128 A4 – 0.134 A5 + 0.049 A6 – 0.072 A7 + 0.069 A9
(–5.78) (–7.98) (–6.82) (3.13) (–2.72) (2.54)
+ 0.118 A15 – 0.101 A18 + 0.0336 D(ISM) + 0.0252 D(ISM(–1))
(3.31) (–2.51) (4.72) (4.72)
+ 0.0168 D(ISM(–2)) + 0.0084 D(ISM(–3)) – 0.181 AR(1) + 0.162 AR(3)
(4.72) (4.72) (–3.34) (2.95)
+ 0.181 AR (4) + 0.142 AR(5) + 0.168 AR(6) + 0.115 AR(9)
(3.02) (2.56) (3.47) (2.26)

R^2 = 0.691, SEE = 0.407, F = 43.48, D.W. = 1.987, Jarque-Bera = 2.97, Jyung-Box Q (2) = 1.83, Q (12) = 5.85, Breusch-Godfrey LM (2) = 4.34, LM (12) = 16.82, ARCH (1) = 1.55, n = 349 (November 1973-November 2002)

Notes: A1, …A18 are the principal components, and AR(1)...AR(9) are the autoregressive errors.

Equation A 12.3

D(EMPLOYMENT) = – 641.3 + 30.015 Z2 + 11.892 Z5 – 19.754 Z6
(– 6.96) (8.27) (2.08) (– 3.66)
+ 14.218 Z11 – 20.512 Z13 – 31.66 Z14 + 22.737 Z19 + 6.752
(2.00) (– 2.04) (–3.17) (1.89) (9.13)
ISM_EMP (–1) + 5.064 ISM_EMP (–1) + 3.3763 ISM_EMP (–2)
(9.13) (1.89)
+ 1.6881 ISM_EMP (–3) + 0.945 AR (1) – 0.843 MA (1)
(1.89) (30.67) (–12.52)

R^2 = 0.643, SEE = 123.12, F = 62.40, D.W. = 2.14, Jarque-Bera = 444.4, Jyung-Box Q (2) = 4.84, Q (12) = 7.80, Breusch-Godfrey LM (2) = 4.53, LM (12) = 7.79, ARCH (1) = 59.0, n = 357 (March 1973–November 2002).

Notes: Z2, Z5, … Z19 are the principal components, and AR (1) …MA (1)–autoregressive-moving average error terms.

Equation A 12.4

DLOG (SANDP500) *100 = 0.716 + 0.141 P1 + 0.496 P5 – 0.983 P8
(21.39) (3.86) (6.00) (-4.16)
+ 0.371 P10 + 1.852 P17 + 2.647 P18 + 3.103 P21 + 0.157 D (UBS)
(1.54) (3.36) (9.38) (6.82) (18.44)
+ 0.118 D (UBS (–1)) + 0.078 D (UBS (–2)) + 0.039 D (UBS (–3))
(18.44) (18.44) (18.44)
– 0.84 AR (2) – 0.54 AR (4) – 0.71 MA (1) – 0.272 MA (3) – 0.518
(–7.75) (–4.30) (–4.81) (–2.85) (–9.76)
MA (5) + 0.516 MA (8)
(3.46)

R^2 = 0.774, SEE = 2.233, F = 12.25, D.W. = 2.346, Jarque-Bera = 0.67, Jyung-Box Q (2) = 2.79, Q (12) = 10.92, Breusch-Godfrey LM (2) = 7.26, LM (12) = 22.41, ARCH (1) = 0.87, n = 65 (July 1997–November 2002)

Notes: P1, P5, …P21 are the principal components, and AR (2) …MA (3)-autoregressive-moving average error terms.

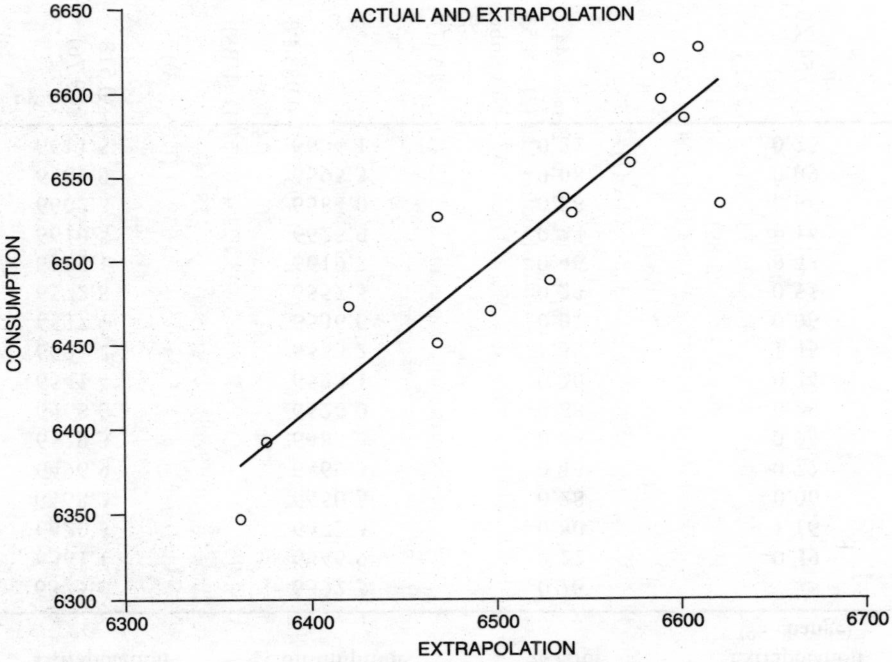

Figure A 12.1: Real Personal Consumption Expenditures—Actual and Extrapolation.
Notes: P1, P5, ..., P21 are the principal components, and AR(2) ... MA(3)–autoregressive moving average error terms.

Table A 12.1: One-period Ahead Extrapolation

Observation	Extrapolation	Consumption	% error	Extrapolation (% change)	Consumption (% change)
2001:08	6375.6	6392.3	-0.26		
2001:09	6361.1	6346.9	0.22	–0.49	–0.71
2001:10	6420.3	6472.3	–0.80	1.16	1.98
2001:11	6468.2	6450.3	0.28	–0.06	–0.34
2001:12	6496.9	6469.3	0.43	0.72	0.29
2002:01	6529.3	6487.4	0.64	0.93	0.28
2002:02	6468.6	6526.0	–0.88	–0.29	0.59
2002:03	6541.4	6528.1	0.20	0.24	0.03
2002:04	6621.2	6533.2	1.35	1.43	0.08
2002:05	6537.1	6536.6	0.01	0.06	0.05
2002:06	6572.8	6557.5	0.23	0.55	0.32
2002:07	6589.1	6619.7	–0.46	0.48	0.95
2002:08	6610.3	6625.9	–0.24	–0.14	0.09
2002:09	6602.3	6584.0	0.28	–0.36	–0.63
2002:10	6589.9	6595.3	–0.08	0.09	0.17
2002:11	6611.5	6626.1	–0.22	0.25	0.47

Source: Computed by author.

References

Klein, Lawrence R. (2000), 'Essay on the Accuracy of Economic Prediction', *International Journal of Applied Economics and Econometrics*, Vol. 9, Spring, pp. 29–69.

—— (1990), 'Cyclical Indicators in Econometric Models', in Philip E. Klein (Ed.), *Analyzing Modern Business Cycles*, pp. 97–106 , Armonk M.E. Sharpe Inc.

Nagar, A.L and Sudip Ranjan Basu (1999), 'Weighting Socio-Economic Indicators of Human Development (A Latent Variable Approach)', National Institute of Public Finance and Policy, New Delhi.

Stone, Richard (1947), 'On the Interdependence of Blocks of Transactions', *Supplement to the Journal of the Royal Statistical Society* Vol. IX, pp. 1, No. 1–45.

Palanivel T., and Lawrence R. Klein (2002), 'Economic Reforms and Growth Prospects in India', in M. S. Ahluwalia *et al.* (Eds), *Macroeconomics and Monetary Policy*, Oxford: Oxford University Press.

Thampy Mammen (1999), *India's Economic Prospects: A Macroeconomic and Econometric Analysis*, Singapore: World Scientific Publishers.

13

Indicators of Business Recessions and Revivals in India 1951–82

Vikas Chitre

Introduction

It is not always possible to come to a definite conclusion about the presence or absence of conditions of business recession or revival by looking at the movement of only one aggregative indicator such as the index of industrial production (even after the influence of trend is removed). The diffusion of the recessionary or the expansionary trends may not be widespread enough particularly in the early stages, and in

The statistical work based on monthly indicators, reported in this paper and most of the write-up of the paper, except the fifth section, were completed by February 1986 (See Chitre 1986). I had the rare privilege to discuss the preliminary results of this study in March 1986 with late Professor Geoffrey H. Moore and Victor Zarnowitz, both leading lights in this field of study, when I visited the US. I am extremely grateful to them for their valuable comments and suggestions.

I am thankful to Pami Dua of Delhi School of Economics, for her having insisted upon my getting this paper prepared for publication. I am extremely happy that Pami Dua and Anirvan Banerji of Economic Cycle Research Institute, New York, have once again revived interest in business cycle research for India.

some cases even in the later stages, and the movement in the index of industrial production of all the commodities may conceal these important incipient or sectoral trends. Moreover, recessionary or expansionary trends are quite often revealed through movements (relative to trend) of economic processes other than production, for example, prices (of industrial raw materials and manufactured products), security prices and yields, change in credit, change in stocks, exports and imports of selected groups of commodities, etc.

In the post-World War II period, cyclical fluctuations in economic activities have been dominated by growing trends. Hence much, if not all, work on business cycles in recent years has been carried out in terms of Burns–Mitchell type of fluctuations in the growth rates of economic activities or in economic activities 'adjusted for their long-run trends.'[1] These have been called growth cycles (see Mintz 1974). Growth cycles based on fluctuations in growth rates of economic activities are termed step cycles while those based on the deviations from the respective long-run trends are called deviation cycles.[2]

Our study of short-run fluctuations in India's economic activity showed that a large number of key economic processes such as net national product outside agriculture, industrial production, factory employment, capital formation by public and private sectors, inventory changes, money stock, bank credit, financial assistance by term lending institutions, interest rates, commodity and security prices, profits of public limited companies, exports, imports, and Reserve Bank of India's holding of foreign securities, show more or less synchronous movements around their respective long-term trends. These movements appear to be sufficiently pervasive, temporally cumulative, and self-reversing to justify our viewing them as exhibiting underlying growth cycles in the overall economic activity, or business cycles adjusted for long-term trends in the economy (See Chitre 1982). In that study based on a number of annual time series, we identified 15 indicators of growth cycles in India and on the basis of these we characterized the Indian economy as having passed through five such growth cycles in overall economic activity during the period from 1951 to 1975.

It was found in studies conducted by the National Bureau of Economic Research (NBER) in the United States that no single series could summarize the cyclical fluctuation of the economy over the entire period of time covered by the study of business cycles.

A major objective of this paper, therefore, is to prepare a

systematic list of indicators of business recessions and revivals in India. The idea is that an index based on these indicators will enable us to conclude with some confidence that the recessionary or revival trends have become sufficiently widespread so that the general situation may be described properly as being one of business recession or revival.

Second, we shall also study the leads and lags of the turning points of the cycle in individual series in relation to the turning points of the cycle in the overall economic activity, the latter being determined by using the index of the above mentioned indicators.

For this purpose, in the present study, we have analysed 94 monthly time series for India for the period 1951–82, the length of each series being determined by the availability of comparable data. The present study of India's business cycles is based on the concept of deviation cycles mentioned earlier.

The statistical analysis to which the data are subjected involves the following steps. First, each series is deseasonalized using the procedure evolved by NBER for this purpose, namely, the X–11 variant of the Census Method II (See Shiskin, Young, and Musgrave 1967). Second, the deseasonalized series is detrended using centred 72-month moving average, and the deviations in each series are obtained, defined as the ratio of actual value of the series to its trend value given by the 72-month moving average of it. Third, the cyclical peaks and troughs in each series are located following a uniform set of rules developed by NBER for this purpose. We have located cyclical turning points of the time series with the help of computer programmes, prepared by us, based on procedures developed by the NBER (see Bry and Boschan 1971, pp. 20–1). The peaks and troughs in the specific economic series mark the cycles in that series and are called specific cycles. The overall business cycle, which is called the reference cycle, describes the alternating periods of expansion and contraction in the overall economic activity separated by turning points, that is, peaks and troughs, in the index of selected indicators of overall economic activity. The reference cycle should reflect the simultaneous expansion and contraction, if any, in major economic processes such as national income, total production, total employment or unemployment, personal income, total consumption, the overall trade, general price index and. Finally, economic indicators of business cycles are classified on the basis of peculiarity of their timing with respect to overall business cycle. The indicators whose turning points coincide with those of the reference cycle are called coincident indicators. The indicators which turn before the turning points of the reference cycle are called leading indicators and those which turn after the turning points of the reference cycle are called lagging indicators. Using this information about the timing relation of major economic processes observed in their past cyclical behaviour, we attempt to arrive at additional short lists of leading, coincident, and lagging economic indicators, consisting of indicators showing a stable lead, coincidence, lag, respectively at the reference cycle peaks and troughs. Separate lists of indicators need to be prepared for peaks and troughs in order to broaden the coverage of economic processes and also to obtain earlier and more regular indicators of recoveries since consistent and sizeable leads at troughs have been less common in recent cycles. These short lists of indicators are expected to be used to forecast downturns and upturns in economic activity in the immediate future. Indeed, the lags in the availability of data on some key indicators being what they are, we might even have to be content with devising a system of leading indicators which could enable us to characterize the current state of overall economic activity appropriately.

Coverage of Time Series and Limitations of Data

While considering the series to be included in the study, those which would be representative of the overall economic activity and would be indicative of turning points of business cycles in India were chosen when they were available on a monthly basis. These series have been listed in Table 13.1. The study examined in all 83 series the number being 94 if broken segments of series are counted as separate series.[4] The break-up of these series, according to the classification given by Geoffrey Moore and Julius Shiskin (1967) which divides the series into eight categories by economic processes, is also given in Table 13.1.

Reference Dates for the Indian Growth Cycle

After considerable experimentation, 11 economic indicators were selected to determine the reference dates that give the cyclical turning points in India's overall economic activity. These indicators have been listed in Table 13.2. The reference dates for the cyclical turning points for India based on these indicators are given in Table 13.3.

Table 13.1 Classification of Included Series according to Economic Process and Breadth of Coverage

Type of Economic Process	Broad Series	Number*	Narrow Series	Number*	Total Number*
Employment and Unemployment		0		2	2
Marginal employment adjustments		—			
Job vacancies	—				
Employment	—		Av. daily number of persons employed in cotton mills (1)		
Unemployment	—		No. of applicants on the live registers of employment exchanges (1)		
Production, income, consumption and trade		1		28	29
Production	General index of industrial production (1)		Sectoral indixes of industrial production (5)		
			Production of individual commodity lines (21)		
Income	—		Railway traffic, total number of wagons loaded (1)		
Consumption and trade	—		Railway traffic, coal and coke wagons loaded (1)		

Contd.

Type of Economic Process	Broad Series	Number*	Narrow Series	Number*	Total Number*
Fixed capital investment		5		1	6
Formation of business enterprises	New companies registered (1)	—			
	Companies liquidated (1)				
	Net addition to registered companies (1)				
New investment commitments	Letters of intent (1)				
	Industrial licenses issued (1)				
Backlog of investment commitments	—		Cement capacity utilization (1)		
Investment expenditure	—				
Inventories and inventory investment		0		0	0
Inventories	—	—			
Inventory investment and purchasing	—	—			
Prices, costs and profits		5		19 (+1)	24 (+1)
Sensitive commodity price indices	—		Domestic gold price (1) +1		
			Domestic price of silver (1)		
Stock price indexes	Index of security prices (government and semi-government securities) (1)				
	Index of security prices				

Contd.

Type of Economic Process	Broad Series	Number*	Narrow Series	Number*	Total Number*
	(preference shares) (1)				
	Index of security prices (ordinary shares) (1)				
Wholesale price indices	Index of wholesale prices (all commodities) (1)		Indexes of wholesale prices for commodity groups (17)		
Retail price indices	—		—		
Unit labour costs	—		—		
Profits and profit margins	Ratio, wholesale price index of manuf. products to industrial raw materials (1)	—			
Money and credit		11 (+9)		4	15 (+9)
Flows of money and credit (Stocks of money and deposits)	Cheque clearance (5)		Changes in bank credit, all scheduled commercial banks, last Friday (1)		
	Money supply, last Friday (1)	+2	Bank credit, all scheduled commercial banks, last Friday (1)		
	Currency with the public (1)	+1	Bank credit, all scheduled commercial banks, average of Fridays (1)		
	Net demand deposits (1)	+2			

Contd.

Type of Economic Process	Broad Series	Number*	Narrow Series	Number*	Total Number*
	Time deposits (1)	+2			
	Other deposits with Reserve Bank of India (1)	+1			
	Aggregate monetary resources (1)	+1			
Bank reserves	—		—		
Money market interest rates	—		Call money rate (1)		
Interest rates on business loans and mortgages Credit	—		—		
difficulties	—				
Foreign trade and payments		5		2 (+1)	7 (+1)
	Value of exports (1)				
	Value of imports (1)		Value of imports, industrial raw materials (1)		
	Quantum of exports (1)				
	Quantum of imports (1)				
	Reserve Bank of India holding of foreign securities (1)		International price of gold	(1)	(+1)
Federal government activities	—		—	0	0
Total Number*		27 (+9)		56 (+2)	83 (+11)

Note: *Additional broken segments in parentheses.

Source: Author.

As Table 13.2 shows, the reference dates based on the 11 monthly indicators listed in Table 13.2—computed by three different methods, namely, the diffusion index, the composite index, and the first principal component index [5]—all yield reference dates which are more or less similar to each other and also match with those identified in the earlier study (Chitre 1982) with the annual time series.

It may be of interest, and possibly also useful, to make explicit the rationale behind the selection of the 11 indicators. *A priori*, we had implicitly started with an impulse—propogation view of the business cycle as well as the growth cycle. The impulse could come from construction activity, investment in machinery and equipment or exports, from any of these sources (listed as the first three indicators in Table 13.2) in isolation or in combination. As this, in turn, stimulates a sympathetic movement in production, key inputs such as intermediate goods, electricity, transport and changes in bank credit (that is, indicators 4–7 in Table 13.2) would show the propogation of the cyclical impulse. When the diffusion of the cyclical movement is sufficiently widespread, it would show up in the cyclical change in the value of (cheque) payments, consumption and import demand, and overall industrial production (indicators 8–11 in Table 13.2). Thus, when the cyclical movement is sufficiently diffused, at least one indicator showing the cyclical impulse, two or three of the indicators showing propogation and two or three indicators showing wider diffusion might be expected to show a change in the direction of cyclical movement, adding to six or more of the eleven indicators. This would show up in the diffusion index locating the turning point of the reference cycle. If the panel is expected to track the turning points of the growth cycle of the non-agricultural sector, it should show up overall industrial production to be a coincidental indicator. Of course, the cyclical movement in all economic processes, including those representing the impulse and those representing propagation and diffusion, takes place more or less synchronously and does not follow a rigid or invariable sequence or timing relation. As it emerged from the statistical analysis of the cyclical behaviour of the indicators, contrary to the time sequence visualized in the above description of the likely sequence of economic processes during the cycle, cheque clearance shows a median lead at peaks and troughs of the overall growth cycle while cement production and railway traffic, (total number of wagons loaded) show a median lag. This means that, empirically, construction

TABLE 13.2: Indicators of Growth-Cyclical Turning Points for India

Name of Series	Period Covered	Median Lead (–) or Lag (+) in Month at Peaks	Median Lead (–) or Lag (+) in Month at Troughs	Timing at Peaks: Leading	Timing at Peaks: Coincident	Timing at Peaks: Lagging	Timing at Troughs: Leading	Timing at Troughs: Coincident	Timing at Troughs: Lagging	Lag in availability (in data months)
Cement production ('000 metric tons)	Jan 51 to Feb 82	+5.0	+10.5			✓	–	–	–	4
Quantum of exports (1970–1 = 100)	Jan 51 to Mar 80	–9.0	+3.0	✓	–	–	–	32		
Index of industrial production, capital goods. (1970 = 100)	Jan 51 to Dec 81	+4.0	-1.5	–	–	–	–	–	–	6
Index of industrial production, intermediate goods (1970 = 100)	Jan 51 to Dec 81	0.0	0.0	–	–	–	–	–	–	6
Electric energy generated (in million kilowatt/hours)	Jan 51 to Sept 81	0.0	-3.0	–	–	–	–	–	–	9
Railway traffic-total no.of wagons loaded (in thousands)	Jan 52 to Dec 81	+6.0	+5.0	–	–	–	–	–	–	6

Contd.

Name of Series	Period Covered	Median Lead (–) or Lag (+) in Month at Peaks	Median Lead (–) or Lag (+) in Month at Troughs	Timing at Peaks: Leading	Timing at Peaks: Coincident	Timing at Peaks: Lagging	Timing at Troughs: Leading	Timing at Troughs: Coincident	Timing at Troughs: Lagging	Lag in availability (in data months)
Changes in bank credit (last Friday) (Rs. crore)	Feb 51 to Jan 82	+2.0	0.0	–	–	–	–	–	–	5
Cheque clearance (all centres) (amount, Rs. crore)	Jan 52 to Apr 78	-2.5	-2.5	–	–	–	–	–	–	15
Quantum of imports (1970–71 = 100)	Jan 51 to Mar 80	+1.5	+3.0	–	–	–	–	–	–	27
Index of industrial production, consumer goods non-durables (1970–100)	Jan 51 to Dec 81	+1.5	+5.5	–	–	–	–	–	–	6
Index of industrial production, general Index (1970–100)	Jan 51 to Dec 81	0.0	0.0		✓			✓		6

Note: Not classified by timing class.
Source: Author.

activity may not have provided the cyclical impulse during the period of analysis or that cement production itself may have been a lagging indicator of construction activity; and transportation of goods may represent transportation of finished goods to meet final demand or the transportation of industrial raw materials after the existing stocks of raw materials with the firms are used in production. Also, whichever economic process provides the impulse, it immediately shows up in a change in financial, trade, and income payments, reflected through cheque clearance. The panel with two or three indicators which lead and three indicators which are coincidental, at the peaks and the troughs of the growth cycles, and which includes seven indicators with median leads or lags of 3 months or less at peaks and eight indicators with median leads or lags of 3 months or less at troughs, should quickly reflect a change in the direction of the overall growth cyclical movement. (See Table 13.2).

Leading, Coincidental, and Lagging Indicators for the Indian Growth Cycles

Selected panels of leading, coincidental, and lagging indicators, and the turning points in the indexes based on these indicators are given in Tables 13.4, 13.5 and 13.6. It may be noted that the diffusion index of indicators leading at peaks (troughs) shows only leads or coincidences with a median lead of 4 months (3.5 months) at reference cycle peaks (troughs). The diffusion index of indicators coincidental at peaks (troughs) shows a median lag of 1.5 months (zero months) at reference cycle peaks (troughs). The diffusion index of indicators lagging at peaks (troughs) shows only lags or coincidences with a median lag of 2.5 months (8.5 months) at reference cycle troughs.

Geoffrey Moore's Observations

The earlier work on growth cycles in the Indian economy and the results reported in the present paper were discussed in March 1986 with Geoffrey Moore and Victor Zarnowitz, both doyens and world authorities in this field, when the author had an opportunity to visit them at the Centre for International Business Cycle Research, Rutgers University at Newark and at the Graduate School of Business, University of Chicago, respectively. Both of them welcomed this work.

Table 13.3: Reference Dates for Growth-cyclical Turning Points for India

Diffusion	P	52–1	56–6	61–3	65–3	70–4	72–2	76–11	78–5
Index	T	53–11	58–6	62–2	68–1	70–11	75–1	77–10	80–4
Composite	P	56–6	65–6	70–4	71–11	76–5			
Index	T	53–8	58–6	68–1	70–9	74–5	80–4		
First Principal Component	P	55–11	64–11	69–9	71–7	75–10			
24.58 %	T	53–1	57–11	66–9	71–1	74–11	76–12		
Annual Data°	P	56	60	64	69/70*	73			
	T	53	58	62	68	72	74		

Source: Reference data from annual data 'Growth Cycles in the Indian Economy', *Artha Vijnana*, 1982.

Note: * For reference step cycle, the years are financial years, for example 56 represents the financial year (that is April–March) 1956–7.

Table 13.4: Leading Indicators

Name of Series Leading at Peaks	Conformity probability for Expansion	Conformity probability for Contraction	Median timing (in months)	Probability of timing class	Lag in the availability of data (in months)
Pig iron production (in '000 metric tonnes)	0.5000	0.0352	–5.00	0.0846	1
Electric energy generated (in million kilo watts per hour)	0.0078	0.0039	0.00	–	9
Cheque clearance (Bombay + Calcutta + Madras) (in Rs crore)	0.7734	0.6367	-8.00	0.2519	5
Production of radio receivers (in '000 nos)	0.2734	0.2188	-3.00	0.2519	4
Ratio of index of wholesale prices, manufactured products/ wholesale prices, industrial raw materials	0.9375	0.9648	-15.00	0.2519	5

Reference cycles	P	52–1	56–6	61–3	65–3	70–4	72–2	76–11	78–5	
Diffusion Index	T	53–11	58–6	62–2	68–1	70–11	75–1	77–10		80-4
Diffusion Index for Indicators Leading at Peak	P	52–1 (0)	56–2 (–4)	60–11 (–4)	63–10 (–17)	69–5 (–11)	72–2 (0)	76–5 (–6)	78–5 (0)	80-2
	T	54–1	58–3	62–8	67–7	71–3	73–6	77–5	78–12	80–12

Contd.

Name of Series Leading at Troughs	Conformity Probability for Expansion	Conformity Probability for Contraction	Median timing (in months)	Probability of timing class	Lag in the availability of data (in months)
Pig iron production (in '000 metric tonnes)	0.5000	0.0352	–1.0	–	1
Electric energy generated (In million kilo watts/hour)	0.0078	0.0039	–3.0	0.2724	9
Cheque clearence (Bombay + Calcutta + Madras) (in Rs crore)	0.7734	0.6367	–10.0	0.0218	
Production of aluminium (in '00 tonnes)	0.2266	0.3633	–7.0	0.0218	6
Ratio of index of wholesale prices, manufactured products/wholesale prices, Industrial raw materials	0.9375	0.9648	–12.5	0.0949	5
Index of industrial production, capital goods (1970 = 100)	0.0625	0.0352	–1.5	–	
Production of motor cycles (in nos.)	0.5000	0.3438	–1.0	–	6

Reference cycles	P	52–1	56–6	61–3	65–3	70–4	72–2	76–11	78–5
Diffusion Index	T	53–11	58–6	62–2	68–1	70–11	75–1	77–10	80–4
Diffusion Index for	P	51–8	56–2	60–11	63–10	69–4	72–5	76–5	78–5
Indicators	T	52–11	58–3	62–1	67–10	70–7	73–8	77–10	79–10
Leading at Trough		(–12)	(–3)	(–1)	(–3)	(–4)	(–17)	(0)	(–6)

Source: Author.

TABLE 13.5: Coincidental Indicators

Name of Series	Conformity probability for Expansion	Conformity probability for Contraction	Median timing (in months)	Probability of timing class	Lag in the availability of data (in months)
Coincident at Peaks					
Production of automobiles	0.0625	0.0352	1.5	0.0078	9
Electric energy generated (In million kilo watts per hour)	0.0078	0.0039	0	0.1594	9
Index of industrial production, general	0.0078	0.0039	0	0.0078	6
Index of industrial production, consumption goods, non-durable	0.0625	0.0352	1.5	0.1594	6

Reference cycles	P	52–1	56–6	61–3	65–3	70–4	72–2	76–11	78–5
Diffusion Index	T	53–11	58–6	62–2	68–1	70–11	75–1	77–10	80–4
Diffusion Index for indicators coincidental at peak	P	53–3 (+14)	56–6 (0)	61–5 (+2)	65–3 (0)	70–5 (+1)	77–2 (0)	78–5 (+18)	82–6 (+36)
	T	54–5	58–6	63–4	67–7	75–6	77–7	80–5	

Contd.

Name of Series	Conformity probability for Expansion	Conformity probability for Contraction	Median timing (in months)	Probability of timing class	Lag in the availability of data (in months)
Coincident at Troughs					
Index of industrial production	0.0078	0.0039	0	0.0377	6
Index of industrial production, intermediate goods	0.0625	0.0039	0	0.1433	6
Changes in bank credit (last Friday)	0.2266	0.1445	0	0.1433	5
Pig iron production (in '000 metric tonnes)	0.5000	0.0352	−1	0.1433	6

Reference cycles	P	52–1		56–6		61–3		65–3		70–4		72–2		76–11		78–5		
Diffusion Index	T		53–11		58–6		62–2		68–1		70–11		75–1		77–10		80–4	
Diffusion Index for	P	52–1		56–3		60–11		56–3		69–7		73–2		77–2		78–12		81–11
Indicators	T		53–8		58–6		62–2		67–10		71–5		75–1		77–10		80–11	
coincidental at Troughs			(–3)		(0)		(0)		(–3)		(+6)		(0)		(0)		(+7)	

Source: Author.

Table 13.6: Lagging Indicators

Name of Series	Conformity probability for Expansion	Conformity probability for Contraction	Median timing (in months)	Probability of timing class	Lag in the availability of data (in months)
Lagging at Peaks					
Total cotton cloth production (in lakh metres)	0.2266	0.3633	6.00	0.1443	8
Cement production (in thousand metric tons)	0.0625	0.0352	5.00	0.1443	4
Bank credit (last Friday) (Rs Crore)	0.2266	0.1445	3.00	0.3599	5
Railway traffic—wagons loaded, coal and coke (in '000 tons)	0.5000	0.6367	3.50	0.1443	6
Production of sugar (in '000 tons)	0.0625	0.0352	2.50	0.1443	6
Index of industrial production, consumer goods, durable (1970 = 100)	0.2266	0.3633	6.50	0.1443	6
Index of security prices (ordinary shares) (1970–1 = 100)	0.5000	0.6367	2.50	0.6415	8

Reference cycles	P	52–1	56–6	61–3	65–3	70–4	72–2	76–11	78–5
Diffusion Index	T	53–11	58–6	62–2	68–1	70–11	75–1	77–10	80–4

Contd.

Name of Series	Conformity probability for Expansion	Conformity probability for Contraction	Median timing (in months)	Probability of timing class	Lag in the availability of data (in months)
Lagging at Troughs					
Diffusion Index for Indicators Lagging at Peak: P 52–6 (+5), 56–3 (+2), 61–6 (+3), 65–4 (+1), 70–9 (+5), 72–4 (+2), 76–11 (0), 79–1 (+8); T 53–12, 58–10, 64–1, 68–6, 71–4, 75–2, 77–11, 80–6					
Total cotton cloth production (in lakh metres.)	0.2266	0.3633	5.00	0.2798	8
Cement production (In thousand metric tonnes)	0.0625	0.0352	10.50	0.5463	4
Bank credit (last Friday) (Rs Crore)	0.2266	0.1448	8.00	0.0982	5
Railway traffic—wagons loaded, coal and coke (in '000 tonnes)	0.2266	0.0352	5.00	0.5463	6
Production of radio receivers (in '000 nos.)	0.2734	0.2188	5.00	0.0982	4
Index of security prices (ordinary shares) (1970–1 = 100)	0.5000	0.6367	1.00	0.2798	8
wholesale prices basic metals (1970–1 = 100)	0.5000	0.1445	8.00	0.2798	4

Contd.

Name of Series Lagging at Troughs	Conformity probability for Expansion	Conformity probability for Contraction	Median timing (in months)	Probability of timing class	Lag in the availability of data (in months)
Ratio of index of wholesale prices, manufactured products/ wholesale prices industrial raw materials (inverted series used)	0.9375	0.9648	–12.50	–	5

Reference cycles	P	52–1	56–6	61–3	65–3	70–4	72–2	76–11	78–5
Diffusion Index	T	53–11	58–6	62–2	68–1	70–11	75–1	77–10	80–4
Diffusion Index for	P	57–1	61–3	65–10	70–9	74–8	76–11	79–4	
Indicators lagging at Troughs	T	54–8 (+9)	59–6 (+12)	63–9 (+19)	68–7 (+6)	73–2 (+27)	75–6 (+5)	78–5 (+7)	80–12 (+8)

Source: Author.

Moore in a letter written to the author on 15 December 1986, recognized that we have made good progress on a very important piece of work and that India would be an important country to add to international economic indicators report if comparable data could be compiled.

The following specific comments which Moore made in his letter are worth quoting not only because they give us a flavour of this kind of business cycle research and its relevance for India, but also because they evince the very keen interest which he took in business cycle research for different countries and in the possibility of developing this kind of research for India. He observed in his letter:

> I found that nine of your annual series matched fairly closely those that we had selected some years ago in order to develop comparable sets of indicators for different countries. We started with the US list, classified by cyclical timing on the basis of US information, and tried to duplicate the list for each of the other countries. In this way we can not only test whether the indicators behave similarly in different countries but obtain information that is reasonably comparable across countries. Although your data were annual, I was pleased to find that the results for the nine matching series corresponded quite well with those for the twelve other countries we have studied (see Table 1, enclosed). I don't know how many of our series you could match on a monthly or quarterly basis, but I should be very much interested to know.
>
> The monthly chronology of deviation cycles that you gave in your lecture notes shows a fairly close relationship to the chronologies we have constructed for the US and for eight other countries (taken as a group). See Table 2, enclosed. I am concerned, however, that the Indian cycles show a tendency to lead, and I wonder whether this would be true if you based your chronology on a group of series that matched our list of coincident indicators as closely as possible.

We have reproduced the Tables 1 and 2, in Geoffrey Moore's letter as Tables 13.7 and 13.8 respectively, in this paper.

Moore noted the correspondence of the growth cycle peaks and troughs for India and other countries (Table 13.7), but was concerned about the timing of the peaks and troughs of the Indian growth cycle emerging from our monthly indicators, because of the median lead shown by the Indian growth cycle in comparison with the peaks and troughs of the growth cycle for the US and for eight other countries taken as a group (Table 13.8).

Discussions with Moore in March 1986 and his comments

Table 13.7: Leads and Lags of Matching Indicators at Growth-cycle Peaks and Troughs: India and Twelve other Countries

Timing Classification and Series Titles based on US Data	Series Code Number	Number of Timing Comparisons at Peaks and Troughs, India			Average Lead (–) or Lag (+), in months			
					At Peaks		At Troughs	
	India	Leads	Coin	Lags	India	12 other counttries	India	12 other counttries
1. Individual Indicators								
a. Leading								
Stock Price Index	12	4	2	2	+3	–6	–9	–7
Change in Credit Outstanding	13	5	6	0	–5	–9	–6	–6
Change in Inventories	38	2	6	2	+2	0	–2	–1
b. Coincident								
Non-farm employment	13	4	3	+2	+1	–2	+2	
Real GNP	21	8	1	+2	0	–2	0	
Industrial Production	43	4	2	+3	0	–5	0	
c. Lagging								
Credit outstanding	48	1	3	5	+9	+4	+2	+3
Interest rates, bus. loans	52	0	3	4	+20	+5	+9	+11
Plant and equip. investment	10	0	5	4	+6	+3	+5	+6
2. Group Totals or Averages								
a. Three Leading	11	14	4	0	–5	–6	–5	

Contd.

Timing Classification and Series Titles based on US Data	Series Code Number	Number of Timing Comparisons at Peaks and Troughs, India			Average Lead (–) or Lag (+), in months			
					At Peaks		At Troughs	
	India	Leads	Coin	Lags	India	12 other countries	India	12 other countries
b. Three Coincident	7	16	6	+2	0	−3	+1	
c. Three Lagging	1	11	13	+12	+4	+5	+7	
3. Correlation Coefficients, Individual Indicator Leads and Lags, India vs 12 Other Countries								
a. At Peaks (9 obs.)					+.77			
b. At Troughs (9 obs.)							+.96	
c. At Peaks and Troughs (18 obs.)						+.71		

Note: Results for India are based on annual data; results for other countries are based on monthly and quarterly data. For the Indian analysis, see V.S. Chitre, *Growth Cycles in the Indian Economy*, Gokhale Institute of Politics and Economics, Pune, India, Appendix Tables C-1 and C-2. For the twelve-country figures, see CIBCR, *International Economic Indicators*, June 1986, Appendix B1 and B2. The twelve countries are United States, Canada, United Kingdom, West Germany, France, Italy, Belgium, Netherlands, Sweden, Japan, Australia, and Taiwan.

Source: Author, Centre for International Business Cycle Research, Columbia Business School, December 1986.

Table 13.8: Growth-cycle Peaks and Troughs : India, US, Eight Other Countries

India		United States		Eight other Countries		Leads (-) and Lags (+), in months, India vs. United States		Eight other Countries	
Peak	Trough	Peak	Trough	Peak	Trough	Peak	Trough	Peak	Trough
	8/53		8/54		n.a		–12		ntc
6/56		2/57		5/57		–8		–11	
	6/58		4/58		3/59		+2		–9
–		2/60		–		ntc		ntc	
	–		2/61		–		ntc		ntc
–		5/62		3/61		ntc		ntc	
	–		10/64		2/63		ntc		ntc
6/65		6/66		2/64		–12		+16	
	1/68		10/67		5/68		+3		–4
4/70		3/69		6/70		+13		–2	
	9/70		11/70		2/72		–2		–17
11/71		3/73		11/73		–16		–24	
	5/74		3/75		11/75		–10		–18
5/76		12/78		2/80		–31		–45	
	4/80		12/82		4/83		–32		–36
Median Lead (–) or Lag (+), at Peaks						–12		–11	
at Troughs							–6		–17

ntc = no timing comparison

Note : Dates for India are based on composite index of 11 monthly indicators compiled by V.S. Chitre, Gokhale Institute of Politics and Economics, Pune, India. The other dates are from the Centre for International Business Cycle Research, *International Economic Indicators*, June 1986, Appendix A-3. The eight other countries are Australia, Canada, France, Italy, Japan, Taiwan, United Kingdom and West Germany.

Source: Author; Centre for International Business Cycle Research, Columbia Business School, December 1986.

suggested that (i) we should make a special effort to compile even a quarterly series of employment in public and private sectors and take that into account in determining the turning points of the reference cycle and examine its behaviour in relation to the reference cycle; (ii) two nominal series used in our panel of eleven monthly indicators be deflated by the wholesale price index to identify the reference cycle; and (iii) the then recently developed method of phase average trend be used for removing the trends, rather than a simple 72-month moving average as we have done.

Accordingly, we compiled the important time series on the quarterly estimates of employment in public and private sectors for India for the period from January 1967 to December 1987. This was seasonally adjusted (using a simple ratio to 4-quarter moving average method and a linear trend of quarterly seasonal factors, as the X-11 programme was not readily available at the time) and detrended using 72-month moving average. Months showing turning points in the detrended series were identified assuming the (seasonally adjusted) employment to be constant for three months centred on the last month for each quarter (since the available data gives employment at the end of each quarter). Comparing the turning points of this series with those of the index of industrial production (general), we find that the latter seems to show a lead over the former. Correlations between these two series with leads (–) and lags (+) of between (–)18 to (+)18 months, however, show that the deviations in employment appear to lead the deviations in industrial production by a period of about 10 months with, surprisingly, a negative correlation. Considering the unusual behaviour of total employment in the organized (public and private sectors) in India, one is not very surprised to find that Dua and Banerji (1999) in their recent study of the business cycle chronology for India note that they had to abandon this important series 'since it does not show cycles'.

The 11 monthly indicators used by us to identify the reference cycles for India contained two nominal value indicators, namely, cheque clearance at all centres and change in bank credit, average of Fridays. On Moore's suggestion, we deflated these two series, using the wholesale price index, and constructed a diffusion index of the eleven indicators including these and compared the turning points for the reference cycle obtained from these with those using our original panel. While a number of turning points are different, the median lead or lag of the panel with deflated indicators with the original panel is zero months for both peaks and troughs. Thus, using deflated indicators may not help resolve the question of the timing relation of the Indian growth cycle with the growth cycle in other countries.

We attempted to work on Moore's suggestion for detrending the time series used in our various panels by using the phase average trend method during the Workshop on Business Cycles in Asia, organized by the Institute of Developing Economies, Tokyo, Japan, on 26 January 1989, by using the software available with the institute. Unfortunately, the results of this work did not appear to be comparable with our earlier findings but neither could they be fully analysed for want of time.

The question of the timing relation of the Indian growth cycle with the growth cycle in the market economies of the world was examined by us in some detail but with annual data (Chitre 1982, 1990, 1991). It was noted in Chitre (1982) that the growth cycles in the index of the GDP and the index of industrial production of the market economies of the world and the index of industrial production, North America, showed perfect conformity with the Indian growth cycle over the period from 1950–75. In particular, the peaks and the troughs of the growth cycle in the index of industrial production of the market economies of the world matched with all the five peaks and troughs identified for the Indian growth cycle with no extra cycles and only one skipped trough and showed a median timing of zero lead or lag (see Chitre 1982, Table C–2 for more details). We observed in a subsequent study (Chitre 1991) that for the period from 1950–1 to 1980–1 the growth cycle in the index of industrial production, North America, showed a remarkably close correspondence with the Indian growth cycle when the influence of fluctuations in agricultural income and gross fixed investment of the public sector on the Indian growth cycle was removed through an appropriate simulation exercise. The turning points of the growth cycle in the index of industrial production for North America almost always lead the corresponding turning points of the Indian growth cycle, adjusted as mentioned above, by one year and sometimes coincide with them. Only in one case, that is, for the peak of 1973–4 of the latter, does it show a lag of one year. The median timing relation is of a coincidence at peaks and one year's lead at the troughs (see Chitre 1991, p.124). However, our study for the period from 1962–3 to 1983–4 (Chitre 1990), using both business cycle methodology and regression analysis, shows that after removing the contribution to the growth cycles in India's non-agricultural income due to the deviations from trend in agricultural income and gross public sector fixed investment, the growth cycle in India's non-agricultural income moves with a lag but contra-cyclically to the industrial cycle in the market economies of the world. It may be further seen from the study that the timing relation of the Indian growth cycle (adjusted as mentioned) with the world growth cycle is affected by a change in the turning points for the Indian growth cycles corresponding to the world growth cycles of 1971–5 and 1975–9, which may possibly have been due to domestic political developments in India during the period, associated with the declaration of Emergency in 1975 and its end in 1977. Thus, the relation of the Indian growth cycle with the world growth cycle may be expected to undergo a change with changing domestic and world environment.

Dua and Banerji (2001 a, b) also address this important question in a different way by studying the behaviour of an index of leading indicators for the business cycle and the growth rate cycle for India for the period 1976–99. They claim that with the post-1991 liberalization of the Indian economy, the cycles in the Indian economy have become more similar in character to those of other market economies. This is testified by a more reliable timing relation of lead with respect to the Indian business cycle and growth rate cycle observed for the post-1991 period for their leading index based on the set of leading indicators, which have proved to be dependable leading indicators of business cycles and growth rate cycles for other market economies. The result reflects the greater liberalization of the domestic economy as well as greater integration of the Indian economy with the world economy. It is intriguing though that an unchanging list of indicators will define a good leading index for all the time for any country, be it India or the market economies of the world.

Endnotes

[1]Mintz (1969), (1974). Recent discussions of the business cycles of 1973–5 (Blinder 1979) and of the 1979 recession are important exceptions. Also see A.G. Frank (1986). These business cycles are of the classical type, that is, involving cycles in economic activities without adjustment for their long run trends.

[2]Also, see Dua and Banerji (1999) for a discussion of a still more recently developed concept of growth rate cycles and its relation to the classical business cycle as well as to the growth cycle.

[3]*Business Conditions Digest*, May, 1975 p.viii, US Department of Commerce, Bureau of Economic Analysis.

[4]A full report, giving a survey of the indicators used in the earlier NBER studies on business cycles, the cyclical characteristics of the Indian time series examined by us, and the experiments with various panels of indicators, are under preparation and are expected to be published separately. A detailed discussion providing the rationale for including the series listed in Table 13.1 in the present study, the limitations of these series and the existing gaps in the available database for business cycle research on India are included in a slightly longer original version of this paper which appeared in Chitre (2001).

[5]Briefly, the diffusion index identifies turning points of the reference cycle by locating the dates when a majority of the indicators in the panel change the direction of movement. The composite index locates the turning points of a cumulative index which takes into account the extent of change in the component series after these changes are standardized for differing amplitudes of cyclical movement of the different indicators so that the average absolute percentage change over the cycle is equal to unity for all indicators. The first principal component index uses the weights of the first principal component of the indicators (standardized by dividing the values of each indicator by its standard deviation over a period common for all the indicators) to construct a weighted index of the values of the standardized values of the indicators to obtain the index, the turning points of which are used to locate the turning points of the reference cycle.

References

Blinder, A.S. (1979), *Economic Policy and the Great Stagflation*, New York: Academic Press.

Bry, G. and C. Boschan (1971), 'Cyclical Analysis of Time Series: Selected Procedures and Computer Programs', National Bureau of Economic Research, Technical Paper 20, New York.

Centre for Monitoring Indian Economy (1984), 'Production and Capacity Utilisation in 650 Industries: 1970 to 1983', CMIE, Mumbai.

Chitre, V.S. (1991), 'Fluctuations in Agricultural Income, Public Sector Investment, World Economic Activity and Business Cycles in India', in H. Osada and D. Hiratsuka (Eds), *Business Cycles in Asia*, Institute of Developing Economies, Tokyo.

—— (1990), 'Transmission of World Growth Cycle to the Indian Economy', *Artha Vijnana*, Vol. 32, Nos 3 and 4 (September–December), pp. 281–97.

Chitre, V.S. (1986), 'Indicators of Business Recessions and Revivals in India', Gokhale Institute of Politics and Economics, Pune, unpublished mimeo, February.

—— (1982), 'Growth Cycles in the Indian Economy, *Artha Vijnana*, Vol. 24, No. 4 (December), pp. 293–450. Also reprinted as *Artha Vijnana* Reprint Series No. 7.

——and R. Paranjpe (2001), 'Indicators of Business Recessions and Revivals in India: 1951–1982', *Indian Economic Review*, Vol. XXXVI, No. 1, pp. 79–105.

—— (1987), 'Keynesian, Monetarist and New Classical Economics and Short Run Dynamics of Output and Inflation in India', *Prajnana*, Vol. 16, issue 4, p. 431, National Institute of Bank Management.

Dua, P. and A. Banerji (2001a), 'A Leading Index for the Indian Economy', Centre for Development Economics, Delhi, Working Paper No. 90.

—— (2001b), 'An Indicator Approach to Business and Growth Rate Cycles : The Case of India'; *Indian Economic Review*, VOL. XXXVI, pp. 55–78.

—— (1999), An Index of Coincident Economic Indicators for the Indian Economy, *Journal of Quantitative Economics*, 15, No. 2 (July), pp. 177–201.

Frank, A.G. (1986), 'Is Reagan Recovery Real or the Calm before a Storm', *Economic and_Political Weekly*, 24 May, pp. 920–7 and 31 May, pp. 972–7.

Hymans, H.S. (1973), On the Use of Leading Indicators to Predict Cyclical Turning Points, *Brooking Papers on Economic Activity*, Vol. VIII.

Mintz, Ilse (1974), 'Dating United States Growth Cycles', *Explorations in Economic Research*, Vol. 1, pp. 1–113.

—— (1969), *Dating Postwar Business Cycles: Methods and Their Application to Western Germany, 1950–67*, National Bureau of Economic Research, New York.

Mitchell, W.C. and A.F. Burns (1938), 'Statistical Indicators of Cyclical Revivals', *Bulletin* Vol. 69, National Bureau of Economic Research, New York, reprinted in G.H. Moore (1961), *Business Cycle Indicators, Vol. I: Contributions to the Analysis of Current Business Conditions*, National Bureau of Economic Research, New York.

Moore Geoffrey H. (1950), 'Statistical Indicators of Cyclical Revivals and Recessions', Occasional Paper 31, National Bureau of Economic Research, New York, reprinted in G.H. Moore (1961) (Ed.), *Business Cycle Indicators, Vol I: Contributions to the Analysis of Current Business Conditions*, National Bureau of Economic Research, New York.

—— and Julius Shiskin (1967), *Indicators of Business Expansions and Contractions*, National Bureau of Economic Research, New York.

Shiskin, Julius (1961), 'Signals of Recession and Recovery: An Experiment with Monthly Reporting', Occasional Paper 77, National Bureau of Economic Research, New York.

—— Allan H. Young, and John C. Musgrave (1967), 'The X–11 Variant of the Census Method II Seasonal Adjustment Program, Bureau of Census Technical Paper No. 15.

Zarnowitz, Victor and Charlotte Boschan (1975a), 'New Composite Indexes of Coincident and Lagging Indicators', *Business Conditions Digest,* May, reprinted in US Department of Commerce, Vol. No. v-xxiv, Bureau of Economic Analysis (1977).

—— (1975b), 'Cyclical Indicators: An Evaluation and New Leading Indexes', *Business Conditions Digest*, November, v-xxii, reprinted in US Department of Commerce, Bureau of Economic Analysis (1977).

14

Monitoring and Predicting Business and Growth Rate Cycles in the Indian Economy

Pami Dua and Anirvan Banerji

Introduction

This paper applies the indicator approach to predicting business and growth rate cycles—attributed to Geoffrey H. Moore and his associates—to the Indian economy. The indicator analysis technique employs systematic methods of interpreting economic indicators to monitor the pulse of the economy as well as to predict future movements in the economy. This approach is based on the premise that in a market-oriented economy, cycle after cycle, economic indicators reach turning points in a known sequence. Basically,

This is an updated version of Dua and Banerji (2001a). The authors are grateful to the Centre for Development Economics, Delhi School of Economics and the Economic Cycle Research Institute, New York, for research support. The authors gratefully acknowledge support from the ICICI Research Centre for the ongoing maintenance of the leading and coincident indexes. The authors are also grateful to Geoffrey H. Moore for his early encouragement and guidance, and to Vikas S. Chitre for invaluable help in the initial stages of the project. Mi-Suk Ha, Shuchita Mehta and Manish Agarwal provided competent research assistance.

leading indicators turn before coincident indicators, which turn before lagging indicators.

One of the earliest systems of this kind was devised shortly before World War I, known as the Harvard ABC curves. The A curve represented speculation, more specifically stock prices. The B curve denoted business activity, measured by the volume of cheques drawn on bank deposits. The C curve represented the money market and was measured by the rate of interest on short-term commercial loans. Warren Persons at Harvard University showed that these three curves typically moved in sequence—stock prices first, bank debits second, and interest rates last, with the lagging movements in interest rates preceding the opposite turns in stock prices. This work was continued by researchers at the National Bureau of Economic Research (NBER) founded in 1920 and is discussed in Burns and Mitchell (1946); Klein (1983); Klein and Moore (1985); Lahiri and Moore (1991); Mitchell and Burns (1938); Moore (1950, 1958, 1961, 1975, 1990); Moore and Cullity (1994); Moore and Shiskin (1967); and Zarnowitz (1991, 1992).

This study aims to analyse business cycles and growth rate cycles in the Indian economy using coincident and leading indexes. The paper is organized as follows. The second section describes the indicator approach to business cycles and distinguishes between classical, growth, and growth rate cycles. The third section describes the construction of the leading index. The fourth section analyses Indian business and growth rate cycles. The fifth section examines the Indian leading index and the following section reflects on the usefulness of the leading index pre and post liberalization. The last section concludes the paper.

Indicator Approach to Monitoring and Predicting Business Cycles, Growth Cycles, and Growth Rate Cycles

Numerous methods have been developed to identify turning points with varying degrees of technical sophistication. These include the indicator approach, the sequential signalling procedures that use leading indicators (Zarnowitz and Moore 1981; Neftci 1982), Stock and Watson's (1989) experimental indicators, and the Markov switching model (Hamilton 1989).

Perhaps the most popular rule-of-thumb designates a recession as at least two successive quarters of decline in the gross domestic product (GDP). Lost in that quest for simplicity are the essential characteristics of a recession—that it consists of a pervasive and pronounced downswing in a variety of measures of economic activity (Banerji 1999). Not surprisingly, such shortcuts can produce anomalous results. In fact, while two successive quarters of decline in GDP occur in most recessions, this is neither a necessary nor a sufficient condition for a recession.

For example, it is well known that in the mid-1970s, Japan experienced its worst recession since World War II in the aftermath of the jump in oil prices. At the time, there were severe and prolonged declines in Japanese industrial production, employment, retail sales, and wage and salary income. Yet Japanese GDP plunged in the first quarter of 1974, rose for the next two quarters, and then dipped again in the fourth quarter, clearly not satisfying the 'two-down-quarters-of-GDP rule'.

In the US, the NBER officially identified a recession that lasted from January to July of 1980. Until 1995, the data showed only one quarter of decline in GDP during that period. Only the 1995 switch to chain-weighted GDP data produced two successive declines in GDP during that recession, belatedly vindicating NBER's original decision. Clearly, the popular rule-of-thumb would have delayed the recognition of that recession by more than a decade! Also, the official US recession of 1960–1 does not show two successive quarters of decline in GDP.

In the US recession of 2001, initial data showed a GDP decline only in the third quarter of 2001 that many ascribed to the events of 11 September . Based on this apparent one-quarter decline in GDP, some economists, as well as certain high officials in Washington, insisted as late as July 2002 that there had been no recession at all in 2001, since GDP had not declined for two quarters. It was only in late July 2002—16 months after the start of the recession—that revised data showed that GDP had actually declined in each of the first three quarters of 2001, finally silencing the denial of the recession. Since the two-down-quarter rule results in such dangerously delayed recession recognition, particularly from the point of view of policy makers, it is clearly inadequate.

In fact, theoretically, a recession is more than a decline in just output (which GDP measures) and empirically, the two-quarter GDP decline rule is not a necessary or sufficient condition for a recession to occur. Thus, such GDP declines are not always accompanied by pronounced, pervasive, and persistent declines in output, income, employment, and retail and wholesale trade that mark a business cycle recession, or the complex processes that are the antecedents of a genuine recession. As a result, the symptoms that precede a real recession, as captured in the appropriate leading indicators, may not be seen ahead of such a mistakenly identified 'recession'. Such anomalies can lead not only to an erroneous dating of recessions, but also to difficulties in the proper selection of leading indicators of recessions and recoveries (Layton and Banerji 2001).

For the Indian economy, GDP data until recently were available only on an annual basis. Thus the two-quarter rule-of-thumb was not applicable. It may be tempting to use another variable, say, the industrial production index, as a substitute. Apart from the obvious problem that industrial production is a far narrower measure of the Indian economy than a properly constructed coincident index, the use of any simplistic rule based on a single economic time series can lead to the problems already outlined.

We, therefore, focus on the indicator approach to cyclical analysis that uses the composite index of coincident indicators to date recessions and selects leading indicators on the basis of historical leads and economic rationale. A composite index of leading indicators is then constructed to provide a collective call on upturns and downturns in the economy. A pronounced, pervasive, and persistent decline in the leading index is expected to predict downturns in the economy.

Leading, Coincident, and Lagging Indicators

The indicator approach to macroeconomic measurement has a long and successful history. This approach works because in a market-oriented economy, cycle after cycle, economic indicators reach turning points in a known sequence. Basically, leading indicators turn before coincident indicators, which turn before lagging indicators.

The NBER, formed in 1920 to address measurement problems in economics, pioneered research into understanding the repetitive sequences that underlie business cycles. Wesley C. Mitchell (1927), one of the founders of the NBER, first established a working definition of the business cycle that he along with Arthur F. Burns (1946), later characterized as follows:

> Business cycles are a type of fluctuation found in the aggregate economic activity of nations that organize their work mainly in business enterprises: a cycle consists of expansions occurring at about the same time in many economic activities, followed by similarly general recessions, contractions and revivals which merge into the expansion phase of the next cycle; this sequence of changes is recurrent but not periodic; in duration business cycles vary from more than one year to ten or twelve years; they are not divisible into shorter cycles of similar character with amplitudes approximating their own.

To examine these repetitive sequences, the indicator approach consists essentially of classifying economic indicators into leading, coincident, and lagging categories and then combining the relevant components into corresponding composite indexes. The coincident index, comprising indicators that measure current economic performance, is then used to represent the level of current economic activity. Such indicators include measures of output, income, employment, and sales, which help to date peaks and troughs of business cycles.

The leading index, on the other hand, combines series that tend to lead at business cycle turns and provides a summary measure of what can be expected in the near future. Leading indicators generally represent commitments made with respect to future activity or are factors that influence such commitments. Examples are average weekly hours, placement of new orders, housing permits, consumer expectations, stock prices, interest rate spreads, and changes in profitability.

The lagging index, a composite of indicators that reach their turning points after the peaks and troughs of the coincident indicators, helps to clarify and confirm the underlying pattern of economic activity identified with the help of coincident and leading indexes. For instance, the levels of stocks, instalment credit outstanding, commercial and industrial loans outstanding, interest rates, and average duration of unemployment, depict previous changes in the economy.

As noted, to track business cycles, a composite index of a group of economic time series—that show similar characteristics (timing) at business cycle turns but represent different activities or sectors of the economy—is preferred to individual series. This is because the composite index represents a broad spectrum of the economy. Furthermore, the performance of an individual series may vary over different business cycles. Specifically, the components that perform best in each cycle may vary and it is not possible to gauge beforehand which of the variables is better for each turning point. Moreover, a composite index also reduces the measurement error associated with a given cyclical indicator. As noted by Moore (1982):

> Virtually all economic statistics are subject to error, and hence are often revised. Use of several measures necessitates an effort to determine what is the consensus among them, but it avoids some of the arbitrariness of deciding upon a single measure that perforce could be used only for a limited time with results that would be subject to revision every time the measure was revised.

Furthermore, Zarnowitz and Boschan (1975) point out that some series, 'prove more useful in one set of conditions, others in a different set. To increase the chances of getting true signals and reduce those of getting false ones, it is advisable to rely on all such potentially useful (series) as a group.'

The individual indicators are combined into a composite index using well-established procedures developed at the NBER by Geoffrey H. Moore, founder of the Economic Cycle Research Institute (ECRI), and Julius Shiskin (Moore and Shiskin 1967) and refined at ECRI. Earlier, Moore and his NBER colleagues worked on the development of the diffusion index, which measures the proportion of indicators of economic activity in the overall economy or in a sector that are experiencing expansion over a given span of time (Moore 1955). Moore later devised the method of constructing composite indexes (Moore 1958) by extending the idea of the diffusion index to take into account the magnitude of these cyclical movements.

The emphasis on the indicator approach thus is on the concerted nature of the upswings and downswings in different measures of economic activity. In fact, the business cycle is a consensus of cycles in many activities, which have a tendency to peak and trough around the same time (Niemira and Klein 1994, p.4). For each coincident series, a specific cycle, that is, a set of turning points can be determined. A reference cycle chronology can then be determined, based on the central tendency of the individual turning points in a set of coincident economic indicators that comprise the coincident index. This reference chronology helps to date recessions as well as to identify leading indicators and their historical leads.

Classical Cycles, Growth Cycles, and Growth Rate Cycles

The above discussion describes 'classical' business cycles that measure the ups and downs of the economy with absolute levels of the variables entering the coincident index. A second NBER definition of fluctuations in economic activity is termed a growth cycle. A growth cycle traces the ups and downs through deviations of the actual growth rate of the economy from its long-run trend rate of growth. In other words, a speedup (slowdown) in economic activity means growth higher (lower) than the long-run trend rate of growth.

Economic slowdowns begin with reduced but still positive growth rates and can eventually develop into recessions. The high growth phase coincides with business cycle recovery and expansion midway while the low growth phase corresponds to expansion in the later stages leading to recession. Some slowdowns, however, continue to exhibit positive growth rates and result in renewed expansions, not recessions. As a result, all classical business cycles associate with growth cycles, but not all growth cycles associate with classical cycles. Growth cycle chronologies based on trend-adjusted measures of economic activity were first developed by Mintz (1969, 1972, 1974). Burns and Mitchell (1946) noted the following about growth cycles:

> If secular trends were eliminated at the outset as fully as are seasonal variations, they would show that business cycles are a more pervasive and a more potent factor in economic life... For when the secular trend of a series rises rapidly, it may offset the influence of cyclical contractions in general business, or make the detection of this influence difficult. In such instances (the classical business cycle method) may indicate lapses from conformity to contractions in general business, which would not appear if the secular trend were removed.'

Following Mintz's work, when the Organization for Economic co-operation and Development (OECD) developed leading indicators for its member countries it decided to monitor growth cycles. Growth cycle analysis also formed the basis for the international economic indicators (IEI) project (Klein and Moore 1985) started at the NBER in the early 1970s.

Of course, growth cycles, measured in terms of deviations from trend, necessitated the determination of the trend of the time series being analysed. The phase average trend (PAT), calculated by averaging business cycle phases, was used as the best trend measure by the OECD as well as in the IEI project, in order to measure growth cycles. However, one problem with the PAT (Boschan and Ebanks 1978) as a benchmark for growth cycles is that it is subject to frequent and occasionally significant revisions, especially near the end of the series.

In other words, while growth cycles are not hard to identify in a historical time series, it is difficult to measure them accurately on a real-time basis (Boschan and Banerji 1990). This is because the trend over the latest year or two is not accurately known and must be estimated, but the PAT estimates tend to be very unstable near the end (Cullity and Banerji 1996). More generally, any measure of the most recent trend is necessarily an estimate and subject to revisions, so it is difficult to come to a precise determination of growth cycle dates, at least in real time.

This difficulty makes growth cycle analysis less than ideal as a tool for monitoring and forecasting economic cycles in real time, even though it may be useful for the purposes of historical analysis. This is one reason that by the late 1980s, Moore had started moving towards the use of growth rate cycles for the measurement of series which manifested few actual cyclical declines, but did show cyclical slowdowns (Layton and Moore 1989).

Growth rate cycles are simply the cyclical upswings and downswings in the growth rate of economic activity. The growth rate used is the 'six-month smoothed growth rate' concept, initiated by Moore to eliminate the need for the sort of extrapolation of the past trend needed in growth cycle analysis. This smoothed growth rate is based on the ratio of the latest month's figure to its average over the preceding twelve months (and therefore centred about six months before the latest month). Unlike the more commonly used 12-month change, it is not very sensitive to any idiosyncratic occurrences 12 months earlier. A number of such advantages make the six-month smoothed growth rate a useful concept in cyclical analysis (Banerji 1999). Cyclical turns in this growth rate define the growth rate cycle.

The growth rate cycle is related to Mintz's earlier work on the 'step cycle' except that the former is based on the smoothed growth rate as mentioned above. Also, in concept, the growth rate cycle does not suggest that the growth rate passes through high growth and low growth steps, but moves, instead, from cyclical troughs to cyclical peaks and back again. At the ECRI, growth rate cycles rather than growth cycles are used along with business cycles as the primary tool to monitor international economies in real time. The growth rate cycle is, in effect, a second way to monitor slowdowns in contrast to downturns. Because of the difference in definition, growth rate cycles are different from growth cycles. Thus, what has emerged in recent years is the recognition that business cycles, growth cycles, and growth rate cycles, all need to be monitored in a complementary fashion. However, of the three, business cycles and growth rate cycles are more suitable for real-time monitoring and forecasting, while growth cycles are more suitable for historical analysis (Klein 1998).

In this paper we examine the performance of the coincident and leading indexes with respect to the classical business cycle and the growth rate cycle of the Indian economy. The classical business cycle as well as the growth rate reference chronologies are reported in our earlier work—Dua and Banerji (1999). The growth rate reference chronology has been revised recently and is reported in this paper. Since the construction of the coincident index is described in Dua and Banerji (1999), we focus here on the leading index.

Method for Constructing the Leading Index

The leading index provides valuable information about the future path of the economy, combining information from several economic series and collectively forecasting future movements in the economy. Each series in the leading index contains some information about the future turning points but it is unlikely that the individual series will show identical turning points. The combined information in the leading index produces better predictions about future turning points than any one of the individual series in the index can generate on its own.

The construction of the leading index follows well-established procedures developed by Moore and Shiskin, with some modifications. The various steps of the classical approach are outlined below.

Determination of reference chronology based on coincident indicators

Classical Business Cycles

1. The cyclical turning points of the coincident indicators are first determined.
2. The composite coincident index is constructed.
3. The cyclical turning points of the coincident index are then determined.
4. The business cycle peak and trough dates are selected based on the consensus of turning point dates of coincident indicators.
5. The coincident index turning points are used to resolve ties.

Growth Rate Cycles

The cyclical turning points of the smoothed growth rates of the coincident indicators and of the coincident index are used in an analogous fashion to determine the growth rate cycle chronology.

The reference chronology is already reported in Dua and Banerji (1999). The growth rate cycle chronology, however, has been revised since then and the revised chronology is used in this study. The next step involves the construction of the leading index.

Leading Index

1. Based on economic theory, empirical observation in other economies, and the special characteristics of the Indian economy, some variables are expected to lead the cyclical movements of the Indian economy. To verify whether or not they actually lead, their cyclical turning points are compared to the reference chronology. If the lead is significant and consistent, and the data are available in a regular and timely manner, the variable can be considered a satisfactory leading indicator and selected to be part of the leading index.

2. The selected leading indicators are then combined into a composite leading index for the Indian economy. The leads of the index with respect to the reference chronology are determined by matching cyclical turns in the leading index and the reference chronology.

3. This is done both for the classical business cycle and the growth rate cycle.

Determination of Turning Points

The choice of turning points is made by mechanical procedures supplemented by rules of thumb and experienced judgment. The initial selection of turning points employs a computer program based on the procedures and rules developed at the NBER (see Bry and Boschan 1971). The selection of a turning point must meet the following criteria: (i) at least five months opposite movement must occur to qualify as a turning point; (ii) peaks (troughs) must be at least 15 months apart; and (iii) if the data are flat at the turning point, then the most recent period is selected as the turning point. These rules of thumb trace their roots to Burns and Mitchell (1946) and continue to be applied at ECRI. Finally, turning points must pass muster through the experienced judgment of the researcher. Turning points can be rejected because of special one-time events that produce spikes in the data, indicating turning points. Experienced judgment also excludes non-cyclical exogenous shocks.

A specific cycle, that is, a set of turning points for each series, is thus obtained. The turning points of the coincident indicators help date the reference cycle or chronology. For the coincident index, the Bry–Boschan turning points of measures of output, income, employment, and sales are 'clustered,' that is, the reference cycle turning points are selected on the basis of the best consensus among the turning point dates of the individual indicators. This clustering of turning points represents the cyclical co-movement of various economic activities that is the hallmark of an economic cycle. The leading index thus leads the turning points in the reference cycle. Therefore, the lead is determined on the basis of the central tendency of the individual turning points in a set of leading economic indicators. Leads for the highs and lows of the growth rate cycle are derived from the growth rates of the leading indicators.

Construction of the Composite Leading Index

The construction of the index follows traditional NBER methodology with some modifications. The basic steps involve the transformation of each series, standardization of each transformed series using standardization factors, and combination of the standardized series into a raw index. The raw index is adjusted for trend and finally rebased.

First, the logarithm is computed for each component series for which such a transformation is required to achieve the 'stationarity of cyclical amplitude' (Boschan and Banerji 1990). Amplitude stationarity requires invariance of cyclical amplitude measured over complete cycles. Where amplitude stationarity is not a concern, including for series that are growth rates or include negative quantities, the log transformation is not performed.

To prevent the more volatile components from dominating the index, the series are then divided by the standardization factor, which is the standard deviation of the detrended trend-cycle component of the series over a number of whole cycles.

Next, the standardized series are averaged with equal weights across all components in the index. The process of scaling the series to prevent the more volatile series from dominating the index implicitly provides a weighting scheme in the index. Trend adjustment is then performed for this series by multiplying it by a suitable factor that scales the trend up or down to match the target trend, which is often the GDP trend over a whole number of cycles. The antilog of this series is then calculated.

The modified (new) procedure now used at ECRI makes two notable changes to the traditional procedure (see Boschan and Banerji 1990). First, it ensures that the standardization factor measures only the cyclical amplitude. The old method lumped together trend, cycle, and irregular components, so that a high-trend cyclical component would be de-emphasized as compared to a trendless component for no good reason. Also, the new method uses a multiplicative trend adjustment instead of the traditional additive trend adjustment, which shifts turning points in the raw index. This ensures that the final index turning points are the same as those of the raw index. Cullity and Banerji (1996) show that the ECRI method outperforms the traditional procedure as well as the OECD method using the same set of indicators.

Indian Economic Cycles

An earlier paper (Dua and Banerji 1999) established the dates of Indian business cycles and growth rate cycles, with the help of a coincident index created for the purpose. In this study, we report the revised chronology and introduce a leading index for the Indian economy, designed to anticipate those cycles.

The index of leading economic indicators is a composite of different indicators that collectively predict future economic activity. It is designed to peak and trough earlier than the coincident index that measures current economic activity. It is therefore a very important and useful forecasting and planning tool for policy makers, financial analysts, financial investors, and businesses. Together with the coincident index (Dua and Banerji 1999), it can help to monitor the Indian economy better and to provide early warning signals of future economic activity.

For a leading index to be useful, economic cycles should be driven by endogenous factors. In fact, most early theories of business cycles are endogenous, that is, concentrating on the internal relations of the economic system. Some later theories have paid more attention to exogenous shocks and their propagation. It is amply clear from an examination of the phenomenon in a variety of economies, however, that a business cycle is driven by a combination of endogenous and exogenous factors.

Even in the 1700s in England, bad harvests tended to adversely affect the demand for manufactured goods from small farmers, depressing the wages of industrial workers and leading to recessions resulting from the propagation of these shocks within an increasingly interdependent economic system. Ashton (1959) compiled a reference chronology of cyclical turning points for eighteenth century England. In some ways, until the recent decade, recessions in the Indian economy were analogous to those experienced in eighteenth century England, which were driven mainly by weather and wars before the industrial revolution of the 1780s.

As noted in our earlier paper (Dua and Banerji 1999), over the last four decades, India has experienced six business cycle recessions characterized by pronounced, pervasive and persistent declines in output, income, employment and trade. These are as follows the details are reproduced in Table 14.1.

1. November 1964 to November 1965;
2. April 1966 to April 1967;
3. June 1972 to May 1973;
4. April 1979 to March 1980;
5. March 1991 to September 1991;
6. May 1996 to February 1997.

It is clear from Table 14.1 that expansions have generally been longer than contractions. Indian business cycles have averaged over six years in length, with recessions averaging just under a year and expansions averaging just over five years. This finding is consistent with evidence for the post-war US economy that shows relatively longer expansions and shorter contractions (see Diebold and Rudebusch 1992; Vilasuso 1996).

Table 14.1: Business Cycle Chronology for India

Dates of Peaks and Troughs		Duration (in months)	
Trough	Peak	Contraction (peak to trough)	Expansion (trough to peak)
	November 1964		
November 1965	April 1966	12	5
April 1967	June 1972	12	62
May 1973	April 1979	11	71
March 1980	March 1991	11	132
September 1991	May 1996	6	56
February 1997		9	
Average (months)		10.2	65.2
Median (months)		11.0	62.0
Standard Deviation (months)		2.3	45.3

Source: Authors.

However, until the 1970s, these recessions were triggered in large part by the failure of the monsoon—a critical factor in an economy where agriculture accounted for over 40 per cent of GDP. The agricultural sector continued to play an important role in determining economic growth until the early 1990s. The 1991 recession was caused by an unprecedented macroeconomic crisis, also triggered by an exogenous shock, the Gulf crisis. It was not until 1996–7 that there was a recession that could be traced in greater measure to endogenous factors.

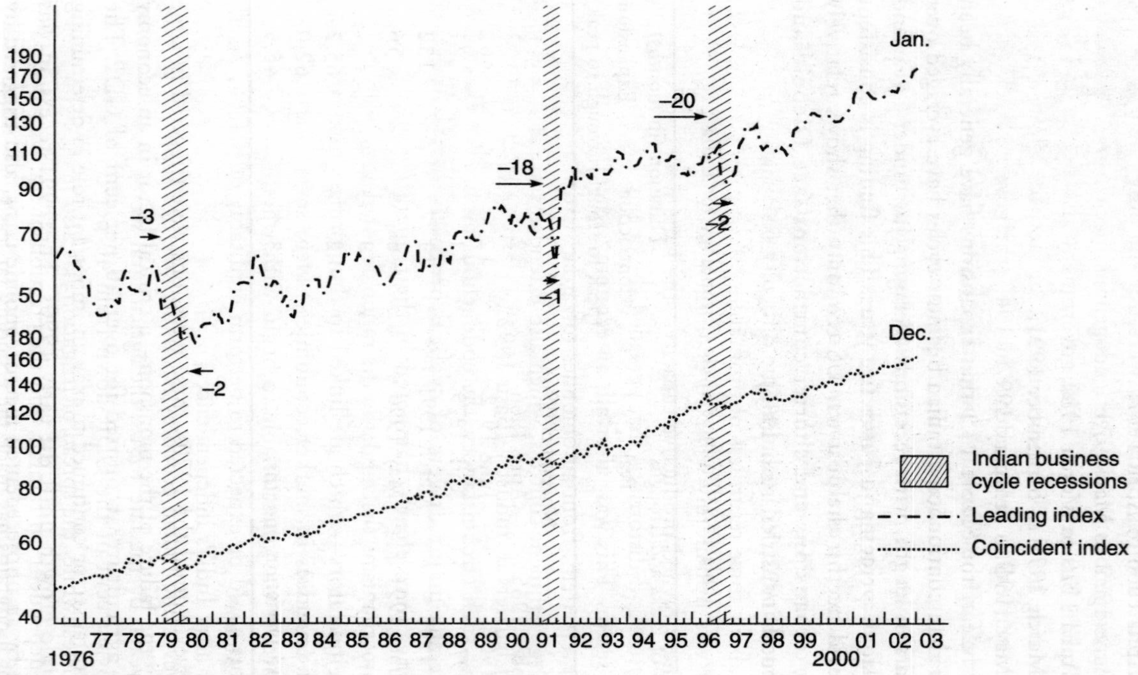

Figure 14.1: Indian Leading and Coincident Indexes.

The dominance of the agricultural sector and its susceptibility to weather-related shocks, however, were not the only circumstances favouring exogenous shocks over endogenous mechanisms as drivers of the Indian business cycle. The government also dominated the 'commanding heights of the economy'. In fact, for the first four decades after India's independence in 1947, the government owned roughly half of the economy's productive capacity.

Myriad regulations and rampant distortions of the free market hemmed in even the private sector. Such distortions took the form of controls on prices and interest rates and extensive licensing procedures for the establishment of new factories or expansion of existing capacity. Generally, there were major barriers to entry and exit in most industries, including the difficulty of laying off any part of the labour force regardless of profitability.

This was not merely a mixed economy, with a large role for government-owned productive capacity—the issue was the extent of the controls and distortions that pervaded the operations of even the private sector. This was, after all, an economy where 'the prices of almost every item, from automobiles to zarda, (had) been tampered with' by government controls, which also extended to extensive entry and exit barriers in industry (Basu 1992).

Under such circumstances, the endogenous cyclical mechanisms that are the major drivers of cyclical processes in free market economies were clearly hampered in their operation. Thus, the market mechanisms that underlie the rationale for the functioning of leading indicators—which are linked to the normal antecedents of cyclical processes in market economies—were severely distorted. Therefore, it was questionable to begin with whether any leading indicators could be expected to perform creditably during the early decades after India's independence.

However, the Indian economy has undergone profound changes in recent years. By the late 1990s, the agricultural sector accounted for only 25 per cent of the GDP, down from 40 per cent in the late 1970s. Meanwhile, the spread of irrigation has also made agriculture far less dependent on rainfall, and the creation of substantial buffer stocks of foodgrains has made the economy far less vulnerable to crop failures. Thus, the economy as a whole is now much less susceptible to weather-related shocks.

Separately, especially after the crisis of 1991, the Indian economy began a far-reaching process of liberalization, which continues to unfold. As a result, many of the extreme distortions of free market mechanisms have already been substantially mitigated. Under such circumstances, it is likely that leading indicators would start to function expected.

Of course, while leading indicators lead at business cycle turning points, their deviations from trend also lead at growth cycle turning points, while their growth rates lead at growth rate cycle turning points. A chronology of growth cycles for the Indian economy for 1951–75 was established by Chitre (1982, 2001).

However, as already discussed, because growth cycles are based on deviations from trend, monitoring them in real time requires the determination of the current trend, which is an uncertain exercise, and thus of dubious value. Therefore, for the purpose of real time monitoring rather than historical analysis, growth rate cycles, based on the smoothed growth rates of the underlying variables (Banerji 1999), are more useful.

The growth rate cycle chronology giving the growth rate cycle downturns is as follows.

1. September 1960 to May 1961;
2. February 1962 to November 1962;
3. May 1964 to November 1965;
4. April 1966 to March 1967;
5. April 1969 to February 1974;
6. February 1976 to December 1979;
7. November 1980 to February 1983;
8. August 1984 to October 1987;
9. June 1988 to March 1989;
10. March 1990 to September 1991;
11. April 1992 to July 1993;
12. April 1995 to February 1997;
13. January 1998 to October 1998;
14. December 1999 to July 2000; and
15. November 2000 to June 2001.

Details are given in Table 14.2. In all, 15 growth rate cycles here been identified from January 1957 onwards compared to 6 classical business cycle recessions. The duration of the slowdowns is generally

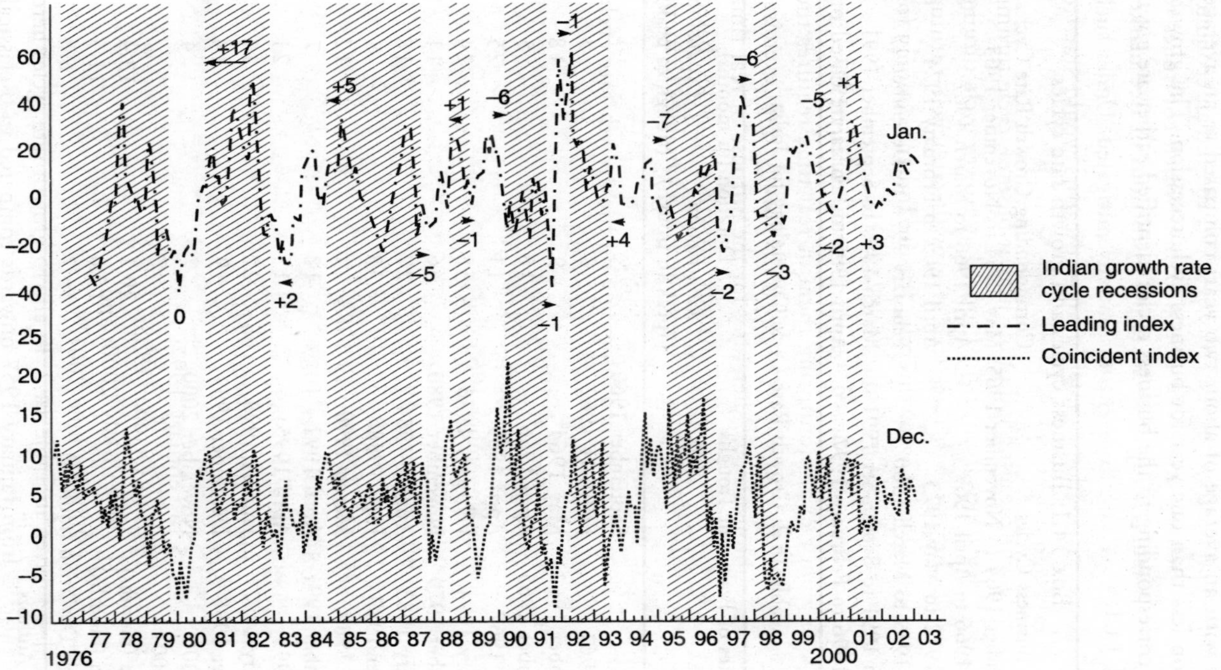

Figure 14.2: Indian Leading and Coincident Indexes, growth rates (%).

higher with an average of about two years compased to an average duration less than one year for business cycle recession. The growth cycles corresponding to the business cycles identified earlier are given in box 14.1.

Box 14.1: Business cycles and growth rate cycles

Business Cycles	Corresponding Growth Rate Cycles
November 1964 to November 1965	May 1964 to November 1965
April 1966 to April 1967	April 1966 to March 1967
June 1972 to May 1973	April 1969 to February 1974
April 1979 to March 1980	February 1976 to December 1979
March 1991 to September 1991	March 1990 to September 1991
May 1996 to February 1997	April 1995 to February 1997

Table 14.2: Growth Rate Cycle Chronology for India

Dates of Peaks and Troughs		Duration (in months)	
Trough	Peak	Contraction (peak to trough)	Expansion (trough to peak)
	September 1960		
May 1961	February 1962	8	9
November 1962	May 1964	9	18
November 1965	April 1966	18	5
March 1967	April 1969	11	25
February 1974	February 1976	58	24
December 1979	November 1980	46	11
February 1983	August 1984	27	18
October 1987	June 1988	38	8
March 1989	March 1990	9	12
September 1991	April 1992	18	7
July 1993	April 1995	15	21
February 1997	January 1998	22	11
October 1998	December 1999	9	14
July 2000	November 2000	7	4
June 2001		7	
Average (months)		20.1	13.4
Median (months)		15.0	11.5
Standard Deviation (months)		15.7	6.8

Source: Authors.

Note that except for the April 1966 recession, the growth rate cycle peaks lead their comparable business cycle peaks, highlighting the distinction between a slowdown and a full-fledged recession. This distinction is not marked for troughs. The average duration of growth rate cycles is less than three years with an average downturn lasting two years and an average upturn a little less than a year.

The business cycle and growth rate cycle turning points reported above represent the targets that leading indicators and their growth rates, respectively, are meant to forecast.

An Indian Leading Index

The obvious approach to the identification of leading indicators for the Indian economy is based primarily on their empirical ability to forecast past economic cycles. However, as we have discussed in the previous section, the structure of the Indian economy and the likely relationships between leading indicators and the Indian economic cycle have undergone profound changes over the last couple of decades. Therefore, any approach based on historical data fitting is likely to be doomed to failure. Even if the performance of any such indicators appear to be good over past decades, it is doubtful that such performance would persist, given the structural shifts that have accured.

The alternative would be to identify a robust set of leading indicators that are likely to work in any free market economy. Fortunately, such an approach is feasible. It is based on the findings of Klein (1983), Klein and Moore (1985); and Moore and Cullity (1994) who demonstrate that leading indicators selected on the basis of an understanding of the key drivers of economic cycles consistently work in a variety of market economies. Klein (1983) shows that while the list of leading indicators originally proposed by Moore and Shiskin (1967) was revised over time, the variables included in the first five sets of leading indicators exhibit remarkable consistency in timing.

Moore and Cullity (1994) show that the first-ever list of leading indicators of recession and recovery (Moore 1950), which Moore had picked 50 years ago, based on economic rationale as well as empirical performance between 1870 and 1938, continued to work very well in the second half of the twentieth century, not only in the US, but also in 10 other economies ranging from Germany to Japan, Korea,

Taiwan, and New Zealand. In other words, leading indicators that had correctly predicted turning points in the nineteenth century US economy continued to perform well not only in the US but also in diverse market economies despite structural differences. This empirical robustness of the leading indicator approach refuted the criticism that the indicator approach represented 'measurement without theory' (Koopmans 1947). Without the soundness of economic rationale, it would be difficult for the same indicators that worked in the post Civil War US economy to continue working in late 20th century Korea, which is structurally so different.

Similar results were obtained by Klein and Moore (1985) in their IEI project started at the NBER in the 1970s. Their work on developing international economic indicators focused mainly on growth cycles based on the deviations of indicators from trend. Their analysis shows that a set of roughly equivalent leading indicators consistently led growth cycle turning points in diverse market-oriented economies. Recent work at ECRI on an even more diverse group of countries has confirmed the effectiveness of such an approach.

Accordingly, as in the case of every other country examined by ECRI, we selected roughly equivalent indicators, instead of choosing indicators according to the degree of statistical fit. This approach was made possible by our extensive experience in analysing economic cycles in a wide variety of international economies, and choosing the most robust indicators, or those that work in all countries covered.

Following this practice of using comparable indicators across countries, we constructed an indian leading index based on indicators from different sectors of the economy such as the monetary (for example, money supply, interest rates), construction (including housing) and corporate sectors (for example, performance of companies).

The composite index construction procedure is that used at ECRI. The design of the procedure is based on a detailed review of the issues that concern composite index construction (Boschan and Banerji 1990), so that it incorporates the strengths and avoids the weaknesses of a variety of approaches used around the world in the past decades.

The leading index is constructed from January 1976 through January 2003. As Figure 14.1 and Table 14.3 show, the leading index had an average lead of fourteen months at business cycle peaks, zero months at troughs and seven months overall. As Figure 14.2 and Table 14.4 show, the growth rate of the Indian leading index had an average lead of four months at growth rate cycle peaks, one month at troughs, and three months overall. These cyclical peak and trough dates were determined on the basis of the classical algorithm (Bry and Boschan 1971) developed at the NBER.

A closer look suggests that the leads were rather elusive until recent years (shaded cells). Until the early 1990s, the leading index was roughly coincident with business cycles, while the leading index growth rate was roughly coincident with growth rate cycles. However, in the last few years a clear pattern of leads has emerged.

Table 14.3: Lead/Lag Record of Indian Leading Index against Indian Business Cycle Chronology

Indian Business Cycle Turning Points		Indian Leading Index Turning Points		Lead (-) / Lag (+) in Months	
Troughs	Peaks	Troughs	Peaks	Troughs	Peaks
	4/1979		1/1979		−3
3/1980		5/1980		2	
			4/1982		extra
		6/1983		extra	
			1/1985		extra
		4/1986		extra	
	3/1991		9/1989		−18
9/1991		8/1991		−1	
	5/1996		9/1994		−20
2/1997		12/1996		−2	

	Troughs	Peaks	Overall
Average	0.0	−14.0	-7.0
Median	−1.0	−18.0	−2.5
Per cent Lead	67	100	83
Standard Deviation	2.1	9.3	9.5

Source: Authors.

This experience is consistent with the logic of leading indicators, which is predicated upon the existence of a free market economy. In the case of India, where the government had long distorted the free market, such an assumption had questionable validity until economic liberalization began in the early 1990s. Also, in earlier decades, a dominant agricultural sector vulnerable to the vagaries of the monsoon made crop failures the key cause of recessions. It is difficult for leading indicators to predict cyclical turns caused primarily by such exogenous shocks.

Under such circumstances, it is understandable that the leading indicators did not lead in a systematic manner, and also exhibited some extra cycles. However, a close look at Figure 14.2 suggests that virtually all these extra cycles corresponded to smaller, roughly contemporaneous fluctuations in the Indian coincident index introduced in Dua and Banerji (1999), most of which did not exhibit the pronounced, pervasive, and persistent declines that mark true cyclical downturns.

What is clear is that the Indian economy grew at a relatively staid and steady pace in the decades after independence, and recessions, caused mainly by bad monsoons, were relatively shallow. Such behaviour was consistent with a command economy, where the role of endogenous free market processes was limited and government action tended to smooth out cycles.

Leading Indicators in a Changing Economy

The Indian economy has changed profoundly in recent decades. The agricultural sector, which accounted for over 50 per cent of GDP until the early 1960s and over 40 per cent of GDP until the late 1970s, represented just 25 per cent of GDP by the end of the 1990s. Meanwhile, the spread of irrigation reduced the vulnerability of agriculture to the vagaries of the monsoon, while a sustained nationwide build-up of buffer stocks of foodgrains broke much of the linkage between crop failures and economic downturns. As a result, the Indian economy is now far less dependent on good monsoons to sustain growth than it was earlier.

Also liberalization began in earnest in 1991 after a balance of payments crisis. By the late 1990s, the economy had been partially liberalized and the leading indicators began to show consistent leads,

Table 14.4: Lead/Lag Record of Indian Leading Index Growth against Indian Growth Rate Chronology

Indian Growth Rate Cycle Turning Points		Leading Index Growth Rate Turning Points		Lead (-) / Lag (+) in Months	
Troughs	Peaks	Troughs	Peaks	Troughs	Peaks
12/1979		12/1979		0	
	11/1980		4/1982		17
2/1983		4/1983		2	
	8/1984		1/1985		5
		4/1986		extra	
			1/1987		extra
10/1987		5/1987		−5	
	6/1988		7/1988		1
3/1989		2/1989		−1	
	3/1990		9/1989		−6
9/1991		8/1991		−1	
	4/1992		3/1992		−1
7/1993		11/1993		4	
	4/1995		9/1994		−7
2/1997		12/1996		−2	
	1/1998		7/1997		−6
10/1998		7/1998		−3	
	12/1999		7/1999		−5
07/2000		5/2000		−2	
	11/2000		12/2000		1
6/2001		9/2001		3	
				Troughs	Peaks
				Overall	
			Average	−1	0
				0	
			Median	−1.0	−1.0
				−1.0	
			Percent Lead	65	56
				61	
			Average, 1994–2003	−1	−4
				−5	
			Median, 1994–2003	−2.0	−5.5
				−2.5	
			Percent Lead, 1994–2003	75	75
				75	

Source: Authors.

Table 14.5: Lead(–)/Lag(+) of Indian Leading Index at Cyclical Turning Points Until 1993 and Later

Period	Median Lead at Business Cycle		Median Lead at Growth Rate Cycle		Per cent Leat at Growth Rate Cycle	
	Troughs	Peaks	Troughs	Peaks	Troughs	Peaks
1993 and earlier	0.5	–10.5	–0.5	1.0	58	40
After 1993	–2.0	–11.0	–2.0	–5.5	75	75

as in other free market economies (Table 14.4). In fact, the average lead of the Indian leading index growth rate in the two most recent growth rate cycles (shaded cells) has improved to five months.

How much liberalization does it take, then, for leading indicators to start working? It seems, based on our results, that after 1993 a sufficient degree of liberalization had occurred for the leading index to show more consistent leads (consider the statistics shown in Table 14.5).

The percentage of time that the leading index growth rate shows leads at growth rate cycle turns has increased from 50 per cent to 75 per cent. Meanwhile, the median lead has increased by 2.5 months and 0.5 months respectively at business cycle troughs and peaks, while it has increased by 1.5 months and 6.5 months, respectively, at growth rate cycle troughs and peaks. Does this mark a true shift in the behaviour of the leading index or is it just a statistical fluke?

It is important to note that it is not a simply a change in the relationship of the leading index with the coincident index that is at issue here. The question is whether there is a change in the behaviour of the leading index at business cycle and growth rate cycle turning points. This is because the primary purpose of a leading index is to anticipate cyclical turns in the economy, not necessarily to forecast economic conditions at other times.

Unfortunately, there is a very limited number of turning points that can be examined—just five and six, respectively, at growth rate cycle peaks and troughs until 1993, and four each after 1993. With such a small number of data points, it is not feasible to arrive at a definite conclusion about a post-liberalization shift in cyclical behaviour.

Conclusion

The foundation for this research was the determination of business cycle and growth rate cycles for the Indian economy, based on a traditional NBER-type approach. Earlier research involved the creation of an index of coincident economic indicators, and the determination of the reference chronologies based on a consensus of the turning points of this index and its components.

An obvious approach might have been to start with a plausible set of leading indicators, and to check what worked well in predicting past cyclical turns. The problem, however, was that the Indian economy had undergone major structural changes in recent years, and past performance might have had very little implication for future success.

Instead, we adopted a different approach inspired by the work of Klein and Moore (1985) and Moore and Cullity (1994), as well as more recent work at ECRI for a variety of economies, on robust sets of leading indicators. This work showed that, based on an appreciation of the key drivers of the business cycle, it was possible to identify leading indicators that were robust enough to work in a variety of market economies. Such sets of roughly equivalent indicators are monitored monthly by ECRI for 16 countries including both developed and developing economies, and have been shown to have good historical as well as real time performance. This was the robust set of indicators used for India.

Since the Indian economy has been undergoing major structural changes in the liberalization process, we believe that pre-liberalization performance may not be relevant to the future success of the index. Instead, our approach has been to focus on the array of robust leading indicators that work consistently in other market economies, and show that these are now working in the Indian economy.

Clearly, what we are assuming by following this approach is that the new Indian economy has more cyclical features in common with other market economies than with its own earlier incarnation. Our consistent success in a variety of other market economies gives us the confidence to adopt this approach. The results are consistent with this view—after all, these same indicators work in country after country and also in the new Indian economy—but do not work in pre-liberalization India.

Our procedure is at clear variance with more data-driven approaches. In any case, in the post-liberalization period there simply is not enough data which could be fitted in a way that is likely to work in the future—and such an approach is risky, given the structural shifts. In effect, what we have is an 'out-of-sample' test for the same indicators that we have used in many other countries, and it works in the period where it is expected to.

Our results provide an indirect window into India's progress towards a market economy. In a sense, the emergence of leads since the mid-1990s is evidence that the free market is starting to dominate the Indian economy. In this liberalized economy, it may be expected that in spite of their indifferent record before the mid-1990s, the leading index and its components will successfully anticipate future cycles in the Indian economy.

The creation of coincident and leading indexes for the Indian economy represents only the first step in designing a system of cyclical indexes for India. The fact is, in the decades since the creation of the original indexes of leading and coincident indicators by Moore and Shiskin, the general approach has been refined under Moore's guidance. This has culminated in a multidimensional framework (Banerji and Hiris 2001) encompassing key aspects of the economy, such as employment, inflation and foreign trade. In the context of this framework, we have already created a leading index of exports for the Indian economy (Dua and Banerji 2001b). In future, we hope to use this framework to create indexes that relate to other aspects of the economy, so as to permit a more nuanced and fine-grained view of Indian economic cycles.

References

Ashton, T.S. (1959), *Economic Fluctuations in England, 1700–1800*. Oxford: Clarendon Press.

Banerji, A. (1999), 'The Three P's: Simple Rules for Monitoring Economic Cycles', *Business Economics*, Vol. XXXIV, No. 4, pp. 72–6.

Banerji, A. and L. Hiris (2001), 'A Framework for Measuring International Business Cycles', *International Journal of Forecasting*, Vol. 17, pp. 333–48.

Basu, K. (1992), 'Markets, Laws and Governments', in B. Jalan (Ed.) *The Indian Economy: Problems and Prospects,* New Delhi: Penguin Books.

Boschan, C. and A. Banerji (1990), 'A Reassessment of Composite Indexes', in P.A. Klein (Ed.) *Analyzing Modern Business Cycles: Essays Honoring Geoffrey H. Moore,*. Armonk, NY: M.E. Sharpe.

Boschan, C. and W.W. Ebanks (1978), 'The Phase-Average Trend: A New Way of Measuring Growth', Proceedings of the Business and Economic Statistics Section, American Statistical Association, Washington D.C.

Bry, G. and C. Boschan (1971), *Cyclical Analysis of Time Series: Selected Procedures and Computer Programs,* National Bureau of Economic Research, Technical Paper No. 20, New York.

Burns, A.F. and W.C. Mitchell (1946), *Measuring Business Cycles,* National Bureau of Economic Research, New York.

Chitre, V.S. (2001) 'Indicators of Business Recessions and Revivals in India', *Indian Economic Review,* Vol. XXXVI, No. 1, pp. 55–78.

—— (1982), 'Growth Cycles in the Indian Economy', *Artha Vijnana,* Vol. 24, pp. 293–450.

Cullity, J.P. and A. Banerji (1996), 'Composite Indexes: A Reassessment', presented at the meeting on OECD Leading Indicators, Paris.

Diebold, F.X. and Rudebush, G.D. (1992), 'Have Postwar Economic Fluctuations Been Stabilized', *American Economic Review,* Vol. 82, No. 4, pp. 993–1005.

Dua, P. and A. Banerji (2001a), 'An Indicator Approach to Business and Growth Rate Cycles: The Case of India', *Indian Economic Review,* Vol. XXXVI, pp. 55–78.

—— (2001b), 'A Leading Index for India's Exports', Development Research Group Study No. 23, Reserve Bank of India, Mumbai.

—— (1999), 'An Index of Coincident Economic Indicators for the Indian Economy', *Journal of Quantitative Economics,* Vol. 15, pp. 177–201.

Hamilton, J. (1989), 'A New Approach to Economic Analysis of Nonstationary Time Series', *Econometrica,* Vol. 57, pp. 357–84.

Klein, P.A. (1998), 'Swedish Business Cycles—Assessing the Recent Record', Working Paper 21, Federation of Swedish Industries, Stockholm.

—— (1985), 'Monitoring Growth Cycles in Market-Oriented Countries, Developing and Using International Economic Indicators', *NBER Studies in Business Cycles,* No. 26, Cambridge, MA: Ballinger.

—— (1983), 'The Neglected Institutionalism of Wesley Clair Mitchell: The Theoretical Basis for Business Cycle Indicators', *Journal of Economic Issues,* Vol. 17, pp. 867–99, reprinted in P.A. Klein (1994), *Beyond Dissent,* New York: M.E. Sharpe.

—— and G.H. Moore (1985), *Monitoring Growth cycles in Market-oriented countries: Developing and using International Economic Indicators,* for NBER, Cambridge, MA:

Koopman, T. (1947), 'Measurement Without Theory', *Review of Economics and Statistics,* Vol. 29, pp. 161–72.

Lahiri, K. and G.H. Moore (Eds) (1991), *Leading Economic Indicators: New Approaches and Forecasting Record*, New York: Cambridge University Press.

Layton, A.P. and A. Banerji (2001), 'Dating the Indian Business Cycle: Is Output All that Counts?' *Indian Economic Review*, Vol. XXXVI, No. 1 pp. 231–40.

—— and G.H. Moore (1989), 'Leading Indicators for the Service Sector', *Journal of Business and Economic Statistics*, Vol. 7, pp. 379–86.

Mintz, I. (1974), 'Dating United States Growth Cycles', *Explorations in Economic Research*, Vol. 1, pp. 1–113.

—— (1972), 'Dating American Growth Cycles', in V. Zarnowitz (Ed.), *The Business Cycle Today*, NBER, New York.

—— (1969), 'Dating Postwar Business Cycles: Methods and their Application to Western Germany, 1950–67', Occasional Paper No. 107, National Bureau of Economic Research, New York.

Mitchell, W. (1927), *Business Cycles: The Problem and its Setting*', National Bureau of Economic Research Studies in Business Cycles, No. 1 and General Series No. 10.

—— and A.F. Burns (1938), 'Statistical Indicators of Cyclical Revivals and Recessions', *Bulletin*, Vol. 69, National Bureau of Economic Research, reprinted in G.H. Moore (Ed.) (1961), *Business Cycle Indicators: Contributions to the Analysis of Current Business Conditions*, Vol. I, National Bureau of Economic Research.

Moore, G.H. (1990), 'Leading Indicators for the 1990s', Homewood, Illinois: Dow-Jones-Irwin.

—— (1982), 'Business Cycles' in D. Greenwald (Editor in Chief), *Encyclopaedia of Economics*, New York: McGraw Hill Book Company.

—— (1975), 'The Analysis of Economic Indicators', *Scientific American*, pp. 17–23.

—— (1961), *Business Cycle Indicators*, Vols I and II, Princeton, New Jersey: Princeton University Press.

—— (1958), 'Forecasting Industrial Production—A Comment', *Journal of Political Economy*, February, Vol. xvi, No. 1, pp. 74–83.

—— (1955), 'The Diffusion of Business Cycles', in R.A. Solow (Ed.), *Economics and the Private Interest*, pp. 35–8, New Brunswick, New Jersey, Rutgers University Press, reprinted in Moore (1961).

—— (1950), *Cyclical Indicators of Revivals and Recessions*, National Bureau of Economic Research, Occasional Paper No. 31.

—— and P.A. Klein (1967), 'The Quality of Consumer Instalment Credit', National Bureau of Economic Research, New York.

—— and J. Shiskin (1967), *Indicators of Business Expansions and Contractions*, National Bureau of Economic Research, New York.

Moore, G.H. and J.P. Cullity (1994), 'The Historical Record of Leading Indicators-An Answer to 'Measurement Without Theory', in K.H. Oppenlander and G. Poser (Eds) *The Explanatory Power of Business Cycle Surveys*, Papers presented at the 21st CIRET Conference Proceedings, Stellenbosch, 1993, Aldershot, UK: Avebury.

Neftci, S. (1982), 'Optimal Prediction of Cyclical Downturns', *Journal of Economic Dynamics and Control*, pp. 225–41.

Niemira, M.P. and P.A. Klein (1994), *Forecasting Financial and Economic Cycles*, New York: John Wiley and Sons.

Siegel, S. (1956), *Nonparametric Statistics for the Behavioral Sciences*, New York: McGraw-Hill.

Stock, J. and M. Watson (1989), 'New Indexes of Leading and Coincidental Economic Indicators', *National Bureau of Economic Research Macroeconomics Annual*, pp. 351–94.

Vilasuso, J. (1996), 'Changes in Duration of Economic Expansions and Contractions in the United States', *Applied Economic Letters*, Vol. 2, No. 10, pp. 403–5.

Zarnowitz, V. (1992), *Business Cycles: Theory, History and Forecasting*, Chicago: University of Chicago Press.

—— (1991), 'What is a Business Cycle?', NBER Working Paper Series, No. 3863, Cambridge, MA, National Bureau of Economic Research.

—— and C. Boschan (1975), 'Cyclical Indicators: An Evaluation and New Leading Indexes', in *Handbook of Cyclical Indicators*, Washington, D.C: Government Printing Office.

Zarnowitz, V., C. Boschan, and G.H. Moore (1981), 'Sequential Signals of Recession and Recovery', *Journal of Business*, Vol. 55, pp. 57–85 reprinted in G.H. Moore (1983), '*Business Cycles, Inflation and Forecasting*', Second edition, Cambridge, MA: Ballinger.

15

Dating Business Cycles
Why Output Alone is not Enough!

Allan P. Layton and Anirvan Banerji

Introduction

Since 1996, India has moved from annual estimates of gross domestic product (GDP) to quarterly estimates. It is natural to ask what implications this might, or should, have for determining and maintaining an Indian business cycle chronology. Some have argued recently, for instance, that if one is interested only in a quarterly chronology then quarterly GDP is all that is needed. Others have gone further to argue that, if monthly GDP data were available (as is the case—at least experimentally—in a few countries), then this single series would be all that would be required to establish a monthly business cycle chronology. In fact, there have been some suggestions in the past in India that since fairly prompt readings of the index of industrial production (IIP) have long been available on a monthly basis, that series alone may be a reasonable basis for determining the Indian business cycle chronology.

Geoffrey H. Moore, we are certain, would have taken strong exception to these suggestions concerning the sufficiency of GDP or

We should point out that the current paper draws significantly on Layton and Banerji (2001) where we have made the same arguments as well as provided a detailed analysis of using GDP alone to date post-World War II US business cycles.

IIP alone in dating the business cycle. Moore worked closely with Burns and Mitchell (1946) at the National Bureau of Economic Research (NBER), was a member of the NBER's official business cycle dating panel[1] and a strong believer in the use of a range of series, in addition to GDP, to arrive at a chronology.

We felt it was important to write this paper for two reasons. First, there currently appear to be somewhat diverging views as to what properly constitutes a recession. Second, largely as a result of this, in many countries there is no single widely-accepted business cycle chronology for the country in question. This is potentially quite serious. The existence of a commonly accepted chronology allows proper analysis of previous business cycle episodes giving very valuable insights into the conduct of policy then and in the future. To be most useful, such analyses require a general acceptance of the specifics of the country's chronology.

The most widely quoted conceptual definition of the business cycle is that due to Burns and Mitchell (1946 p. 3): Business cycles are a type of fluctuation found in the aggregate economic activity of nations… : a cycle consists of expansions occurring at about the same time in many economic activities, followed by similarly general recessions, contractions, and revivals which merge into the expansion phase of the next cycle; this sequence of changes is recurrent but not periodic.

A critical aspect of the above definition is: What should we understand as 'aggregate economic activity'? Some have recently suggested that 'aggregate economic activity' can be well represented simply by GDP.

We argue that such an approach is both inadequate and at odds with the approach taken by the NBER and should not, therefore, be used. In addition to an output dimension, we argue that there are also other important dimensions to aggregate economic activity which need to be considered, viz., income, sales and employment. These latter measures may well show similar patterns to output over the longer term, however, in particular macroeconomic episodes, their short term movements are often quite different from measured GDP. Their short-term cyclical movements are, therefore, quite often of material importance in precisely dating the peaks and troughs in the business cycle. Our perspective would seem to be at odds with, for example, Pagan (1997), Harding and Pagan (1999), and Boehm and Summers (1999). However, our approach, we believe, is more consistent with Moore (1967,1982), Stock and Watson (1991), the US Federal Reserve System, and the NBER itself.

The paper is organized as follows. In the next section we provide our reasons for arguing against using GDP, or, for that matter, IIP, alone to date the business cycle. We contend that such an approach is, at the very least, entirely at odds with those NBER researchers who pioneered the study of the business cycle. Some Indian empirical work follows with brief conclusions provided in the fourth section.

The Business Cycle

The Business Cycle Concept

As has been noted, the core of the issue boils down to a practical, workable definition of aggregate economic activity. As noted in the introduction, some argue that a satisfactory proxy for this is now GDP, being as it is the most comprehensive measure we have of a nation's total production in a given period. It is certainly true that GDP is about as aggregate a measure of output as we can get. Nonetheless, it still measures only output.

What are the supporting reasons put forward by those in favour of GDP (or IIP) alone being used as a proxy for aggregate economic activity? The essence of the argument seems to be that only annual estimates of US GDP were available in the 1920s and 1930s when Mitchell began his work of developing a US business cycle chronology. What was wanted was a monthly chronology and so it was necessary for many alternative, but imperfect, macroeconomic time series to be studied. Little changed with the introduction of quarterly GDP estimates since Mitchell (and Burns) wanted a monthly chronology and this still required a range of alternative monthly measures of economic activity to be considered to identify the precise month of the relevant turning point.

On this output-based view of the concept of aggregate economic activity a quarterly chronology, if that was all that was wanted, would simply require quarterly GDP. Furthermore, if an accurate monthly estimate of GDP were to become available then it would be all that would be required. Burns and Mitchell (1946) themselves said on this issue (pp. 72–3):

> Aggregate activity can be given a definite meaning and made conceptually measurable by identifying it with gross national product. However, for the

purposes of analyzing business cycles, it is better to restrict the total to the portion of the national product that passes through the 'market'... . Similar restrictions apply to other measures of aggregate activity that might be used, such as the physical volume of production or the volume of employment... Unfortunately, no satisfactory series of any of these types is available by months or quarters for periods approximating those we seek to cover.

Given their explicit reference to employment, we believe that, if available for direct comment today, Burns and Mitchell would argue that GDP is not, by itself, sufficient to capture what they meant by aggregate economic activity. At the very least, employment variation is another important dimension to the business cycle. In fact, according to the NBER's business cycle dating committee[2], 'employment is probably the single most reliable indicator' of recessions.

In contrast to this, Boehm and Summers (1999, p.13) philosophically subscribe to the view that the 'ideal measure' for business cycle dating purposes would be monthly GDP. They argue that the only reason for analysing series other than GDP and combining them (along with GDP) into a composite index is the absence of a reliable monthly measure of real GDP. This is at odds, we believe, with the NBER, the original progenitors of business cycle analysis, as well more modern exponents such as Stock and Watson. It is also at odds with the thinking of Geoffrey Moore, that other great proponent of the economic indicator approach to business cycle analysis.

One point needs to be clarified before proceeding. Clearly, one significant advantage of analysing a range of roughly coincident macroeconomic series is that almost all such time series are measured with error and are often revised, sometimes very significantly. Thus, the existence of such measurement error alone is strong justification for avoiding reliance on any single macroeconomic time series to determine a business cycle chronology.

A recent, and very stark, example of the folly of this over-reliance on one indicator—namely GDP—is the 2001 US recession. The official date of the onset of that recession was determined late in 2001 by the NBER dating panel as the month of March.[3] This date was selected mainly on the basis of movements throughout late 2000 and early 2001 in US employment, unemployment, industrial production and retail sales as well as GDP growth. However, at the time of dating by the NBER panel, there had been only one quarter of negative growth in GDP (the September quarter) and so there was some considerable debate in the second half of 2001 and into 2002 as to whether the US had actually entered into recession at all during 2001!

It was not until the June quarter 2002 US national accounts figures were released in July, 2002 that subsequent revisions to the 2001 GDP data confirmed that the US had, in fact, actually experienced three consecutive quarters of negative growth (March, June, and September) in 2001! Thus a full 15 months after the actual onset of the 2001 US recession, was it finally evidenced in revised GDP data—completely vindicating the much earlier determination by the NBER.

In passing, this latest US recessionary episode provides a vivid example of how simple ex-post correlation analyses of GDP growth data against the official US business cycle chronology can easily give quite a misleading impression of the very significant added value of analysing a range of series other than GDP when determining the phase of the business cycle in real time. In 20 years from now, the final data will simply show that the 2001 US recession officially began in the first quarter of three consecutive quarters of negative GDP growth. A new generation business cycle analyst looking at the data in 2022 would have to be very thorough indeed (and have access to original unrevised data vintages and real time debates and commentary) to uncover the actual circumstances surrounding the dating of this most recent US business cycle turning point.

The same is also almost certainly true of many other earlier turning point dates. For instance, it is not widely known that the fixed-weight GDP estimates used in the US until 1995 showed only one down quarter of GDP in the officially recognized recession of 1980. But it was not until 1995 that the adoption of chain-weighted GDP estimates revealed, 15 years after the fact, that the 1980 recession had shown two successive quarterly declines in GDP.

Whilst the above certainly provides a powerful justification for looking beyond any single putative measure of aggregate economic activity, we believe the motivation for looking at a range of measures other than GDP—irrespective of its frequency of measurement—is much more profound than simply allowing for measurement error. Rather it involves the essential philosophical question of what should constitute aggregate economic activity, and, therefore, the business cycle. We believe it should be recognized as being much more than simply a downturn in measured output. Most crucially, it must also encompass employment dimensions.

Thus, the analysis of series such as retail sales, industrial production and GDP may be regarded as attempts to gauge the current state of demand and output production in the economy. However, the inclusion of series such as household income, employment and the unemployment rate is an explicit recognition of the impact of variation in output and demand on community welfare and is, therefore, very much an integral aspect of any business cycle.

Some would argue that the inclusion of output measures indirectly captures these latter effects. However, in different cycles and over the course of any given cycle, the relationship between output growth and employment is not very stable or precise. For example, the early 1990s recession in Australia was characterized by GDP beginning to grow again after five quarters. However, for quite a long period, such growth was very slow. The result was that, even after GDP had begun growing again, there was virtually no employment growth for quite some time with the result that the unemployment rate continued to climb for almost another year!

Another clue to what was in the minds of Burns and Mitchell is evident from this quote from Burns (1952, p. 36), 'and if business cycles are... a congeries of interrelated phenomena, any distinction between the problem of how business cycles run their course and how our economic organization works cannot but be artificial'.

It should be noted from this that, in business cycle analysis, has always been the co-movement of a number of key macroeconomic time series of crucial importance. Those who favour using GDP alone for business cycle dating appear to have forgotten this very important aspect of business cycles since the use of a single measure such as GDP can never hope to capture this critical aspect of the nature of business cycles. And again from Burns (1952, p. 36):

> To Mitchell a business cycle meant more than a fluctuation in a single aggregate such as national income or employment. It also meant that the fluctuation... is diffused through economic activity... appearing, as a rule... in markets for... commodities and labor, in processes of saving and investment, in finance as well as in industry and commerce.

And, finally, we have from Moore (1982, p. 98):

> No single measure of aggregate economic activity is called for in the definition because several such measures appear relevant to the problem, including

output, employment, income and [wholesale and retail] trade... Use of several measures necessitates an effort to determine what is the consensus among them, but it avoids the arbitrariness of deciding upon a single measure...

Here, Moore quite clearly indicates there are several important dimensions to the concept of a business cycle (rather than just produced output). Whilst he also recognizes that the use of several series complicates the dating process, this is to be preferred to the use of a single series. We also note that the NBER itself continues to state,[4] 'the NBER does not define a recession in terms of two consecutive quarters of decline in real GNP. Rather, a recession is a period of significant decline in total output, income, employment, and trade, usually lasting from six months to a year, and marked by widespread contractions in many sectors of the economy'.

Furthermore, James Stock and Mark Watson of the NBER have continued the work begun by Burns, Mitchell, and Moore and, although they employ more modern statistical methods in their approach, they too acknowledge the fundamental importance of looking at a range of complementary indicators rather than relying simply on GDP as the proxy for the business cycle (see, for example, Stock and Watson (1991, pp. 64–5).

Importantly, the US Federal Reserve System also recognizes the importance of going beyond GDP in looking for a business cycle chronology. For example, Crone (2000) had this to say about dating the business cycle:

When someone asks, 'How's the economy doing?', it's often not clear which measure to point to. Should we refer to the unemployment rate, job growth, or some broader measure like the change in gross domestic product (GDP)... Each of these statistics has some information. But none has all the information we are looking for, and they sometimes give conflicting signals about where we are in the business cycle... A partial solution to this dilemma is to combine several measures into a composite index of current... economic activity. (pp. 3–4).

In sum, we feel that the evidence is overwhelmingly strong in favour of the view of Burns, Mitchell, and Moore, current NBER researchers, and the US Federal Reserve System that there needs to be more to dating the business cycle than just using GDP. Further, we would argue that this is not simply the recognition of the existence of measurement error in macroeconomic time series, nor is it the unavailability of a monthly measure of real GDP. Rather, it is critically to do with the fundamental philosophical view that the proper characterization of the 'business cycle' or the 'state of the economy' involves an employment and income dimension as well as measured output. gross domestic product, even if available monthly and without error, is certainly not all that would be required as the 'ideal measure' for business cycle dating.

DATING THE BUSINESS CYCLE

How should we determine the chronology of the business cycle, viz., the set of dates of turning points (peaks and troughs) in aggregate economic activity? One currently popular way of doing this is to use the 'at least two consecutive negative quarterly growth rates' rule to determine the beginning of a recession; the peak being the period immediately before the first of the negative growth quarters. An analogous rule is used to date the trough.

Elsewhere (Layton and Banerji 2001), we have argued strongly that this practice was not and is not that used by the NBER, has no persuasive basis of support, and can lead to quite anomalous outcomes as far as determining a business cycle chronology is concerned. Instead, we would urge practitioners interested in determining turning points to use the computer algorithm developed by Bry and Boschan (1971). This algorithm was written with the goal of capturing the intent and practice of those at the NBER who were the originators of business cycle dating research (Burns, Mitchell, Moore, Shiskin). The interested reader is referred to Layton and Banerji (2001) for more on this issue.

Thus, in summary, we argue that, in dating recessions, it is necessary to do three things. First, analysts must look to more than just GDP, or monthly IIP, or any other single series. Rather, a range of measures, covering employment, income, and sales in addition to output measures need to be investigated to determine whether a business cycle turn has occurred. Second, turning points in these individual series need to be determined but not by the 'two consecutive quarterly growth rate rule'. Rather, we recommend that the widely used and accepted algorithm developed by Bry and Boschan (1971) be used. Third, a consensus date is then selected from the turning point dates for each of the series in question and this becomes the business cycle turning point.

Some Indian Empirical Work

As noted in the previous section, we believe that it is totally inappropriate to base the determination of a country's business cycle chronology purely on an output measure, whether this measure is quarterly GDP or monthly IIP. In this section we illustrate this issue in relation to the Indian economy.

The question is whether output is a satisfactory basis for determining the dates of Indian business cycles. Since Indian GDP has become available only quite recently on a quarterly basis, an empirical analysis showing the consequences of choosing business cycle dates on the basis of GDP is not possible.

However, it has been suggested in the past that the monthly IIP, a far narrower measure of output, could be used instead as the basis for determining the dates of Indian business cycles. As Table 15.1 shows, however, according to the Bry–Boschan (1971) procedure—an algorithmic codification of the NBER rules for selecting cyclical turns—the IIP picks up only one of the six recognized cycles in the Indian business cycle chronology, and misses the other five. In contrast, the indian coincident index (ICI) described in Dua and Banerji (1999)—which is a much broader activity measure than the IIP—misses only one of the six cycles according to the Bry–Boschan procedure.

Even if we tried manually to pick the local highs and lows in the IIP and ICI corresponding to the Indian business cycle chronology, in order to judgmentally supplement the Bry–Boschan procedure's picks, the timing of the turns is still revealing. As Table 15.1 shows, the turning points in the ICI correspond quite closely to the timing of the business cycle turns, with the median leads at peaks, troughs, and overall, all being zero. In contrast, the turns in the IIP do not correspond all that closely to the business cycle turns, and have a median lead of three months at troughs and a median lag of one month at peaks.

Not surprisingly, the standard deviation of the leads of the IIP is almost four times that of the ICI, even if we assume that all those turns had been correctly picked up. Of course, as we have pointed out, the IIP does not in fact show cyclical turns in almost all the cases and is, therefore, a highly unsuitable basis for the determination of business cycle dates.

In sum, it is empirically clear that measures of output alone would

Table 15.1: Turning Point Analysis of Indian Business Cycle

Indian Business Cycle		Indian Coincident Index								Indian Industrial Production			
				Lead(–)/ Lag(+) (months)		% Change	Duration of Decline (months)			Lead(–)/ Lag(+) (months)		% Change	Duration of Decline (months)
T	P	T	P	T	P			T	P	T	P		
	Nov 64		Nov 64		0				Jun 65		7		
Nov 65		Jan 66		2		–4.7	14	Jan 66		2		–8.0	7
	Apr 66		*Apr 66*		0				May 66		1		
Apr 67		*Mar 67*		–1		–7.1	11	Feb 67		–2		–5.6	9
	Jun 72		*Jun 72*		0				Oct 72		4		
May 73		*May 73*		0		–5.4	11	Feb 73		–3		–4.5	4
	Apr 79		*Apr 79*		0				*Mar 79*		–1		
Mar 80		*Mar 80*		0		–5.5	11	*Dec 79*		–3		–8.4	9
	Mar 91		*Mar 91*		0				Mar 91		0		
Sep 91		*Sep 91*		0		–8.8	6	Jul 92		10		–9.3	4
	May 96		*May 96*		0				May 96		0		
Feb 97		*Nov 96*		–3		–9.1	6	Nov 96		–3		–3.4	6
Average at T				0						0			
Average at P					0						2		
Average Overall				0						1			

Contd.

	Indian Business Cycle		Lead(–)/ Lag(+) (months)		Indian Coincident Index		% Change	Duration of Decline (months)	Lead(–)/ Lag(+) (months)		Indian Industrial Production		% Change	Duration of Decline (months)
	T	P	T	P	T	P			T	P	T	P		
Median at T					0						–3			
Median at P						0						1		
Median Overall					0						0			
Standard Deviation at T					1.6						5.2			
Standard Deviation at P						0.0						3.1		
Standard Deviation Overall					1.1						4.2			

Source: Indian business cycle chronology as determined by Dua and Banerji (1999).

Notes: T = Trough, P = Peak; For ICI and IIP, only those turning points in italics were properly identified by the Bry–Boschan (1971) algorithm.

have had a dubious record of picking the appropriate business cycle turning points in the case of the Indian economy.

Final Remarks

As noted in the introduction, the existence of a commonly accepted business cycle chronology allows a proper analysis of previous recessionary or expansionary episodes. Such analyses provide very valuable insights into the conduct of macroeconomic policy at the time, and for the sake of consistency, it is desirable to have a general acceptance of the specifics of the country's chronology.

In this paper we have argued that the proper conceptual definition of the business cycle requires more than simply an analysis of quarterly GDP (or monthly IIP). We have argued that other measures, particularly employment measures, but also sales and income measures, should figure prominently in any analysis and dating of a country's business cycle.

This is not because of the non-availability of a monthly measure of GDP. We argue that fundamentally a business cycle must be defined in terms of more than just the measured output of an economy. A careful analysis of the seminal writings on the topic strongly points to the necessity of incorporating dimensions other than output into a proper definition of the business cycle. This view precludes, but even more emphatically, the use of the IIP as the sole basis for determining the Indian business cycle chronology. After all, for the Indian economy, industrial production represents less than a third of total output.

The most recent recession in the US is the most telling example in recent times of how an over-reliance on just one series such as the GDP can lead to seriously incorrect conclusions in respect of the business cycle. The official start date of this most recent US recession is March 2001 with a most likely end date of December 2001 or January 2002. However, up until July 2002, there had not as yet been two consecutive negative growth rates in reported US GDP. Until then, the only negative quarterly growth was reported to have occurred in the third quarter of 2001. Thus, according to the 'two negative quarterly growth rates in GDP' rule, the US would not be regarded as entering into recession in 2001 and would have actually continued its 1990s expansion up to June 2002! This is despite the fact that, since late 2000, employment growth had stagnated and US unemployment had increased by around 50 per cent from its cyclical trough.

Of course, the US most certainly entered into recession in early 2001, the early warning indicators of which were in evidence since mid to late 2000. (ECRI first warned of the impending US recession in its *US Cyclical Outlook* in September 2000.) It was precisely because of that impending recession that the US Federal Reserve began aggressively easing monetary policy in January 2001 (but probably a little too late as it turned out) and eventually reduced interest rates to generational lows. Then finally, after 16 months, in July 2002 with the release of newly revised GDP data, it was finally in evidence that GDP had in fact actually experienced three consecutive quarters of negative growth during 2001, commencing in the March quarter.

Further to this very timely example, we have also shown elsewhere that the empirical evidence for the US strongly corroborates the basic premise of this paper; viz., that an output measure alone, whether available quarterly or monthly, is a poor way to determine the start and end dates of recessions. We have also sought to demonstrate this in the case of the Indian economy in this paper section.

As noted in the second section, at the core of the matter is the philosophical notion of what defines 'an economy'. We argue that it is much more than a broad measure of output. On the contrary, business cycles are characterized by cyclical co-movements of key coincident indicators such as output, income, sales, and employment, whose turning points collectively demarcate the periods of recession and expansion.

In practical rather than philosophical terms, a short-cut definition of recession based on output alone is likely to miss the essence of what a recession is, and thus improperly identify it. The danger is that such a mistaken identification of business cycle dates would lead to the selection of inappropriate leading indicators that would fail to anticipate recessions by any definition. As Prakash Loungani (2001) of the International Monetary Fund (IMF) concludes from a review of private and public sector forecasts in 63 industrialized and developing countries, 'the record of failure to predict recessions is virtually unblemished'. By contrast, ECRI's outstanding record of success in predicting recessions in the US and elsewhere suggests to us that while defining recessions properly is not a sufficient condition for accurately predicting recessions, it is probably a necessary condition.

In sum, it is not appropriate to use a single measure of output, regardless of frequency, as the unique basis for determining the dates of recessions. Rather, what is called for is the determination of the consensus of such coincident indicators about the date of each cyclical turning point. Such an analysis has been carried out for the Indian economy by Dua and Banerji (1999) and the resulting business cycle chronology determined (see Table 15.1).[5] We would encourage the various policy agencies to use this chronology as the basis of the Indian business cycle chronology.

Endnotes

[1]A country's business cycle chronology is the set of dates (desirably, monthly) corresponding to the aperiodic peaks (the month economic activity switches from expansion to contraction) and troughs (the month economic activity switches from contraction to expansion) in its business cycle. In the US, an official business cycle dating panel—under the auspices of the NBER—determines these dates.

[2]See the last question and answer in the NBER's 2001 recession announcement, at http://www.nber.org/cycles/november2001/

[3]It is worth noting that ECRI had been publicly predicting a 2001 recession since late 2000 and had tentatively picked March as the start date from as early as May 2001.

[4]This quote is taken from NBER website *http://www.nber.org/cycles.html* as at 9 May 2001.

[5]The recession start and end dates based on such a procedure, comparable to the NBER approach, is available for 16 other economies at *http://www.businesscycle.com/research/intlcycledates.html*

References

Bry, G. and C. Boschan (1971), 'Cyclical Analysis of Time Series: Selected Procedures and Computer Programs', Technical Paper 20, NBER, Columbia University Press.

Boehm, E. and P.M. Summers (1999), 'Analysing and Forecasting Business Cycles with the Aid of Economic Indicators', *Melbourne Institute Working Paper Series,* WP No. 18/99.

Burns, A. F. (1952), 'Wesley Clair Mitchell: The Economic Scientist', New York: NBER.

—— and W. Mitchell (1946), *Measuring Business Cycles*, New York: NBER.

Crone, T.M. (2000), 'A New Look at Economic Indexes for the States in the

Third District', *Current Business Review*, Federal Reserve Bank of Philadelphia, November–December, pp. 3–14.

Dua, P. and A. Banerji (1999), 'An Index of Coincident Economic Indicators for the Indian Economy', *Journal of Quantitative Economics*, Vol., 15 No. 2 July, pp. 177–201.

Harding, D. and A. Pagan (1999), 'Dissecting the Cycle', Melbourne Institute Working Paper Series, WP No. 13/99.

Layton, A.P. and A. Banerji (2001), 'What is a Recession?: A Reprise', International Economic Competitiveness Policy Discussion Paper No. 95, School of Economics and Finance, Queensland University of Technology.

Loungani, P. (2001), 'How accurate are private sector forecasts? Cross-country evidence from *consensus forecasts* of output growth', *International Journal of Forecasting*, Vol. 17, No. 3, July–September, pp. 419–32.

Moore, G.H., (1982), Extract on 'Business Cycles' from Douglas Greenwold *Encyclopedia of Economics*, New York: McGraw-Hill.

—— (1967), 'What is a recession?' *American Statistician*, October.

Pagan, A. (1997), 'Towards an Understanding of Some Business Cycle Characteristics', *Australian Economic Review*, Vol. 30, pp. 1–15.

Stock, J.H. and M.W. Watson (1991), 'A Probability Model of the Coincident Economic Indicators', in Kajal Lahiri and Geoffrey H. Moore (Eds), *Leading Economic Indicators*, Yew York and Melbourne: Cambridge University Press.

16

Economic Indicator Approach and Sectoral Analysis

Predicting Cycles in the Growth of Indian Exports

Pami Dua and Anirvan Banerji

Introduction

With greater globalization of the Indian economy, policy makers, businesses, and financial analysts are closely tracking the external sector. A key driver of this sector is the level of exports, which has, of late, grown significantly relative to GDP by almost 10 per cent. Since exports growth affects fluctuations in the growth of overall economic activity, it is essential to construct an accurate and reliable tool for forecasting fluctuations in exports. This study reports such a measure—the leading index for exports—whose growth rate predicts cyclical shifts in the growth rates of real exports, the price of exports, and the value of exports, respectively.

The leading indicator approach to business and economic forecasting is based on the premise that market-oriented economies experience business cycles consisting of 'expansions occurring at about

This paper is an updated and revised version of Dua and Banerji (2001a). We are grateful to the Development Research Group, Reserve Bank of India for providing support for an earlier version of this study. We are also grateful to Mi-Suk Ha and Sumant Kumar Rai for competent research assistance.

the same time in many economic activities, followed by similarly general recessions, contractions and revivals that merge into the expansion phase of the next cycle; this sequence of changes is recurrent but not periodic' (Burns and Mitchell 1946). The leading indicator approach, therefore, predicts these repetitive sequences of the business cycle.

This paper focuses on the external sector of the Indian economy. Since that sector is driven largely by other countries' economic cycles, it is typically not in sync with domestic business cycles, thus a leading index of the domestic economy may not be a good predictor of the external sector. Hence, a separate, specialized leading index is needed to forecast cycles in the external sector. This study constructs such an index to predict movements in exports.

The second section describes the underlying rationale for constructing a leading index for exports and outlines the methodology. The third section comments on its performance in predicting each of the three target variables: real exports, price of exports, and value of exports over the past 25 years. The fourth section evaluates the growth rate of the leading index using lead profiles and the concluding section sums up and notes the limitations of this study.

With the enormous fluctuations experienced in the exports sector in the past, a key question is whether it is possible to provide an early warning signal for at least some of these changes. This study aims to create such a signal for cyclical movements in the exports sector.

Rationale and Methodology

The construction of the leading index for exports is based on the premise that peaks and troughs in the business cycle and/or growth rate cycle[1] in the domestic economy are likely to be associated with exports to and imports from respective trading partners. For any economy, these cyclical upswings and downswings can be predicted by leading indices, typically six to nine months in advance. These cyclical changes in domestic demand also encompass the demand for imports. This implies that a leading index of a trading partner can provide useful information on the exports of any exporting country. This notion can be extended to a group of countries importing goods from an exporting country. Thus, a weighted average of the leading indexes of importing countries can be used to predict fluctuations in the exporting country's exports (Moore 1976; Klein and Moore 1978, 1980).

In addition to cyclical fluctuations in the economies of a given country's trading partners, exchange rate movements are also a vital harbinger of future exports. Of course, cyclical expansions in the trading partners' economies would herald an increase in the given country's exports. If, however, the value of its currency rises, the net impact on exports will be blunted or offset by the erosion in price competitiveness. Therefore, exchange rate fluctuations must also be taken into account along with cyclical factors in a country's trading partners to accurately predict cyclical swings in exports.

In a study of US exports, Cullity, Klein, and Moore (1987) combine exchange rates with conventional leading indices to predict US exports. They note that exchange rates have almost half a year's extra lead over exports compared to that of leading indices.

In a more recent study, the Economic Cycle Research Institute (ECRI 1997; Hiris *et al.* 1995) constructed a leading index of US exports that includes a broad-based, trade-weighted effective exchange rate index, as well as ECRI's long leading indices of ten industrial economies that include most of the major US trading partners. Long-leading indexes improve on the traditional leading indices by increasing the lead time to over a year, on average.[2] That is, long-leading indices have about half a year's extra lead over traditional leading indices. This implies that exchange rates as well as long-leading indices have about the same lead over exports and can be combined into a composite exports leading index.

In that study, the long-leading indices of ten countries were combined into a single index by weighting each country's index by the respective average share of US exports. This composite long-leading index was combined further with the 131-country trade-weighted real exchange rate index compiled by the Federal Reserve Bank of Dallas to yield the leading index for exports.

Cyclical activity in ECRI's leading index for US exports is measured in growth rate form. This is because cyclical declines in the level of exports are rare whereas movements in growth rate are relatively more frequent. Economic cycle research institute's leading index for US exports, therefore, predicts growth rates in exports. Cycles are thus expressed in terms of growth rates where the growth rate is measured by the 'six-month smoothed growth rate', which is based on the ratio of the latest month's figure to its average over the preceding twelve months, annualized and centred about six months before the latest month. Unlike the more commonly used 12-month change, it is not very sensitive to idiosyncratic occurrences 12 months earlier. A number of such advantages make the six-month smoothed growth rate a useful concept in cyclical analysis (Banerji 1999).

The exchange rate index as well as the composite leading index have cyclical movements around a trend that determine the cyclical movements of future exports. Note, however, that the multi-country composite leading index is itself a weighted average of several composite indices. The real exchange rate index represents a composite exchange rate and has completely different units from the leading index. Therefore, the two cannot be combined by simply using a weighted average. Instead, the composite index procedure—especially designed to combine the movements of a number of such heterogeneous cyclical time series—is used. Given the difference in units as well as the cyclical volatility of the exchange rate index and the composite leading index, it is important to ensure that the variable which moves in wide swings does not have a larger influence on the movement of the combined index than one which typically moves in narrow swings. This is achieved by the process of standardization, which involves adjusting the amplitudes of the two components by dividing each by its own historical cyclical volatility. After standardization, the cyclical movement of each component is expressed in units of its own cyclical volatility. The two standardized components are then aggregated, and trend and the amplitude of the combined series are adjusted to optimize cyclical performance.

To evaluate the predictive ability of the exports leading index (level or growth form), a reference chronology that dates the downturns in the export sector is required. For this, a single or composite time series is used as the 'target' variable and its turning points are determined. These turning points apply to contemporaneous economic activity. For a leading index to be useful, its turning points must precede those of the reference series. The first step in this analysis is, therefore, to determine the turning points of the reference series and the historical turning points of the leading index.

Turning points are chosen using mechanical procedures, supplemented by rules of thumb, and experienced judgment. The initial selection of turning points employs a computer program based on the procedures and rules developed at the National Bureau of Economic Research (NBER) (see Bry and Boschan 1971). The selection of a turning point must meet the following criteria: (i) at least five months opposite movement must occur to qualify as a turning point: (ii) peaks (troughs) must be at least fifteen months apart; and (iii) if the data are flat at the turning point, then the most recent period is selected as the turning point. These rules of thumb trace their roots to Burns and Mitchell (1946) and continue to be applied by the ECRI. Finally, turning points must pass muster through the experienced judgment of the researcher. Turning points can be rejected because of special one-time events that produce spikes in the data, indicating turning points. Experienced judgment also excludes non-cyclical exogenous shocks.

The methodology described above is applied to the Indian economy and two leading indices are constructed—one in level and the other in growth form. Dua and Banerji (2001a) evaluate these indices with reference to the levels and growth rates of three target variables—real exports, price of exports, and the product of the two, the total value of exports. In this study, which updates those results, for the sake of brevity we focus only on the performance of the growth rate of the leading index.

Leading Index for Indian Exports

The leading index for the level of future Indian exports comprises the real effective exchange rate (REER) and a 17-country long leading index. The REER index (RBI 1993) used is based on export weights and official exchange rates from January 1975 to February 1992 with base 1985=100. (Annual indices are available from 1960.) From March 1992, Foreign Exchange Dealers' Association of India (FEDAI) indicative rates are used and the base moves to 1993–4=100. The REER index is basically the weighted average of the bilateral nominal exchange rates of the home currency in terms of foreign currencies adjusted by domestic to foreign relative local-currency prices. The exchange rate of a currency is expressed as the number of units of special drawing rights (SDRs) that equal one unit of the currency (SDRs per currency). A fall in the exchange rate of the rupee against SDRs, therefore, represents a depreciation of the rupee relative to the SDR. Similarly, a rise in the exchange rate represents appreciation of the rupee. The nominal effective exchange rate (NEER) and REER indexes are based on bilateral export weights and total trade (exports plus imports) weights. The number of countries used is 36—representing 65 per cent to 70 per cent of total exports/trade during 1975 and 1991. Given that 36 countries are used, the weights are normalized accordingly for constructing the REER and NEER indexes for India. The large number of countries smoothens out the year-to-year variations in the share of any country and ensures that the pattern of trade is representative over a long span of time.

The 17-country index is a weighted average of the ECRI long leading indices for 17 countries that trade with India—US, Canada, Mexico, Germany, France, UK, Italy, Spain, Switzerland, Austria, Sweden, South Africa, Japan, Korea, Taiwan, Australia, and New Zealand, which collectively account for about half of India's total exports. The weights used in the 17-country long leading index are the percentages of India's exports accounted for by each of these countries in 1995, according to the Direction of Trade Statistics of the International Monetary Fund (IMF). The choice of the year 1995 was based on the fact that it was a relatively recent year where the direction of trade flows was not unduly distorted by the Asian crisis or other similar developments. Three target variables are used:

1. Real exports measured by the quantum index of exports;
2. Price of exports measured by the unit value index of exports; and
3. Total value of exports which is the product of the above two variables.

The leading exports index is used to predict each of these variables. The economic rationale is simple. The leading exports index has two basic components—the exchange rate, which determines price competitiveness, and the 17-country long leading index covering the export markets, which determines the cyclical movement of demand in the consuming countries. It follows that both these variables predict the movements in exports.

Traditionally, a leading exports index has been used to forecast real exports. In the case of India, we extend the analysis to encompass the price of exports as an additional target variable.

The logic is as follows. When the rupee weakens, the unit value of future exports in rupees tends to rise, and *vice versa*. Further, when demand in the consuming countries rises, so does the price, raising the unit value of the exports. Another motivation for using the unit value series as a target variable is the numerical quotas (rather than value) that many Indian exports such as textiles have traditionally faced. The implication is that exporters would try to export higher unit value items.

The analysis is further generalized by using the total value of exports as an alternative target variable. If the economic rationale holds for real exports and the price of exports, it must also be valid for the product of the two.

As noted in the previous section, cyclical declines in the level of exports are relatively rare whereas cyclical movements in the growth rate of exports are more prevalent. Our analysis, therefore, focuses on the growth rate of the leading index to predict the three target variables in growth form. The leading index in growth form is simply the 'six-month smoothed growth rate' of the leading index already described.

The estimations begin in 1975 since REER is not available before this period. The leading index for exports is constructed with base 1992=100. Since the components of the leading index are available monthly, the leading index is estimated on a monthly basis. The target variables are, however, currently available only on a quarterly basis and are converted to monthly series by simple step interpolation, that is, the quarterly series is repeated three times corresponding to the months of the quarter. Although monthly data on export variables is available up to 1985, this is converted to quarterly to conform to data available after 1985 as well as to smoothen the series. The data for the entire period are seasonally adjusted using the Census X-11 procedure.

The reference chronologies of the three target variables are determined using the procedure described in the previous section. The turning points of each target variable are evaluated relative to those of the leading index. The results are shown in Tables 16.1 to 16.3. The main findings given in the following sub-sections.

Target Variable: Growth Rate of Quantum Index of Exports

Table 16.1 and Figure 16.1 report the downturns in the growth rate of the quantum index of exports. These downturns are the periods from a peak to the following trough as shown in Table 16.1, and the corresponding periods marked off by shaded areas in Figure 16.1. The growth rate of the leading index leads the quantum index growth rate at 83 per cent of peaks and 71 per cent of troughs, with an average lead of seven months at peaks and four months at troughs.

Target Variable: Growth Rate of unit value index of exports

Downturns in the growth rate of the unit value index of exports are shown as the periods from a peak to the following trough (Table 16.2),

Table 16.1: Turning Points of Growth Rate of Leading Index of Exports *vis-à- vis* Growth Rate of Quantum Index of Exports

Quantum Index of Exports, Growth Rate		Leading Index of Exports, Growth Rate		Lead(–)	OR	Lag(+)
Troughs	Peaks	Troughs	Peaks	Troughs		Peaks
05/1977		10/1976		–7		
	05/1979		04/1978			–13
05/1980		03/1980		–2		
			01/1983			extra
	08/1985			extra		
	08/1987		04/1986			–16
05/1988		09/1987		–8		
	02/1989		11/1988			–3
05/1990		06/1989		–11		
	11/1991		07/1991			–4
05/1992		11/1992		6		
			05/1994			Extra
		07/1995		Extra		
	08/1996		01/1996			–7
05/1997		08/1997		3		
	11/1998		01/1999			2
08/1999				Miss		
	05/2000					Miss
11/2001		04/2001		–7		
				Troughs	Overall	Peaks
		Average		–4	–5	–7
		Median		–7.0	–7.0	–5.5
		Per cent Lead		71	77	83
		Std. Deviation		6.3	6.4	6.7

Source: Authors.

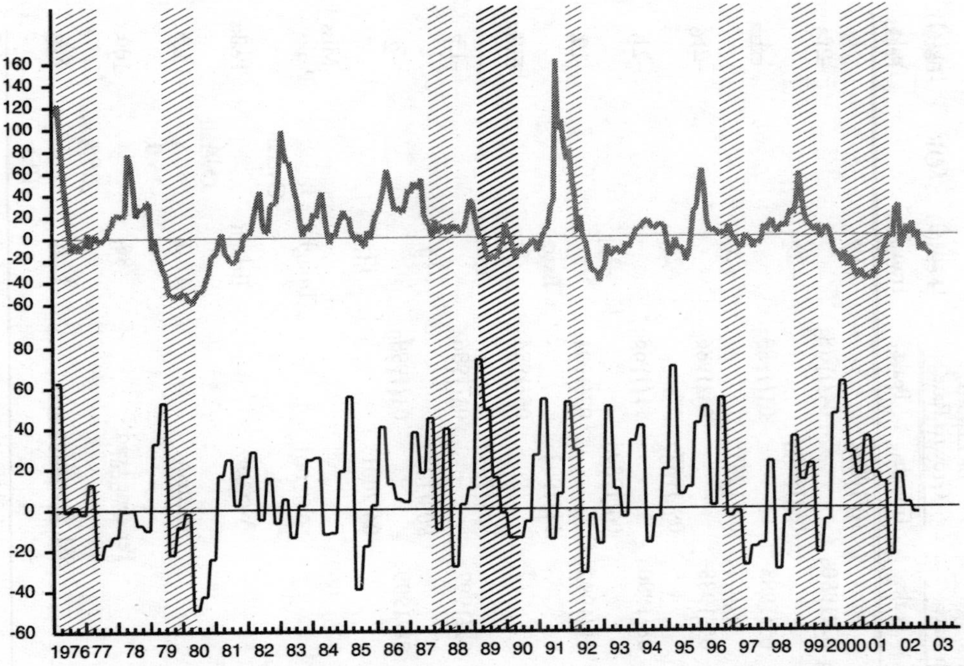

Figure 16.1: Growth Rate of Leading Index of Exports vs Growth Rate of Quantum Index of Exports.
Note: Shaded areas represent downturns in the growth rate of the quantum index of exports.

Table 16.2: Turning Points of Growth Rate of Leading Index of Exports *vis- à- vis* Growth Rate of Unit Value Index of Exports

Unit Value Index of Exports, Growth Rate		Leading Index of Exports, Growth Rate		Lead(–)	OR	Lag(+)
Troughs	Peaks	Troughs	Peaks	Troughs		Peaks
05/1978		10/1976		–19		
	02/1980		04/1978			–22
08/1982		03/1980		–29		
	05/1983		01/1983			–4
11/1985		08/1985		–3		
	05/1988		04/1986			–25
05/1989		09/1987		–20		
	08/1990		11/1988			–21
05/1991		06/1989		–23		
	05/1992		07/1991			–10
		11/1992		Extra		
			05/1994			Extra
08/1996		07/1995		–13		
	02/1997		01/1996			–13
11/1998		08/1997		–15		
	08/1999		01/1999			–7
05/2000		04/2001		11		
				Troughs	Overall	Peaks
		Average		–14	–14	–15
		Median		–17.0	–15.0	–13.0
		Per cent Lead		88	93	100
		Std. Deviation		12.6	10.4	8.1

Source: Authors.

and the corresponding periods marked off by shaded areas (Figure 16.2). The growth rate of the leading index leads the unit value index growth rate at 100 per cent of peaks and 88 per cent of troughs, with an average lead of 15 months at peaks and 14 months at troughs.

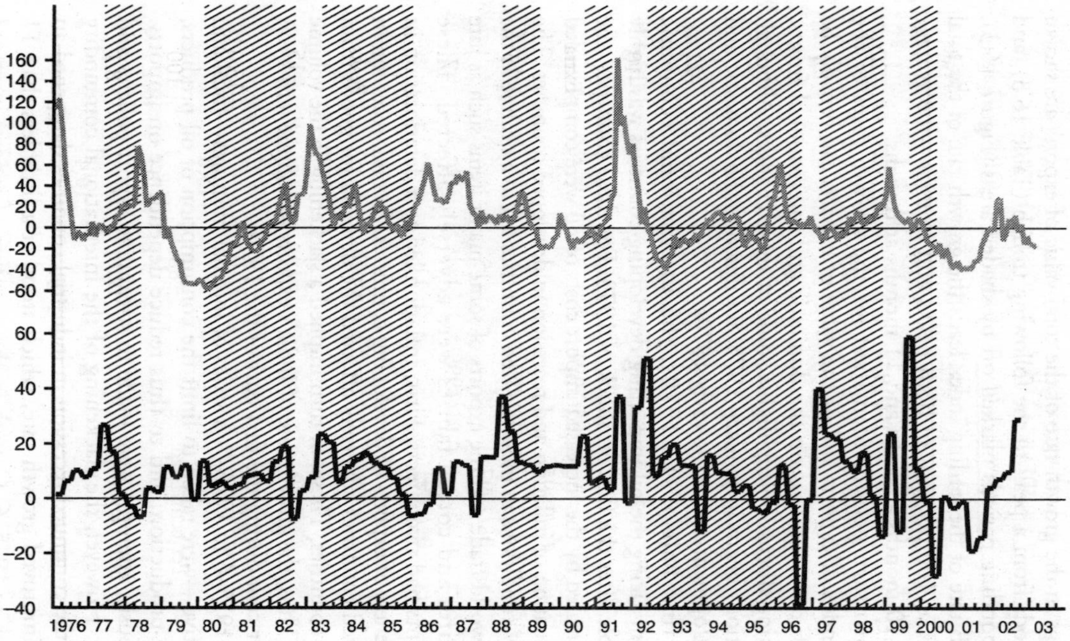

Figure 16.2: Growth Rate of Leading Index of Exports vs Growth Rate of Unit Value Index of Exports.
Note: Shaded areas represent downturns in the growth rate of the unit value index of exports.

Target Variable: Growth rate of total value of exports

Downswings in the growth rate of the total value of exports are shown as the periods from a peak to the following trough (Table 16.3), and the corresponding periods marked off by shaded areas (Figure 16.3). The growth rate of the leading index leads the growth rate of the total value index at 100 per cent of both peaks and troughs—the average lead being 10 months at peaks and 11 months at troughs.

The downturn periods identified for the growth rates of the quantum index of exports and of the value of exports can broadly be linked with developments on the domestic and international fronts. The following discussion highlights some of these changes. Although the estimations begin in January 1975, we describe the domestic and global developments since the early 1970s.

In the first half of the 1970s, the international economic environment facing the oil importing developing countries was highly unfavourable after the first oil shock of 1973. For these countries, the problems created by the increased import costs of oil were compounded by a combination of inflation and recession in developed countries. The recessionary conditions in industrialized countries led to a decline in the volume of world trade and the exports of some major items such as jute manufactures and cotton fabrics were adversely affected. These developments had two effects. First, inflation led to a deterioration in competitiveness of exports of developing countries. Second, recession in industrialized countries adversely affected the demand for goods from developing countries. These, in turn implied a slackening in the volume of exports. Thus, the growth rate of India's exports in volume terms was under 6 per cent during the first part of the 1970s.

During 1975–6 to 1976–7, a series of internal measures—fiscal and administrative—were taken to limit the consumption of oil products, to increase production, and to thus reduce dependence on imports. Simultaneously, attempts were made to streamline export policies and procedures. However, the slackening of the international commodity boom and the continued recession in industrial countries dampened an otherwise improved growth rate, which stood at a little less than 11 per cent during 1975–6. Growth in the quantum of exports increased to more than 18 per cent during 1976–7 spurred by the recovery of economic activity and the replenishment of inventories in developed countries.

Table 16.3: Turning Points of Growth Rate of Leading Index of Exports *vis- à- vis* Growth Rate of Total Value of Exports

Total Value of Exports, Growth Rate		Leading Index of Exports, Growth Rate		Lead(–)	OR	Lag(+)
Troughs	Peaks	Troughs	Peaks	Troughs		Peaks
11/1977		10/1976		–25		
	05/1979		04/1978			-13
05/1980		03/1980		-2		
			01/1983			Extra
		08/1985		Extra		
	02/1987		04/1986			-10
05/1988		09/1987		-8		
	02/1989		11/1988			-3
02/1990		06/1989		-8		
	02/1993		07/1991			-19
05/1994		11/1992		-18		
			05/1994			Extra
		07/1995		Extra		
	02/1996		01/1996			-1
05/1998		08/1997		-9		
	02/2000		01/1999			-13
11/2001		04/2001		-7		
				Troughs	Overall	Peaks
		Average		–11	–10	–10
		Median		–8.0	–9.0	–11.5
		Per cent Lead		100	100	100
		Std. Deviation		7.8	7.1	6.8

Source: Authors.

Soon after, exports slackened in 1977–8 in the wake of recessionary conditions and protectionist tendencies in the major industrial countries. Furthermore, the restrictions placed by the government on exports of certain agriculture based mass consumption goods also

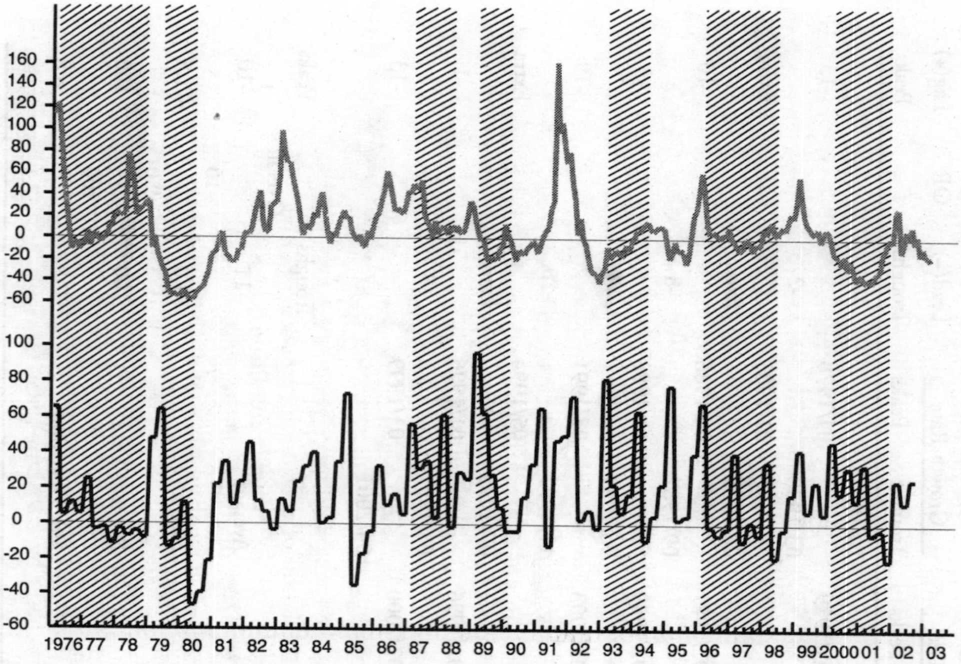

Figure 16.3: Growth Rate of Leading Index of Exports vs Growth Rate of Total Value of Exports.
Note: Shaded areas represent downturns in the growth rate of the total value of exports.

added to the worsening of real exports, with the volume index of exports showing a negative growth of 3.7 per cent during 1977–8. In level terms also the volume index declined during 1977–8, attaining a level of 93.2 as compared to 96.8 during 1976–7.

Though the growth rate in the quantum index of exports improved to 7.3 per cent during 1978–9, it decelerated in 1979–80 to 6.2 per cent. The reasons for this sluggish performance can be attributed to both domestic as well as external environment. On the domestic front, the strong pull of the highly profitable domestic market did not encourage aggressive export orientation. Further, in the area of domestic policy, the emphasis on export promotion had declined compared with the situation in the wake of the oil crisis of 1973. This was made worse by the unfavourable international trading environment compared to the past because of slower growth in world trade and an accompanying increase in protectionism. This period witnessed an increasing resort to a host of measures such as quota, excessively restrictive and cumbersome quality control, and countervailing duties. All these non-tariff barriers limited access to developed country markets and increased the uncertainty faced by exporters. The domestic economy also suffered from severe drought conditions in 1979 and the consequences of the global oil price rise.

During the first four years of the Sixth Plan (1980–5), exports in volume terms showed a lower growth. This was a continuation of the performance witnessed in the latter years of the 1970s. This has to be viewed against the background of recessionary conditions in the world economy, continuation of protectionist tendencies in world markets, and the impact of severe drought conditions in the country during 1979–80 and 1982–3. In volume terms, world trade grew by just 1.5 per cent in 1980, stagnated in 1981, and then fell by 2 per cent in 1982 (*Economic Survey* 1984–5). Some of the important markets for India in West Asia were facing disturbed conditions and there was also a slowing down of economic activity in these countries, following the decrease in the volume of their oil exports and international prices. Also, lower purchases by East European countries contributed to the slow growth in exports.

The government undertook a series of corrective measures during the course of 1985–6 and 1986–7 to boost the growth of exports and curb the increase in imports. A wide range of exports-enhancing initiatives was launched during this period. This resulted in a marked improvement in the growth of real exports that was significant in the face of sluggish expansion in the volume of world trade. The global economic environment was also affected by the stock market crisis of 1987 and the turmoil in the world foreign exchange market with the US dollar declining against a majority of currencies. On the domestic front, the unprecedented drought of 1987 exerted strain on the balance of payments. It also necessitated additional imports of essentials and reduced exports of agro-based commodities.

In the early part of the 1990s, the country passed through a severe balance of payments crisis. The Gulf crisis coupled with the recessionary trends discernible in some major industrial economies constrained export growth during 1990–1. The early 1990s also witnessed political and economic upheavals in Eastern Europe. These economies had earlier provided a sheltered market for a large variety of Indian goods. The exports growth thus decelerated during the early 1990s.

Other factors that accounted for the poor performance in the growth rate of real exports included import curbs introduced during the early 1990s in response to the foreign exchange shortage, which affected export-related imports. Further, movements in the exchange rate, which were broadly supportive of exports since 1986–7 became adverse, thus affecting the competitiveness of exports. There was also a slowdown in the expansion of world trade and recessionary conditions in some major industrial countries. Exports were also adversely affected by a tight monetary policy that affected export credit and imports of raw materials and components. Industrial production growth could not be sustained once the accumulated inventories were drawn down resulting in a decline in industrial production during 1991–2, and affecting export surpluses available.

During 1993–4, the growth rate of real exports recovered, reflecting in part the strength of the reforms in trade and industrial policies adopted since 1991. This recovery shows that exports responded positively to the removal of the anti-export bias of a protectionist environment. This was bolstered by the resurgence in world output, which increased by 3.6 per cent during 1994 after a growth of 2.5 per cent in 1993 (Economic Survey 1995–6).

This recovery was, however, not sustained for long and there was a rapid decline in the growth from 1996–7 to 1997–8. This decline in export performance must be viewed in the backdrop of a steep decline in non-petroleum-oil-lubricants (POL) import growth during 1996–7. The decline reflects a modest slowdown in industrial activity compared to the economic dynamism of earlier years. This wass compounded by several external developments, including a fall in import demand by industrial countries, regional groupings of the developed economies, and the effect of large movements in cross- country exchange rates on exports.

Apart from these, a noticeable decline in the growth of world trade in 1996 and 1997 and an appreciation of the rupee in REER terms were other contributory factors. The unprecedented depreciation of currencies of competitors in Southeast Asia such as the Philippines, Indonesia, and Thailand was another factor responsible for the decline.

The deceleration in the growth of India's exports (in US $) continued for the third year in succession in 1998–9. The fallout of the crisis in East Asia continued to deepen and broaden in 1998, resulting in a sharp contraction in domestic demand in these countries. Exports, however, recovered in 1999, growing by 10.8 per cent in 1999 (in US $ value). The effects of the East Asian crisis were minimal in 1999. Further, low inflation in the domestic economy strengthened India's export competitiveness in the global market. A new chapter was incorporated in the export–import (EXIM) policy to boost exports of services. Free trade zones (FTZs) replaced export processing zones (ePZs).

India's exports were almost stagnant in 2001–2 due to a marked deceleration in world output and trade and a slowdown in the domestic economy. Domestic factors such as the appreciation of the Rupee in REER may have also affected the competitiveness of exports. The robust expansion in global economic activity witnessed in 2000 was followed by a marked slowdown in 2001. The year 2001 thus experienced the deepening and reinforcing of the global economic slowdown that had begun to set in during 2000. The global slowdown was accentuated further by the terrorist attacks in the US on 11 September 2001 and the subsequent retaliation by the US in Afghanistan, and it assumed a synchronized, self-reinforcing dimension with adverse implications for world trade.

Evaluation of the Leading Index: Lead Profiles

The hallmark of a cyclical leading indicator is the property that its cyclical turning points lead cyclical turning points in the economy. However, there are no well-known methods to test whether these leads are statistically significant. Furthermore, the leading index for exports covers a small number of cycles. Thus the evaluation of its cyclical leads at turning points by parametric statistical methods is not easy. The need to make a heroic assumption that the probability distribution of the leads has a standard functional form also precludes the use of parametric tests of statistical significance. The solution is a series of non-parametric statistical tests, which yield the lead profile (Banerji 2000).

The lead profile is a graphical depiction of the leads in strictly probabilistic terms, which aids meaningful comparisons between two indexes or an index and the reference cycle. It can be graphically represented in terms of bar charts or 'lead profile charts'. The question answered by this chart is whether the difference between the leads of the two indices (or an index and the reference cycle) is statistically significant.

The advantage of lead profile charts is that they use as input just the information on the length of the leads at each turning point. However, by gleaning statistical inferences from the data rather than relying solely on averages, and by displaying the results graphically, they afford additional insights into the significance of the leads.

Another major advantage of lead profiles lies in the explicit statistical inferences that can be made about the significance of leads without making any assumptions about the probability distribution of leads, or any restrictions on sample size. These inferences can be made about the leads of a given cyclical indicator over a reference cycle, such as a set of business cycle turning points. They can also be made about the leads of one cyclical indicator over another, to assess whether one has significantly longer leads than the other. Moreover, it is convenient to put lead profiles in the form of bar charts, for easy and effective visual appraisal of the significance of lengths of leads.

Non-parametric tests are often called 'distribution-free' because they do not assume that the observations were drawn from a population distributed in a certain way, for example, from a normally distributed population. These tests also do not require the large samples needed to reliably estimate parameters of distributions assumed in parametric tests. Such tests should, therefore, be uniquely suited to testing the significance of leads, which may be small in number, and for which the probability distribution function is clearly unknown.

Since the leads in question are differences in timing at cyclical turns (between corresponding pairs of turning points in the leading index growth rate and exports growth, for example), the appropriate non-parametric tests are those applicable to matched pairs of samples.

One appropriate test to assess the significance of such leads is the Randomization test for matched pairs (Fisher 1935). The first step is to calculate the leads of one indicator over another. The null hypothesis, that these differences are not statistically significant, is to be tested against the alternative hypothesis that the leads are significant.

Now, some of the differences calculated in the first step may be positive, others negative. If the null hypothesis is true, the positive differences are just as likely to have been negative, and *vice versa.* So if there are N differences (from N pairs of observations), each difference is as likely to be positive as negative. Thus, the observed set of differences would be just one of 2^N equally likely outcomes under the null hypothesis.

Also, under the null hypothesis, the sum of the positive differences would, on average, equal the sum of the negative differences, so the expected sum of the positive and negative differences would be zero. If the alternative hypothesis was true, and the leads were positive and significant, the sum would very likely be positive.

The second step, therefore, is to sum the differences, assigning positive signs to each difference; then to switch the signs systematically, one by one, to generate all the outcomes which result in sums as high or higher than that observed. If there are *R* such outcomes, then the probability of the observed outcome (or a more extreme outcome) under the null hypothesis is $(R/2^N)$. In other words, the null hypothesis can be rejected at a confidence level of $100(1-(R/2^N))\%$.

So far, the discussion has focused on the confidence level at which the null hypothesis ('leads not significantly different from zero') can be rejected in favour of the alternative hypothesis ('leads significantly greater than zero months'). Now, even if it is established that the leads are significantly greater than zero months, it might be interesting to know how much greater than zero months the leads are likely to be—for example, whether the leads are also significantly greater than one month.

This is easy to determine. All one needs to do is to subtract one month from each of the differences in timing at turns (already calculated in the first step of the Randomization test). Then, as before, one finds the confidence level at which the null hypothesis is rejected in favour of the alternative hypothesis that the difference in timing at turns significantly exceeds one month.

In this way, one can also determine the confidence levels for the hypotheses that the leads exceed 2,3,4, ... *K* months—by simply subtracting 2,3,4, ... *K*, respectively, from the original differences before performing the Randomization test. We call this full set of confidence levels a 'lead profile'.

Figures 16.4 to 16.6 show the lead profiles of the Indian exports leading index growth rate against alternative reference cycles. Figure 16.4 shows the leading index *vis-à-vis* the quantum index growth rate reference cycle and is based on the leads shown in Table 16.1. The first bar represents a test of the null hypothesis that the lead of the composite index is zero months, against the alternative that it is greater than zero, that is, at least one month. Analogously, the second bar represents another test, of the null hypothesis that the lead is one month against the alternative that it is greater, that is, at least two months. Figure 16.4 shows that the null hypothesis of zero lead cannot be rejected, and, in fact, the confidence level is over 90 per cent for leads up to 3 months.

Figure 16.5 depicts the lead profile of the Indian exports leading index growth rate against the growth rate of the unit value of exports, based on the leads shown in Table 16.2. Figure 16.5 shows that the null hypothesis of zero lead cannot be rejected, and, in fact, the confidence level is close to 100 per cent up to 7 months and more than 90 per cent up to 11 months.

Figure 16.6 gives the lead profile of the Indian exports leading index growth rate against the growth rate of the total value of exports, based on the leads shown in Table 16.3. Figure 16.6 shows that the null hypothesis of zero lead cannot be rejected, and, in fact, the confidence level is close to 100 per cent up to 6 months and more than 90 per cent up to 8 months.

On the basis of these lead profiles, we can conclude that the Indian exports leading index growth rate has a statistically significant lead at cyclical turning points of the three target variables. The longest lead is against the growth rate of the unit value of exports, the shortest lead against the growth rate of the quantum index of exports, and an in-between lead, as expected, is against the growth rate of the product of those two variables, that is, the growth rate of the total value of exports.

Summary and Limitations

The findings of the study indicate that the growth rate of the leading index for exports leads the growth rates of the quantum index, the unit

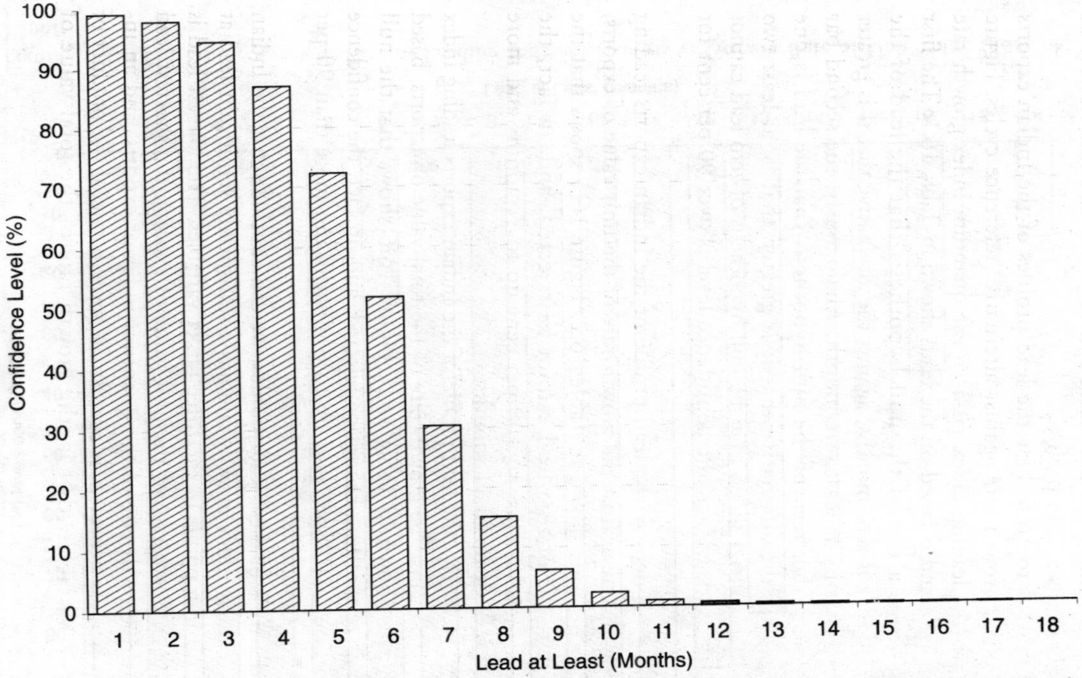

Figure 16.4 Lead Profile: Growth Rate of Leading Index of Exports vs Growth Rate of Quantum Index of Exports.

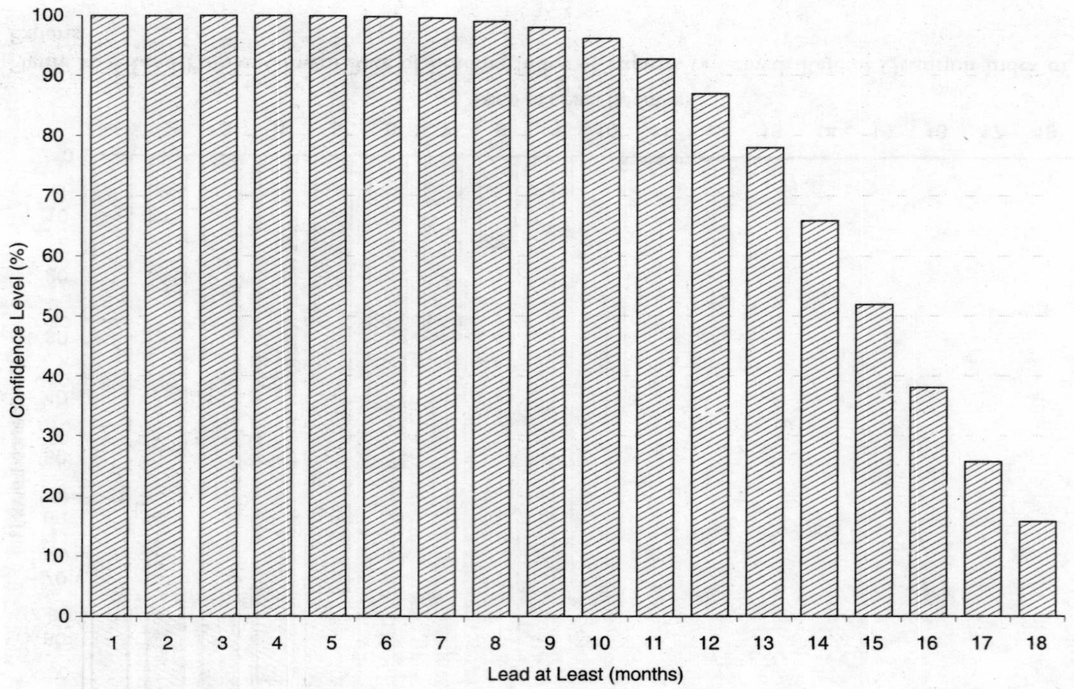

Figure 16.5: Lead Profile: Growth Rate of Leading Index of Exports vs Growth Rate of Unit Value Index of Exports.

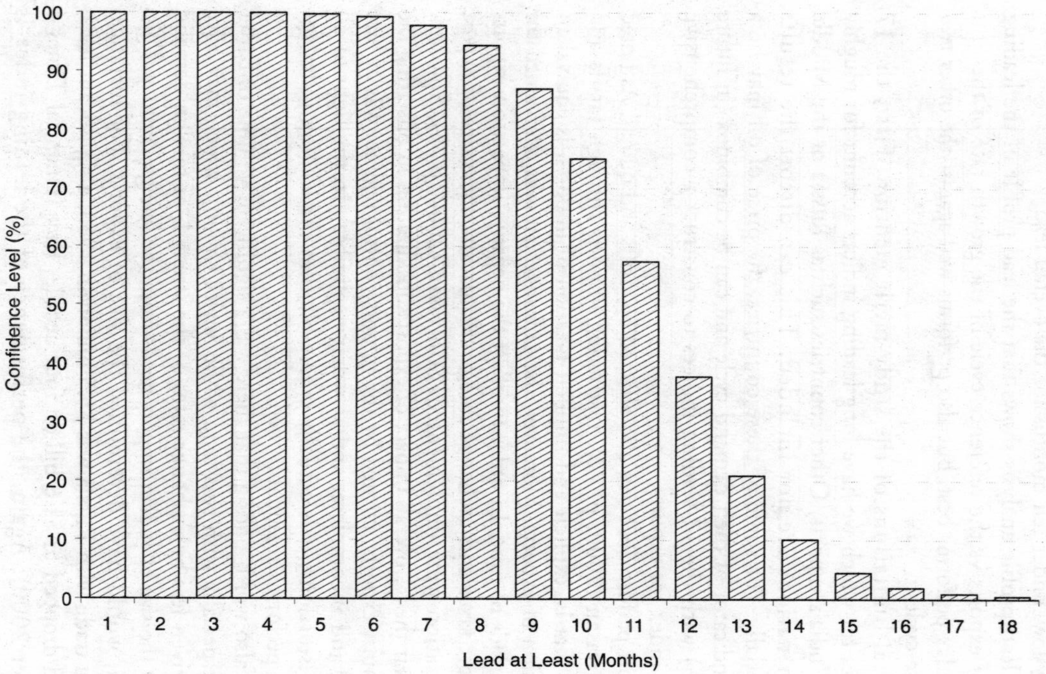

Figure 16.6: Lead Profile: Growth Rate of Leading Index of Exports vs Growth Rate of Total Value Index of Exports.

value index, and the total value index. These findings are very encouraging considering the volatility of the series. The results are also robust in the sense that the standard deviations of the leads are typically low, under ten months for the overall lead.

The lead profile analysis shows that the lead profile of the leading index of exports vs the reference cycle of the growth rate of the unit value index performs best, but also performs well against the other two reference cycles.

Several limitations of the study merit mention. First, the 17 countries for which we have long leading indices account for roughly half of India's exports. Other countries such as Russia or the Middle Eastern nations are not included. This can distort the results substantially. For some of these countries, the price of oil may be a useful indicator of their demand cycle and can be combined (in future research) with the 17 leading indices to construct a comprehensive leading index for exports.

Export performance was also affected by tariffs and quotas. As noted by Srinivasan (2000, p. 72), restricting imports through tariffs and quotas, that is, explicit and implicit taxation of imports, is equivalent to taxation of exports. Moreover, the exchange rate was overvalued for long periods of time. In order to offset the negative impact on exports of import taxes and exchange rate overvaluation, measures of export subsidization were implemented. Srinivasan (2000, p.73), however, notes that the '...overall impact of export subsidization in offsetting the bias against exports, created by the import control regime, was at best modest and incomplete, and at worst negligible'. In the light of all these distortions, it is actually creditable that the leading index for exports performs reasonably well.

It is also worth noting that there was a significant volume of barter trade (especially with Russia ... while Soviet Union), which may have been driven less by exchange rates or the strength of foreign demand than by the size of Indian import needs from the foreign country. This, in turn, would have determined the size of exports. For instance, bilateral trade with Russia was \$5.5 billion in 1960, a significant level, but had dropped to \$1.6 billion four decades later (Financial Times 4 October 2000). Again, the performance of the leading index is creditable given that the components of this index may not have incorporated these changes in trade.

Moreover, the composition of exports may also adversely affect the predictive ability of the leading index for exports and its growth rate.

For instance, especially in the past, a significant portion of India's exports have included items like tea, the demand for which may not have much to do with the business cycle in the consuming countries. We, therefore, expect the performance of the leading index for exports to improve in the future with India moving into the cyclically sensitive (investment-driven) high-tech areas.

A major problem with predicting Indian exports is the long publication lags in the target variables. At the time of writing, the most recent export related data measuring the target variables are available up to September 2002 only, implying about nine months lag in the availability of data. For a leading index to be useful, meaningful and reliable, data must be available on a timely basis—and in fact, the components of the leading index (17 country leading index and REER) are available on a timely basis. The lag is in the availability of the target variables movements which are predicted by the leading index. Thus, the exports leading index predicts cyclical turns in the target variable not just months before they occur, but even longer before those turns become evident from the available data.

The fact that only demand factors have been taken into account in the construction of the leading index also merits mention. This can, however, be justified on the following grounds. First, supply factors are generally not cyclical. Second, apart from those that are not predictable (for example, shocks), supply factors usually change more slowly than demand factors. This means that demand factors are generally the drivers in economic cycles. Finally, with further liberalization of trade, demand factors are expected to become more dominant than supply constraints, implying that they will primarily drive the cycles.

In sum, the construction of the leading index for exports in the past was beset with data limitations and other problems experienced by a developing country dominated by the public sector and import-substituting industrialization. Nevertheless, the growth rate of the index performed reasonably well and its performance can only be expected to improve further in the future.

Finally, while earlier leading exports indexes for other countries were designed only to predict cyclical turns in real exports, the current work done in the Indian context also demonstrates that the leading exports index can predict cyclical turns in export prices as well as those in nominal exports. This may be especially important for developing economies that run up against numerical quotas in their export markets, which may artificially limit the physical quantity of exports.

References

Banerji, A. (2000), 'The Lead Profile and Other Non-Parametric Tools to Evaluate a Survey Series', in K.H. Oppenlander, G. Poser, and B. Schips (Eds), *Use of Survey Data for Industry, Research and Economic Policy,* Aldershot, England: Ashgate.

—— (1999), 'The Three Ps: Simple Tools for Monitoring Economic Cycles', *Business Economics,* Vol. XXXIV No. 4, October, pp. 72–6.

Bhagwati, J. and P. Desai (1970), *India:Planning for Industrialization,* Oxford: Oxford University Press.

Bhagwati, J. and T.N. Srinivasan (1993), 'Indian Economic Reforms', *Working Paper,* Ministry of Finance, Government of India.

Boschan, C. and A. Banerji (1990), 'A Reassessment of Composite Indexes', in P.A. Klein (Ed.), *Analyzing Modern Business Cycles,* New York: M.E. Sharpe.

Bry, G. and C. Boschan (1971), 'Cyclical Analysis of Time Series: Selected Procedures and Computer Programs', National Bureau of Economic Research, Technical Paper No. 20, New York.

Burns, A.F. and W.C. Mitchell (1946), *Measuring Business Cycles,* National Bureau of Economic Research, New York.

Chitre, V.S. (1986), 'Indicators of Business Recessions and Revivals in India', Gokhale Institute of Politics and Economics Working Paper, Pune.

—— (1982), 'Growth Cycles in the Indian Economy', *Artha Vijnana,* Vol. 24, pp. 293–450.

Cullity, J.P. and A. Banerji (1996), 'Composite Indexes: A Reassessment' presented at the meeting of the OECD Expert Group on Leading Indicators, Paris. 17–18, October.

Cullity, J.P. and G.H. Moore (1987), 'Developing a long-leading composite index for the United States', CIRET Conference, Zurich, Switzerland, September.

Cullity, J.P., P.A. Klein, and G.H. Moore (1987), 'Forecasting US Trade Flows with Exchange Rates and Leading Indicators', presented at the meeting of the International Association of Forecasters, Boston, May.

Dua, P. and A. Banerji (2001a), 'A Leading Index for India's Exports', Development Research Group Study, No. 23, Reserve Bank of India, Mumbai.

—— (2001b), 'An Indicator Approach to Business and Growth Rate Cycles: The Case of India', *Indian Economic Review,* Vol. XXXVI, pp. 55–78.

—— (1999), 'An Index of Coincident Economic Indicators for the Indian Economy', *Journal of Quantitative Economics,* Vol. 15, pp. 177–201.

ECRI (Economic Cycle Research Institute) (1997), 'A New Predictor of U.S. Exports Growth', *International Cyclical Outlook,* October, New York.

Financial Times (2000), 'India, Russia Sign Strategic partnership', 4 October.

Fisher, R. A. (1935) *The Design of Experiments,* Edinburgh: Oliver & Boyd.

Granger, C. W. J. and P. Newbold. (1986) *Forecasting Economic Time Series,* San Diego, California: Academic Press.

Hajra, S. and D.L. Sinate (1997), 'Fifty Years of India's Foreign Trade: Issues and Perspectives', *RBI Occasional Papers,* Vol. 18, Nos. 2 and 3, pp. 421–52.

Hiris, L., A. Banerji, and B.W. Taubman (1995), 'An Index to Forecast US Exports of Goods and Services', in R. Moncarz (Ed.), *International Trade and the New Economic Order,* Pergamon: Elsevier Science.

Joshi, V. and I.M.D. Little (1994), *India: Macroeconomics and Political Economy – 1964–1991,* Oxford: Oxford University Press.

Kapur, M. (1997), 'India's External Sector Since Independence: From Inwardness to Openness', *RBI Occasional Papers,* Vol. 18, Nos. 2 and 3, pp. 385–419.

King, R.G. and C.I. Plosser (1989) 'Real Business Cycles and the Test of the Adelmans', unpublished manuscript, University of Rochester.

Klein, P.A. (1998), 'Swedish Business Cycles – Assessing the Recent Record', Working Paper 21, Federation of Swedish Industries, Stockholm.

—— and G.H. Moore (1985), *Monitoring Growth Cycles in Market-oriented Countries: Developing and Using International Economic Indicators,* for NBER, Cambridge, Massachusetts: Ballinger.

—— (1980), 'Further Applications of Leading Indicators to Forecasting Foreign Trade Flows and Balances', in W.H. Strigel, (Ed.), Business Cycle Analysis, England: Gower Publishing Co.

—— (1978), 'Forecasting Foreign Trade with Leading Indicators', in W.H. Strigel (Ed.), *Problems and Instruments of Business Cycle Analysis,* New York: Springer-Verlag, pp. 159–81.

Marjit, S. and A. Raychaudhuri (1997), *India's Exports: An Analytical Study,* Oxford: Oxford University Press.

Moore, G.H. (1982), 'Business Cycles' in D. Greenwald (Editor-in-Chief), *Encyclopaedia of Economics,* New York: McGraw Hill Book Company.

—— (1976), 'Forecasting Foreign Trade Flows with Leading Indicators', presented at the Second Conference of the International Federation of Associations of Business Economists, Cambridge, England, April.

—— (1961), 'Measuring Recessions', in *Business Cycle Indicators,* Vol. 1, pp. 120–61, Princeton: Princeton University Press.

—— (1958), 'Forecasting Industrial Production—A Comment', *Journal of Political Economy,* February, Vol. No. 1, pp. 74–83.

—— and J. Shiskin (1967), *Indicators of Business Expansions and Contractions,* NBER, New York.

OECD (1987), *OECD Leading Indicators and Business Cycles in Member Countries, 1960–1985,* OECD, Paris.

RBI (1993), 'The Nominal Effective Exchange Rate (NEER) and the Real Effective Exchange Rate (REER) of the Indian Rupee', *Reserve Bank of India Bulletin,* July.

Shiskin, J. (1961), *Signals of Recession and Recovery,* NBER, New York.

Siegel, S. (1956), *Nonparametric Statistics for the Behavioral Sciences,* New YOrk: McGraw Hill.

Srinivasan, T.N. (2000), *Eight Lectures on India's Economic Reforms,* New Delhi: Oxford University Press.

—— (1999), 'Foreign Trade Policies and India's Development', in U. Kapila, (Ed.), *Indian Economy since Independence,* 1999–2000, New Delhi: Academic Foundation.

—— and S. Tendulkar (1999), *India in the World Economy,* unpublished manuscript.

Watson, M. W. (1994) 'Business Cycle Durations and Postwar Stabilization of the US Economy', *American Economic Review,* Vol. 84, pp. 24–46.

Zarnowitz, V. and C. Boschan (1975), 'Cyclical Indicators: An Evaluation and New Leading Indexes', in *Handbook of Cyclical Indicators,* Washington, DC: Government Printing Office.